Southern Literature

and Literary Theory

D1525319

Edited by Jefferson Humphries

Southern

Literature

and Literary

Theory

The University of Georgia Press   *Athens & London*

"James Dickey: From 'The Other' through *Early
Motion*" by Harold Bloom was first published in
the *Southern Review* (Winter 1985). "Zora Neale
Hurston and the Speakerly Text" by Henry Louis
Gates is from *The Signifying Monkey: A Theory
of Afro-American Literary Criticism* by Henry
Louis Gates, Jr. Copyright Henry Louis Gates, Jr.
1988. Reprinted by permission of Oxford University Press, Inc.

Printed in the United States of America

94 93 92 91 90 C 5 4 3 2 1

96 95 94 93 92 P 5 4 3 2 1

Library of Congress
Cataloging in Publication Data
Southern literature and literary theory / edited by
   Jefferson Humphries.
      p. cm.
   Includes bibliographical references.
   ISBN 0-8203-1189-8 (alk. paper)
   ISBN 0-8203-1486-2 (pbk.: alk. paper)
   1. American literature—Southern States—
History and criticism—Theory, etc.
   2. American literature—Southern States—
History and criticism.   3. Southern States in
literature.   I. Humphries, Jefferson, 1955− .
PS261.S5287   1990
810.9'975—dc20   89-20282
                  CIP

British Library Cataloging in
Publication Data available

Contents

Introduction:

On the Inevitability of Theory

in Southern Literary Study

JEFFERSON HUMPHRIES

In a recent essay entitled "The State of Southern Literary Scholarship," Lewis P. Simpson refers to a "Southern Literary Establishment," a group of critical elders whose principal legacy to southern studies is *The History of Southern Literature*, published by the Louisiana State University Press in 1985.

A landmark volume in which some fifty scholars and critics have pooled their resources to produce for the first time a narrative history of southern letters from 1585 to the present, *The History of Southern Literature* is dominated editorially by [Louis D.] Rubin and five senior associates—in other words, by what I believe, by virtue of his long centrality in southern literary studies, may be called the "Rubin generation." We realize, I believe, our generational limitation. From the point of view of younger scholars and critics our book (I say our, for I am one of the editors) is lacking in its failure to respond— save perhaps incidentally, and certainly in no programmatic fashion —to the approach to literary history through theories of language and literature like "deconstruction." Adapted largely from European sources, this approach is in important ways reshaping American literary and historical thought at this moment. Looked at from this point of view, I'm sure our effort may seem to be a testament to past ways of thinking and feeling. That is to say, the 1985 *History of Southern Literature*—even though it clearly revises the "genteel" version of southern literary history that is the basis of *The Library of Southern*

Literature and that still speaks in Hubbell's *The South in American Literature*—must already yield to the endless process of historical revision that is the life blood of modern society. [p. 250]

While *Southern Literature and Literary Theory* cannot possibly compete, in any sense, with the monumental *History of Southern Literature,* the present volume can be taken as weighty and incontrovertible proof that the Rubin generation of southern writers, scholars and critics will not have been the last.

How we, the post-Rubin generation of southernists, understand and apply cultural and literary "theory" varies widely, from the avowed Marxism of Carl Freedman, to the feminism of Michelle Collins, to the deconstructive poetry and poetics of James Applewhite, to Fred Chappell's concept of fictional characters as specular tropes of their author's personal investment in them, and back again to the Afro-American deconstruction of Henry Louis Gates. Each of us speaks from a unique theoretical vantage point that may appear hermetic to the uninitiated, or, as in Fred Chappell's case, very much the opposite. But we have in common one thing that sets us apart from our elders in our conception of the South and our approach to southern literature and history: the basic assumption that the meaning and significance of literature is not in the immanence of the literary object, or in history, but in the complex ways in which the literary, the historical, and all the "human sciences" that study both, are interrelated. The traditional "practice" by southernists of history as literary study, and of literary study as history, cannot accommodate the insights of continental philosophy since Hegel. So we have turned to exploring the unspoken assumptions, the invisible intellectual architecture, which make literary and historical practice possible—to theory, from the classical Greek word *theoria* meaning "a looking at, viewing, contemplation, speculation," and also "a spectacle" (OED), hence the contemporary notion of literary theory as an art on its own.

The very pluralism evident in this volume may make it impossible for there ever to be a reply to *The History of Southern Literature* to which all of us could subscribe. For we do not believe in the kind of global synthesis practiced in traditional history. There is not one truth, but many, and all of them change while you look at them. The answer to "What happened?" depends just as much on who and how and when you ask, as the answer to "What will happen?" Some of our colleagues in our own discipline, and most of our colleagues in American history departments scoff at such "relativism," saying that it comes from an ill-advised and illogical infatuation with European philosophy—which, they say, ought to have nothing to do with American, and particularly southern, history and literature. But the merging of southern and post-Romantic European minds is, as I will argue later, a logical, even inevitable development, because both are expressions of cultures grounded in loss and defeat. If we have been more sensitive to common ground between southern and European experience than our elders, it may be because we grew up in post–World War II America, where Europe no longer seemed distant. The first World War had not convinced the United States as a nation that it had an *inevitable* stake in events across the Atlantic—witness American reluctance to enter World War II. But Hitler changed the nation's and so the South's sense of itself in the world. Many of us were taught at some point in our college educations by refugees from that war, who assumed the central importance of continental philosophy. And there was the example of older southern writers like Allen Tate, who wrote about the affinity he felt with the French poet and thinker Paul Valéry, and William Faulkner, whose earliest literary efforts reflected the profound influence of French poetry. There was the example of Edgar Allan Poe, far more celebrated in the translations of Baudelaire and Mallarmé, in France, than in America.

We all have in common that we have come of professional age—as poets, novelists, and/or critics—no earlier than the 1960s. This is significant not only because it means we are separated from the Rubin generation by age, but also for the different sense of southern history our lived experience has given us. Lewis Simpson speaks for the Rubin generation in expressing the fear that younger southern literati may lack the powerful sense of history that came for our elders from temporal proximity to the Civil War, and that was so essential for their strong sense of southern identity. He outlines four "vital mandates for the continued humanistic inquiry into the history and literature of the American South":

1. A continued effort to recover the character of the white society of the Old South—a society that, while it did not truly grasp its own motives, aspired to be a modern slave society and to develop a justification of slavery that would perpetuate this ancient institution as the chief (some Old South writers said the "sole") agency of civilization.

2. A continued effort to recover the character of the Afro-American society (the world of the slaves) in the Old South as a culture in

its own right—a culture of great moral and spiritual resourcefulness that bears a relation to the subsequent development of all American culture.

3. A continued effort to recover the life and thought of the women of the South, black and white.

4. A continued effort to understand the meaning of the central event in American history, the war some southerners still call the War for Southern Independence but is today almost uniformly called the Civil War. [pp. 250–51]

Of all these mandates, we may only, I think, be found lacking on the fourth. The white slaveholding society still existed, practically if not legally, when we were children. My parents, like many others, had a black cook and yardman. I had a black nurse. My grandmother had a staff of black servants who lived on her property in what had been slave quarters. All were paid unbelievably little but provided with meals and "looked after" if they fell sick, were arrested, or needed money. We have as much reason as any other generation of southerners to attempt to understand that society, for it was ours too, however much we may have been, or may be now, retrospectively, appalled by it. As for mandates two and three, among the contributors, and the writers considered here, there are blacks and there are black and white women. But the Civil War is, undeniably, less immediate to us than to the Rubin generation. This is why Simpson says that "the chances are better [for the continued vitality of southern studies] among students of the South who are in departments of history than for those who are in literary departments."

I say this because the literary historians have been motivated to study the South chiefly by the complex drama of southern history projected by twentieth-century novelists, poets, and (to a limited extent) dramatists, but by now the depletion of this source of motivation has become obvious. I say this not because writers born in the South in the sixties do not constitute another definable generation of skillful literary craftsmen who use the southern setting effectively. . . . What one senses is missing is the literary power generated by the encounter between the imagination of a Faulkner, a Warren, a Lytle, a Caroline Gordon, a Richard Wright and the historical society of the South. The tension produced by this encounter—the quarrel within the self of the artist and between the artist and society that Yeats saw as the essential condition of great poetry and drama—had charged the notable writers of New England in the nineteenth century, but it had been largely absent in the writers living in the closed society of the Old South. . . . When the literary imagination of the South at last became openly responsive to the tensions it experienced, it was capable of . . . producing another classic scene in Faulkner, when near the end of *Intruder in the Dust,* Chick Mallison recalls one of his Uncle Gavin Stevens's eloquent homilies on the South, in which Stevens said that every southern boy has at his memory's instant command the moment at Gettysburg before Pickett began his charge. The literary imagination cannot remedy the fact that the southern writer born in the 1960s has had to find out about Gettysburg from a textbook rather than from the memory of an uncle. . . . At best by the 1960s personal links with the memory of the Civil War had become insubstantial. So had personal links with the memory, black or white, of slavery and its overthrow by the Civil War. [pp. 251–52]

But another cataclysm in southern history, of almost equal significance, may be more meaningful to us than to our elders because we experienced it as children and young adults. I am speaking of the great civil rights upheaval of the 1950s and 1960s that finally put an end to the old agrarian, slavery-based society that still existed, de facto, well into the 1950s. The civil rights movement was a historical event whose righteousness all of us recognized as soon as we were old enough, but we nonetheless could not escape the sense that something was being destroyed, that the very culture was crumbling around us. I felt so probably as much as anyone of my generation, growing up in rural Greene County, Alabama, which before the Civil War had been a wealthy center of the slaveholding, cotton-growing southern culture, and whose population has remained overwhelmingly black and poor—the descendants of slaves. These blacks had been essentially disenfranchised by the few white families, descended from slaveowners, who controlled local politics until the 1960s and still own the land. The heritage of the Old South, its economy and social structure, and the consequences of the Civil War, were thus as immediately real to me—and to many southerners of my generation—as to anyone with an uncle who fought at Gettysburg. However much we may have recognized and welcomed justice in the demise of the old regime, it left an indelible mark on us, black and white. The tensions that it brought to the surface exceeded anything we are ever likely to see again, and they still live inside us. It is those tensions, occasioned by the great second defeat of the Old South in the fifties and sixties, that have produced a new generation of southern writers and critics: James Applewhite, Josephine Humphreys, Gail Godwin, Bobbie Ann Mason, Robb Forman Dew, Andrew Hudgins, and many others.

Simpson has identified the conditions necessary for literature to be produced, for a genuine literary culture to exist. The historical circumstances are clearly there for the "post-Rubin generation." For us, the attention focused by older scholars on the Civil War, and by the older generation of writers on the culture of the Old South, seems, indeed, of more historical than personal significance. But the tremendous, ground-shaking tremors from the Civil War, which did not reach us until the fifties, and the consequent "Americanization" of the South, have received little attention from the older scholars, for whom nothing could approach the mythic greatness of the Civil War. While they were looking back to the period between 1860 and 1865, we were ourselves living through the most violent consequences of that war since the experience of the war itself. That has given us a sense of tension with southern culture, and within ourselves, which may even be more intense and more vital, even fresher than that of our elders, who are often heard to say that their "tensions," which define southernness for them, are growing ever fainter, more ethereal, more purely intellectual —more historical than literary. For literature can thrive only on an immediate, a present sense of tension. And that is why I disagree with Lewis Simpson when he says that the students of history, rather than those of literature, will carry the burden of southern identity for the next generation. The conflict between Old and New South, the sort of tensions we lived through, and still feel, while different from those occasioned by the economic and material devastation of the Civil War and Reconstruction, are too powerful to find expression in the quieter, cooler mode of history alone. Only literature can accommodate them.

And yet, for many theorists, myself included, history has become a primary concern, a fact reflected in most, if not all of the essays in this book. It is no longer possible to separate the literary from the historical. Each is the other's alter ego. My thinking on the question of their interrelatedness was set forth in Losing the Text (1986), where I argued at some length that history is nothing but memory elevated to the status of myth, a kind of literature in reverse. The relation between literature and history is a tautological chiasmus—each a mirror image, a reversal, of the other. I do not wish to repeat that argument here—it is much too long, for one thing —but I stand by it. I do not think that my stance is atypical of the literary scholars and critics of my generation who are committed to theory. The focus of literary theory has changed so much over the past ten years that it might more properly be called cultural theory, for the same phenomena that occur in the acts of reading and writing also occur whenever we engage in communication of any kind. And communication is the basis of all human culture.

It seems entirely appropriate, as I mentioned earlier, that European modes of thinking about literature, culture, and history should have appeared congenial to the newest generation of southern writers and critics. This is why the reader will find essays by European, and European-influenced, non-southern contributors in this volume alongside those by native southerners. For me, the fusion of southern studies with European modes of close reading represents the final stage of escape from the organic nationalism of the Old South. I will explain why I think so. I will start by repeating that European thinkers have a lot to share with southerners, because their culture has known defeat, decline, and loss at least as deeply as ours. This historical experience gives our cultures something in common which America as a country does not know, or did not begin to know until the war in Vietnam.

The burden of the Old South's injustices, which every white southerner cannot help feeling somewhere, sometime, in some way, is comparable in many ways to the guilty memory of German National Socialism harbored by many Europeans. Now, lest the analogy be misconstrued, I do not mean to suggest that Jefferson Davis, or the southern ideology that he represented, is akin to Adolf Hitler's fascism except to the extent that both reflect ideological stances that most people today would agree are morally repugnant. The comparison that I wish to make centers on the essentially *ideological* nature of the southern and German regimes, the persistence of ideology in certain European and southernist discourses, and the essentially anti-ideological force of theory.

A great deal of publicity has recently been given to the fact that Paul de Man, the most powerful literary theorist of his generation in America, wrote articles sympathetic to Nazi ideology when he was a young man in Europe. Most of the reaction has been from de Man's enemies, who have been quick to assert that his later work must reflect their author's early profascist views. Christopher Norris, however, has pointed out what seems to me the only plausible way of understanding de Man's mature work—which represents deconstruction in its purest form—in its relation to these early essays: the later work is clearly a reaction against the nationalistic organicism of those early reviews, and a monumental intellectual edifice against the destructive, delusional power of organicist ideologies of all kinds—including the one according to which the Old South was a great, if doomed, civilization, and the South a kind of benightedly chosen people. Ideologies depend on the assumption that language—that the language of ideology—can state and reveal unmediated Truth. They must then also believe that literature can accomplish the same end. It is no accident that ideological regimes always profess themselves to be highly literary, though in fact I would argue that they must be the opposite. De Man's mature work aims at showing one thing, over and over: that ideology's organicist claims for the word, literary or ideological, are lies. "Thus according to de Man, 'as soon as the word is uttered, it destroys the immediate and discovers that instead of stating Being, it can only state mediation'" (Norris, p. 8). It is in the realm of such mediation that whole nations can be deluded. But the value of great literature, true literature, if it is read closely, is that it erodes any such pretension, including, if necessary, its own, to reveal an unmediated truth.

[De Man's] point is again that Heidegger [whose Nazi sympathies are well known] falls into error in so far as he thinks that language can articulate such truths in a mode of immediate apprehension that would finally transcend history, reason and the antimonies of conscious thought. Such is de Man's chief objection to Heidegger's readings of Hölderlin: that they presume to state explicitly what the poet can only suggest through a language that everywhere acknowledges its own inevitable failure to reconcile these disparate realms. This strikes de Man as a form of hermeneutic violence, a will to penetrate to the truth of a text whose truthfulness lies in its way of avoiding such premature and dangerous absolutes. . . . Heidegger's desire to have poetry achieve an authentic overcoming or transcendence of man's divided condition is complicit with his will to identify language—and the German language preeminently—with the voice of revealed truth. In both aspects his thinking courts the danger of confusing history [and literature as a phenomenon of history, I would add] with processes of natural evolution and growth, a confusion which de Man was later to track through its numerous showings in the discourse of post-Romantic critical thought. [Norris, p. 9]

If I—and I dare not speak for anyone but myself here—have a quarrel with my elders of the Rubin generation, it is precisely that they have retained too many vestiges of a similar organicist, totalizing tendency, which characterized and characterizes old southern ideology as it does any ideology, which is clearly visible in romanticized views of the Old South such as are reflected in *The Library of Southern Literature* and J. B. Hubbell's *The South in American Literature*, both mentioned by Simpson as exemplary of what the Rubin generation has been reacting against. True, they have distanced themselves from such romanticizations of southern history and literature, but most—Simpson himself is a notable exception—have retained a faith in the transparency and organic Truth, the immediacy, of literary language that leaves little, if any room for the mediation of very close, philosophically informed reading prescribed by de Man. For critics such as Rubin, de Manian skepticism represents a kind of literary apostasy, precisely because it denies the integrity and immediacy of the literary object. According to Rubin, the mediation of any critical enterprise is to prepare us for the blinding ascesis afforded only by the literary object itself: "The purpose of literary criticism is to enable us to experience the work of literature with greater richness and depth than might otherwise be possible" (p. 19). George Core, editor of the *Sewanee Review*, more pointedly expresses the same sentiment: "These days criticism has become a desperate ontological and metaphysical manoeuvre, and the structuralists and poststructuralists expect us to admire their preening and pirouetting and to forget that the object of literary criticism is properly literature" (p. 136). No one can blame these gentlemen for denouncing theoretical criticism; if I shared their organicist ideology, I would probably react in similar fashion. It is not surprising that Rubin, Core, and many of their colleagues should accuse "structuralism" (a catch-all term by which Rubin denotes all alien critical perspectives) of distorting texts to suit its own whim: it does so in their view at the outset, by assuming that the text is not an organic, integrated whole which gives access to some pure distillate of True Being. It seems to me, however, that Rubin, and the New Criticism of Brooks and Warren, which imbues the thinking of most of the Rubin generation, distort literature most grievously by confusing its achieved, and admitted mediatedness with unmediated Truth. This is only a thinner, watered-down version of the nationalist, ideological organicism of the Old South, which led it to believe in its own infallible and true virtuousness, and in its destiny to preserve western civilization through slavery, and vice-versa, and which led the first generation of scholars of southern

literature to a rather sentimental and celebratory view of the past. That
there are still vestiges of this old southern ideology left in the work of the
Rubin generation means that there is work—important work—left to be
done in southern literary scholarship. There is still a threshold, beyond
ideology, to be crossed. To cross it is the purpose of this book.

In a certain sense, my argument here, that there is a viable, necessary
next stage in southern literary study, only repeats Lewis Simpson's teleological view of the progress of southern literary identity. In one sense
we, the post-Rubin generation, have postponed the apocalypse only long
enough to give ourselves time to speak. But this may be unavoidable, for I
believe that all fertile literary cultures are grounded in a sense of ongoing
loss and defeat. By this I mean that before the Civil War the South did not
exist in the sense that it does and has since 1865, but only in embryo, in
the latency of its paranoid belligerence in the defense of an institution that
had to be defended so stoutly because it was indefensible, and because it
posed real dangers, dramatically demonstrated by the slave uprisings of
Nat Turner and others, and by Toussaint L'Ouverture's bloody revolution
in Haiti. The only pre–Civil War southern writer with real, deep affinities
with twentieth-century southern literature is Poe—also the first of many
to strike a deeply resonant chord in European readers—and this is because
his mind was characterized by a sense of loss and defeat which, while personal rather than historical, was nevertheless powerful enough to control
his literary vision. Literature's value, and its power to compel attention,
are similarly grounded in a sense of its evanescence. Simpson is not the
only, or the youngest living scholar to assert that the modern West has no
need of literature and the man of letters, that literature is rapidly losing
its value as a commodity in an age of television and personal computers:
"American society today does not conceive literacy to be a central need in
the maintenance of civilizational order. The motive of literary alienation
—the keeping alive of 'the spirit of the letter'—is draining away" (*Man of
Letters in New England and the South,* p. 254). In fact, similar assertions
have been made for centuries, since the Middle Ages at least. As long as
such assertions are made, we can be sure that literary culture is alive, for
Simpson's statement reflects, is motivated by, the very literary alienation
that it claims to be "draining away." The vitality of Simpson's own work,
and its grounding in a sense of alienation too powerful and too profound
to be anything but literary, denies most emphatically that the demise of
southern literary culture is at hand. But it is part of our pleasure in literature to believe in and assert its fragile evanescence, to assert that, as a

literary culture, we are near the end in the South. So I will not bother to state outright what I have already implied, that southern identity may not survive the passing of the post-Rubin generation. I will say only that if we did not at least tacitly believe so, it would not have survived in us.

I should repeat here what I said at the outset: this collection is intended to suggest the possible range of theoretical approaches to southern literature, and to demonstrate the validity, indeed the *necessity,* of such approaches; it most emphatically does not pretend to exhaust those possibilities and it rejects any idea that they should be defined in a homogeneous manner. This book represents a beginning, and, because of the nature of literary theory, a highly heterodox one.

The debt which I, and the younger generation of southernists, owe to Lewis Simpson is apparent from the volume of his words reproduced in this essay. He, of all his generation, has practiced, and urged by example, a skepticism in critical thought, and I have explained why and how skepticism leads directly to theoretical concerns. He has identified himself as a member of the Rubin generation, but I will claim that in spirit, he is one of us. For this reason, this volume of essays is dedicated to Lewis P. Simpson, scholar, man of letters, theorist.

My great thanks are due to the American Council of Learned Societies; I do not know how or why they decided to support this project, but they did. Without their financial encouragement, the project might never have been completed. Thanks also to Oxford University Press for permission to reprint here an essay that first appeared, in slightly different form, in my book *The Puritan and the Cynic* (1986), and to Michael Dennison, who served as my editorial assistant for the project. I should also acknowledge that a quite different form of this introduction appeared in the fall 1989 edition of the *Yale Journal of Criticism.*

WORKS CITED

Core, George. "Agrarianism, Criticism, and the Academy." *A Band of Prophets: The Vanderbilt Agrarians After Fifty Years,* pp. 117–40. Baton Rouge: Louisiana State University Press, 1982.

Norris, Christopher. "Paul de Man's Past." *London Review of Books,* 4 February 1988, pp. 8–11.

Rubin, Louis D. "Robert Penn Warren: Critic." *A Southern Renascence Man,* edited by Walter B. Edgar. Baton Rouge: Louisiana State University Press, 1984.

Simpson, Lewis P. "The State of Southern Literary Scholarship." *The Southern Review* 24, no. 2 (Spring 1988): 245–52.

——. *The Man of Letters in New England and the South: Essays on the History of the Literary Vocation in America*. Baton Rouge: Louisiana State University Press, 1973.

Southern Literature

and Literary Theory

Sd: for an African Chronicle

Here, below the line,
Is our ancestral yard,
Replete with codicils and broken-necked guitars;
Pine-needle bed of history.

Above the bar,
An endless play of signifiers,
Harmonica bridges,
Gut-bucket connectives that
Span black time,
All blue.

—Houston Baker

Constructing the River

The sequences of the river write themselves
Anew every day. It is a flow which dries
In lines from my pen. Fine dogwood twigs
End in periods of buds, limb-type prints
Phonemes of foam on air. Words are things.
I feel them in my brain's blood, forming with my
Running. I am accompanied through a narrowing
Where path comes close to rocky shallows by a
Continuous murmuring of the many streams' tongues
The rapids form. I use *foam, stream,* and *tongue*
For their sound. So language refers to itself.
Millipede with tail in its mouth, it circles
In these woods and every word is a leg touching
Water or tree. The cliff shows an intrusion of quartz,
Crystalline vein continuing even where
Softer stone has rotted to loam. Word is not
Object but both exist and align. This poem
I am writing is not precisely the one in my head
As I was running. This presence is an illusion.
The relation between word-thing and quartz vein
Is something seen, clear air, quintessential
As metaphor. It was not there before. Poor
As we are, this affluent gleam at the speed
Of light vibrates between noun and thing, almost
Joining them. Grandsons of Freud, we handle
The mental toy, make it disappear like mother,
Fort/da, fort/da. We visit our own funerals with
Huck Finn. The word-river cherishes time that was,
That is, that will never again be. Is elegy.
                                        —James Applewhite

Mark Twain, William Wells Brown,

and the Problem of Authority in

New South Writing

WILLIAM L. ANDREWS

Until the late 1960s the history and criticism of southern literature in America proceeded from the unwritten assumption that the literature of the South was the product of white, predominantly male southerners. Black writers from the South belonged to a separate province of letters that was reconstructed into Negro American literature mainly by the literary historians and critics who taught in the black colleges of the South. Owing to the enormous influence of his myth and his message on both sides of the color line, Booker T. Washington was one of the few black writers who held a secure niche in both southern and Negro literature before the onset of the civil rights movement in the late 1950s. Charles W. Chesnutt, a figure of the first importance to students of Negro literature, footnoted Joel Chandler Harris in standard accounts of southern literature. In Faulkner's shadow lurked Richard Wright, but Wright's perspective on the South was judged parochial next to Faulkner's much-vaunted universality. White southern criticism chose Faulkner more than any other single writer to explain southern race relations to the world. Black critics accepted Richard Wright as a brave new spokesman for their side of the controversial issue. But until very recently virtually no published discourse ensued between the two literary camps.[1]

As the study of Afro-American history, literature, and culture boomed in the 1960s and 1970s, the significance of the black writer in the literature of the South underwent considerable reevaluation. Not surprisingly, the desegregation of southern literary history and criticism received its impetus from black researchers and commentators. It was they who first began to argue that the autobiographical writing of ex-slaves like Frederick Douglass and William Wells Brown served as a critique of the plantation tradition of antebellum southern literature.[2] In their analyses, the fiction of Chesnutt had to be read as a corrective to the excesses of Harris and Thomas Nelson Page.[3] James Weldon Johnson, Jean Toomer, and Zora Neale Hurston offered insights into the folk traditions of the South that could not be found in DuBose Heyward, Paul Green, or Erskine Caldwell. Faulkner's "Negro" was a mythic construct of white southern society filtered through the divided consciousness of the artist.[4] One could learn more about southern history from Margaret Walker's Vyry Brown than from Margaret Mitchell's Scarlet O'Hara. As a consequence of these changing perspectives, the southern affiliations of a host of black writers, ranging from the eighteenth-century poet George Moses Horton to the contemporary novelist Ernest J. Gaines, have become matters of serious investigation to southern literary criticism.[5]

The impact of these developments on the long-assumed plenary status of white writing in the literary history of the South is not difficult to summarize. The margin and the center have been reversed in a few areas of southern literary history, such as in the narrative of antebellum life, where Douglass now takes precedence over John Pendleton Kennedy as an authority on plantation life, and the slave narrative generates more critical inquiry than the *Partisan Leader* or the *Yemassee*. One could argue that Gaines's Miss Jane Pittman is no more historical or representative than William Styron's Nat Turner, but the respectability earned by the one compared with the suspicion that still clings to the other testifies to the moral authority that black southern literature has been gaining in competition with much white southern literature for this era's interpretation of the racial past. Is it advisable, however (to reapply a phrase of Ralph Ellison's), simply to slip the yoke of marginality from one group of writers to another without changing the joke that southern literary historians and critics have for too long been playing on themselves and their readers, namely, that a single race or sex or mode of southern writing can be awarded plenary or representative status?

Let us grant the fact that black and white writers of the South have usually treated the racial competitor as an alien, the better to picture oneself and one's people at the moral, and often the historical and intellectual, center of things. We still should recognize that such marginalization is a rhetorical strategy that informs certain traditions in southern literature; it is not a determining or structuring principle of southern literary history. Underlying this rhetorical strategy is an assumption of a degree and kind of authority without which the strategy cannot be invoked. In this essay I propose to examine not the rhetoric of marginalization but the problem of literary authorization that underlies it. To avoid the rhetoric of marginalization in my own essay, I want to focus on a transitional point in southern literary history—the early 1880s—when "the southern quest for literary authority" (to use Lewis P. Simpson's phrase) confronted major black and white writers with a common problem: how to authorize a brand of first-person narration largely alien to the southern literary tradition at a time when the South's own authority, indeed, its very identity, lay very much in doubt.[6]

William Wells Brown's *My Southern Home* (1880) and Mark Twain's *Life on the Mississippi* (1883), perhaps the first important literary expressions of the "new," that is, the post-Reconstruction, South, are fundamentally concerned with this problem of authorizing a new kind of southern writer and writing. Critics have often complained that a lack of consistency and proportion and a disjunctiveness of form in these books vitiate their literary quality and rhetorical authority.[7] It is possible and more useful, however, to consider each text as a field of experiment and play with the idea of authority itself.

The end of Reconstruction found the South casting about for a new raison d'être, one that would accommodate its increasingly grandiose vision of its future and its moral ambivalence toward its past.[8] Antebellum southern authors who became more self-consciously "southern" after the war than before it—men like William Gilmore Simms and Paul Hamilton Hayne—struggled, often futilely, to retain their authority in the eyes of northern readers.[9] The new southern writers, epitomized in the late 1870s and early 1880s by George W. Cable, Joel Chandler Harris, Mary Boykin Chesnut, and Brown and Clemens, realized that with the collapse of the Confederacy they had lost a firmly defined, coherent, and morally defensible myth and image of the South on which they could depend for a tradition, a sense of order, a structure of values, and a reason for their own literary being. All these resources from which the southern writer had traditionally drawn his or her authority had to be reconstructed, if not reinvented, by the postbellum southern writer. While this posed many problems for this new generation of writers, their marginal relationship to both the old and the inchoate new social orders did have one advantage. It placed them in what Allen Tate has called "the perfect literary situation."[10]

For all its uncertainties, the post-Reconstruction literary scene was wide open enough to allow new southern writers to test and exploit the "author-function" of certain modes of ironic discourse, particularly in the guise of first-person narration, that had not been admitted to or authorized in the official—that is, the apologetic—literature of the antebellum South. [11]

In the early dialect fiction of Cable and Harris and in the revision of her diary that Chesnut undertook in the early 1880s we discover the post-Reconstruction southern litterateur engaged in experiments with narrative personae (Harris's Uncle Remus), generic conventions (Chesnut's "diary"), and modes of treatment of material (Cable's local color realism) that could endow his or her writing with an authority that the name of its creator could not readily confer. All these devices serve to heighten the sense of objectivity in these texts. It's not the new southern writer we seem to hear—it's a black relic of slavery; it's the knights and ladies of the Confederacy; it's the quaint old New Orleans Creoles. The problem of how to render the New South and how to realize the new southerner as a morally and historically viable self in his or her own right is not so much confronted as circumvented in the early fiction of Cable, Harris, and Chesnut.

By contrast, the narrators of *My Southern Home* and *Life on the Mississippi* approach their readers in an unabashed autobiographical vein as new southerners untouched by the guilt, bitterness, pugnacity, or nostalgia for the old days that so easily undermined the authority of southern writers in the postwar era. Both of these books seem to be advertisements for a new kind of southern self, one whose proven roots in the antebellum world and progressive views of the postbellum scene enable it to bridge the chasm between the Old and New Souths.

The decision of the Civil War placed the New South writer "under a maximum obligation to memory," Lewis Simpson argues. Deprived by history of their ideal of a national identity, the people of the postbellum South clung to the past with "a compulsive need" that evolved into "a revealed faith" in "a metaphysics of remembrance" that would show them who they had been and were to be.[12] The quasi-autobiographical form of *My Southern Home* and *Life on the Mississippi* invites us from the outset to invest a similar kind of faith in the revelatory power of each of these writers' memories. The title of Brown's book suggests that his will be a rosy reminiscence, but his preface warns us that he will not indulge our "imagination" or emotions, nor will he transform the people of his past into "heroes or heroines." While telling us how he became a riverboat pilot, Mark Twain extols the wonderful exactness of the pilot's memory, which allows him to surpass the ordinary man's "I think" with a resounding "I know."[13] Statements like these seem designed to authorize each writer as a realistic and reliable first-person historian of self and region. Readers of Brown and Mark Twain are asked to place themselves "under a maximum obligation" to a particular writer's memory instead of venerating the standard objects of the postbellum southern literary memory, such as the courtly code, the organic social hierarchy, or the agrarian ideals of the Old South. The subject in both *My Southern Home* and *Life on the Mississippi* often displays a marked resistance to the veneration of much of the subject matter of these two books.

Because of their newness on the postwar literary scene and their consequent anxieties about offending the sensibilities of their dual audience; both writers resort to what Freud called "tendency-wit" as a way to displace and dispose of those cultural and literary authorities whose precedence restricted the new southern writer's self-promotion.[14] The Old South in both men's books is not taken as seriously as it is in the scores of reverent reminiscences of the antebellum order, fictional as well as autobiographical, that flooded late-nineteenth- and early-twentieth-century America. But then how seriously, one is compelled to ask, should we take the narrators of these two often profane personal histories of the antebellum scene and satiric commentaries on the contemporary South? We shall be better able to answer this question after we have examined the basic motif that structures the dramatic action in both *My Southern Home* and *Life on the Mississippi:* the contest for power and mastery between possessors of and aspirants to authority.

The act of imaginative recollection—the organization of remembered particulars of experience into a meaningful whole, a *storia*—cannot take place, according to Vico, unless the mind has access to a master image of human experience that can accommodate both the materials of individual experience and their potential significances.[15] For William Wells Brown and Mark Twain, the master image of their personal histories centers on the making and unmaking of masters in the Old South. In *Life on the Mississippi* we are introduced to the master pilot of the Mississippi River, a man of "boundless authority," "the only unfettered and entirely independent human being that lived in the earth." We are shown how a cub pilot was initiated into the august company of these "absolute monarchs" of the river, and we discover the ex-pilot's nostalgia for his lost freedom and authority when Mark Twain compares his former status on the river to his current vocation as a literary man. "Writers of all kinds are manacled servants of the public. . . . In truth, every man and woman and child has a master, and worries and frets in servitude; but in the day I write of, the Mississippi pilot had *none*" (313–14). In *My Southern Home*, it is the subversion and unmaking of mastery on an antebellum Missouri plantation that we witness repeatedly. Dr. John Gaines and his wife, Sarah, master and mistress of Poplar Farm, ten miles north of St. Louis, are introduced by the narrator as pious, respectable people who presided over "a happy family" of white and black dependents. The narrator remarks Dr. Gaines's paternalistic concern for the eternal welfare of his slaves' souls, and he notes that corporal punishment was meted out on Poplar Farm only to the degree that it "was actually needed to insure respect to the master, and good government to the slave population" (3–4, 82). Nevertheless, in chapter after chapter of the book, the narrator records instances of the witty guilefulness and resistance to masterly authority endemic in Gaines's slaves. "We had three or four trustworthy and faithful servants," the narrator recalls, but "most of the negroes on 'Poplar Farm' . . . thought that to deceive the whites was a religious duty." The master and mistress "were easily deceived by their servants." "Indeed, I often thought that Mrs. Gaines took peculiar pleasure in being misled by them; and even the Doctor, with his long experience and shrewdness, would allow himself to be carried off upon almost any pretext" (52–53). When compared with the rigid mastery exerted by whites over blacks in the post-Reconstruction South, one emanating from "a reign of terror" and accepting nothing less than "complete submission to the whites" (165–66), the freer play of authority on the Gaines plantation gives Brown reason to sound a nostalgic note for the antebellum era.

What the two writers' master images of antebellum southern life hold in common is an attention to the discursive, rather than the institutional or ideological, underpinnings of authority in the Old South. Masters of the river as well as the shore were not born but made—and unmade—and made and unmade again, according to verbal rituals and combats of wit that bonded superior and subaltern in a perpetual competition for mastery of the moment. *My Southern Home* and *Life on the Mississippi* celebrate the masters of these kinds of discursive authority in order to prepare their readers to accept the implicit claims that each text ultimately makes to a radical discursive authority of its own.

The hallmark of a riverman, Mark Twain informs us throughout the story of his initiation as a cub pilot, is his marvelous facility with language. "I wished I could talk like that," he tells us after describing the picturesque profanity of the imperious mate who so disdainfully ignored him during his first trip down the river. The callow cub longs to acquire the style of river speech, but more important, he covets the authority that such profane utterance both signifies and punctuates. The profanity of rivermen is an index of their contempt for the standards and manners held sacred by landspeople. Pilots like Mr. Bixby, the cub's instructor in river matters, are masters of profanity because they have "no respect for anything or anybody" (316), not even their own, a fact that is underscored by the example of "Stephen W.," who profanes the friendship of a fellow pilot by borrowing shamelessly from him and then lying to him in the most extravagantly obvious way about his determination to repay him. The pilot is the epitome of self-important egoism and the enemy of self-confidence in anyone else. He trains his cub by frequent "strategic tricks" that humiliate whatever pride in his own authority the apprentice may develop.

Perhaps the key moment of initiation for the cub comes when Bixby introduces him to the subtleties of bluff reefs and wind reefs. The former signal catastrophe if struck head-on by a steamboat, while the latter are merely the product of wind gusting over the water. Yet it is impossible for the uninitiated to tell one from the other. When asked how he distinguishes between the two, Bixby says it is an instinctual power that pilots " 'just naturally' " develop, but it is impossible " 'to explain why or how you know them apart' " (283). Once he can claim this intuitive power for his own, however, the cub assumes the most authoritative of all the linguistic skills of the river. He moves from talking to reading like a pilot; he becomes a "master [of] the language" of the "wonderful book" of the river (284). Through discourse with the river, he achieves the necessary confidence, the self-endorsed authority, to discriminate between the romantic appearances and underlying realities that characterize the narrative flow of the river, according to the pilot-narrator.

The pilot's authority, therefore, depends on his mastery of the arts of speaking and reading. He uses speech to profane all authorities other than his own and that of the river itself, with which he apparently holds constant discourse, both conscious and unconscious. From his intuitive communion with the river he receives a supposed ineffable power to read its secrets, the knowledge of which becomes the special gnosis that gives him an elite status and qualifies him to give orders where others must only request, to say "I know" where others can only hazard an "I think." For reasons that Mark Twain's reader only gradually realizes, the pilot is as careful to cultivate the mystique of his own authority as he is to demolish anyone else's. This is because he knows that the mystification of authority is just as necessary as its profanation to any speaker (or writer) who desires to displace his audience's self-confidence with his own authority.

When Mark Twain needed to authorize himself as the guide to the reading of the Mississippi of his book, he reapplied the lessons he had learned from the pilots of his past. After displaying Bixby the pilot in all his self-mystifying glory and showing enthusiasm over "the rank and dignity of piloting," Mark Twain sets about profaning the memory of pilots en masse in the chapter entitled "The Pilots' Monopoly." There he demystifies the sources of the pilot's marvelous gnosis: his ability to navigate the river successfully depends not on the mysteries of intuition but on a simple mechanism of information gathering and storage. Monopoly pilots (like Mark Twain himself) kept notes on the changes in the river that affected navigation, and they deposited that information in a series of wharf-boxes provided by the pilots' monopoly for the use of its members up and down the river. The more we learn of the methods of the monopoly, the more questionable we find Mark Twain's earlier claims for the pilot's untrammeled freedom and independence. As for any given pilot's authority as a reader of the river—that, it seems, was merely provisional and fleeting; it was revised and replaced daily, even hourly, by the reports of every successive pilot who arrived at a wharf-box with fresh notes on the state of the river as he saw it. Instead of the romantic image of Bixby, the last pilot we see in Mark Twain's narrative of the antebellum river era is the mean-spirited Mr. Brown, against whose authority the cub finally rebels, exposing his purported master as merely a verbal blusterer, a coward, and a fool.

Which side of the pilot are we finally to believe in—Bixby or Brown? To what extent does Mark Twain's satiric portrait of Brown reflect his unacknowledged resentment of Bixby and of all the masters of the river whose authority he needed to cast off in order to come into his own? Where is Mark Twain being comic and ironic; where is he straightforward and serious in his making and unmaking of the image of the pilot? Such questions, as James M. Cox has wisely pointed out, are ones that Mark Twain elicits regularly in his work, not to fulfill but to frustrate his reader's expectations that he or she will finally discover the "real" Mark Twain somewhere behind all the masks and impersonations.[16] A reading of *Life on the Mississippi* may very well lead us to conclude that its narrator really was a steamboat pilot, but we are hardly justified in deducing from that apparent fact that the narrator is reliable or authoritative in what he tells us about himself or about life on the river. We must remember that, by the narrator's own admission, "your true pilot cares nothing about anything on earth but the river" (268). This suggests that to the "true pilot" telling the truth—and the authority that being deemed a truth-teller would give him—is of secondary importance to giving voice to all that the river signifies. When this literary pilot talks about the river we can assume only that like all pilots he aims to be "always interesting" (268), not consistently truthful.

The issue is, what effect does this attitude of the narrator's have on the way in which we read *Life on the Mississippi* and on the authority of either narrator or text? If the pilot-narrator's purpose and standards as a writer bind him not to truth-telling but only to being "interesting" about the river, is he actually making an appeal to authority at all? Clearly, the more we read of *Life on the Mississippi,* the more we discover the narrator's disrespect for many sources of authority, particularly those emanating from the Old South and justified by an appeal to romantic idealism. Like the profane "pet parrot" that presides over the postwar Mississippi's dominant vessel, the tugboat (507), Mark Twain cannot resist an ironic parroting—that is, parodying—of even his own pretensions to special powers of insight into the marvels of the river. In chapter 24, significantly entitled "My Incognito Is Exploded," Mark Twain shows us a pilot yarning grandly on the mysteries of "alligator water" reading, explaining, in terms that burlesque Mark Twain's earlier mystification of the pilot's occult powers of "water-reading," that to " 'judge of alligator water . . . was n't a thing a body could *learn,* you had to be born with it' " (374). As in *Innocents Abroad* and *Roughing It,* we learn by reading *Life on the Mississippi* that we invest confidence and authority in Mark Twain's narrator only at our peril.

But there is something profounder to be learned from Mark Twain about the reading process than this alone. Through the experience of reading his book about the Mississippi, the reader is thrust into a situation analogous to that of anyone who attempts to read the "wonderful book," the magnificent text, of the river itself. The only way to suggest to the landsman-reader what it is like to experience that text is to reenact an analogous scene of reading—the reading of *Life on the Mississippi*—in which a written text evokes something like the complex of responses elicited by the act of reading the river itself. What Mark Twain tries to do, therefore, is to make his book *about* the river *read like* the text of the river. This leads him to produce in *Life on the Mississippi* a variant of Roland Barthes's "text of bliss," [17] a book that challenges readers just as the river dares army engineers to "make [it] over again" (398), to reconstruct and "boss" it into fixed and controllable channels the better to ensure steady and confident navigation of its narrative flow.

Like Barthes's "text of bliss," the river and Mark Twain's river-text demand that their readers learn to read according to the dictates of the text. Like a text the river profoundly unsettles and discomfits the cub as he tries vainly to decode all its signifiers and record them and their "meaning" conveniently for his memorandum book. The reader of *Life on the Mississippi* encounters similar kinds of problems. What the cub pilot realizes is also what Mark Twain's reader must realize: that everything about the river is ungrounded; all its signifiers are in flux, "eluding and ungraspable," "dissolving and changeful" (278). Just as a text defies generic codification, so the river and Mark Twain's river-text "play havoc with boundary lines and jurisdictions" (228). Reading the text of the river and the river-text imposes something like what Barthes calls a "state of loss" for the reader of any text of bliss; one loses one's capacity to indulge unselfconsciously in the "romance and beauty" of the world supposedly recapitulated by the text. What is gained, however, are the manifold "pleasures of the text," the chief of which is the capacity to be "always interesting" (as the pilot is when expatiating on the river), to be as "absorbing," as "unflagging," and as "sparklingly renewed with every re-perusal" (283–84) as the river is whenever it is reread. These are the qualities that make *Life on the Mississippi* as perpetually provocative as the text of the river itself.

Most of Mark Twain's southern literary contemporaries tried to authorize themselves as interpreters of southern reality via acts of literary reconstruction, such as that attempted by white "plantation writers" like Thomas Nelson Page who recreated slavery so as to authorize themselves as the true and reliable elucidators of this dark and misunderstood subject. Mark Twain, on the other hand, did not attempt simply to reconstruct Mississippi River life as a tribute to his powers of literary comprehension; his text also testifies to the capacity of the river—indeed, of any text—to deconstruct the authority of interpretive attempts to comprehend it. Like the river, Mark Twain's text is a law unto itself. It authorizes itself by de-authorizing its narrator, southern life and history, even its reader's expectations, as priorities to which it must bind itself and appeal in order to assume an "author-function" in the new literary scheme of things. What

Life on the Mississippi authorizes is a fundamental skepticism about any authority that fails to acknowledge its own provisionality. At the same time, the text demonstrates an exuberant comic awareness of the advantages that this kind of textual freedom can have for the new southern writer in search of a way to capitalize on his own marginality vis-à-vis the authorities of traditional southern literary expression.

In *My Southern Home* the unmaking or, rather, the unmasking of the pretensions of white mastery on the antebellum plantation goes hand in hand with black attempts to become masters of their own fate, often at the expense of their owners. As a sketchbook of mostly comic episodes involving southern character types—the indulgent master, the pompous preacher, the witty slave, the beautiful quadroon, the hypocritical slave trader, and so forth—the opening chapters of *My Southern Home* sound like the work of a local colorist who is especially knowledgeable about slave lore, as instanced in the number of slave songs, corn-shucking verbal games, and hoodoo practices that he discusses. With the exception of the speculators in slaves, the antebellum whites recalled for us are not pictured as inhuman or depraved by their status as slave masters. What disqualifies them from the authority that southern writers traditionally accorded the plantation master and mistress is not so much a moral blot as a comic predilection for self-deception. The whites in the Gaines's circle are made ridiculous by the ironic disparity between their actual behavior and the myths that they appropriate from southern tradition to help them justify and aggrandize themselves in a society much less genteel than it appears to be. Mrs. Gaines boasts publicly about her blue blood and her family's social superiority, but to her slaves Dolly and Susan she acts more like poor white trash. " 'You can't speck nothin' more dan a jump from a frog,' " Susan reminds Dolly while commenting on her mistress's so-called breeding. " 'Missis says she is one ob de akastocacy; but she ain't no more of an akastocacy dan I is. Missis says she was born wid a silver spoon in her mouf; ef she was, I wish it had a-choked her, dat' what I wish' " (46).

Brown's extensive use of Negro dialect in *My Southern Home* sounds much in the vein of postwar southern local color. When Susan substitutes "akastocacy" for "aristocracy" in her comment on Mrs. Gaines, one could easily take her for the sort of malaprop-mouthing Negro exploited in the "darkey humor" of late-nineteenth-century popular American literature.[18] The usual motive behind such malformed speech is conceit, which the error in pronunciation helps to expose and ridicule. However, Susan does not wish to promote herself to the "akastocacy"; she intends to demote her mistress from it. In the process of doing this, her rendition of "aristocracy" into "akastocacy" provides a parodic translation and comic reinterpretation of a word held sacred to her mistress and the world of antebellum southern gentility. What is the southern "akastocacy" if not, quite literally, *a caste-ocracy?* This is but one example of the way in which the slaves profanely redefine the very language of authority as the whites employ it in *My Southern Home.* When a slave posing as a physician dons Dr. Gaines's coat in order to " 'look suspectable' " to any Negro who might come to the office for medical advice, we realize that the joke is as much on the reliability of the doctor's medical knowledge as it is on his slave's.

Throughout Brown's reminiscences of the Old South slaves vie verbally with their masters and each other for mastery of situations. Authority rarely emanates from a fixed and acknowledged source; authority is transactional, a product of discourse, especially of wit contests in dialogue. A quick-witted slave like Cato, who appears repeatedly in *My Southern Home,* plays a role in Gaines's household similar to that of a Renaissance court fool. When called upon to toast his master, he does so in a mocking, ironic bit of doggerel:

> "De big bee flies high,
> De little bee makes de honey,
> De black man raise de cotton,
>   An' de white man gets de money."

That Cato only plays the fool becomes clear in his successful hoodwinking of slavecatchers and a treacherous fellow slave who vainly try to stop him from escaping to freedom later in the narrative. Dinkie, the resident conjurer on Poplar Farm, could give lessons to his master in the art of the mystification of authority. Dinkie alone among all the men on the plantation does no work, yet he commands universal respect from whites and blacks because he knows how to turn their superstitious fears of the devil to his own advantage. Dinkie's only weapon is talk, but against his powers of suggestion even a hard-bitten overseer loses his nerve. The conjure man "was his own master" (71) because he plays the role better than Dr. Gaines does and enforces his authority more convincingly than either the doctor or his overseer can. Reinforcing Brown's image of an antebellum South that recognizes no higher authority than self-preservation is Pompey, the servant of the Mississippi slave trader James Walker. Walker's practice is to cheat prospective buyers of his merchandise by advertising slaves as younger and healthier than they actually are. Pompey carries out his master's will by teaching the advertised slaves how to lie about their ages and conditions. Pompey assures the whites who deal with him that there is "no bogus" about him, but when his master decides to have him flogged in the New Orleans slave prison because of carelessness, Pompey proves himself a master practitioner, as well as teacher, of the art of self-misrepresentation. First he tricks a black freeman into taking his punishment; then he tricks his master into thinking that he received the beating that Walker intended for him.

Unlike Mark Twain, who grows almost rhapsodic when he recalls the glory of the pilot's authority, Brown recounts the struggles for power and prestige among whites and blacks in the slaveocracy in a deadpan, detached tone that seldom betrays his identification with either the Pompeys and Catos or the Walkers and Gaineses of the Old South. In fact, the further one reads in *My Southern Home* the more intriguing the identity of its narrator becomes. On what authority does he recount the most private conversations of slaves in the kitchen of the plantation big house and the preaching and praying of the poor whites at their nearby place of worship? This narrator never specifically identifies his place in the world of Poplar Farm, but phrases like "we in the great house" (19), "we had three or four trustworthy and faithful servants" (52), and "our city negroes" (122), interspersed among scenes in which the narrator and the whites of the Gaines circle appear on very close terms, imply that the point of view is that of a white southerner. Like many postwar whites who wrote reminiscences of their antebellum southern youth, this narrator puts the best possible face on some aspects of slavery made infamous in abolitionist attacks on the South. "Cruelty to negroes was not practiced in our section," he remarks; "if a servant disobeyed orders, it was necessary that he should be flogged, to deter others from following the bad example" (82). The narrator also can take the condescending tone that white southerners often adopted in generalizing authoritatively about "the negro." "Sympathetic in his nature, thoughtless in his feelings, both alimentativeness and amativeness large, the negro is better adapted to follow than to lead." He continues: "History shows that of all races, the African was best adapted to be the 'hewers of wood, and drawers of water'" (91).[19]

These conclusions about blacks and slavery are entered into *My Southern Home* in the form of what Bakhtin has called "authoritative discourse," the expression of generally acknowledged or official truths that stem from some prior authority and are usually demarcated in a text in a special way, either through quotation marks or through prefatory allusions to the authority from which the discourse has issued.[20] The narrator of *My Southern Home* turns his judgment of "the African" into a variant of this "authoritarian enforced discourse" by citing "history," the contemporary science of phrenology, and the bible as intellectual and ideological sanctions for his comments. No one who reads the history of the South as presented in this text, however, can ignore the fact that these conclusions about the Negro are not supported by the example of Dinkie, or by Pompey's facility at manipulating his master, or by the success of Cato in planning and executing his flight to freedom. As is typical of "authoritative discourse," the narrator's judgment of the Negro distances itself from its own narrative context, confronting the reader's consciousness in such a way as to demand either total affirmation or total rejection of its premises. To accept the "authoritative discourse" about blacks and slavery one must ignore the counterauthority of the text itself. Yet the narrator himself is responsible for entering the "authoritative discourse" into the text. Does this not imply his endorsement of it, especially since he himself seems to be a white southerner?

It is difficult for the reader of the first half of *My Southern Home* to conclude otherwise. The narrator does picture southern whites as rather less masterful than the traditional image of patriarchal slavery maintained; he also describes blacks as a good deal more canny and resourceful than "history," science, or his biblical authorities state. He may be a rather liberal southerner, given his dismissal of the charge that granting civil rights to former slaves will "make it incumbent upon us to take these people into our houses, and give them seats in our social circle, beyond what we would accord to other total strangers" (163). But not until he begins to recount his travels in the post-Reconstruction South does the narrator start violating the confidence based on an implied identity of interests that he set up in the first half of his book between himself, the ostensible white southerner, and his white northern reader.

In the role of southern critic of the New South, the narrator of *My Southern Home* pontificates on the errors of Reconstruction as authoritatively as Mark Twain on the excesses of southern romanticism. Despite the many faults of the black-dominated state legislatures during Reconstruction, the narrator asserts that the standard of government they introduced "surpassed" that of "the whites that had preceded them" (183). As for the new white supremacist governments of the South, theirs is a "cause of oppression scarcely second in hatefulness to that of chattel slavery" (225). These comments, of course, evidence a degree of heresy against the myth of the new southern order that even Cable in his most censorious writing about the South never approached. Given this reactionary political environment, the narrator advises the newly freed Negroes to curb their love of "extravagance" in everything from clothing to religion, to stop aping the whites uncritically, to dedicate themselves to education, and to start cooperating in social and economic spheres so as to build up racial "self-reliance." The more the narrator of My Southern Home warms to his role as critic and adviser of southern blacks, the more openly he identifies with them. "The colored people of the South" become "our people." "To elevate ourselves and our children," the narrator preaches in the latter pages of his book, "we must cultivate self-denial" (233). He includes himself in the general observation that blacks "have no confidence in each other. We consider the goods from the store of a white man necessarily better than can be purchased from a colored man" (237). My Southern Home ends with an admonitory exemplum about a black man who, objecting to being labeled as a Negro, demands instead to be addressed as "an American." Should an Irishman deny his brogue and by implication his ethnic identity in order to be regarded as an American, asks the narrator? Why then should a Negro disavow his color? "Black men," the narrator urges in the final lines of My Southern Home, "don't be ashamed to show your colors, and to own them."

This is a consummate irony. A narrator who has masked his own color through the first half of his text, even to the point of virtually contradicting the harsh image of southern slavery that Brown had painted in his antebellum slave narrative, concludes by exhorting other black men not to be ashamed to acknowledge their color.[21] After having obscured—one might say deliberately mystified—his status in the Old South so that he might reinforce his narrative with the authority of a white southerner, the narrator gradually removes the veil from his reader's eyes and by the end of his story lays claim to the authority of a black southerner who lectures his people from a progressive, northern vantage point. This claim to the authority of the Yankeefied black southerner would seem to nullify the narrator's earlier implicit claim to authority as a white southerner. Indeed, the narrator would seem to have forfeited virtually any pretense to authority at all by this revelation of his color(s), since he has exposed himself to his white reader as a black literary confidence man and to his black reader as a self-contradictory, if not hypocritical, preacher of secular salvation.

It is unlikely, however, that a writer as skilled and experienced as Brown would have brought his text to such a final aporia without having deliberately planned to place his reader in a quandary.[22] When the narrator of *My Southern Home* exhorts blacks to show their colors boldly, he puns ironically on the idea of colors as a flag or symbol of one's position or opinion, to be owned or disowned at will, and on the idea of color as an indelible, inescapable signifier of one's race which a racist society demands be owned in the manner dictated by that society. How can colored men escape being owned by the color signification of racist America so that they can identify themselves according to colors that signify what *they* determine? If there is an answer, it lies in the idea of claiming and displaying "colors" other than black, other than the one (in fact, the no-color) allotted to blacks by white American culture. The narrator of *My Southern Home* provides an example of one way this activity might proceed in discourse. In the first half of his text he shows how an Afro-American can take possession of and display the point of view of whites, even though their color was assumed the binary opposite of his own. There he also shows how white "authoritative discourse" can be more effectively challenged through subversion of its status within a text than through direct attack from some outside authority. From this perspective, the narrator's impersonation of white in the first part of his text looks more like an act of appropriation and empowerment through, than an act of betrayal of, color. Reading the narrator's behavior in this way makes his adoption of a black persona in the second half of *My Southern Home* a confirmation, rather than a contradiction, of the authority that the concluding lines of the text seek to summarize for all blacks.

The doubleness and deliberately acknowledged duplicity of the narrator of *My Southern Home* call attention to the options that Brown saw available to the black storyteller in the new postbellum era. More than ever before the new black writer had opportunities to exploit the ambiguities of narrative voice, to make the gestures of and to authority without being bound by it. The new black southern writer could more freely reclaim the southern past and exploit southern voices (including southern black dialect) without feeling morally obliged to authenticate himself as a reliable Negro, as the great black writers of the Old South, the slave narrators, had been required to do.[23] As long as his text remained true to its colors, its internal standard of authenticity, the black writer could assume the freedom to play white as well as black, to straddle or efface the color line, to play both sides against the middle, that is, against any marginal region of his own imagining. This is just what Charles W. Chesnutt and James Weldon Johnson, Brown's major successors in the first-person narrative tradition of black southern literature, went on to do in *The Conjure Woman* (1899) and *The Autobiography of an Ex-Coloured Man* (1912). They exploited the potential of narrative to authorize various kinds of duplicitous color displays without leaving their readers any clear assurances about the degree of authorial endorsement of the racial views taken by their often-masked narrators. *My Southern Home* does not delve into the ironic possibilities of these kinds of impersonations as fully or as artfully as Chesnutt and Johnson did. Its importance was to point the way and help set the course of new black southern narrative toward an accelerating novelization of form and voice that freed subsequent writers like Chesnutt and Johnson to play with the "authoritative discourse" of official New South literature. [24]

   My Southern Home is a literary experiment similar to *Life on the Mississippi* in its predication of authority on an internal rather than external standard, a standard not just within the text but a function of the text as a duplicitous narrative show (modeled on Brown's Janus-faced narrator) or as a shifting and elusive narrative flow (modeled on Mark Twain's Mississippi). The authority that each text lays claim to inheres neither in the reliability of its narrative voice (they are multiple and contradictory) nor in the factuality of its narrative assertions (many are ironic, deliberately exaggerated, and outright fabrications). The authority of the text is a function of its free play with, its profanation of, (1) authorities imported into the text from extratextual sources and (2) authorities created within the text, by the narrative voice, for instance, or the logic of the narration itself. The mark of a text's authority, therefore, is the freedom with which it plays with the very idea of authority itself.
   It was crucial to the development of a new southern literature in the postbellum era that *My Southern Home* and *Life on the Mississippi* display this kind of textual freedom, though it meant profaning some of the most reverenced southern authorities and subverting the moral authority of the narrator himself without explaining what new standard of authority the new southern writer would espouse. The postbellum writer had to follow the "southern quest for literary authority" to its source, to the

meaning of authority itself, particularly as it was manifested in the South, which after the war seemed much in need of liberation from the repressive authority of the past. The new southern writer had to take a skeptical look at what was present behind the many masks that re-presented themselves as authoritative in his or her world. At its source, both Brown and Mark Twain suggested, authority derived its power from acts of impersonation and mystification that could be appreciated as verbal display, as masterful gamesmanship, as sheer *style* or witty show. However, neither writer treated authority as though it deserved to be invested with an essential prestige or precedence that, as an artificial creation, both writers kept showing that it lacked.

Brown and Mark Twain conduct an extensive comic analysis and narrative demonstration of the art of self-authorization in various characters and in the narrators of *My Southern Home* and *Life on the Mississippi*. They invite their readers, particularly the southern ones (we may suspect), to see how the game is played, how it has been played in the past, and how it can be played still, openly and with gusto, to the amusement and even the instruction of its witnesses. But these two writers do not let their readers leave the game with the illusion that it is something more profound or less artificial than a contest sanctioned by culture. By contrast the more orthodox southern literary contemporaries of Brown and Mark Twain not only leave the illusion intact but try to introduce new forms of "authoritative discourse" into the literature of the New South in an effort to conserve and mystify the idea of authority for new purposes. The fact that today we take much more interest and pleasure in the texts of writers like Brown and Mark Twain than in the work of figures like Daniel Webster Davis or Thomas Nelson Page testifies to the triumph of what we might call a de-authorizing tradition of comic skepticism in post–Civil War and modern southern literature, a tradition launched under the narrative colors of *My Southern Home* and *Life on the Mississippi*.

NOTES

1. A sign of a much-welcome change is Craig Werner's "Tell Old Pharaoh: The Afro-American Response to Faulkner," *Southern Review* 19 (Autumn 1983): 711–35.

2. The earliest discussion of this matter was Charles H. Nichols's "Slave Narratives and the Plantation Legend," *Phylon* 11 (Fall 1949): 201–10.

3. See Sterling A. Brown, *The Negro in American Fiction* (Washington, D.C.: Associates in Negro Folk Education, 1937), 78–82.

4. See Thadious M. Davis, *Faulkner's "Negro": Art and the Southern Context* (Baton Rouge: Louisiana State University Press, 1982).

5. In Louis D. Rubin's landmark *Bibliographical Guide to the Study of Southern Literature* (Baton Rouge: Louisiana State University Press, 1969), James Weldon Johnson, Jean Toomer, and Ralph Ellison joined Chesnutt and Wright among the writers deemed important enough to merit individual treatment. *Southern Literary Study: Problems and Possibilities,* ed. Rubin and C. Hugh Holman (Chapel Hill: University of North Carolina Press, 1975), recommends a "collected edition of George Moses Horton" be undertaken, along with a "critical edition of Sterling Brown's *Southern Road"* and a critical biography of Sutton E. Griggs. For a sample of the kind of specialized critical attention that black southern writers have begun to receive, see J. Lee Greene, *Time's Unfading Garden: Anne Spencer's Life and Poetry* (Baton Rouge: Louisiana State University Press, 1978), and the special issue of *Callaloo* 1 (May 1978), devoted to Ernest J. Gaines, especially Michel Fabre's "Bayonne or the Yoknapatawpha of Ernest Gaines," 110–23.

6. Lewis P. Simpson, *The Man of Letters in New England and the South* (Baton Rouge: Louisiana State University Press, 1973), 129.

7. For a survey of some of the more negative estimates of *Life on the Mississippi,* see Horst H. Kruse, *Mark Twain and "Life on the Mississippi"* (Amherst: University of Massachusetts Press, 1981), xv–xvii, 1–4. Much less attention has been devoted to *My Southern Home.* Although J. Saunders Redding praised the book for its craftsmanship, Vernon Loggins regretted its crudities of style and preachiness of tone. William Wells Brown's biographer doubts the literary quality of *My Southern Home* and considers it one of his inferior books. See Redding's *To Make a Poet Black* (Chapel Hill: University of North Carolina Press, 1938), 27; Loggins's *The Negro Author* (New York: Columbia University Press, 1931), 171–72; and William Edward Farrison's *William Wells Brown* (Chicago: University of Chicago Press, 1969), 446–51.

8. The standard discussion of the postwar South's new raison d'être is Paul M. Gaston's *The New South Creed* (New York: Knopf, 1970).

9. The fate of Simms and Hayne is discussed in Jay B. Hubbell's *The South in American Literature, 1607–1900* (Durham, N.C.: Duke University Press, 1954), 709–10, 712–14, 748–57.

10. Allen Tate, "Emily Dickinson," in his *The Man of Letters in the Modern World* (New York: Meridian, 1955), 222–23.

11. The term "author-function" is drawn from Michel Foucault's essay "What Is an Author?" in his *Language, Counter-Memory, Practice* (Ithaca: Cornell University Press, 1977), 113–38. Foucault argues that authority is a function of certain types of discourse that a culture chooses to authorize. A piece of writing that has an author enjoys an enlarged status in modern society. An author's name helps to

endow a piece of writing with a definable origin, an individualized existence vis-à-vis other forms of writing, the importance of an object of property, the potential of authenticity, and, when studied alongside other writings under the same signature, the power of psychological indicativeness, of identifying the author. For further discussion of the idea of authority invested in texts, see Edward W. Said, *Beginnings: Intention and Method* (New York: Basic Books, 1975), 83–85.

12. Simpson, "O'Donnell's Wall," in *The Man of Letters in New England and the South,* 196–97.

13. William Wells Brown, *My Southern Home; or, The South and Its People* (Boston: A. G. Brown, 1880), iii. Mark Twain, *Life on the Mississippi,* ed. Guy Cardwell, in *Mississippi Writings* (New York: Library of America, 1982), 305. Further quotations from these books will be taken from these editions.

14. In a general sense my discussion of the wit of Brown and Mark Twain will draw on Freud's discussion of "the tendencies of wit" in *Wit and Its Relation to the Unconscious,* ed. and trans. A. A. Brill in his *The Basic Writings of Sigmund Freud* (New York: Random House, 1938), 668–708.

15. See *The New Science of Giambattista Vico,* trans. Thomas Goddard Bergin and Max Harold Fisch (Ithaca: Cornell University Press, 1948), paragraph 145; and Donald Phillip Verene, *Vico's Science of Imagination* (Ithaca: Cornell University Press, 1981), 107–10.

16. James M. Cox, *Mark Twain: The Fate of Humor* (Princeton: Princeton University Press, 1966), 56–59.

17. Roland Barthes, *The Pleasures of the Text,* trans. Richard Miller (New York: Hill and Wang, 1975), 14.

18. See Albion Tourgee, "The South as a Field for Fiction," *Forum* 6 (Dec. 1888): 409, and Rayford W. Logan's discussion of "The Negro as Portrayed in the Leading Literary Magazines" of the postwar era in his *The Betrayal of the Negro* (New York: Macmillan, 1965), 242–75.

19. This kind of patronizing characterization of blacks in New South literature was standard, as William L. Van Deburg notes in his *Slavery and Race in American Popular Culture* (Madison: University of Wisconsin Press, 1984), 73–74. One such southern writer to use the same biblical language as Brown to define the Negro's low social status was Victoria V. Clayton, *White and Black under the Old Regime* (Milwaukee: Young Churchman, 1899), 124.

20. M. M. Bakhtin, *The Dialogic Imagination,* ed. Michael Holquist, trans. Caryl Emerson and Michael Holquist (Austin: University of Texas Press, 1981), 342–44.

21. A reading of *The Narrative of William W. Brown* (Boston: Anti-Slavery Office, 1847) reveals a picture of plantation life in the area of Missouri where Brown grew up that is very different from that pictured in *My Southern Home.* Before his escape from slavery on January 1, 1834, Brown witnessed a great deal of cruelty on the plantation of his master, Dr. John Young (on whom Dr. Gaines is

modeled), and elsewhere in the St. Louis region. The antics and adventures of Cato in *My Southern Home* parallel in several important ways experiences that Brown had in slavery. For further information on this matter, see Farrison's *William Wells Brown.*

22. Besides writing one of the most widely selling slave narratives of the ante-bellum era, Brown was also the first Afro-American novelist (with *Clotel; or, The President's Daughter* in 1853) and the first Afro-American dramatist (with *The Escape; or, A Leap for Freedom* in 1858) in addition to publishing a pioneering book of travel essays (*Three Years in Europe,* 1852) and three volumes of Afro-American history in the postemancipation era. I use the term "aporia" to apply to the kind of obstacle to interpretation that we discover at the end of *My Southern Home.* The self-contradictoriness of this conclusion, which deconstructs whatever pretension to authority the narrator has built up, resists resolution of the problem of what Brown "really means." Instead this irresolution points toward the question of the authority of color itself as a signifier of a presumed signified within the context of a narrator's display of his colors as part of his bid for his reader's comprehension and trust.

23. For discussions of the authentication devices and strategies of antebellum black autobiographers, see Robert B. Stepto, *From behind the Veil: A Study of Afro-American Narrative* (Urbana: University of Illinois Press, 1979), 4–31.

24. I use "novelization" here in Bakhtin's sense of the word. The "salient features" of genres that have undergone novelization are: "They become more free and flexible, their language renews itself" by incorporating various levels of literary and so-called nonliterary language, they become "permeated with laughter, irony, humor, elements of self-parody" and, most important, with "an indeterminacy, a certain semantic openendedness, a living contact with unfinished, still-evolving contemporary reality" (*The Dialogic Imagination,* 6–7).

The Near Landscape and the Far:

Nature and Human Signification

JAMES APPLEWHITE

The first poem of my first book was written behind the wheel of an automobile. I sometimes fantasize that happy state of affairs in which a poet could become sufficiently well known to justify a historical marker by the roadside: "killed in this curve, writing a poem, while driving." But in the case of this poet and this poem, the relatively deserted South Carolina roads, the flat land, the sandy, wintry fields with pecan trees, barns, a few horses in the distances, let me encounter, instead of another driver, a "buried" landscape. The ash-colored rows around the car became a translucent snowfield, a kind of solid ocean through which the artifacts of my region's history could appear.

> Snow as if holding the country houses
> Apart to be inspected, unsilvered
> Mirror that lets float out of its depths
> As from an old ocean of no dimension
> Unlimited objects, leather tack and
> Spokes of surreys, china
> Long broken, whittled horses
> Everything their hands would have touched.

I was born and lived, until the time of going away to college, in a tobacco-farming town in eastern North Carolina—a town of a thousand persons, where the farmed land started immediately behind those cross-arms of streets that marked, in simplest outline, *place*. The fossil shells from the clifflike streambank across fields behind my home had impressed upon me, a good many years earlier, the fact that I lived on an ancient seafloor. But encountering the *likeness* of this immemorial field with its

historic accretions there in South Carolina—in, really, a geologically similar situation—was a necessary occasion for the poem. Recalling this early
example of composition in relation to place, I might distinguish four landscapes, four ways the earth-prospect may impinge upon our consciousness in poetry: "natal field," "middle earth," "other land," and "infernal
regions."

The "natal field" is a place or view so close to early life experience,
so associated with an intuitive and traditional response that, by itself, it
does not tend to help originate poems. This for me is the local roads with
pickups in autumn, the Wilson tobacco market ten miles away, of the first
poem of my second book. These are scenes which may be seen as a poem
if through some distancing lens, as when, in the case of "Tobacco Men,"
I had returned from England, from visiting, among other sites, the location and outsized urn of the "country churchyard" at Stoke Poges where
Gray's elegy is supposed to have been written. Intending to visit my home
and Wilson that autumn, I "saw" that landscape first through the air of
England and elegy. The poem is that vision.

The "middle earth" is this place where I live now, in this present that
incorporates the past but is not obsessed or suffocated by it. Middle earth
is my house in northern Durham County, with Seven Mile Creek running across the foot of the wooded lot, and the interrupted, stretched
Eno State Park running along the river beyond the ridge. This is the earth
whose riverbank I run in winter, when the poison-ivy leaves have fallen.
Here I read a texture of twig-characters, dogwood buds like periods, the
marvelous nouns of kinds as spelled in bark color and scale, crown con-
formation: ironwood, sycamore, white oak, river birch.

Here there is no imprinting of my own earlier life history: no barely discernible watermark of Oedipal displacement, incestuous love for a cousin
merged into the secluded yard. No Onan-legacy spilled into the field, no
perilous escape from capsized boat dimensioning the slick creek, no map
of camp building and adolescent bravado with a twenty-two rifle and the
sawmill noon whistle threading the pine thicket, past the boundary of Big
Ditch and millstone. Benjy's section of The Sound and the Fury captures
perfectly that aspect of the land-mapped psyche of earlier life that impris-
ons one in the past. Middle earth is free of the place of the discovery of
fire, where the Boy Scout twigs turned the broom sedge a leaping orange.
Free of the place of the dark wetness of water, where under a capsized boat
I tried to breathe a liquid glistening dark as the leaves shed by autumn. It
has not the place of first sight of a girl's sex, the firm white hairless lips

expressionless, an enigmatic mark. Has not the Snake through the gatelike bushes over what had been our own pond, our Water Eden.

Middle earth is not, then, a mythology arranged topographically. No lit height of service station with its bulb-squared portico of bulbs at one end of town, to balance swift creek of dream downhill at the other—like technological North versus slumberous South. Yet middle earth cannot avoid being text as well as texture, since the psyche which constructs it as experience is itself a landscape with aspects of the mystic writing pad. The journal-poem I have written while jogging this past year finds itself echoing, perhaps in figure more than phrasing, the accumulation of the years' teaching—from the quick sun-declension at the end of the *Canterbury Tales* to Pope's snake-vigorous root of self-love. Texts of one day's poem carry over to the other. Though I stop well short of Derrida's version of the unconscious as language traces alone—since experience, for me, is so largely sensory, with a visual *structure*—I have been deeply impressed, since my visit to "Gray's field," by the contribution of texts to landscapes. The stanzas of the "Elegy" inscribed on the great urn made it impossible to be sure of the effect of those maternal, hovering elms alone. It *seemed* the most familiar of home fields. But like a more recent Illinois landscape on the road to Cairo, the element of familiarity may have been literary as much as visual. There in Illinois, my head was full of Huck and Jim on the raft, and of Huck's coming "home" to Aunt Sally's—as if back from the dead. Yet the silos and leaf-hills and bronzed light in Illinois, within smell of the river, corresponded to the text—in fact, called it up.

Middle earth is a place you may or may not see as numinous. From the path there next to the Eno River, I have occasionally seen deeply into the sun's orb, its essential pool as of molten platinum. It has printed its greenish dot of Other. There ego-consciousness has seen its own small circle, the tiny blank in the All occasioned by its identity. The river, risen after a storm, has slapped and dashed with waves, and resin of broken pine limbs has smelled like new paint. Contact with these pure elements through the overlay of previous texts—whether literary and thus verbal, or the psyche's own spatialized mix of verbal and visual—produces a sense of fresh generation. One feels what may be a necessary illusion: words sprung freshly, as if directly from *things*.

> All the way to the bridge,
> I ran through airs
> And humidities like sheets

Hung on a line. Breathed
Washed accents of language.

The landscape, of course, may refuse to open itself. Usually does refuse. The "other land" is nature as indifferent, as pure bulk, possible sublimity, perhaps harshness, maybe indifferent beauty. The landscape that doesn't relate. This is the Grand Canyon when you visit and it looks a flat picture, or Mont Blanc, a soulless image upon the eye for Wordsworth. I will formulate this condition as *place*—as the places you visit as tourist, or as places you feel threatened by and so see as part of that "inanimate cold world allowed" to us in our ordinary beings of self-enclosure and limited concern. Though the other land may tend to be embodied in famous vistas attended by crowds, or landscapes simply too harshly unfamiliar to be assimilated, it is in essence a condition of reaction (or nonreaction) on our parts more than a condition of nature. Middle earth may be, on occasion, the other land. When I had first moved next to the woods, I worried about ticks, chiggers, poison ivy, perhaps snakes. The woods in wet weather looked forboding. Strange rustles abounded, the flocks of black birds as dark as formations of Stukas.

So even middle earth *can* be the fourth circle of landscape: the "infernal regions." We have a capacity for seeing damnation, the char-black of devastation and desecration. Burnt-out shells of apartment buildings in Queens, boarded-up shop fronts in Philadelphia suburbs, the westward fringes of Dayton, Ohio, hung mournfully with powerlines, patrolled by ghoulishly large cars: as if eaten out insidiously inside by rust, like the human life from within Count Dracula.

The different modes of nature in relation to us, and us in relation to it, are no doubt countless. I have suggested four possibilities, four ways of human psyche and landscape relating or not relating, which may stand as abstractions representing the actual complexity. There is no doubt that mind and land are bound together, to interact and mutually alter. Through some inconceivable accident or symbolic correspondence or evolved perceptual structure, the face of the planet seen as a three-dimensioned plane matches the mind's way of organizing experience. Structuralists confuse spatial metaphor with literary meaning, says Derrida, seeming not entirely displeased. He would only remind us of the *primacy* of language's significations—in respect to the visual field from which are taken individual metaphors, as well as the larger metaphor of structure. I would remind the deconstructionists that the visual language came first, and that it *is* a language. The unconscious "primary process" (Freud) is a maker of plots whose cinematic sequences conduct us through rooms and landscapes to our primal aversions and desires. Kings College Chapel and Salisbury Cathedral arrest in stone a new species of dream-animals. In earlier centuries, it was probably never questioned that space and color, like harmonized sound, were language elements for the actualization of our psyche's poles of heaven and hell. Both Dante and Milton move from a pit *below* to a paradise *above*. The abstract shape of mind-meaning behind the landscapes of experience is made more evident in Dante, as the degrees of moral degradation and perfection are stationed in concentric circles or spiral curves or spheres-within-spheres. Beatrice's eyes see the poet in the full contour of his spatialized journey toward meaning, and her lips' words symbolize those which record the poet's ontological geometry.

But when all this is said, nature remains stubbornly literal. The resistance of northern Durham County's clay soil brings blisters to my palms when I dig it. Sometimes it refuses my design for flowerbeds, continues its own signs of trout lilies, oak roots, ferns, honeysuckle. The soil's signification is often averse to our wishes, says *acid*, will grow azaleas or coreopsis but not the roses I intend. But this is not to say that the soil has no order of being. Full of microorganisms, it will soon reduce a buried rat or opossum to bones. Underneath my mowed yard, a well casing siphons down, brings up, from down in the blue shale stone, the water which feeds this house. Soil downhill on the other side of the house accepts and transforms the flow from our septic tank. Relatively stable earth crust, water, a temperature range close to the optimal for human life (considering the possibilities in the wider universe), sustain us in existence, accept, even, the imprint of our meanings. Earth has its own, other language, which we are beginning, stumblingly, to read. Knowing this interdependence of mind-life and land-life, as well as the human tendency to impose only the anthropocentric Logos, I found myself wishing for a poetry of landscape less prefabricated and prejudged by prior verbal texts on the one hand, and less marked by prior psychological concerns on the other. The very concept of *natal landscape, middle earth, other land,* and *infernal regions* grew out of this project to move on, perceptually, experientially, from old texts to new textures—from the words and scenes of my obsessions to the previously unread characters of twig and bud.

With Derrida's quotation from Nietzsche in mind ("only those thoughts that come when you are walking have any value"), I thought of my running and dodging between trees as producing such "a dance of the pen." Close proximity every day to a river with no literary pretensions coincided with Derrida's evocation (in *Of Grammatology*) of that writing which arises provisionally, repetitively, but less formally than the predetermined Logos.

As I've said, this landscape and these poems suggested the idea of middle earth—a psychic condition in relation to landscape suggesting the *adult* state of transactional analysis. I had staked cedar steps into the ridge beyond Seven Mile Creek at the end of my lot. I had recleared an overgrown logging path along the ridge that led eventually to the old wagon road down to a mill site and to a ford. I could walk among trees and run for miles beside the river, with no interruption except from bobwhite or blue heron or squirrel or hog-nosed water snake or turtle going under from a rock in the current. Or much less frequently, from the sight of a beaver or white-tailed deer. There were evidences in plenty of previous habitation: names and dates cut into the bark of beeches (most of the legible dates from the turn of the century to the 1920s), a couple of abandoned homesteads where jonquils still bloomed in spring, near old bottles and rusting roof-tin. One graveyard, with several graves in deep woods marked only by boulders. A single white legible tombstone. Running this landscape, I encountered a pattern of nineteenth- and earlier twentieth-century rural history, but a history not personally my own. The stone of Catharine Dunnagan—Born March 7, 1826, died January 6, 1914—under the periwinkle carpet next to where the jonquils would appear in February, to be seen by no one save a few lucky hikers, did not mark the grave of a relative. I felt toward these memorial human presences only the elegiac respect due members of my own species.

I do not argue that the middle-earth landscape can be free of psychological association and projection. Part of the time last year during which I was running the river and writing, my own mother seemed close to death, and inevitably a woman's tombstone or jonquils in the trees called up that fact. But it was a distanced fact, a fact in relation to this objectivity of other lives seen now as a pattern, and as in process of assimilation: by pine forest becoming hardwood, and the old erosion-scars of farming healing under the layerings of woods mold. This landscape was scene of an intense self-encounter, but one which appeared to take place in new terms, as discovery (and perhaps growth) instead of mere repetition. In those early winter days, my own sense of middle-aged time pressure and professional crises tended to coalesce with the need to get out on the path for my run after work, and yet home before dark. I hadn't realized my habitual sense of *belatedness* on the trail until rereading Harold Bloom's

The Anxiety of Influence and *Poetry and Repression*. But out there pursuing a long overdue self-definition, I found the texts from my twenty-plus years of teaching shining newly from rock and water surface, regenerated presences because of the sharp bright detail of the *otherness* of the environment. My consciousness seemed to identify with the water surface roughened by rock and wind, marked in vees by snags, given characteristic swirls by current deflected from submerged ledges. The interlinked flow and fracture of Pheromone, impelled by blood in my brain as I ran, merged with the Eno as it changed its luster over gravel, tensioning in wide bends under light.

My middle-earth landscape by the Eno has meant for me the opportunity to encounter those hidden constraints and entanglements which contradict expression and deaden or pervert feeling. I really do believe that imaginative experience of nature may become the means toward a more comprehensible Freudian insight, toward an exploring of the unconscious in poetry. The self in words may be constructed each day through a deconstructive stripping away of habit, assumption, illusion. I went again and again to the river in order to encounter my *self*. Under the river was the *es* to my *ich*. It was simultaneously nature and the unconscious. The current became my luminous inkblot for a winter-long Rorschach. The providentially provided set of steel lines over the water (the power company as providence is not farfetched) completed my habitually enacted metaphor, my tightwire walk over the void. I adjusted the tensed lines of words, replica of what mind was aware it thought, as it vibrated in harmony with below-surface forces. Language in my mind while running became the acted-on actor, figure whose image from above moved with the reflections from below.

In book 14 of *The Prelude*, Wordsworth entertains the possibility that nature sometimes "Thrusts forth upon the senses" an inevitable metaphor for—and "genuine counterpart" of—the "glorium faculty" of human imagination (1805 text, lines 86–89). Modern critics such as Geoffrey Hartman and Paul de Man, however, see the Romantics' true destiny in their discovery of Imagination's self-subsistent thrust *beyond* the forms of landscape. Thus, the episode of crossing the Alps in *The Prelude*, book 6, becomes for Hartman the thematic conclusion of the poem, for there the poet is disappointed in nature and completes the experience imaginatively. The "awful Power" that "rose from the mind's abyss" (1850, line 594), when the poet realizes that his further path points only downward, is exalted also by de Man, who sees the Romantics as putting into question for the first time "the ontological priority of the sensory object" and so leaving the poetry of today "under a steady threat of extinction" (*Romanticism and Consciousness,* ed. Harold Bloom, p. 77). I have no quarrel with the idea that, stimulated by the landscape, unconscious powers may come into play and project a completing structure into an outline provided by sensory experience. But these authors seem uncomfortable with the fact that the structure of human signification and that of sensory experience so closely correspond. Or perhaps they worry that this "fit" (or perhaps "fitness of things") was mythologized by Wordsworth (and others) as evidence of a "Wisdom and Spirit of the universe" (*Prelude* 1, 1850, line 401), a power which impressed itself upon both minds and objects and made these correspondent halves of the marriage-union of perception (see the Prospectus to *The Excursion*) able mutually to interact. They seem obliged to read our first great poetry of landscape in the most skeptical terms available. Well, if we go back to Descartes's account of mind and matter and substitute psyche for his aspatial soul, tied into extended matter through the subtle knot of the pineal gland, we simply have again the paradox of modern attempts to portray consciousness through physical causation. Neither Descartes's terminology nor more recent talk of the synaptic transfer of certain chemical messages does much in the way of explaining our *experience* of consciousness. Our *experience* is that mind and matter, thought and image, poet and landscape, interact and interdepend. Language, even, has a necessary body—these words, which are originally sound-pulse, and which are pushed through the brain by the blood in a rhythm, especially when imagination heats and we are in motion. Critics would do better to see that Wordsworth and later poets of landscape operated experientially, phenomenologically, if you will, and refused to allow theoretical impossibilities to prevent the synergistic feedback-loop of objects and signifiers from creating the spatial structures of poetry.

Derrida's "Force and Signification" suggests that the domination exerted over critical analyses (and perhaps, also, artistic creation) by spatial metaphor can be so great as to cause an essential confusion. Though strictly speaking "the notion of structure refers only to space, geometric or morphological space, the order of forms and sites," the critical (and, I think, creative) mind is subject to a "*topographical* literality" whereby the difference between metaphor and meaning is forgotten. Because "language can determine things only by spatializing them," critic (and writer) run the risk "through a kind of sliding as unnoticed as it is *efficacious,* of confusing meaning with its geometric, morphological, or, in the best of cases, cinematic model" (*Writing and Difference,* translated by Alan Bass, pp. 15, 16). The movie of our dreams is visual/spatial, with a verbal component, and Derrida worries that this primary signification—which is that of our three-dimensioned sensory experience and its replication and editing—will subjugate the self-referential linguistic flow. Derrida wishes to make of words, as both signifiers and signifieds, the true psychic interiority, and would take Freud's late metaphor picturing the unconscious as "mystic writing pad" to be his central model ("Freud and the Scene of Writing," *Writing and Difference,* pp. 196–231). Yet Freud's metaphor-system representing the psyche remained largely topographical, and even the writing-pad image (which Derrida would adapt to his own purposes) preserves, with its earth-brown base corresponding to the unconscious and its retentiveness of sensory experience, the *layered* quality of landscape imagery. From the time that Thomas Gray symbolized, to the oversophisticated middle of the eighteenth century, more emotionally immediate forebears beneath the uncouth memorials of a country churchyard, landscapes have been offered us by artists in a memorial aspect, as if to reaffirm a threatened relationship between the mind and the land. From "The Ruined Cottage" to "Poems on the Naming of Places," Wordsworth suggested time and again the reciprocal action of human personality and land in forming one another. Earth becomes, with its artifacts, its overgrown wells, broken mud walls, ruined sheepfolds, and paths worn by anxious feet, a spatially extended physical memory having an almost geological layering. The human imagination, imprinted by these patterns, becomes like an earthen palimpsest of overlaid scenes. From the mounds and fissures of such experiential deposits, through which one has acquired not only the depth of one's own life but the experience of many generations —"not the lifetime of one man only / But of old stones that cannot be deciphered" (Eliot, "East Coker")—come the oozings of creativity. Possessing a past and an identity affirmed in part by this sequence of history which is experienced topographically, the artist can imagine a future and the art which helps create it. From the Romantics to us, the earth has imaged that memory-bank source, whether for Mendelssohn in the Hebrides, Wordsworth in Grasmere, or Gauguin in Tahiti. I suspect that the image of the soil, whether exotic place to which one travels, or terrain of earliest experience, tends to energize for the preconscious a connection with the cosmos which rationality has denied our more conscious intellection.

James Dickey:

From "The Other"

through *The Early Motion*

HAROLD BLOOM

I first read James Dickey's early poem "The Other" some twenty years ago. Having admired his recently published book, *Drowning With Others,* I went back to his first book, *Into the Stone,* at the recommendation of a close friend, the poet Alvin Feinman. Though very moved by several of the earlier poems, I was affected most strongly by the one called "The Other." It has taken me twenty years to understand why the poem still will not let me go, and so I begin with it here. I don't think of Dickey as a poet primarily of otherness, but rather as a heroic celebrator of what Emerson called "the great and crescive self," indeed of the American self proper, which demands victory and disdains even great defeats. Dickey, as I read him, is like what Vico called the Magic Formalists or Blake named the Giant Forms. He is a throwback to those mythic hypotheses out of which strong poetry first broke forth, the bards of divination whose heroic vitalism demanded a literal immortality for themselves as poets. But even a Magic Formalist learns that he is at best a mortal god.

The pain of that learning is the central story of Dickey's poetry, and I choose to evade that pain here in order to emphasize Dickey's countersong of otherness. Since I will take him scarcely into his middle years, I will be ignoring all of his most ambitious poetry, "the later motion," as he has called it. Though his work from 1965 to the present clearly is more problematic than the poems I will discuss, its achievement quite possibly is of a higher order. But it is too soon to prophesy Dickey's final stature, and criticism must discourse on what it loves before it broods upon the limits of the canonical. What I know and love best, so far, in Dickey's poetry is "the early motion," and the counter-song of otherness in that motion moves me most. I have circled back to that poem, "The Other," and turn to it now to locate an origin of Dickey's quest as a poet.

That origin is guilt, and guilt ostensibly of being a substitute or replacement for a brother dead before one was born. Freud, I think, would have judged such guilt to be a screen memory, and I am Freudian enough to look or surmise elsewhere for the source of guilt in the poems of *Into the Stone*. From the beginning of his poetic career, Dickey was a poet of Sublime longings, and those who court the Sublime are particularly subject to changeling fantasies. The poem he titled "The Other" is manifestly Yeatsian, whether directly or through the mediation of Roethke, but the argument already is Dickey's own, and in all respects it is the meter-making argument, and not the derived diction and metric, that gives this poem its great distinction. Indeed Dickey, an instinctive Emersonian from the start, despite his southern heritage, literalizes Emerson's trope of a meter-making argument by the extraordinary device of packing the seventy-seven lines of this lyrical reverie into what has always felt to me like a single sentence. How could there be a second sentence in a poem that identifies itself so completely with the changeling's will to be the other, when the other ultimately is the god Apollo?

Somewhere, Dickey identified his triad of literary heroes as the unlikely combination of Keats, Malcolm Lowry, and James Agee, presumably associated because of their early or relatively early deaths, and because of their shared intensity of belief in what could be called the salvation history of the literary art. But Dickey is very much a poet of Sensibility, in the mode that Frye once defined as *the* Age of Sensibility, the mode of Christopher Smart and of William Collins, among other doomed poets whose threshold stance destroyed them upon the verge of High Romanticism. The Keats who moves Dickey most, the Keats of the letters, is the culmination of the major theme of the poets of Sensibility, the theme that, following Collins, I have called the Incarnation of the Poetical Character. Lowry and Agee, though I don't recall Dickey mentioning this, were curiously allied as verse writers by the overwhelming influence that Hart Crane exerted upon both of them. Dickey seems to prefer Crane's letters to his poems, which oddly parallels his preference of Keats's letters. But Keats and Crane, like Lowry and Agee in their verse, represent fully in their poems the Incarnation of the Poetical Character, where the poet, in the guise of a young man, is reborn as the young god of the sun. That is clearly the genre of Dickey's "The Other," but the clarity is shadowed by Dickey's early guilt concerning what the poem accurately names as "my lust of self."

What self can that be except the magic and occult self, ontological rather than empirical, and in Yeatsian or Whitmanian terms, self rather than soul? The guilt that shadows Dickey's marvelous seventy-seven-line utterance is the guilt induced by what Freud came to call the above-I or the over-I (the superego), a rather more daunting though no less fictive entity than Emerson's Oversoul. Emerson had the shrewdest of eyes for anxiety, but Freud's eye, as Wallace Stevens once wrote, was the microscope of potency. The guilt of family betrayal must ensue from the changeling fantasy of the family romance, and for Freud (as for Kenneth Burke), all romance is family romance. But the family romance of the poet *as* poet tends to depart from the domain of the merely biographical family. Dickey's assertion of self as person was the desire to rise from the "strength-haunted body" of a "rack-ribbed child" to the Herculean figure he has been since, a titanic form among contemporary poets. But since poems can attempt the truth only through fictions or tropes, the poem of "The Other" is compelled to treat the child's aspiration as the drive towards becoming Apollo, poetry itself. The youthful Henry James, reviewing *Drum-Taps,* scorned Whitman as an essentially prosaic temperament trying to lift itself by muscular exertion into poetry. The elderly Henry James, weeping over the great *Lilacs* elegy, scorned his own youthful review; but, properly modified, it can give us a critical trope for reading Dickey: an essentially poetic temperament lifting itself by muscular exertion into poetry.

Dickey's most curious characteristic, from "The Other" through *Puella,* is his involuntary but striking dualism, curious because so heroic a vitalist ought not to exemplify (as he does) so Pauline and Cartesian a mind-body split, or even so prevalent a sense of what Stevens termed the dumb-foundering abyss between ourselves and the object. What the poem surprisingly shows for and to Dickey is that his own body becomes his brother, or Apollo, or "the other." If the body is the divine other, then pathos becomes both sublime and grotesque, because the body must change, and the final form of that change is death. "The Other" is almost the first of Dickey's poems, and in some ways he has never surpassed it, not because he has failed to develop, but because it is unsurpassable. The whole of Dickey is in it already, as the whole of Shelley is in *Alastor,* or the whole of Yeats is in *The Wanderings of Oisin.* I repeat that this does not mean that Dickey simply has unfolded; so restless and reckless an experimentalist is outrageously metamorphic. But all his changes quest hopelessly for a disjunctiveness his temperament refuses to allow him. The "holes" that space out the poems of his major phase never represent discursive gaps or even crossings from one kind of figuration to another. Instead, they impressively mark or punctuate the exquisite desperation of the will to live, the lust of self that is not to be railed at, because it does represent what Keats called "a sickness not ignoble": the sickness unto death of heroic poetry.

"The Other," like so much of Dickey's best work, is very clearly a Southern American poem, and yet its Incarnation of the Poetical Character is necessarily universal in its imagery and argument. This is the universal purchased at the high cost of what was to be a permanent guilt, the guilt of a poet who as poet greatly desired *not* to be egocentric, despite the demands of the mythology that found him from the start. Those demands are felt even in the opening movement of "The Other":

> Holding onto myself by the hand,
> I change places into the spirit
> I had as a rack-ribbed child,
> And walk slowly out through my mind
> To the wood, as into a falling fire
> Where I turned from that strength-haunted body
> Half-way to bronze, as I wished to.

Dickey's natural religion always has been Mithraism, the traditional faith of soldiers, and certainly the most masculine and fierce of all Western beliefs. Despite the Persian origins of Mithra, Rome assimilated him to Apollo, and Dickey's major alteration is to make the Incarnation of the Poetical Character into a Mithraic ritual. The "bronze" of this first stanza will be revealed, later in the poem, as both the statue of Apollo and the body of the sacrificial bull slain by Mithra. As the boy Dickey slings up the too-heavy ax-head, he prays

> To another, unlike me, beside me:
> To a brother or king-sized shadow
> Who looked at me, burned, and believed me:
> Who believed I would rise like Apollo
>
> With armor-cast shoulders upon me:
> Whose voice, whistling back through my teeth,

Counted strokes with the hiss of a serpent.
Where the sun through the bright wood drove
Him, mute, and floating strangely, to the ground,
He led me into his house, and sat
Upright, with a face I could never imagine,

With a great harp leant on his shoulder,
And began in deep handfuls to play it.

"Burned" is the crucial trope here, since the brother, as god of the sun, leads only into the heat and light that is the house of the sun. The oracular hiss is Pythian, though the voice truly becomes Dickey's own. What Dickey, *in the poem*, develops most brilliantly is the figure of downward movement, which is introduced in the second stanza as the combined fall of sweat and leaves, and further invoked in the fall of light. Later in the poem, music falls, followed in the final line by the casting down of foliage. All these fallings substitute for the hidden ritual in which the bull's blood falls upon the Mithraic adept, the warrior in the act of becoming Apollo:

My brother rose beside me from the earth,

With the wing-bone of music on his back
Trembling strongly with heartfelt gold,
And ascended like a bird into the tree,
And music fell in a comb, as I stood
In a bull's heavy, bronze-bodied shape
As it mixed with a god's, on the ground,
And leaned on the helve of the ax.

The "great, dead tree" of the poem's second stanza might be called Dickey's first major fiction of duration, the origin of his quarrel with time. Being Dickey's, it is the liveliest of dead trees, yet it cannot propitiate this poet's poignant longing for a literal immortality:

Now, owing my arms to the dead
Tree, and the leaf-loosing, mortal wood,
Still hearing that music amaze me,
I walk through the time-stricken forest,
And wish another body for my life,
Knowing that none is given
By the giant, unusable tree

And the leaf-shaped lightning of sun,
And rail at my lust of self
With an effort like chopping through root-stocks:
Yet the light, looming brother but more
Brightly above me is blazing,
In that music come down from the branches
In utter, unseasonable glory,

Telling nothing but how I made
By hand, a creature to keep me dying
Years longer, and coming to sing in the wood
Of what love still might give,
Could I turn wholly mortal in my mind,
My body-building angel give me rest,
This tree cast down its foliage with the years.

"This tree" is at last Dickey himself as fiction of duration, the poet become his own poem, indeed "made / By hand," and so a house made by hands, a mortal body. When desire can turn monistic, for Dickey, it can become only a mortal turn, a trope knowing it is only trope. The other is divine, but only as Apollo or Mithra was divine, rather than as Jesus or Jehovah. A poem "about" a body-building child has transformed itself into the Sublime, into the body-building angel who has never since given Dickey any rest.

Retrospectively, I suppose that the poem "The Other" first moved me because so few American poems of twenty years ago had anything like Dickey's remarkable ability to be so humanly direct and yet so trustingly given to the potential of figurative language. The Dickey of the early motion seemed to have found his way back, almost effortlessly, to the secrets of poetry. I remember that the first poem by Dickey that I read was the title poem of *Drowning With Others,* a title that is itself an unforgettable trope, worthy of Emily Dickinson's apprehension that an acute consciousness, even when aware of neighbors and the sun, of other selves and outward nature, still died quite alone, except for its own identity, a totemic single hound. What is Sublime in the self finally is capable only of "drowning with others," but that is only part of what is central in what remains one of Dickey's most singular and enduring poems.

If I remember aright, Dickey himself doesn't much like this poem, and thinks it obscure rather than strong. Indeed, I recall his insistence that he wrote the poem only so as to give status to his book's title. His account of the poem's referential aspect was strangely literal, but I think this is one of his poems that sneaked by him, as it were:

> There are moments a man turns from us
> Whom we have all known until now.
> Upgathered, we watch him grow,
> Unshipping his shoulder bones
>
> Like human, everyday wings
> That he has not ever used,
> Releasing his hair from his brain,
> A kingfisher's crest, confused
>
> By the God-tilted light of Heaven.
> His deep, window-watching smile
> Comes closely upon us in waves,
> And spreads, and now we are
>
> At last within it, dancing.
> Slowly we turn and shine
> Upon what is holding us,
> As under our feet he soars,
>
> Struck dumb as the angel of Eden,
> In wide, eye-opening rings.
> Yet the hand on my shoulder fears
> To feel my own wingblades spring,
>
> To feel me sink slowly away
> In my hair turned loose like a thought
> Of a fisherbird dying in flight.
> If I opened my arms, I could hear
>
> Every shell in the sea find the word
> It has tried to put into my mouth.
> Broad flight would become of my dancing,
> And I would obsess the whole sea,
>
> But I keep rising and singing
> With my last breath. Upon my back,
> With his hand on my unborn wing,
> A man rests easy as sunlight

> Who has kept himself free of the forms
> Of the deaf, down-soaring dead,
> And me laid out and alive
> For nothing at all, in his arms.

I read this as another lyric of poetic incarnation, a rather less willing assumption of the divine other, perhaps even a defense against the Orphic predicament, but still a revision of the poem "The Other." Indeed, I wonder if one way of characterizing Dickey's obsessive strength as a poet is to say that he cannot stop rewriting that essential early poem. For the man who turns from us in the opening line of "Drowning With Others" is the Orphic Dickey, poet and divine other. Like the rich-haired youth of Collins, or Coleridge's youth with flashing eyes and floating hair, or Stevens's figure of the youth as virile poet in "Mrs. Alfred Uruguay," this other Dickey has hair released into "a kingfisher's crest, confused / By the God-tilted light of Heaven." Apollo is reborn again, but as Orphic drowning man, fit version of the poet of Sensibility in America, be he Hart Crane or Roethke or Agee or Dickey. But if the man turning from us in this poem is Dickey in the act of Sublime apotheosis, then whoever is that "I" rather desperately chanting this hieratic spell? Perhaps that is why Dickey as commentator judged this grand lyric too obscure, despite its palpable strength.

Our poet is weird in the true sense, one of the Fates (as Richard Howard, lexicographer among bards, might remind us), and his natural mode is the uncanny. What he has done here may be obscure to his spectral self, but his magic or occult self gathers his spectral self, until even that "I" keeps "rising and singing / With my last breath." And so truly neither self dies, or can die, in this soaring lyric of divination. Perhaps there is a touch, not indeliberate, of Dylan Thomas in the metric here, and even allusive overtones of Thomas at moments in the diction. That resemblance may even be a hidden cause of Dickey's distaste for his poem, but I remark upon it to note the difference between the poets, rather than their shared qualities. On mortality, the warrior Dickey cannot deceive himself, but a poet whose totem seems to be the albatross does not fear death by water. Few lines are as characteristic of Dickey as "And I would obsess the whole sea."

I take it that "drowning with others" is a trope for "winging with others," and that the dominant image here is flight, and not going under. Flight of course is Freud's true trope for repression, and an Orphic sensibility never ceases to forget, involuntarily but on purpose, that its vocation is mortal godhood, or not dying *as a poet*. Drowning with others, then, as a trope, must mean something like dying only as the immortal precursor dies or writing poems that men will not let die. Though its scale is small, this is Dickey's *Lycidas,* even as *The Zodiac* will be his cosmological elegy for the self. The child building up a Mithra-like body is still here in this poem, but he is here more reluctantly, caught up in the moments of discovering that a too-closely-shared immortality becomes mortality again, the stronger the sharing is known.

Dickey, being one of our authentic avatars of the American Sublime, exemplifies its two grand stigmata: not to feel free unless he is alone, and finally to know that what is oldest in him is no part of the Creation. After two poems wrestling with otherness, I need to restore his sense of solitude, his Emersonian self-reliance, and the great poem for this in his early motion is "In the Mountain Tent," which appropriately concludes the book *Drowning With Others.* I remember that Dickey contrasts this with the more famous "The Heaven of Animals," a lovely poem, but not one with the power of this meditation:

> I am hearing the shape of the rain
> Take the shape of the tent and believe it,
> Laying down all around where I lie
> A profound, unspeakable law.
> I obey, and am free-falling slowly
>
> Through the thought-out leaves of the wood
> Into the minds of animals.
> I am there in the shining of water
> Like dark, like light, out of Heaven.
>
> I am there like the dead, or the beast
> Itself, which thinks of a poem—
> Green, plausible, living, and holy—
> And cannot speak, but hears,
> Called forth from the waiting of things,
>
> A vast, proper, reinforced crying
> With the sifted, harmonious pause,
> The sustained intake of all breath
> Before the first word of the Bible.

At midnight water dawns
Upon the held skulls of the foxes
And weasels and touseled hares
On the eastern side of the mountain.
Their light is the image I make

As I wait as if recently killed,
Receptive, fragile, half-smiling,
My brow watermarked with the mark
On the wing of a moth

And the tent taking shape on my body
Like ill-fitting, Heavenly clothes.
From holes in the ground comes my voice
In the God-silenced tongue of the beasts.
"I shall rise from the dead," I am saying.

Whether a Christian or not, this speaker appears to entertain a belief in the resurrection of the body. Even in this solitude of spirit, the uncanny in Dickey, his *daimon,* enters with the poem's implicit question: Whose body, mine or that of the other? Is it every man who shall rise in the body, or is it not a more Gnostic persuasion that is at work here? The Gnostic lives already in the resurrected body, which is the body of a Primal Man who preceded the Creation. What a Gnostic called the Pleroma, the Fullness, Dickey calls beautifully "the waiting of things." The dead, the animals, and Dickey as the poem's speaker, all hear together the Gnostic Call, a vast crying out of the waiting of things. Without knowing any esoteric Gnosticism, Dickey by poetic intuition arrives at the trope of the Kabbalistic holding in of the divine breath that precedes the rupture of Creation. What Dickey celebrates therefore is "The sustained intake of all breath / Before the first word of the Bible." That word in Hebrew is *Beresit,* and so the vision of this poem is set before the Beginning. At midnight, not at dawn, and so only in the light of a rain image reflected from the beasts, Dickey speaks forth for the beasts, who have been silenced by the Demiurge called God by Genesis. In Dickey's own interpretation, the man experiences both a kinship with the beasts and a fundamental difference, since he alone will rise from the dead. But I think the poet is stronger than the poet-as-interpreter here. To rise from the dead, in this poem's context, is merely to be one's own magical or pneumatic self, a self that precedes the first word of the Bible.

It isn't very startling to see and say that Dickey, as poet, is not a Christian poet, but rather an Emersonian, an American Orphic and Gnostic. This is only to repeat Richard Howard's fine wordplay upon what could be called the Native Strain in our literature. What startles me, a little, is to see and say just how doctrinal, even programmatic, Dickey's early Orphism now seems. The Orphism has persisted, emerging with tumultuous force in the superbly mad female preacher of Dickey's "May Day Sermon," which I recommend we all read directly after each time we read Jonathan Edwards' rather contrary sermon, "Sinners in the Hands of an Angry God." Rhetorically, though, that is a very different Dickey than the poet of *The Early Motion,* whose Orphism perhaps is the more persuasive for being almost overheard, rather than so emphatically heard.

I turn my charting of the early motion to Dickey's next book, *Helmets,* which so far may be his most distinguished single volume, a judgment in which I would neither want nor expect him to concur. "Helmet," as a word, ultimately goes back to an Indo-European root that means both "to cover and conceal," but also "to save," which explains why "helm" and "helmet" are related to those two antithetical primal names, Hell and Valhalla. Dickey's book, of course, knows all this, Dickey being a preternaturally implicit knower, both as a poet and as a warrior—or, combining both modes, as an archer and hunter. Had I time and space, I would want to comment on every poem in *Helmets,* but I will confine myself to its two most ambitious meditations, "Approaching Prayer" and the final "Drinking from a Helmet." Certain thematic and agonistic strains that I have glanced at already can be said not to culminate but to achieve definitive expression in these major poems. I qualify my statement because what is most problematic about Dickey's poetry is that nothing ever is allowed to culminate, not even in *The Zodiac,* or "Falling," or "May Day Sermon." So obsessive a poet generally would not remain also so tentative, but Dickey's is a cunning imagination, metamorphic enough to evade its exegetes.

As a critic himself obsessed with the issue of belatedness, I am particularly impressed by the originality of "Approaching Prayer," which Dickey rightly called "the most complicated and far-fetched poem I've written." I should add that Dickey said that some fifteen years ago, but it is good enough for me that his observation was true up to then. The far-fetcher was the good, rough English term that the Elizabethan rhetorician Puttenham used to translate the ancient trope called metalepsis or transumption, and "Approaching Prayer" is certainly an instance of the kind of poem that I have learned to call transumptive. Such a poem swallows up an ever-early freshness as its own, and spits out all sense of belatedness, as belonging only to others. "Approaching Prayer" is at moments Yeatsian in its stance and diction, but what overwhelmingly matters most in it can only be called "originality." I know no poem remotely like it. If it shares a magic vitalism with Yeats and D. H. Lawrence, its curious kind of wordless, almost undirected prayer has nothing Yeatsian or Lawrentian in its vision. And it is less like Dickey's true precursor, Roethke, than it is like Robert Penn Warren's masterful "Red-Tailed Hawk and Pyre of Youth," which, however, was written long after it and perhaps may even owe something to it.

Originality in poetry, despite Northrop Frye's eloquent assertions, has little to do with the renewal of an archetype. Instead, it has to do with what I would call a struggle against facticity, where "facticity" means being so incarcerated by an author, a tradition, or a mode that neither author nor reader is aware of the incarceration. Dickey calls his poem "Approaching Prayer," but as his revisionist or critic, I will retitle it "Approaching Poetry" or even "Approaching Otherness." I grant that Dickey has said, "In this poem I tried to imagine how a rather prosaic person would prepare himself for the miraculous event which will be the prayer he's going to try to pray," but surely that "rather prosaic person" is a transparent enough defense for the not exactly prosaic Dickey. No one has ever stood in Dickey's presence and felt that he was encountering prose. The poem's speaker is "inside the hair *helmet*" (my emphasis), and this helmet too both conceals and saves. At the poem's visionary center, the boar's voice, speaking through the helmet, gives us the essential trope as he describes his murder by the archer: "*The sound from his fingers, / Like a plucked word, quickly pierces / Me again.*" The bow, then, is poetic language, and each figuration is a wounding arrow. Who then is slaying whom?

Like any strong poet, Dickey puts on the body of his dead father, for him, let us say, the composite precursor Yeats / Roethke. Shall we say that the strong poet, in Dickey's savage version, reverses the fate of Adonis, and slays the boar of facticity? I hear the accent of another reversal, when Dickey writes:

> My father's sweater
> Swarms over me in the dark.
> I see nothing, but for a second

> Something goes through me
> Like an accident, a negligent glance.

Emerson, in his famous epiphany of transmutation into a Transparent Eyeball, chanted: "I am nothing; I see all; the currents of the Universal Being circulate through me; I am part or particle of God." Dickey's surrogate sees nothing, but for a second is all, since that something going through him, glancingly negligent, accidental, also makes him part or particle of God. Addressing beasts and angels, this not so very prosaic personage speaks both as beast and as angel. But to whom? To part or particle of what is oldest, earliest in him, to the beyond that comes straight down at the point of the acceptable time. But acceptable to whom? The God of the hunt is hardly Yahweh Elohim. Dickey's closing chant salutes the God through the trope of "enough": a violent enough stillness, a brain having enough blood, love enough from the dead father, lift enough from the acuity of slaughter—all enough to slay reason in the name of something being, something that need not be heard, if only "it may have been somehow said." The apocalyptic Lawrence of the last poems and *The Man Who Died,* and the Yeats of the final phase, celebrated and so would have understood that "enough." As an American Orphic, as pilot and as archer, Dickey is less theoretic, more pragmatic, in having known just that "enough."

If I were writing of the later Dickey, the poet of "The Firebombing," "Slave Quarters," "Falling," and *The Zodiac,* then I would invoke Blake's Proverbs of Hell on the dialectics of knowing enough by knowing more than enough. But I am going to conclude where Dickey himself ends *The Early Motion,* with the gracious approach to otherness that characterizes the nineteen fragments that constitute "Drinking from a Helmet." Dickey remarks that the fragments are set between the battlefield and the graveyard, which I suspect is no inaccurate motto for the entire cosmos of what will prove to be the Whole Motion, when we have it all. Though it is a suite of war poems, "Drinking from a Helmet," even in its title, moves toward meaning both of Dickey's major imaginative obsessions: divination through finding the right cover of otherness, and salvation from the body of this death through finding the magic body of the poet.

A survivor climbs out of his foxhole to wait on line at a green watertruck, picking up another's helmet to serve as a drinking vessel. Behind him, the graves registration people are laying out the graveyard for those still fighting. The literal force of this is almost too strong, and conceals the trope of divination, defined by Vico as the process of evasion by which the poet of Magic Formalism achieves godhood—a kind of mortal godhood, but immortality enough. Drinking from a helmet becomes the magic act of substitution, fully introduced in the luminous intensity of fragment VIII:

> At the middle of water
> Bright circles dawned inward and outward
> Like oak rings surviving the tree
> As its soul, or like
> The concentric gold spirit of time.
> I kept trembling forward through something
> Just born of me.

The "something" is prayer, but again in the peculiar sense adumbrated in the poem "Approaching Prayer." Dickey always has been strongest at *invention* (which Dr. Johnson thought the essence of poetry) and his invention is triumphant throughout the subsequent progression of fragments. We apprehend an almost Blakean audacity of pure vision, as the speaker struggles to raise the dead:

> I swayed, as if kissed in the brain.
> Above the shelled palm-stumps I saw
> How the tops of huge trees might be moved
> In a place in my own country
> I never had seen in my life.
> In the closed dazzle of my mouth
> I fought with a word in the water
> To call on the dead to strain
> Their muscles to get up and go there.
> I felt the difference between
> Sweat and tears when they rise,
> Both trying to melt the brow down.

I think one would have to go back to Whitman's *Drum-Taps* to find an American war poetry this nobly wrought. Vision moves from Okinawa to rural America, to the place of the slain other whose helmet has served as the vessel of the water of life:

> On even the first day of death
> The dead cannot rise up,
> But their last thought hovers somewhere

For whoever finds it.
My uninjured face floated strangely
In the rings of a bodiless tree.
Among them, also, a final
Idea lived, waiting
As in Ariel's limbed, growing jail.

Ariel, imprisoned by the witch before Prospero's advent, then becomes
the spirit of freedom, but not in this poem, where only to "be no more
killed" becomes freedom enough. "Not dying wherever you are" is the
new mode of otherness, as vision yields to action:

Enough
Shining, I picked up my carbine and said.
I threw my old helmet down
And put the wet one on.
Warmed water ran over my face.
My last thought changed, and I knew
I inherited one of the dead.

Dickey at last, though only through surrogate or trope, is at once self
and other. What was vision becomes domesticated, touchingly American:

I saw tremendous trees
That would grow on the sun if they could,
Towering. I saw a fence
And two boys facing each other,
Quietly talking,
Looking in at the gigantic redwoods,
The rings in the trunks turning slowly
To raise up stupendous green.
They went away, one turning
The wheels of a blue bicycle,
The smaller one curled catercornered
In the handlebar basket.

The dead soldier's last thought is of his older brother, as Dickey's longing
always has been for his own older brother, dead before the poet was born.
Fragment XVIII, following, is the gentlest pathos in all of Dickey:

I would survive and go there,
Stepping off the train in a helmet

> That held a man's last thought,
> Which showed him his older brother
> Showing him trees.
> I would ride through all
> California upon two wheels
> Until I came to the white
> Dirt road where they had been,
> Hoping to meet his blond brother,
> And to walk with him into the wood
> Until we were lost,
> Then take off the helmet
> And tell him where I had stood,
> What poured, what spilled, what swallowed:

That "what" is the magic of substitution, and the final fragment is Whitmanian and unforgettable, being the word of the survivor who suffered and was there:

> And tell him I was the man.

The ritual magic of a soldier's survival has been made one with the Incarnation of the Poetical Character. Of all Dickey's poems, it is the one I am persuaded that Walt Whitman would have admired most. Whitman too would have said with Dickey: "I never have been able to disassociate the poem from the poet, and I hope I never will." What Whitman and Dickey alike show is that "the poet" is both an empirical self, and more problematically a real me or me myself, an ontological self, and yet a divine other. Both poets are hermetic and esoteric while making populist gestures. There the resemblance ends, and to pursue it further would be unfair to Dickey or any contemporary; it would have been unfair even for Stevens or for Hart Crane. The Dickey of the later motion is no Whitmanian; if one wants an American analogue, one would have to imagine Theodore Roethke as an astronaut, which defeats imagination. But I end by citing Whitman because his final gestures are the largest contrast I know to James Dickey's ongoing motions in his life's work. Whitman is up ahead of us somewhere; he is perpetually early, warning us: "Will you speak before I am gone? will you prove already too late?" The burden of belatedness is upon us, but if we hurry, we will catch up to him:

> Failing to fetch me at first keep encouraged,
> Missing me one place search another,
> I stop somewhere waiting for you.

Not Dickey; he cannot stop, yet he has taken up part of the burden for us. Whitman is larger, but then no one is larger, and that largeness is a final comfort, like Stevens's "Large Red Man Reading." Dickey speaks only to and for part of us, but that part is or wants to be the survivor; wants no more dying. Words alone, alas, are not certain good, though the young Yeats, like the young Dickey, wanted them to be. But they can help us to make "a creature to keep me dying / Years longer," as Dickey wrote in the poem of "The Other." I conclude by going full circle, by returning to the poem with the tribute that it could prove to contain the whole motion within it. Dickey cannot "turn wholly mortal in [his] mind," and that touch of "utter, unseasonable glory" will be his legacy.

Colonel Tate, in Attack and Defense

GALE H. CARRITHERS, JR.

How may the Southerner take hold of his tradition?
The answer is: by violence.[1]

It's all very well to tell the Colonel to up and at 'em, but fortu-
nately the Colonel, who has a fair notion of the force he is about
to exhibit, isn't so confident that he will defeat the enemy. He is
confident that he has the right plan of attack, but his tactics may
be bad. He feels genuine timidity, and if it weren't arrogant to
say so, humility.[2]

In literature as in life nothing reaches us pure. The task of the
civilized intelligence is one of perpetual salvage.[3]

The military figure Tate uses above seems to have been well established in his inner circle of friends. The published correspondence with
Donald Davidson, for further example, shows him saying "in this kind of
literary warfare, if we hesitated till we were sure, there would be no warfare, for you can't *prove* things like *revenge*, etc; you have to divine them
and let loose. And what is life without war?" (11 Oct. 1924). Or the letter to "General D. Davidson," signed "A. Tate (Colonel)" (18 Jan. 1933).[4]
Sometimes the figure will be understood metaphorically, but perhaps more
often metonymically, given Tate's deep sense of all language as action,
wherein, as we shall see, he remained akin to oral societies. In any case,
the combativeness—"Bellum omnium contra omnes," he jauntily quotes
Hobbes in the letter cited above—the bellicose strategizing, so characterizes much of his working style that one longtime friend standing by his
grave exclaimed "Colonel Tate!" and was instantly understood.[5]
   What the essays and reviews (and even poems) suggest by their frequent
edginess is almost palpable in the fifty-seven boxes of correspondence at

Princeton. He wrote letters "two evenings a week, at least" in 1924 in New York (*DD*, 17 Dec. 1924), and surely at an equivalent rate in ensuing decades. One finds a campaigner for literature, who tirelessly planned, exhorted, acted as liaison, and encouraged with practical instruction, gave reinforcement or a touch of Allen in the night. The bellicosity and sense of besiegement constitute a less-noticed aspect of the Tatian calling to be a man of letters on behalf of "the republic of letters (which is the only kind of republic I believe in, a kind of republic that can't exist in a political republic)" (*JPB*, 23 Dec. 1933). Professor Lewis Simpson, in his definitive series of expositions of that calling and that republic has persuasively emphasized the quasi-priestly aspect of it.[6]

Yet what we might echo Walter Ong in calling the *agonistic* aspect of these writings opens into another realm of discourse and about discourse. That realm of discourse can tell us provocative things about Tate's situation and the world he inhabited—not simply the cultural world of South or New York or (as Simpson helpfully argues) Europe, but his life world, and his postures within it. That conflicted and combative posture, both internally and externally allied and adversarial, is my subject here. What Tate calls his plan of attack and his tactics, which is to say the shape of his war and its battles, his targets and his verbal ammunition, may be held aside for separate treatment.

The agonistic tone of Tate's characteristic expression has some psychic roots in family, roots of quite common American kind. It seems necessary to acknowledge as much, and more might be said. But culturally, as Walter Ong has shown, it associates with a congeries of features which distinguish oral culture from literature culture. The former contrasts with the latter, Ong argues, as (1) additive and aggregative rather than subordinative and analytic; (2) redundant and copious rather than dense or concise or allusive; (3) continuous rather than intermittent; (4) conservative and traditionalist rather than innovative and eclectic; (5) close to the human life world and situational rather than abstract and static; (6) agonistic and vituperative, or correspondingly fulsome in praise, rather than reportorial or judicious; (7) empathetic and participatory rather than objectively distanced: (8) homeostatic in adjusting history to current felt realities rather than seeking to perceive a historical occasion as if through contemporary eyes (however awkwardly those might be donned on particular literate occasions).[7]

It must be added that Ong's work does not only instruct us as to differences in kind between oral cultures and literate cultures, and that in literate cultures orality will be variously residual and "secondary," which is to say framed and altered by literacy. He also alerts us to degrees of difference or intermixture and to persisting degrees of difference, since every infant is without a word and may be reared by circles of people whose thinking and expressive behavior are more *or less* habituated to protocols of literacy. These considerations could well frame separate treatment of Tatian issues in terms of other foci of critical theory.

Several things may well be stirring in the mind of any reader of this who recalls with much vividness writings by Tate.

As conspicuous to Tate's readers as his combativeness is his hypertrophic literacy. All of Ong's features ascribed to (i.e., "written down for") literacy and many he ascribes to orality appear constantly in Tate's diction, his syntax, and his organizational habits beyond the sentence. In writing, he analytically emplaces countless references to other texts and other analyses. This is true even in the relatively conversational letters; but this may be less a paradox than it first seems. For one thing, writing so as to sound (sound?) conversational is a literary skill of marked sophistication, as any reader of college undergraduate papers knows.

The persistence of traits of orality (and not only the agonistic or panegyric) in Tate's elaborate literacy can seem more profoundly paradoxical: his southernness, his espousal of values which he *called* essentially southern, may be conceived as affection strong despite its ambivalence for not only native hearth (in Rebecca West's sense; no traitor he), but for the conservatism and immediacy normal in oral society. These themes run through Tate's work, especially those essays which have a strong social focus—he would have bridled at calling it *functional*—from "Religion and the Old South" in 1930 to "Faulkner's *Sanctuary* and the Southern Myth" in 1968.

The first was Tate's contribution to *I'll Take My Stand*. Tate, Lytle, and Warren objected to that title for the collection (*DD*, app. D), apparently feeling it suggested unreflective rigidity perhaps worse than bellicosity. In any case, he himself and some others who had made *The Fugitive* a significant little magazine in the early mid-twenties had exhibited, in Simpson's words, something like "the pattern of withdrawal and return common in the psychology of visions." [8]

He wrote to Marjorie Swett in 1923: "we fear very much to have the slightest stress laid upon Southern traditions in literature; we who are Southern know the fatality of such an attitude—the old atavism and sentimentality are always imminent."[9] The next year he would not return south from New York unless a job "Red" (Warren) was trying to secure for him became definite: "I simply can't pursue an *ignis fatuus,* especially in the South, a region none too friendly at best" (*DD,* 5 June 1924). By a small irony, one surely not without counterparts in his voluminous correspondence, this crossed in the mail with Davidson's complaint that a review by Tate for the *Nashville Tennessean* used words no more than half a dozen among the paper's readership would understand. By Christmas, Tate was saying with truth enough but more-than-expectable detachment (or is it ambivalence?): "I can never forget you all. But really I shall never return to Nashville; so you must come up here when you can" (*DD,* 17 Dec. 1924).

Somewhat earlier, already in New York, he had pursued with his uniquely deferential assertiveness a corporate definition of a proper Fugitive relationship to home, and the relationship is a written one:

It isn't the old South as material we object to, it seems to me (all Greek literature is a throwback to the fragrant and heroic past), but the fatal attitude of the South toward this material. . . . There's nothing wrong with local color, so far as I can see, except when it drops to mere colored locality—everything must be placed in space and time somewhere, and the South is as good a correlation of emotion as anyplace else; and so I think that the trouble is the damnably barbaric Southern mind, which would be provincial in London, Greenland, or Timbuctoo. (*DD,* 29 June 1923)

Hoi barbaroi the Greeks had called the tribesmen from north and west of them, by a metonymy from how their speech sounded to the Greek ear. Of all Greek literature, that which is most notably "a throwback to the fragrant and heroic past" is not the (textual) poetry of the Greek anthology nor the works in what Ong points out has been the first text-bound genre, the drama, but rather the epic, the more oral and tribal form. The point is that the ethnocentricity of oralism and of tribalism go together as the convex and the concave of a curve, and Tate seems to have thought something like that ("fatal attitude"), even as one exiled by his literacy from the epic garden. *Placing* in space and time is textual or quasi-textual. Most of Tate's visits, likewise, were epistolary.

Moreover, raising the whole constellation of issues to consciousness, so as to achieve awareness of options, precisely an awareness *not* provincial, accords as paradoxically with the nature of the awareness as a map of chaos would accord with "the spirit of the place" (to use Paul Pickrel's deft trope). In a further irony which must have been uncomfortable, Tate partly recognized that, too. After publication of *I'll Take My Stand,* he wrote to Bishop, on the matter of relationship to the land, that "like most of us you are both inside and outside the old tradition, that in a word you are a modern and divided mind" (June 1931). Whatever the justice of Tate's objection to the title, the text did, in contrast to waves and counter-waves of oratory, *take its stand.* As Ong prompts us to keep in mind, any text is intransigent. The text answers questions no more than does a Grecian urn, even though the author may do so in subsequent voice or text.

Readers of "Religion and the Old South" may recall that it is in con-siderable part about a horse. Tate, as if donning the "overhauls" of vil-lage storyteller, copiously propounds a parable (albeit disjointed) of "the whole horse" of viable religion living in the meadow of experience (and one might compare Ortega's "lived-in forest" of *Meditations on Quixote*). Tate mainly distinguished the whole horse from the rationalistic, goal-oriented, and properly mechanistic half-horse of mere horsepower, sec-ondarily from the feckless absurdity of irrational "symbolist poets and . . . Bergson."

But simple narration has been led some intricate measures, with ana-lytic/ironic differentiations of (in Clifford Geertz's term) thickly historical Christ from abstractly historical Osiris, and of horse as Christ from cen-taur, before the argument subsides into unevenness and assertiveness in the last two of the essay's six sections. There may well be a self-consciously ironic relationship of intertextuality between Tate's horse and the Emer-sonian "One Horse Shay" of Calvinism. (He wrote of a friend's fictive characters that "It is the irony which testifies that the author has faced the present" [*JPB,* 12 Mar. 1931]). But more assuredly Tate here concerns himself with the horsepower of northern reductive instrumental thinking. And we concern ourselves here not with his conception of South, North, Bergson, or Jefferson but rather with his attitude toward conceptions he could not live in as reality, yet could half approve as myth, and his attitudes toward southern neighbors and peripatetic self.

Tate began the essay as if mediating between anthropologists in resi-dence and some more-or-less transient third parties, speaking of his own religion as "fable" and "myth," but nevertheless religion: "immediate, direct, overwhelming." [10] After defining the religion of the whole horse by contrast with the above-mentioned religions, which are each half a horse, an argumentative strategy one would have to acknowledge empathetically close to an agrarian life world, he turns to analytic distinctions as highly abstract as anything he attacks for abstraction.

The "religion of the completely workable" is truly a religion, he argues, despite its deficiency in concretely situational and participatory markers like altars and rituals, because it *worships* something it defines as an absolute: logical necessity and human rationality. Tate appeals to the relatively oral life world of experience on the one hand to assert the inadequacy of that, and appeals on the other hand to the literate-abstractive device of the *reductio ad absurdum* to falsify the idolized rationality: "it can predict only success" (*CE*, 307–308). As rhetoric for quarreling with others, this risks self-defeat; as the poetry of quarrel with self, it is poignantly suggestive. [11]

Recognizing limitations in the "image of the horse" and seeking life-worldly immediacy, he proposes a supplementary double "image of history," allegorized (but taxonomized) as a potentially Christian "Short View"—history as a "concrete series" with the same "accident and uncertainty" as the present—and a "Long View"—history as a "logical series," with general identities and rationalistic "natural law," the "cosmopolitan destroyer of tradition." It is not to my purpose to quibble here with his fairness in characterizing historians, or the local details of his logic. Both historical attitudes he identifies have been noticeable; Tate's view of his South seems never to have failed to recognize the spiritual deadliness to whites of slavery or the physical murderousness to blacks of slavery and postemancipation racism. But his epistolary friend Yvor Winters took him immediately to task for the vaguely desperate announcement at essay's end that only violence can now enable the southerner to take hold of his tradition. [12]

Still less would I take issue with Professor Simpson's provocative and consequential point that "Ransom, Davidson, and Tate . . . yearned, it might be said, to complete the spiritualization of the secular. By transforming the South into a symbol of a recovered society of myth and tradition, they would assert the community and spiritual authority of men of letters and make whole the fragmented realm of mind and letters." [13]

But Tate himself insists on "a nice and somewhat slippery paradox here," and it is one which might trouble anyone who from the universal illiteracy of infancy achieves unusual literacy. Even if one's literacy, in all the duality of oral-literate capabilities anatomized by Ong's schema, were not so superbly developed as Tate's, one's own society would as Ong indicates be modified by those capabilities and that doubleness. Even if other things could be equal, a child coming to literacy in a home with literate parents would have differing nurture according to whether *their* parents were literate or not; the degrees of spatializing, analytic thought would differ.

Tate pursues the matter as if in oral debate, by postulating the question "Why must we choose whole horse or half, short view or long?" "Merely living in a certain stream of civilized influence does not compel us to be loyal to it. Indeed, the act of loyalty, even the fact of loyalty, must be spontaneous to count at all. Tradition must, in other words, be automatically operative before it can be called tradition" (*CE,* 311). He closes the section by acknowledging a little ruefully the paradox that both tradition and the Long View prompt "the present defense of the religious attitude." He finds "this conception . . . wholly irrational" and calls irrational his own efforts "to discover the place that religion holds, with abstract instruments, which of course tend to put religion into some logical system or series, where it vanishes" (*CE,* 311–12).

Yet religion did not vanish for Tate himself: he eventually became a Roman Catholic. An asseveration that secular means could not spiritualize the secular? Ong argues that "text-formed thought" about literacy, orality, and identity can (not will but can) deepen a religious sense of the human situation. Was Tate then confused or ironic at age thirty-one? "Religion . . . vanishes" means it vanishes for anyone ill-advised enough to worship reductive rationality. But *how* situate religion with text-formed habits of thought yet not *place* it "into some" reductive quasi-thing? Can "Religion . . . vanishes" mean with a milder and more compassionate irony that it suffers some troubling attenuation? Something of that, though his scorn is real for those who would, as we have learned to say, lapse out of history and back into myth, whether of science or politics or history. He seems generally in step with half a century of Continental argument on behalf of history over myth, most of it still to come when he wrote the essays first treated here, and Continental phenomenologically existential appraisals of lived experience, including religious experience.

Some of his diagnosis presages a good deal of later discourse. He appraises the characteristic early-nineteenth-century New England attitude as "self-conscious and colonial," characteristics which are possible only in a society considerably conditioned by text-formed thought, in contrast to a South whose position seemed to itself "self-sufficient and self-evident," characteristics usual in societies still dominated by oral thought forms. He goes on: "The Southern mind was simple, not top-heavy with learning it had no need of, unintellectual, and composed; it was personal and dramatic, rather than abstract and metaphysical; it was sensuous because it lived close to a natural scene of great variety and interest. . . . They liked very simple stories with a moral in which again they could see an image of themselves" (CE, 319–20). An "alas" just before those lines betokens Virginia-Kentucky-Tennessean Tate's ironic awareness that the southern mind had in fact needed more learning than it recognized. Myth, as he eventually came to define it, means "a dramatic projection of heroic action, or the tragic failure of heroic action, upon the reality of the common life of society, so that the myth *is* reality." [14] The bit about "simple stories" is the decisive diagnosis, even if he did not quite have the more decisive terminology. Ong argues that past ages were not ontologically more heroic than this one but rather that aural apprehension and mnemonic economy in an oral society *demand* sharply differentiated type characters, the oral-aural equivalents of the white hats and black hats in the early Western movie. Northrop Frye long since anatomized the Western as a version of pastoral, and we can note that pastoral seems historically to have thrived in connection with secondary orality. Narrative, Ong observes, "builds less and less on 'heavy' figures until, some three centuries after print, it can move comfortably in the ordinary human lifeworld typical of the novel." [15] To say it can is not to say it regularly does. Tate's words, rather than Ong's, well describe the world of most television serials, soapy and otherwise, a world evidently appealing to minds not much or not long affected by text-formed thought. Likewise, whatever "Southern Gothic" owes to action in southern life worlds, it may be construed to owe something to the oral traditions of heavy characters. Elsewhere Tate praises Bishop's literately ironic treatment of quasi-historical type characters (*JPB*, 11 May 1931).

One should somewhat similarly consider Tate's own consideration of the plight and deformations of the sign, from strictures in 1930 about reason and nature being wrongly equated in what was called naturalism (CE, 314) to "Ezra Pound and the Bollingen Prize" (1949) and later. One should consider Tate's concern with uniting man's "moral nature and his economics . . . that greatest of all human tasks" (CE, 302). One must consider Tate's campaign for "a spiritual community . . . and for the mind's capacity for the perception of transcendence," and one profits from Professor Simpson having done so (1974, especially). But more remains to be said about his continuing struggle, increasingly conscious and informed, with the modes and the issues of orality and literacy. If Ong has been the foremost analyst of those, thus far, Tate may, I think, be called one of the most noteworthy American protagonists.

He wrote "What Is a Traditional Society?" early in 1936, thought it "the best essay" he had "ever done . . . in the field of general ideas" (*JPB*, 31 Mar. 1936), gave it as the Phi Beta Kappa Address in June at the University of Virginia, and published it in the *American Review* in September. Urbanely (or homeostatically?) adjusted to the audience at "Mr. Jefferson's university," it masterfully works the crowd from the most puerile undergraduates to their most senior mentors. A remarkably mixed work.

In the address, one finds "finance-capitalism" posited as a five-day-a-week way of life at odds with a potentially more humane and spiritual way of life often pursued only two days a week. Indeed, he avers that "finance-capitalism, a system that has removed men from the responsible control of the means of livelihood, is *necessarily hostile* to the development of a moral nature" (*CE*, 303, my emphasis). One can only infer here what elsewhere he makes explicit, his religious objection to any practice which treats persons as things, doubly objectionable in the case of the black man both made a thing and situated to alienate the slaveholder who degrades him from the land which might in Tate's view be the medium of that slaveholder's salvation (*CE*, 273). One gets in this address-essay an oratorical expansiveness and devices like anaphora difficult to represent briefly, though "finance-capitalism" hints at the copiousness of orality (cf. the still-current southernism *toad-frog*). [16]

But one does not find explicated such implications about religious belief, which might well elude a listener. A sufficiently analytic listener in 1936 might, like a reader today, flinch at the pastoral neatness of the claim that Virginia gentlemen of the early Republic "knew what they wanted because they knew what they themselves were" (*CE*, 297); as we shall see, he later disavows the ascription of self-knowledge. Or one might fix on his stipulative definition: "An untraditional society does not permit its members to pass to the next generation what it received from its immediate past" (*CE*, 302). *Pass, what, it*—Tate's reified abstractions may seem incautiously unitary. Doesn't the implied opposite traditional society at this point in the essay resemble homogeneous, oral, tribal society? We suppose that more farmers' sons among the people of the Book became farmers than became ministerial or scholarly spokesmen for the Bible. We know as Tate did that families can pass a crazy salad whereby the horn of plenty may be undone. We know, as he perhaps more suspected than knew, that all the overlapping ways of cultural transmission—family attitudes and exempla, family emotional and economic conditions, semipublic experience, public exempla, formal education—may be rearticulated in the wake of literacy components in formal education.

His thought and behavior already suggest a campaign on behalf of "the republic of letters." He had taken at Southwestern University in Memphis the first of several temporary teaching posts. He was editing with Herbert Agar *Who Owns America?*, a collection of essays to be a textbook–campaign manual for enlistees to the cause. And he exhorts his listeners in Charlottesville and the readers of Agar's *American Review:* "traditional property in land was the primary medium through which man expressed his moral nature; and our task is to restore it *or to get its equivalent today*" (*CE,* 303, my emphasis).

What shall metaphoric land be? Whatever, its formulation would seem to depend on literary-ideological efforts of men and women citizens from the republic of letters. The land conceived as medium, tenor, or vehicle for expressing man's moral nature, insofar as land is cultivated, acculturated, abuts on such diverse phenomena as ecology-consciousness, a Miltonic-Puritan sacramental sense of work, and a psychoanalytic sense of adult self-actualization. If metaphoric land is language itself, then the republic of letters requires better distribution of high literacy than ever yet achieved, lest it be a Gnostic cult or oligarchy.

In a kind of simultaneous example and crux of his argument and dramatization of his proposal, he quotes the "Game of Chess" section from *The Waste Land,* and glosses it. We should recall he always honored Eliot as one of his two most influential teachers (Ransom the other). He says, in part: "In ages [like ours] which suffer the decay of manners, religion, morals, codes, our indestructible vitality demands expression in violence and chaos; it means that men who have lost both the higher myth of religion and the lower myth of historical dramatization have lost the forms of human action; it means that they are no longer capable of defining a human objective, of forming a dramatic conception of human nature" (*CE,* 301, my emphasis). *Forms,* here as elsewhere with Tate, means more than "visible shapes." It means something like "modes and principles of arrangement, similarity, and experienced continuity," a religious or near-religious concept for him. Thus, he brilliantly used the text-formed skills of analysis and subordination to attack the discontinuous and abstractive tendencies of any current thought that has run to atomistic extremes. He attacks in defense of "tradition," which is something continuous, participatory, aggregative, homeostatic, and at its best neither exclusive nor repressive. Literacy defending orality? An absurdity or forlorn hope? No: each human being must achieve orality before achieving literacy, and the genius of the former, like ideas in culture, need not die even though it be resituated. That we know our vitality is far from indestructible strengthens his point. Tate may be seen as a prophet and a pioneer (in both agrarian and military senses) on behalf of an enlightened secondary orality, one attempting to discriminate in favor of (if we may revise Matthew Arnold) the best that has been thought and believed. Spiritualizing the secular world will formally be textualizing it for communities necessarily highly literate.

The tricky footwork and occasional awkwardness of that effort appear in a somewhat less focused essay of the year before, "The Profession of Letters in the South," originally in the *Virginia Quarterly Review* in 1935. His reflections on profession, on the South, and on letters range long in time, far in space. Still earlier, he had animadverted privately on Archibald MacLeish's *Conquistador:* "Facing our own past is a way of facing the present. Has MacLeish any Aztec ancestry? It is probably too bad that a man like MacLeish ever received an education, for education is nothing without tradition, and the traditionless educated man will, in spite of himself, work out fictitious and romantic scenes to dramatize his character in, usually in the past. It is a blessing that Ernest never went to a university and took it seriously" (*JPB,* 12 Mar. 1931). Whatever one may think about Hemingway or MacLeish, one acknowledges that writers who have been endowed with education and tradition have frequently projected elements or fantasies of self into historic or quasi-historic scenes. Tate was later and by his own acknowledgment to do some of that in his only novel, *The Fathers* (1936).

Here, he offers an extraordinary delineation of twentieth-century southern difference from the twentieth-century North. He begins by acknowledging "an immensely complicated region," as privately he would acknowledge "the 'North' is a group of sections whose interests should be severally protected from the haphazard impulse of industrial capitalism." [17] But he insists that despite sectional diversity it is "a single culture."

> The South to this day finds its most perfect contrast in the North. In religious and social feeling . . . the greater resemblance is to France.
> . . . Englishmen have told us that we still have the eighteenth-century amiability and consideration of manners, supplanted in their country by middleclass reticence and suspicion. . . . where, outside the South, is there a society that believes even covertly in the Code of Honor?

. . . Where else in the modern world is the patriarchal family still innocent of the rise and power of other forms of society? Possibly in France; probably in the peasant countries of the Balkans. . . . Where else . . . so much of the ancient land-society . . . along with the infatuated avowal of beliefs hostile to it . . . supine enthusiasm for being amiable to forces undermining the life that supports the amiability? . . . its . . . religion . . . a convinced supernaturalism . . . nearer to Aquinas than to Calvin, Wesley, or Knox. (CE, 268–69)

I've quoted at length, even while eliding some oratorical pavanes and divagations, because the passage instances so many of the cultural ambiguities in Tate's position as an ultraliterate southerner, and shows something of his ambivalence breaking through the habit and conviction of mannerliness: "infatuated . . . supine"; compare Othello's "goats and monkeys"!

The suggestion of cultural kinship with "peasant countries of the Balkans" is a shrewd one, however defamiliarizing. In "The New Provincialism," of 1945, he formulates in his most considered fashion a provocative distinction between what he calls regionalism and provincialism:

Regionalism is that consciousness or that habit of men in a given locality which influences them to certain patterns of thought and conduct handed to them by their ancestors. Regionalism is thus limited in space but not in time. The provincial attitude is limited in time but not in space. When the regional man, in his ignorance . . . of the world, extends his own immediate necessities into the world, and assumes that the present moment is unique, he becomes the provincial man . . . without benefit of the fund of traditional wisdom [he] approaches the simplest problems of life as if nobody had ever heard of them before. A society without arts, said Plato, lives by chance. The provincial man, locked in the present, lives by chance. (CE, 286–87)

Ong has argued in *Orality and Literacy* that Plato was really arguing for the new textual literacy, arguing against the old reductive orality embodied in poets and rhetors. Tate hedges: consciousness *or* habit. Tate seduces by metaphoricity: "handed to them by their ancestors." Precisely not by hand do traditional cultures in "peasant countries" of South or Balkans or Africa convey the traditional messages, except insofar as a minatory hand "touched . . . trembling ears" (or body of recalcitrant child, or the like) to reinforce a vocal message.[18] And such vocal messages tend to be more diffuse, harder to taxonomize or systematize than is usual in more literate and linear contexts. Tate praised Yvor Winters's linearity (1928), but also Crane's truth of legend over history (1930).[19]

"Tacky is tacky," remarked a well-bred southern lady of my acquaintance, "and if he doesn't know what it means, there's no use trying to explain." She is university educated but was adverting to a socioaesthetic *gestalt* "handed" to her by mid-teens and probably little addressed in any of her schooling. "Handed" is a metaphor for vocal presence, which is why regionalism can indeed be extended in time but not in space (unless electronic means to "reach out and touch someone" become more internalized?). In a 1933 review complaining of too little action in E. A. Robinson's long poems, Tate concedes "with the disappearance of general patterns of conduct, the power to depict action that is both *single* and *complete* also disappears" (*PR*, 167). But the single patterns of oral culture, the good, the bad, the tacky, can be repressively oversimple. And their completeness and singularity, their very marked boundedness, will likely be eroded by the profuse variety affordable to print culture, opportunity for good or ill in print culture, but sure demoralization to oral culture.

Furthermore, "traditional wisdom" can bear down with an oppressively or stultifyingly heavy hand, eventuating in tribal stasis, degrading linear history into cyclical myth. Tate himself lived for years in partial flight from the South, flight not to the quasi-tribal society of Yankee village or of (say) Queens, but to the New York City literary scene, which he saw as factionalized but not tribalized.

Yet the metaphor of handing on culture admits to the problem which Plato could not resolve. Handing to us can suggest physical presence or something like voice; but, alas, the text or artifact which can be literally handed over can more easily than the live-though-evanescent voice go forever ignored. A society is still "without arts" and the more a slave to chance insofar as the community of persons does not sojourn in the house of the muses, whether museum, library, or pedagogical adjunct to those.

Or as Tate puts it later in "The New Provincialism," and with acknowledgment to Christopher Dawson, and to house and temple: "Man belonged to his village, valley, mountain, or seacoast; but wherever he was he was a Christian whose Hebraic discipline had tempered his tribal savagery and whose classical humanism had moderated the literal imperative of his Christianity to suicidal otherworldliness" (*CE*, 289). That such otherworldliness was not always nor everywhere made a central Christian imperative (as loving one's neighbor, for instance) does not detract from the present point that the imperative tended to be literary, as in the

Pauline epistles, or secondarily oral, as in homiletic argument from them. Worth emphasizing too is one shared aspect of classical humanism and Judaeo-Christian traditions which could nestle comfortably enough with tribalism (and even with its predilection for xenophobic savagery), but which helped articulate Tate's opposition to modern instrumentalisms. That is the preoccupation of Hebraic discipline and (perhaps to a lesser degree) classical humanism with time, with long views and processes. In the Judaeo-Christian instance, the preoccupation with extended history is partly a metaphoric genuflection toward eternity. That fact further marks (rather than attenuates) Tate's estrangement from the taxonomic atemporality of what he tended to stigmatize as positivism. Atemporality is quasi-unmediated, always quasi-local, often visualized. Eternity is infinite timelessness always mediated by an always inadequate imaginative expression.

But the prophet can remind a perhaps reluctant audience that man is the being who has conceived eternity, and who has conceived human kinships which—unlike mechanical control—extend "unchanging" over very long sequences of time. Tate calls the prophet who does that "The Man of Letters in the Modern World" (1952): "His duty to render the image of man as he is in his time. . . . his concern is with what has not been previously known about our present relation to an unchanging source of knowledge" (CE, 384, 389). The man of letters, more pointedly, is prophetic because Tate identifies him (or her, as his championship of more than one woman writer indicates) as the personage peculiarly responsible for "the invention of standards by which this difference may be known," the difference between "communication, for the control of men, and the knowledge of man which literature offers us for human participation" (CE, 380).

That sense of "man" as a being with a very long-term corporate and individual form of identity, a form more exactly describable as a stable range of possibilities, would by itself set Tate's view in opposition to mechanicoplastic proposals for abrupt remodelings of humankind. His belief in an unchanging source of knowledge, a source by definition incompletely knowable, and his conception of man as himself incompletely knowable because a believing being—those paired conceptions jointly honor knowledge but dismiss dreams of totalization. There is a kind of high and difficult middle ground between ignorance and positivism, as he would limn the matter: "Man is the creature that in the long run has got to believe in order to know, and to know in order to do. For doing without knowing is machine behavior . . . with which man's specific destiny has no connection" (*CE,* 383). The prophet as man of letters is obliged like Saint Luke's preacher to *deliver* captives of the myth of the machine, assist *recovery of sight* to those blind to *theres* beyond the *here* and *thens* beyond the *now* or possibilities beyond the mechanically implicit. In short, and as Tate might have been increasingly willing to say in his later career, the man of letters must argue "the acceptable year of the Lord."

"A Southern Mode of the Imagination" (1960) stands as his ripest public and explicit address to this complex of issues. It was retrospective and revisionary, quoting his 1935 essay on "The Profession of Letters in the South," not as Matthew Arnold quoted himself, for choral reinforcement, but to gain a dialectical purchase on new and further thought. Remarkably, it was almost his last substantial essay, though his mind was clear until his death in 1977.[20]

It is here that he puts the finest point he can on the old distinction between rhetoric and dialectic, in order to differentiate the southern mind. The rhetorical mode of discourse, "the traditional Southern mode . . . presupposes somebody at the other end silently listening. . . . Its historical rival is the dialectical mode, or the give and take between two minds, even if one mind, like the mind of Socrates, prevail at the end. . . . Southern conversation is not going anywhere . . . is only an expression of manners, the purpose of which is to make everybody happy" (*CE,* 560). Oral societies are conservative. Strongly hierarchical social structure reinforces that conservatism; those in power like it, and the structure is so stable that even for those not content, prospects of change can scarcely be conceived at all, still less as real options. Change is alien and tends, at least initially, to be feared. Tate has sometimes been unfairly linked with old-line racist opposition to all change because he opposed change in the direction of the machine myth.

But, it may be objected, what about the bellicosity of oral society? What about *flyting?* What, indeed; his remarks occur in a context of argument, opposing a long gray line from Robert E. Lee to Henry W. Grady, opposing in more or less temporary alliance with Twain, Cash, Hemingway, Adams (Henry), Eliot, Trilling, and Marx (Leo). One reflects that the verbal combats of orality were and are rudimentary in comparison with linear argument (tending to forms like "You're a bigger one"). The invective of orality may in Tate's and Ong's terms be seen as a subset of normal rhetoricity in which copious or exaggerated expressions are exchanged by listeners waiting their chance for self-expressions which need not connect.

In the same context cited just above, Tate elaborates: "The Southerner always talks to somebody else . . . [but] the conversation isn't going anywhere; it is not about anything. . . . Educated Northerners like their conversation to be about ideas. . . . The notorious lack of self-consciousness of the antebellum Southerner made it almost impossible for him to define anything; least of all could he imagine the impropriety of a definition of manners" (CE, 560–61). The self-expression of rhetorical talk might reach to self-realization, but not to self-awareness. Nor does it have the goal-directedness fostered by linear, spatialized typographic thought. And goal-directedness can reinforce a certain kind of self-consciousness: the self as an entity moving from here to there, among alternatives or oppositions, reaching a conclusion. Tate, evidently combative since youth, seemingly hyperliterate since puberty, and always self-conscious, would like Socrates prevail at the end if he could. He will distance himself from those antebellum (and later) southerners by defining manners in an ironically distancing way. He will typically, and often charmingly, in addresses and essays observe the code of manners—but just as often observe it in ironic fashion.

He professes puzzlement at the end of "Southern Mode," though, as to "What brought about the shift from rhetoric to dialectic" in southern letters, even as he posits a "New England dialectic . . . in which the inner struggle is resolved in an idea . . . [in contrast with] Southern dramatic dialectic . . . as in . . . Faulkner, in action" (CE, 568). That form, which he saw finally as the genius of the southern literary renaissance had historically to await "perception of the ironic 'other possible case' which is essential to the dramatic dialectic of the arts of fiction" (CE, 568). Forty adult years as a man of letters never out of touch with his native and still profoundly oral South: his health was poor; his satisfactions in family were apparently great. Yet one wonders: was the growing awareness of other possible cases, even ironic personal cases, a great factor crowding the public pen and voice into the intimate and dwindling quasi-silence of letters?[21]

NOTES

1. Allen Tate, "Religion and the Old South" (1930), first published in *I'll Take My Stand*, by Twelve Southerners (New York: Harper, 1931; repr., Baton Rouge: Louisiana State University Press, 1977); cited here from *Collected Essays* (Denver: Alan Swallow, 1959), 322.

2. Allen Tate to John Peale Bishop, 25 Oct. 1935, *The Republic of Letters in America: The Correspondence of John Peale Bishop and Allen Tate*, ed. Thomas Daniel Young and John J. Hindle (Lexington: University Press of Kentucky, 1981); hereafter *JPB* and date.

3. Allen Tate, "Ezra Pound and the Bollingen Prize," *Partisan Review* 16 (1949); cited here from *Collected Essays*, 536; hereafter *CE*.

4. *The Literary Correspondence of Allen Tate and Donald Davidson*, ed. John Tyree Fain and Thomas Daniel Young (Athens: University of Georgia Press, 1974), 126; hereafter *DD* and date. "A. Tate" perhaps echoes in a reflexively mock-heroic vein the familiar "A. Lincoln." Again, when he was preparing a special issue of *American Review*, he said, "fine poetry, backed by some aloof criticism . . . strategy calls for secrecy. We want this number to take 'em by surprise," suggesting infantry attack with support by artillery.

5. Lewis Simpson, "The Critics Who Made Us: Allen Tate," *Sewanee Review* (Summer 1986), kindly shown me in typescript by Prof. Simpson.

6. Ibid., and "The Southern Republic of Letters and *I'll Take My Stand*," in *A Band of Prophets*, ed. William C. Havard and Walter Sullivan (Baton Rouge: Louisiana State University Press, 1982); *The Dispossessed Garden: Pastoral and History in Southern Literature* (Athens: University of Georgia Press, 1975; repr. Baton Rouge: Louisiana State University Press, 1983); Simpson's foreword to *DD*.

7. See Walter J. Ong, *Orality and Literacy: The Technologizing of the Word* (London and New York: Methuen, 1982), esp. 37–57, used here with some adaptation; his notes indicate more extended treatments in his own and others' earlier work.

8. L. P. Simpson, *The Man of Letters in New England and the South* (Baton Rouge: Louisiana State University Press, 1973), 244.

9. Ibid., 245.

10. *CE*, 306.

11. Yeats's distinction, endorsed by Tate (1968) in *Memoirs and Opinions, 1926–1974* (Chicago: Swallow Press, 1975), 146, hereafter *MO*. See the partly similar argument of Michel Serres, *Hermes: Literature, Science, Philosophy*, ed. Josué Harari and David F. Bell (Baltimore: Johns Hopkins University Press, 1982), 15–28.

12. 29 Dec. 1930, Allen Tate Collection, Princeton University Library; by permission of Janet Lewis.

13. Lewis Simpson, "The Southern Republic of Letters," 87–88.

14. "Faulkner's *Sanctuary* and the Southern Myth" (1968), in *MO*, 151.

15. Ong, "Orality and Literacy," 70.

16. See Stephen M. Ross, "Oratory and the Dialogical in *Absalom, Absalom!*" in *Intertextuality in Faulkner*, ed. Michel Gresset and Noel Polk (Jackson: University Press of Mississippi, 1985), esp. 75 and 78, where Ross cites Faulkner as characterizing the style of *AA* in "studbook style: 'by Southern Rhetoric out of Solitude.' "

17. Tate, writing on the back of a letter from George Soule, then one of the editors of the *New Republic,* 18 Nov. 1931; Allen Tate Collection, Princeton University Library; by permission of Helen Heinz Tate.

18. Again, in "The Profession of Letters in the South," "All the great cultures have been rooted in . . . free peasantries" (*CE,* 273).

19. *The Poetry Reviews of Allen Tate, 1924–1944,* ed. Ashley Brown and Frances Neel Cheney (Baton Rouge: Louisiana State University Press, 1983), 67, 101; hereafter *PR.*

20. His short essay (1968) to introduce the New American Library edition of *Sanctuary,* and a memoir (1972) are printed in *MO.*

21. I also gratefully acknowledge the provocative discourse on these matters of my colleague J. Bainard Cowan.

Fictional Characterization as

Infinite Regressive Series:

George Garrett's Strangers

in the Mirror

FRED CHAPPELL

When the author begins, there is a clean page before him like an unpeopled stage. His drama shall almost certainly unfold around a central character; this character will interact with other characters, influencing, penetrating, infusing their different personalities, shaping or failing to shape their purposes to his own ends. The central character cannot be portrayed alone upon the stage; even the monodrama and the dramatic monologue must refer to other personages besides the speaker, to circumstances that other characters operate upon. The personalities of secondary characters reveal and illuminate the central character, and in fact, he does not exist independently of their perceptions of him. Any character in the drama consists of a roster of the other characters he knows, plus whatever he is in himself.

The author projects himself, in greater or lesser degree, into all the characters that shall come onstage. To whatever observed data he has gathered in regard to them, he adds his own imaginative sympathy and emotional involvement. The characters are convincingly portrayed in direct arithmetical relation to the amount of personal involvement the author is able to muster with each of them. It may have little to do with affection or admiration; Shakespeare's Richard III supremely involved his creator by means of horror and disgust.

The entrance of each new character tells the author more about his central character and at the same time reveals to him more about himself. And as soon as the author takes note of this fact, his work becomes self-conscious, analytical. He begins to populate his work with dissemblers: thieves, confidence men, political puppets and cat's-paws, spies, paid informants, actors, poets, and other authors. Each of these sorts of character hides his motives from the world at large, and the more he hides them from the world, the more he reveals them to us, his audience. The more the author clothes himself in different characters, the more naked he becomes, every disguise a revelation.

> Leaving the cocktail party
> I steal the Admiral's hat
> At home I try it on
> See how much it changes me
>
> Now I am purely different
> I am handsome I am jaunty
> I have pride and power on my head
>
> .   .   .   .
>
> Sir I thank you kindly for it
> And I solemnly promise never to stand
> downcast and shifty in front of anyone
> with your hat humble in my hands

These stanzas are from George Garrett's poem, "Little Transformations," and on one level of meaning they indicate that he, as poet, short-story writer, playwright, and novelist, recognizes the fact that he is on-stage, projecting himself into the characters he has placed there, accepting willingly and even cheerfully the changes these disguises effect in his own private character. His recognition marks perhaps a certain extreme of involvement; Garrett as author is loathe to dissociate, or even to extricate, himself from his fictional characters.

In a companion piece, "Another Hat Poem," he explicitly defines his process of imaginative projection as a means of self-discovery, self-understanding.

> I aim to continue
> making strange faces in funny hats
> and hoping that in due time the stranger

in the mirror will choose to wink back
and that on that judgment day we'll know
each other at last for long lost friends.

Each gallery of characters is then a corridor of mirrors, Garrett's own features strongly or faintly discernible in every face reflected in each glass. But it does not stop there; it is what the mathematicians describe as an infinite regressive series, for a great number of Garrett's characters are also highly self-conscious, and the aspects they show one another are disguises too, adopted in the hope that the characters *they* are engaged with will show *their* true faces. A tiring room of mirrors, a stage full of echoes. The germinal notion is perhaps Shakespearean—all the world a stage— but Garrett carries it to a characteristically modern limit.

Fictional characters, like real people, have double roles to fulfill; they are public as well as private secret personalities, as we all are. As public figures, they play roles, they are performers who fulfill imposed duties, and they like to suppose that their private personalities are separate from, and unaffected by, their public ones. In that unforgettable short story "The Old Army Game," Elwood Quince plays so perfectly his role of the sadistic first sergeant that the reader is disappointed and even disgusted when he reveals himself an ordinary vulnerable human being. In fact, Quince is so polished an example of his type that he causes, by equal and opposite reaction, two stubborn recruits to become polished soldiers. But they know they are only playing the part. "Sachs called it being in disguise and referred to his uniform as a costume," the narrator tells us. "He called us both 'the masqueraders.'" In the story "Bread from Stones" the straitlaced banker-narrator finds that his scapegrace cousin Raymond, his opposite in every way, is still necessary to his own sense of well-being. "Not that I believe the same myth that he does," he says. "Not that I think we could change things much one way or the other or would even if we could. I have been living and working in a bank too long to believe anything like that. Still, it makes me feel better that somebody I know believes it."

These sentences show how the matter is complicated. His characters often understand one another by means of the same sympathetic projection that Garrett shows toward them. In "Noise of Strangers" that tough weary Sheriff Riddle has in his power a hapless wandering guitar player who has got involved in a killing. At one point the sheriff realizes that he has pushed his interrogation too far and in a cruel direction. He stops to reflect: "You can take away a lot, but don't take away jail pride. He's done his time, walked in and walked out where many a man couldn't. Don't make light of his suffering and endurance. A man has little enough to comfort himself with." Riddle is not merely second-guessing; it is as if he is overhearing his prisoner's interior monologue. But if his knowledge makes him a more compassionate person, it does not make him a softer sheriff. The public and official role is the one he lives by, and his compassion is only part of a sad knowledge he will be at pains to keep secret.

Often Garrett's characters have developed such belief in their public roles that they end up as performers. In "Don't Take No for an Answer," Stitch performs as a lecturer on seduction technique. Battling Bill Thibault, in "Time of Bitter Children," exhibits himself as a sort of carnival freak; the Wounded Soldier, in the story of that title, makes himself a pure spectacle for one and all. The father and son in "The Rivals" cannot prevent themselves from taking part in a performance that neither really wishes to go through with. In "A Game of Catch" and "Pretty Birdie" the women end up as naked dancers, ballet performers of the fantasies of others. The same thing is true, in his poetry, of Garrett's "Salome" and his "Stripper." The latter says,

> Oh not for pity or pleasure
> I peel myself like a grape.
> Nor for a trick of loaves and fishes,
> to be divided and devoured whole
> by your lost lonely tribe.

The stripper has her own motives; her public persona hides a sadder private situation.

> But when I greet my mirror
> a bored and aging stranger laughs
> and my heart staggers like a drunk.

So we have George Garrett the writer projecting himself into his characters. The characters in turn project themselves into one another and also into the public roles they have developed. It is inevitable then that his stories will themselves be reports of performances and rituals. In "An Evening Performance" the aptly named Stella is allowed after many hindrances and delays to leap from her towering perch into a small tank of burning water. Her feat, with its attendant frustrations, is all that the action of this story amounts to. There has been no fanfare, no proper buildup, but she jumps—and survives unscathed. That is all there is, but it is a long way from being all there is. "But if the evening performance had been brief, it remained with them, haunting, a long time afterwards. Some of the preachers continued to denounce it as the work of the devil himself. The drunkards and tellers of tall tales embroidered on it and exaggerated it and preserved it until the legend of that high dive was like a beautiful tapestry before which they might act out their lives, strangely dwarfed and ashamed."

"A Wreath for Garibaldi" is an account of pure ritual. In this story an American is persuaded, for reasons not really clear to himself, to lay a wreath of flowers, in honor of Garibaldi, at the grave of the poet Lauro di Bosis in a Roman public park. It seems the emptiest of quixotic gestures. The American has no stake in the ceremony, and the Italian authorities allow him to perform it only "with the full understanding that it doesn't mean anything." But after he goes through with it, he comes to find out that the act does have meaning for him, that a genuine ritual is never empty.

> That same night I had a dream, a very simple, non-symbolic dream. In the dream I had a modest bouquet of flowers and I set out to try to find the bust of Lauro di Bosis and leave the flowers there. I couldn't find it. I had a sense of desperation, the cold-sweat urgency of a real nightmare. And then I knew where it was and why I hadn't noticed it. There it was, covered, bank on bank, with a heaped jungle of flowers. In my dream I wept for shame. But I woke then and I laughed out loud and slept soundly after that.

He discovers one of the profoundest purposes of ritual, the reconciliation of the private needs of personality with the public demands of society.

But the public demands of society can be complex, imperious, and total. *Death of the Fox* and *The Succession* are Garrett's most ambitious and extended uses of ritual form. *The Succession* concerns itself with one of the grandest of public rituals, a coronation; *Death of the Fox* with one of the gravest, a public execution. In both novels a large number of characters are at pains to explain from a private position the necessity of their public roles, and both novels are at bottom concerned with the necessary sacrifice of the precious personal psyche in the interests of the preservation of society and the continuance of history. And these are true sacrifices because they are made by people acutely conscious of what they are doing and what the final outcome will be.

Sir Walter Raleigh, in *Death of the Fox,* sacrifices his own life. It seems to him—finally—that he is required to do so. He is determined to do it properly—not merely on his own terms, insofar as that is possible—but in the most becoming public terms as well. The whole longish novel is ritual preparation culminating in ritual performance. The private Raleigh must recoil from his unhappy fate, but the reasoning public Raleigh knows that he must choose to embrace it. At one point he ponders the necessity of the public man:

> Take another figure. Clothed in all his finery, a naked king is invisible. Even unto himself. Clothed only in bare flesh and hair, the anatomy of bones is unknown. But the body beneath clothes and the bones beneath flesh are always there. And after clothing has rotted and flesh in corruption has shredded away, there, intricate enough, yet simple, stands the design of the man who lived. And no robes he wears, royal or rogue's, no form of flesh, clean or filthy, healthy or sick, can work a change upon that inmost architecture.
>
> Just so, the layers of a man's thought and deeds. Bodied forth, clothed as the times permit and require.

As the times permit and require. It often seems to me that Garrett is almost the only serious writer of our decades who understands and sympathizes with the figure of the administrator, who sees the risks of disgrace and contumely the administrator knows and lives with, who admires the sacrifices the able administrator makes. He is one of the few writers of military fiction who sympathizes with the officer as well as the enlisted man; he shares feeling with the queen as well as the bandit, with the courtier as well as the plowman.

Probably it is significant that the play the actor has been performing in *The Succession* is Shakespeare's *Troilus and Cressida* with its famous long speech on "degree."

> Take but degree away, untune that string,
> And hark what discord follows.

Garrett is apostle and disciple of order, and his characters, wearily, grudgingly, give up themselves for the sake of it. This is not to say that he worships simple authority or brutal command; George Garrett is no Ayn Rand, he does not see society as mere opportunity for individual materialist buccaneering. Rather, he seems to see society as a continually endangered system, beset with enemies internal and external. Society, however riddled with flaws and maggot-eaten, is what we have; the alternative is as terrible as it is unknowable. The duty to preserve it requires eternal sacrifice of individual desire and personal integrity. If we wanted to find a writer at the opposite end of the pole from Garrett, we might put up D. H. Lawrence, who was willing to wreck the system, to destroy it in the interest of personal psychic health and integrity. If we looked for a writer whose views are largely consonant with Garrett's, we might choose T. S. Eliot, radically (but not blindly) conservative—even to the point of royalism. *The Succession* can be seen as a celebration of the instauration of James I, a king for whom the author has no admiration whatsoever, but whose kingship is the best hope for society.

James is not paramount; the succession itself, the peaceful handing-on of ultimate temporal authority, is what is important. In the last sentence of the novel Garrett reveals the figure at the center, the person for whom William Cecil hatched his long design, for whose sake all the intricate politicking and even all the treachery have taken place. It was all for "this happy drunken plowman, mud of good English earth thick on his boots, out under the stars, who is wishing for [Queen Elizabeth] and the rest of the world, for the sake of our own sweet Jesus, a good night." The plowman is drunk because it is Christmas time, and he is so happy that he wishes for "the dead, from Adam and Eve until now, their rest in peace." He wishes too for "the living, one and all, from the beggar in his hedge to the Queen in her soft bed." The whole length of the Great Chain of Being is involved, from mud to stars; all history is involved, from the very beginning; and every class and station of society. The Christmas season, with its single long various ritual, already consecrates the succession before it takes place.

But the mechanics of the succession, the way it has to be managed amid highly imperfect circumstance, is a mare's nest of chicanery, deceit, betrayal, and crime both petty and grand. It is a matter of compromising some of the precious inner workings of a society in order to preserve its firm outer structure. Even so, this vision of order, crammed and prickly with detail, is all a dream, a benevolent Machiavellian fantasy. William Cecil, who perpetrated the plan for the succession in the first place, is long since dead. And the messenger, upon whose news the success of the plan depends, had but just started his journey. The 538 pages of the novel actually comprise his imaginative projection of what shall take place, what *must* take place, if the succession is to come about in proper order. There is probably no other novel of comparable length and complexity in all literature which reveals its underlying design so late; certainly there is none which proclaims such faith in the imaginative abilities of people to understand one another.

They understand one another because each knows the roles the others are supposed to fulfill. In their business with the world they are all conscious actors, and while they may use parts of their private lives and personalities in the furtherance of their roles, they do not allow the former to intrude upon and spoil the purposes of the latter. Professional actors are important in *Death of the Fox* and, especially, in *The Succession;* and in his prologue to a work in progress, a novel about Christopher Marlowe, Garrett gives us an inner portrait of an Elizabethan player who is more or less representative of the trade. This portrait will, as we expect, describe equally well all the courtiers, politicians, and spies in his work—on one side of their nature, at least.

> Foolish or not, he chooses not, not yet, to despair. He defers that. In his heart of hearts he knows this world is beyond redemption and so well lost. Knows that, thus, to win the world would be then to possess nothing worth having. In his secret heart, he can see himself clearly, as naked as God made him first; and to see himself thus, a poor creature, pale as a winter root, is to know beyond doubting that he is a fool. But, do you see?, he loves this tired world, worthless as it is and may be. And, calling upon St. Paul and St. Augustine and any others he can think of, he chooses to try to love himself, too. And always to be busily seeking the love of others . . . to confirm his own best fictions.

The final paragraph of the player's portrait can include not only the characters in Garrett's novels but the author of them as well:

> It is these lies, these falsehoods and very present weaknesses, which give to his often desperate life most of its strength and its energy. It is from his deepest falsehoods that his finest moments as a player (in life as much as on the boards) are drawn up to the light like sweet, cold well water which can assuage the most powerful thirst and set your teeth on edge.

The player's gift is drama, fiction—that is to say, his gift is truth, and it does indeed set our teeth on edge. Garrett's vision of civilization as the relentless sacrifice of individual personality for the sake of order and continuance is deeply tragic. (We might remark that it is also deeply southern and carries with it something of the doomed gallantry of the Confederate soldier, as "A Wreath for Garibaldi" points out.) It is tragic because none of Garrett's characters—none at least that I can remember—ever assents to the essential worthiness of the present order. It is merely the best thing, the only thing, that they know. They had no hand in creating present order, and they are powerless to change it in any significant degree. The toll that its guardianship exacts from them is excruciating, and their normal emotional states are those of overburdened weariness or, more rarely, searing outrage. They have been yoked to the heavy dung cart of history, sentenced by inner feelings of responsibility to pull it through the Slough of Despond before them, and they are always painfully aware of the injustice of a situation which they were born into and which they are deliberately defending in order to pass on to others. The dutiful man in his time is like the child among ancestors, in Garrett's poem of that title. History, like the ancestors, is both unreal and relentless.

> Dimensionless, they've left behind
> buttons, daguerrotypes, a rusty sword
> for a small boy to fondle, and the tales
> he hears without believing a word
>
> about the escapades of the tall people.

And probably there is not one among the author's responsible earnest dissemblers who does not applaud, in his secret heart, the final lines of the poem:

> What can be said of the dead? They rise
> to make you curse the day that you were born.

WORKS CITED

All quotations from Garrett's work are from the following editions:

The Collected Poems. Fayetteville: University of Arkansas Press, 1984.
Death of the Fox. New York: Doubleday, 1971.
An Evening Performance: New and Selected Short Stories. New York: Doubleday, 1985.
The Succession. New York: Doubleday, 1983.

The Color Purple:

What Feminism Can Learn

from a Southern Tradition

GINA MICHELLE COLLINS

"Black women are called, in the folklore that so aptly identifies one's status in society, 'the mules of the world,' because we have
been handed the burdens that everyone else—*everyone else*—refused to
carry."[1] When Alice Walker embraces rather than denies the identification
of women as "mules of the world" in black folklore, she shifts our focus
from the immediate negative charge carried by the word *mule* to identify
a peculiar strength embodied in the image. A mule after all, while an ugly,
comical creature, has one outstanding feature: its ability to survive. A talent for survival is the most immediately praiseworthy characteristic of the
women and men who people Walker's fiction, certainly the most often
praised attribute of her best-known character, Celie in *The Color Purple,*
who throughout the novel is first her father's then her husband's "mule."

It is Celie's methods of survival and her potential as a role model for
contemporary feminists that I will address in this essay. Before moving
on to *The Color Purple,* let me reconsider some of the traditionally negative connotations of this identification of black women as "mules of the
world." For when she accepts the label, Walker takes not only its positive attributes but also what is—or what the patriarchy would have us
believe is—wrong about our status as "mules of the world"—our status
as outsiders.

Black women are doubly marked as outside the patriarchal structure,
because of gender as well as race. We are, as Walker puts it, bearers of burdens that no one else will carry. The pejorative connotations of the word

mule however, conceal a particular asset. Because of her singular position as "absolutely" outside patriarchal power structures, the black woman's perspective is particularly well-suited to seeing what is wrong with those structures. This singularity is one of Walker's motivations in choosing to write almost exclusively about the experience of southern black women; it is why Barbara Christian suggests that Walker *capitalizes* upon the status of black women: "Walker approach[es] the forbidden as a possible route to a new world." [2] What she turns to her advantage is the freedom inherent in this position, using it to articulate the unspoken or unspeakable realities of the patriarchal system as a first step toward offering a vision of an alternative social order.

In *The Color Purple* her approach to the "forbidden" is a series of letters written to God by a "nearly illiterate black womanchild," the novel's protagonist, Celie. By not only creating Celie's voice but allowing her to speak directly to us in her letters, Walker not only allows the "victim," the repressed minority, a voice, but she allows Celie to tell her story *in her own language*. This is an important distinction. At the foundation of Walker's strategy is her realization that much, if not all, of the real power of the patriarchy resides in its all-inclusive discourse. Should any member of the minority attempt to speak, there are no *acceptable* words —no socially sanctioned words—with which to describe the experience of oppression. If it can be spoken, the experience itself may already have ceded to genteel ambiguity. If the experience is spoken without compromise, every effort is often made to suppress it. We can see this operative in most if not all the objections that have been made to *The Color Purple*.

In a recent *Ms.* article, Walker discusses an attempt to censor the novel by banning its use in public schools. She cites a Mrs. Green who objected to her daughter's reading the novel because of its explicit sexuality, offering this response to the woman's objections:

> I feel I know what Mrs. Green was objecting to [. . .]: the first five pages of the book. The same five *my* mother objected to, because she found the language offensive. They are the pages that describe the brutal sexual violence done to a nearly illiterate black womanchild who then proceeds to write down what has happened to her in her own language. She does not find rape thrilling; she thinks the rapist looks like a frog with a snake between his legs. How could this not be upsetting? Shocking? How could anyone want to hear this? She spoke of "pussy," "titties," the man's "thang." I remember actually

trying to censor this passage in Celie's voice even as I wrote it. Even I found it almost impossible to let her say what had happened to her as *she* perceived it, without euphemizing it a little. And why? Because once you strip away the lie that rape is pleasant, that rapists have anything at all attractive about them, that children are not permanently damaged by sexual pain, that violence done to them is washed away by fear, silence and time, you are left with the positive horror of the lives of thousands of children (and who knows how many adults) . . . who have been sexually abused and who have never been permitted in their own language to tell about it.[3]

Here Walker's focus is on the very distinction I want to stress: it is not the subject per se that is offensive to readers, but rather her treatment of it. Walker's offense lies in stripping away the polite ambiguities that usually veil even the most "realistic" representations of rape.

Mrs. Green objects not only to the explicit sexuality in the novel, but also to the way in which it reinforces existing racist stereotypes about black people in general and black men in particular. To her way of thinking, even if black men do on occasion commit acts of rape, are in fact on occasion child abusers, it is something that we should not discuss openly for fear of contributing to racism. But silence ultimately reinforces the patriarchy. Who is it that controls language anyway? Who decides just what can or cannot be said? And why? Mrs. Green's objections to the novel, and indeed Walker's reaction to her own prose as described above, provide eloquent testimony of the degree to which they, like so many other women, have internalized and are governed by patriarchal structures. This automatic censoring response can be read as one of the patriarchy's most effective repressive tools. When we accept and encourage the silence which repressive discourse imposes with respect to certain subjects, we are complicit in our own repression. Mrs. Green and all the others like her, by tacitly agreeing that there is something from which our children (and we ourselves) must be shielded, prevent any interrogation of the very source of their anxiety. Walker interprets this will to silence in similar fashion: "it is not by suppressing our own language that we counter racist stereotypes but by having the conviction that if we present the words in the context that is or was natural to them we do not perpetuate those stereotypes but rather expose them."[4] Recontextualizing in order to expose, rather than perpetuate stereotypes: we can argue for the same principle not only with respect to words but also with respect to context, to subject matter. We ought not censor the physical and sexual abuse of black women and children by black men, for in so doing we unwittingly contribute to the system that perpetuates racist and other stereotypes. Instead, Walker insists that we must speak the truth: about rape, child abuse, violence against women, no matter who the perpetrators.

Walker's response to the Mrs. Greens of the world is similar to the stance of French critic Hélène Cixous, long an advocate of the use of repressive, sexist stereotypes in order to "use them up," and thereby rob them of their power over women and prepare the way for a revalorization of the potentially subversive attributes and values that the stereotypes were meant to suppress. Cixous and Walker share a common goal: each in her own way attempting to find a voice with which the repressed minority can tell its story, in its own language and from its perspective. Each of them recognizes that in order to do so, we must be willing to speak what the patriarchy deems unspeakable. The first step in accomplishing this involves distancing ourselves from the value system which imposes the silence. Walker attributes her ability to distance herself from patriarchal values to her heritage as a black woman of the South: "In large measure, black Southern writers owe their clarity of vision to parents who refused to diminish themselves as human beings by succumbing to racism. Our parents seemed to know that an extreme negative emotion held against other human beings for reasons that they do not control can be blinding."[5]

This refusal to adopt the values and attitudes of a racist patriarchy, to believe in its stereotypes, along with a recognition of the destructive, limiting effects of adherence to such values, is the key to the power of a Meridian or a Maggie or a Celie over those who would silence and enslave them. Walker's characters are strong and free despite being downtrodden; her clearest articulation of the source of their power can be found in the distinction she makes between "being a slave and being enslaved."[6] A slave, however limited in terms of physical or material freedoms, can still retain freedom of spirit. The enslaved, however, have succumbed to a far more insidious form of oppression. Those who have been enslaved by their oppressors internalize the values of oppressors. They identify themselves with the very system that represses them and become its willing, though unwitting allies. Or, still more serious, should they manage to free themselves sufficiently to attempt to subvert or destroy patriarchal structures, they adopt the very tools of the patriarchy and in so doing, doom themselves to failure.

Celie, like so many of Walker's protagonists, is essentially a free woman, despite her status as slave, first, to an abusive stepfather, and then to an equally abusive husband. Though for much of the novel she seems to accept their negative images of her, her slavery is more physical than spiritual. Her survival resides in her failure to *internalize* patriarchal structures. Her triumph as defined within that system (emancipation from her husband, acquisition of financial security in the form of property and a thriving business) is the outward manifestation of an inward struggle and is possible only because of her psychic independence. Celie's transformation from slave to free woman is effected through her interaction and identification with a series of nontraditional, female role models. But what is all too easily overlooked is the part that Celie herself plays as role model in the novel; Nettie, Sofia, Shug, and Mary Agnes all learn as much from Celie's example as she from theirs. Celie teaches the most important lesson of all, and it is not until these women, in particular Sofia and Shug, have learned to distance themselves from their identification with patriarchal values that they can serve as role models for Celie. Although each of them is remarkably free and independent by comparison with Celie, they are nonetheless enslaved: trapped by their internalization of a patriarchal value system even as they reject the roles it assigns them. Their position may be much like that of many readers of the novel.

Celie's most salient strengths are thus initially defined as weaknesses, characterized as ignorance. She herself deprecates them as such, as in this conversation with her younger sister:

> Don't let them run over you, Nettie say. You got to let them know who got the upper hand.
> They got it, I say.
> But she keep on. You got to fight. You got to fight.
> But I don't know how to fight. All I know how to do is stay alive.[7]

It is clear from this exchange that the two sisters define strength in patriarchal terms: it means mastery and domination. When Nettie exhorts her sister to fight, to exert her authority over her stepchildren, what she advocates is actually a role reversal in which Celie, in order to assert her power, must practice the same kind of repressive mastery of which she has long been a victim, this time with children as subjects. For Nettie, as for Celie, this is the only model of strength.

Sofia, Harpo's lover and later wife, shares Nettie's vision of Celie as someone who is essentially weak and helpless, someone to be pitied: "I think about how every time I jump when Mr. ——— call me, she [Sofia]

look surprise. And like she pity me."[8] Sofia is the complete antithesis to
Celie: a strong woman endowed with masculine powers who can give
as good as she gets: first when she refuses to be intimidated by Harpo's
father and later when she beats Harpo black and blue when he attempts to
emulate his father and assert his physical authority over her once they are
married. Celie envies Sofia her ability to fight, just as she envies Nettie her
intelligence and independence of spirit. It is to this envy that she attributes
her spontaneous advice to Harpo, that he beat Sofia in order to make
her "mind" him. Celie later realizes that she has sinned against her friend
(succumbing to methods and values of the patriarchy), but what is most
interesting about the incident is Sofia's reaction to Celie's explanation cum
apology of her actions:

> She stand there a long time, like what I said took the wind out of her
> jaws. She mad before, sad now. She say, All my life I had to fight.
> I had to fight my daddy. I had to fight my brothers. I had to fight
> my cousins and uncles. A girl child ain't safe in a family of men. But
> I'd never thought I'd have to fight in my own house. She let out her
> breath. I loves Harpo, she say. God knows I do. But I'll kill him dead
> before I let him beat me. Now if you want a dead son-in-law, you just
> keep on advising him like you doing. She put her hand on her hip. I
> used to hunt game with a bow and arrow she say.[9]

Sofia's reaction denies any system of values that would esteem the ability
to dominate. Walker's final image here, that of Sofia with her hand on
one hip—a quintessentially feminine gesture—calmly declaring herself
capable of murder, underscores that woman's perception of her paradoxical position. Sofia sees her physical strength and her ability to fight as
necessary evils; she appears almost to recognize that her strategy of survival is itself limiting and destructive. Walker proceeds to demonstrate
just how limiting and destructive it is in all of Sofia's interactions. Her
identification with patriarchal values (and repetition of them, by reversal)
is ultimately her downfall. First she leaves Harpo because their home has
become little more than a battlefield, since their struggles, played out in
accordance with his rules, leave no room for discussion, compromise, or
reconciliation. Then she is nearly killed and forced to endure years of imprisonment and servitude because, when insulted by the mayor's wife and
then challenged by the mayor himself, she resorts to the only means of
resistance she knows: she punches the mayor. In each instance, Sofia wins
the battle while losing the war.

Sofia knows how to fight, but she does not know how to survive. She does not yet realize that any attempt to fight the system by its own rules and on its own ground is doomed inevitably to failure. This is why it is so vitally important to oppressors that the oppressed share their values. Survival, on the other hand, something that Sofia knows nothing about, depends upon nonidentification with the oppressive system. Celie survives because she has never completely internalized the values and methods of the patriarchy. As she states it so often, she does not know how to fight by their rules. Her character could have been created as a direct response to the definition of survival offered by Audre Lord:

> *Survival is not an academic skill.* It is learning how to stand alone, unpopular and sometimes reviled, and how to make a common cause with those others identified as outside the structures, in order to define and seek a world in which we can all flourish. It is learning how to take our differences and make them strengths. *For the master's tools will never dismantle the master's house.* They may allow us temporarily to beat him at his own game, but they will never enable us to bring about genuine change. And this fact is only threatening to those women who still define the master's house as their only source of support. [10]

Celie's capacity to "stand alone, unpopular and sometimes reviled" is readily apparent. Walker's descriptions of her endurance of psychological and physical abuse make that point early on. Her capacity to endure such abuse and transcend it is exemplary in comparison to Sofia's complete inability to do so. Sofia's power, at first applauded and welcomed in the face of Celie's passivity, comes from her inability to manipulate the master's tools, to play his game; it is ultimately her greatest weakness. Just as Lord predicts, her victories are temporary. What she does not see is that the game is fixed and so she cannot possibly win. It is only in prison that she learns the harsh lessons of survival, lessons first taught her by Celie's example, as she explains here:

> Everything nasty here she say, even the air. Food bad enough to kill you with it. Roaches here, mice, flies, lice, and even a snake or two. If you say anything, they strip you, make you sleep on a cement floor without a light.
>
> How you manage? us ask.
>
> Everytime they ast me to do something, Miss Celie, I act like I'm you. I jump right up and do just what they say. [11]

And so begins Sofia's long road toward emancipation from enslavement. She has begun to glimpse as we have, if only dimly, the difference between slavery and enslavement; clearly her rebellious spirit, though bent dangerously close to madness, has not been broken, despite her outward appearance of docility. She has also learned a less obvious but equally important lesson: the importance of identifying oneself not with the oppressor, but with the oppressed.

This is the way in which Celie, again less obviously, embodies the other, crucial element in Lord's definition of survival: knowing "how to make common causes with those others identified as outside the structures." We see it generalized to the black community in their efforts to gain Sofia's release from prison; even Mr. ———— participates in the plan while Squeak, Sofia's "rival," willingly exposes herself to physical danger in that cause. It can scarcely be accidental that after this incident Squeak for the first time asserts her own worth, demanding that Harpo tell her if he loves her for herself or only for her pale skin, and announcing that her name is not Squeak but Mary Agnes. This incident also offers yet another glimpse of the way in which internalization of patriarchal values works as a powerful repressive force. When the women unfold their plan to gain Sofia's release, her boyfriend, the prizefighter, dismisses it out of hand. He declares that it sounds suspiciously like "uncle tomming" to him.[12] All the negative connotations inherent in that label conspire to discount the plan as undignified and therefore unfeasible, something which in another context might well be enough to guarantee that it would not be implemented. A most effective means of neutralizing a would-be attempt to subvert patriarchal structures.

But the most compelling model of this kind of solidarity is the relationship between Celie and Shug. More so than Sofia, Shug is an outsider; she can be characterized as an outsider in a community of outsiders, for even the black community has rejected her. Like Sofia, Shug pays dearly for her freedom: she has lost her children, is estranged from her parents; she has no real friends other than Celie. Mr. ———— may be her lover, but he is certainly not her friend, and while he abandoned wife and children for long periods of time for her, he would not defy his father or his community in order to marry her. When Shug falls ill, although men would flock for miles to hear her sing, no one will take her in, except for Celie and Mr. ———— (and even then Mr. ————'s motives are suspect). Celie, however, has been fascinated with Shug Avery for years. Despite the negative reaction of her in-laws and the townspeople, Celie is delighted to welcome the sick woman into her home. Celie's feeling of solidarity with Shug is apparent when her in-laws call to chastise Mr. —— and sympathize with Celie about his unreasonable demands; first we encounter Old Mr. —— :

> He [Old Mr. ——] rise to go. Hand me his glass. Next time he come I put a little Shug Avery pee in his glass. See how he like that.
>
> Celie, he say, you have my sympathy. Not many woman let they husband whore lay up in they house.
>
> But he not saying to me, he saying it to Mr. —— . Mr. —— look up at me, our eyes meet. This the closest us ever felt.
>
> He say, Hand Pa his hat, Celie.
>
> And I do. Mr. —— don't move from his chair by the railing. I stand in the door. Us watch Old Mr. —— begin harrumping and harrumping down the road home. [13]

and then brother Tobias:

> What the world got to do with anything, I think. Then I see myself sitting there quilting tween Shug Avery and Mr. —— . Us three set together gainst Tobias and his fly speck box of chocolate. For the first time in my life, I feel just right. [14]

In each instance Celie's sense of solidarity with Shug extends to include her husband. Mr. —— has become an outsider as well, if only briefly, because of his actions toward Shug. Once he has exchanged his role of oppressor for that of the victim, Celie is able to identify with him just as she identifies with Shug. Conversely, now that Mr. —— has been made to feel like an outcast, he can identify with his wife; theirs is a collaborative effort in expelling Old Mr. —— from their home. In each passage we are left with images of family unity: Celie and Mr. —— together on the porch, watching Old Mr. —— take his departure; Celie, Shug, and Mr. —— seated in a row, a united front against Tobias and the rest of the world. And while these tableaux are seen through Celie's eyes, Walker makes it very clear that the feeling of unity is a shared one.

These passages are also noteworthy because in them we see Celie not only happy, but also outside her now familiar passivity. While she does not confront either her father or her brother-in-law directly, after the fashion of a Sofia or even a Shug, she does not accept their abuse of her husband and her "friend." She defies them, even if only in thought.

This shared sense of family and community is only temporary, however.

Since Shug, like Sofia, still identifies with patriarchal values, even though she has rejected her assigned role, she judges Celie according to the same standard. She is even more harshly critical of Celie than Sofia ever was, as can be seen in their first encounter: "She [Shug] look me over from head to foot. Then she cackle. Sound like a death rattle. You sure *is* ugly, she say, like she ain't believed it," and in her later reactions to Celie's willingness to defend her, her expressions of affection for her: "That real good, for first try, I say. That just fine and dandy. She [Shug] look at me and snort. Everything I do is fine and dandy to you, Miss Celie, she say. But that's cause you ain't got good sense. She laugh. I duck my head." [15] For Shug, Celie is just an ugly woman who "ain't got good sense." Celie is stupid because she returns good for evil, she persists in her affection for Shug in the face of the other woman's abuse. "Good sense" would require that Celie's admiration of Shug be transformed into envy and jealousy, then ultimately disillusionment and resentment in the face of her persistent cruelty. Yet Celie persists.

Shug is trapped just as Sofia is trapped. Her development has been stunted. While she is worldly and sexually experienced, by contrast with Celie's innocence and virtual virginity, she knows little or nothing about sharing, cooperation, or love. In this Celie is her teacher, as demonstrated in her almost maternal attitude toward Shug during her illness and convalescence. And we learn, to our surprise, that Shug envies Celie in this role, just as she envied Annie Julia, her predecessor. What Shug envies, of course, is the relationship that each woman has or has had with Mr. ———. While he is certainly no prize, marriage itself represents the kind of relationship that Shug can never have with him, no matter how desperately they desire one another. Her contempt for Celie and Annie Julia allows Shug to deny her envy of them, but she ultimately comes to realize that envy is the source of her cruelty toward each woman and her encouragement of Mr. ———'s abusive behavior. To cite one example, she tells Celie of those times when she would keep Mr. ——— with her until Annie Julia was forced to come and beg him for money with which to feed their children. Significantly, this realization comes only once Shug and Celie have become not only friends but also lovers; once Shug has begun to learn from Celie and to see Mr. ——— through Celie's eyes: "What was good tween us must have been nothing but bodies, she [Shug] say. Because I don't know the Albert that don't dance, can't hardly laugh, never talk about nothing, beat you and hid your sister Nettie's letters. Who he?" [16] With this brief passage Walker sets in opposition the Shug/

Albert, Shug/Celie couplings. Shug's relationship with Mr. ——, which she now describes as "nothing but bodies," is centered in a struggle for power, specifically, in efforts at mastery and domination. Just as his relationship with Shug is a way for Mr. —— to defy his father, so Shug uses it as a means of demonstrating her power over not only Mr. —— but also Annie Julia and later Celie. She too is thumbing her nose at the patriarchy, all the while using its methods.

Shug's relationship with Celie, on the other hand, is subversive not simply because it is "unnatural," that is, lesbian, but because it is grounded in another value system. Celie's response to Shug's final question about Mr. —— is another indicator. She writes: "I don't know nothing, I think. And glad of it," yet another instance in which she asserts, as weakness, her ignorance.[17] This avowed ignorance is another manifestation of the innocence of which I spoke earlier. Innocence may seem a strange word with which to describe a woman who has been brutalized to the degree Celie has, but innocent Celie is: innocent of any real identification with a patriarchal value system rooted in dominance and mastery. Celie's ignorance of this system of values is her strength, although neither she nor the reader recognizes it as such until well into the novel. Her response to Shug echoes and mirrors her question. When Shug asks, "Who he?" she indicates the degree to which she has begun to identify with Celie; she has begun to see her former lover through Celie's eyes, and we are reminded that while he has always been "Albert" to her, Celie consistently refuses to name her husband. Shug's question marks a shift in her allegiance, away from the patriarchy toward the other, "forbidden" system.

It also marks a necessary stage in Celie's education, for it is only once Shug, and Sofia, have acknowledged her strength, and have learned from her example how to turn their independence to their own advantage, that these women become viable role models. Only then can they begin to teach Celie to appreciate her own worth. Only then is it possible for Celie to leave slavery behind, a process which begins with her affair with Shug, progresses once she leaves her husband to live with Shug in Atlanta, and comes to maturity once she can appreciate herself and her strengths without the crutch of Shug's constant reinforcing presence.

The stage is now set for a generalized reconciliation and reestablishment of family and community ties: Sofia and Harpo reconcile; Shug is finally able to settle in a stable marriage, reconciled with her past by having reestablished relations with one of her children. Celie has become the model for the community as a whole. With the death of her step-

father she regains her heritage, the farm and store left her by her natural
father, and her children are restored to her, as is her beloved sister Nettie.
Celie has even forgiven and become friends with her former oppressor,
Mr. ———, whom she finally calls by name. And he has discovered what
"good company" she is; they spend their evenings together, sitting on the
porch, sewing and talking. Celie even displays on her mantel a ceramic
frog, Albert's gift to her and their own private joke, an emblem of her
feelings about men and her impression of her rapist. The novel's happy
ending is too good to be true, too pat to be believable. Walker draws here
an idealized portrait of an alternate social order, one which is grounded
in the nonhierarchical, cooperative, and nurturing values that Celie represents. The warm, supportive, interdependent community presented at the
end of *The Color Purple* is Alice Walker's utopia, her new Eden.

What then can a contemporary feminist learn from the southern tradition which informs *The Color Purple*? To borrow from an earlier citation,
"that an extreme negative emotion held against other human beings for
reasons that they do not control can be blinding." The modern feminist
all too often shares the plight of a Sofia or a Shug, trapped by her own
unconscious internalization of the values of the system she is working
to dismantle. Feminist ideology has failed to recognize how completely
it identifies with patriarchal values. Consequently our efforts have been
misdirected, channelled toward beating men at their own game, advo-
cating that women emulate male behavior in order to achieve success.
What is overlooked in this drive to adapt the individual to the system is
the automatic assumption that patriarchal structures are the only possible
structures.

Walker reminds us, none too gently, that along that path lies failure.
At best it leads only to a kind of mirror society in which the structures
of power remain the same and only the identities of those who wield
that power have changed. We will have exchanged one sexist society for
another, one just as blinding and destructive as the original. So that while
Walker's male characters may be portrayed as brutal in their treatment
of women and each other, they are not beyond redemption. Because the
male characters' sense of patriarchy as their sole source of support is even
greater than that of their female counterparts, they have still farther to
go in their reeducation. Just how far is graphically demonstrated by the
depth of Mr. ———'s fall after Celie and Shug walk out on him. His
complete disintegration would indicate that they take with them what
little humanity he possesses. This disintegration and slow recovery mark

Mr. ———'s rebirth as a new man, Albert, who is ready and able to participate in Celie's utopian community.

This southern tradition teaches us that disenfranchisement brings with it a power all its own, so long as we do not allow ourselves to be blinded by our own identification with the disenfranchising order's models and values. If we can do nothing else, we can refuse to believe what the master tells us. What we must refuse to believe is not that we are different, but that difference is something which marks us as inferior or ignorant.

NOTES

1. Alice Walker, "In Search of Our Mothers' Gardens," in *In Search of Our Mothers' Gardens* (New York: Harcourt Brace Jovanovich, 1983), 237.

2. Barbara Christian, "Alice Walker: The Black Woman as Wayward," in *Black Feminist Criticism* (New York: Pergamon Press, 1985), 90.

3. Alice Walker, "Finding Celie's Voice," *Ms. Magazine*, Dec. 1985, 71.

4. Ibid., 72.

5. Alice Walker, "The Black Writer and the Southern Experience," in *In Search of Our Mothers' Gardens,* 19.

6. Alice Walker, "A Letter of the Times; or, Should this Sado-masochism Be Saved?" in *You Can't Keep a Good Woman Down* (New York: Harcourt Brace Jovanovich, 1981), 120.

7. Alice Walker, *The Color Purple* (New York: Washington Square Press, 1983), 25–26.

8. Ibid., 43.

9. Ibid., 46.

10. Audre Lord, "The Master's Tools Will Never Dismantle the Master's House," in *This Bridge Called My Back,* ed. Cherrie Moraga and Gloria Anzaldua (New York: Kitchen Table Press, 1981), 99.

11. Walker, *The Color Purple,* 88.

12. Ibid., 94.

13. Ibid., 59.

14. Ibid., 61.

15. Ibid., 50, 60.

16. Ibid., 117.

17. Ibid.

Reading between the Lines:

Fred Chappell's *Castle Tzingal*

KATE M. COOPER

The remarks accompanying Fred Chappell's photograph in Mark Morrow's *Images of the Southern Writer* (University of Georgia Press, 1985) include a wry admission from the prize-winning poet/novelist: "There's something about a disembodied voice that gets me every time. I don't even dare answer the phone unless I know who it is. Salesmen call me up asking me to come look at condominiums or mountain chalets and I always agree to go. Of course, I never show up." Chappell's fetching confession countersigns the attitudes of several other writers depicted in Morrow's volume. When first approached about having a photographic portrait made, Walker Percy pithily but gently demurred: "Thanks, Mark, but I finally had to swear off getting my picture took. To feel foreign for several hours!" Eudora Welty's comment during her own photographic session is more resonant with Chappell's. After objecting to Morrow's choice of her home's hallway for the sitting, Welty finally conceded and settled herself in a chair that she used only when talking on the phone. She explained her opposition to the chair as a portrait site, saying that she associated it "with nothing but resignation and impatience." Reynolds Price's somewhat resolute stare at the camera shows a face half obscured by the shadows of lamplight; the same light that both clarifies and darkens his facial features illuminates the metallic sheen of a small statue near the border of the photograph, a statue that Price salvaged from a going-out-of-business sale in New York. After glossing over topics as diverse as the formation of a writer's sensibility, his experiences as a teacher, the comparatively recent southern literary renaissance, and the role of religion in southern fiction, the acclaimed novelist set aside his worry beads and answered Morrow's question about his own personal religious involvement with a curious reflection: "I'm eastern North Carolina, but that's all."[1]

Remarks such as these are anecdotally reassuring. A Columbia-trained physician and National Book Award winner who anticipates a sense of personal disorientation strong enough to make him beg off from a photo session, a venerable stateswoman of southern letters who prefers a straight-drive Oldsmobile and a crisp relation to the phone, a widely traveled Oxonian scholar who would choose to live no further than sixty-five miles from his home town in North Carolina—all of these descriptions breed the impressions of genteel xenophobia, Arcadian nostalgia, and "rootedness" so often associated with the personalities of the American South and its literature in the twentieth century. Without a doubt, the richly evocative, almost tangible linguistic forms that convey such memorable figures of fiction as Price's Rosacoke Mustian, Percy's Binx Bolling, or Chappell's Virgil Campbell seem to require a reading of homogeneous signification, the assimilation of a language and its purveyors with a comfortable, historically determined notion of place. The familiar content of southern literary production in the twentieth century—this textuality's persistent reflection upon the images of nature and upon the structures of family, race, and church—perhaps encourages the unquestioned mimetism and fulsome sense of community so often apparent in the criticism of southern literature. Just as an Italian reader may risk loss of critical distance when dealing with Dante, the southern reader may be especially vulnerable to the referential lure of much southern writing. But is it not even more absurd to seek dialectical possibilities between this seemingly referential literature and the rarefied sophistication of contemporary language theory?

When speaking of contemporary language theory, I am referring specifically to the conceptual influence that America has acknowledged in the writings of such French theorists as Jacques Derrida, Roland Barthes, Maurice Blanchot, and Jacques Lacan. Since the critical developments of these thinkers are so radically different in orientation, and since their thoughts affect such traditionally disparate disciplines as philosophy, semiotics, linguistics, literature, and psychoanalysis, it is impossible to establish strict homology or analogy between them. I allude to them here as a group only because of their shared focus upon language as a field of inquiry and because of their insistence upon the autonomy of language as both force and form. In approximate terms, all of these theorists emphasize the intransitive character of the linguistic medium, the power of words as signs to defer indefinitely or even to deny the representation of reality in a text. The critical practice of each of these thinkers thus posits textuality (literary or other) as its own object, and shows how linguistic representation invariably asserts its own impure agency, its simultaneous status as vehicle of and obstacle to meaning.

Though the questions provoked by these theoretical stances admit no certain answers, the implications for contemporary critical thought are innumerable. Derridean inquiry, for example, is generally directed toward the historical and cultural significance of writing as that significance is inscribed within various texts. In brilliant readings of Plato and Freud, Nietzsche and Heidegger, Rousseau, Mallarmé and others, Derrida concentrates upon textual examples of the written sign and shows how these representations are both determined and determinative—how they respond to and define the western conceptual tradition.[2] Lacanian thought, on the other hand, is more distinctly concerned with the analytic experience and with linguistic phenomena in relation to the unconscious. Since Lacan's theory reformulates the structures of the unconscious elaborated by Freud, it accords less primacy to the status of the written sign than does Derridean thought. For Lacan, language plays a crucial role not only in the constitution of the human subject, but also in the larger set of human relations in which that subject exists.[3] Yet, of the theorists mentioned, Blanchot is the one who most consistently points to the fundamental ambivalence of language as a dilemma of literature, writing, and reading. His fiction and theoretical writings relentlessly invoke the destructive force of language, the power of words to falsify or annihilate the truth that they attempt to name. His theory repeatedly exposes the fallacies of literary mimesis and obsessively questions the writer's control over whatever it is he is trying to say. According to Blanchot, the act of writing opens an empty space between the world and what is written, a void that always exceeds the writing which creates it. What he calls "l'espace littéraire," the literary space, is paradoxically the place of literature's impossibility: the space emerging yet always retreating from the writer's efforts to appropriate it with words.[4]

These synopses are extremely rough, at the same time partial and overly general. However, they are necessary within this study for two reasons. First, by juxtaposing them to the personal confidences of the writers cited at the beginning of this essay, I hope to stress the superficial eccentricity of a critical reading that proposes discursive coherences between a southern literary text and the questions of French modernism. To call any form of literature "southern" is to ascribe it to a certifiable American tradition and, on some level, to assume a teleological relation between that literature and the locus of its production. As suggested, the often familiar idiom and repeated thematic reflections of southern narrative and poetry perhaps hasten identification between this literature and the area where it was written. Even from a purely demographic perspective, the density of literary production in the southeastern United States during the past forty years argues favorably for generic labeling of the sort that the term "southern" connotes.[5] But if the literature produced in this region is so clearly an evocation of place, is it not then highly questionable to read it through a body of thought that radically problematizes literature's place? Here is where the surface eccentricity of the proposed reading lies.

My second motive for invoking contemporary French theory results from a more careful scrutiny of this eccentricity and a reordering of the questions it implies. Ultimately, to read a literary text merely as the mimetic expression of a geographical region is to consign each to the other and to ignore the specificity of both. Though such a critical practice may have a certain documentary utility, it fails to interrogate adequately the determinations of both literature and place, and thus encloses both in a static conceptual system. To immortalize William Faulkner as the apotheosis of southern literature is to say no more than that Faulkner wrote about the South and that the South of his period furnished him with the material of his opus. This kind of reading can account neither for the fact that Europe recognized him with greater enthusiasm and foresight than did America, nor for the fact that the South has been the site of America's most prolific (though erratic) literary production since the First World War.[6] Since it takes stock neither of the "whys" of a writer's project nor of the conditions subtending a culture's specificity, critical homologizing of this sort can only impair the strength of its own assumptions.

My intention, then, is not to reject a priori the possibility of causal relations between the literary text and the region of its production. Instead, through a reading informed by contemporary French theory, I shall relocate the question of literature's place within the terms of the literary text itself. Another look at the comments cited at the beginning of this discussion confirms the validity of my approach. Ultimately, all the authors quoted are conveying an awareness of the dynamically complex tension between the sign (verbal, written, photographic) and the determinants of an individual's being and place, the tension between linguistic or photo-graphic images and the larger systems of difference (historical, political, ritual, and so on) used to specify a region and the individual's role within it. Walker Percy's statement is illustrative: for the novelist, having his picture "took" is tantamount to being humanly alienated, made "to feel foreign," uprooted from the appurtenances and rights of a culture. Given the fact that his photographic session finally took place on the front porch of his home in Covington, Louisiana, it is safe to say that Percy's under-standing of human alienation in this case has more to do with the violent effect of the camera image than with any sort of physical displacement.[7] The "resignation and impatience" that Welty professes when at the mercy of the telephone betray a similar wary consciousness of the temporal and spatial differences arbitrarily imposed upon human existence by a cultural medium.

What these writers' comments seem to enjoin is a critical view of the literary text that treats the ontological implications of origin, his-tory, and social order as problems of linguistic representation. Rarely have these issues been so forcibly addressed in contemporary American letters as in Fred Chappell's allegorical poem *Castle Tzingal*.[8] Similar to his ac-claimed *Midquest* tetralogy and his more recent poetic collection *Source*,[9] *Castle Tzingal* is a formally structured verse work in which the four clas-sical elements—earth, water, wind, and fire—play highly symbolic roles. But instead of the southern rural landscapes that serve as backdrop in so much of Chappell's poetry, the setting of *Castle Tzingal* is the mythical court of a deranged king, a mad monarch whose obsessive attempts to insure total control over his subjects lead to the dissolution of his own kingdom.

Chappell's achievement in *Castle Tzingal* consists in part of his custom-ary mastery of innumerable verse forms and traditions, combined with the ever-startling novelty of his own style. The overriding singularity of *Castle Tzingal*, however, resides in the insights it lends to a range of cru-cial issues. The intricate series of articulations that this text establishes between nature and culture, language and desire, poetry and power, point not only to the problematics of its own writing but also to the questions of production inherent in every literary undertaking. And if *Castle Tzingal* may be read as a clue to the understanding of southern culture and litera-ture, it also speaks with uncanny explicitness to the issues of contemporary French theory.

The poem is a series of monologues, ballades, dramatic dialogues, and epistles that tell a devastating story of political decay, moral corruption, and loss. The tale relates the search for a poet/harpist named Marco whose prolonged absence has disturbed King Tzingal's court (especially the King's wife, Queen Frynna) and the neighboring realm of the mad King's half brother, King Reynal. Knowledge of Marco's whereabouts and of the circumstances of his disappearance is the goal of a quest that King Reynal has delegated to his emissary and first cousin, Petrus. Petrus's mission leads him within the walls of Castle Tzingal to various encounters with the depraved King's grotesque subjects, encounters which he then resumes in report form for King Reynal. Inside the dank walls of the castle, however, Marco's absence is the disturbing evocation of a melodic, disembodied voice (see Chappell's comment at the beginning of this discussion) that haunts the sleep of King Tzingal's subjects and troubles the depths of their memory. The perturbing lyrics of the disembodied voice conjure madness in those who hear them, and finally impel Queen Frynna and Tzingal's old, pensioned Admiral to their deaths.

Causally, then, Marco's mysterious disappearance and his spectral reemergence in song are the pretext of all speech and activity in the textual world of *Castle Tzingal*. Though the mad King's castle is the site of the entire poem, the effects of Marco's absence upon the respective kingdoms of Reynal and Tzingal give rise to two separate understandings of political rule, social order, and genealogical filiation in the text.

THE COURTS OF HARMONY AND DISCORD

In Reynal's realm, effective political rule and genealogical linking are coterminous. Petrus's relation to the king signals this overlay of royal and familial orders since the emissary is at the same time a titled member of the court and the monarch's first cousin. In this "other" kingdom, Marco's protracted absence represents not only dismemberment of the body politic but also an excision from the royal family tree. Petrus's first letter from Castle Tzingal to his regent comments on this genealogical relation between King Reynal and the poet:

> Of your nephew Marco, whose silent disappearance
> I've come here to trace,—not much.
> I have unveiled some puzzling hints

> And know that he stopped here indeed
> Last year, received the gracious encouragements
> Of Queen Frynna.
>
> (*Castle Tzingal*, p. 13)[10]

Further, under Reynal the solid bonds of polity and kinship are only enhanced by the affective ties that the kingdom's members profess for each
other and for their lost poet. In his first report to Reynal, Petrus comments
on the infected atmosphere of Castle Tzingal and its unsuitability for a
youth of Marco's constitution:

> A lad devoted to sport in open fields, to song
> And skillful love-converse, as Marco was,
> Would have but villeyn company in this place
> And much dour argument.
>
> .   .   .   .   .   .
>
> Marco's affections would not be for this place
> Or for these folk. And I do admit
> Neither is the liking of your close and faithful envoy.
>
> (pp. 13–14)

The concurrence of filial, affective, and political ties linking King Reynal
and his subjects suggests that his reign has been one approaching holism,
one in which the structures of kinship, authority, and desire have achieved
a viable balance. If there is an equilibrium implied by the cohesiveness
of these public and private structures, it is only reinforced by the solidity
of the genealogical relations between the kingdom's members. As first
cousins, Reynal and Petrus share a linear tie to the same ancestors; as
uncle and nephew, Reynal and Marco are descended in different degrees
from the same parents. All three genealogical links (between the King and
his emissary, between Petrus and the poet Marco, between Marco and
the King) imply marital or sibling alliances—lateral bonds—that remain
absent in the language of the text. Bound in relations of both affinity and
consanguinity, the members of this poem's "other" kingdom are allied in
multidimensional terms.

But such is not the case inside the walls of Castle Tzingal. The mad
king's rule is one of strict linearity, a governance that seeks to control even
the erratic supervention of desire. In order to maintain his preeminent authority, Tzingal threatens his subjects with knowledge of their innermost

fears and dreams, with the awareness of their own perverse humanity. In repeated attempts to assert his own supereminence, the obsessive King invokes either the illicit sexual conduct of his court members or their static purposelessness as mere functionaries in his realm. After one particularly brutal evening meal, the court's Astrologer reports the vitriolic tirade launched by Tzingal against the old Admiral:

> "Tell us," he told the Admiral, "how you took
> Zomara, and what you said when they struck
> Their colors. What joy
> That victory must have been! Or were you—
> As I have heard—below, buggering the pretty cabin boy?"
> The Admiral stared unseeing into his plate.
> "I know," the King continued, "of field commissions in battle.
> But to raise a lad from lackey to First Mate?
> I fear you take no prize for being subtle."
>
> (p. 27)

But neither is the Astrologer himself immune to King Tzingal's invective:

> "For you, Astrologer,"
> He said, "all energies of life have lost their savor.
> You are sick and cowardly and have betrayed
> Some best part of yourself. Do you recall
> The earnest scholar once you were and have since unmade?"
>
> (p. 28)

Thus, desire and its vagaries constitute the target of Tzingal's barbarous threats. In the case of the old Admiral, the alleged secret of desire and ensuing act of sodomy make for a faulty and humiliating infraction under Tzingal's law. Perhaps most interesting is the fact that the wretched King views that infraction in terms of a hierarchical displacement ("But to raise a lad from lackey to First Mate?"). On the other hand, the Astrologer is accused by his regent of a lack of desire itself, a stagnation of the vital forces which had formerly infused his work. In either case, in the furtive expression of sexual desire or in the demonstration of its loss, King Tzingal's subjects are called wanton because they want.

The King takes pains to exempt himself from the circuits of desire that he mentions to recriminate his court members. Tzingal's marriage to Queen Frynna, though a plausible locus for the licit expression of sexual desire, is a purely formal and barren relation overridden by the harsh imposition of the monarch's order. The Queen views her own plight as the grotesque inversion of her childhood:

> In Castle Tzingal I sigh long sighs
> And wish I were a silly child again,
> Nestled beneath my father's stout roof
> And never stolen away to be the wife
> Of an iron and fruitless man.
>
> .   .   .   .   .   .
>
> I am not suited for the intricate gloom
> And thorny intrigue of a blackguard time.
> There is a child, a sunny child
> Who dances within my breast and combs
> Her sunny hair and coddles a painted mammet.
> In these bleak years I am defiled
> By the drunken ambitions, the nightmare designs
> Of a petty Mahomet.

(pp. 4–5)

The painted mammet of Queen Frynna's youth, the doll she embraced during childhood play, is now transformed into a false deity who alienates and repugns her with his possessive schemes. The royal couple's alliance is perhaps this poem's clearest expression of the sterilizing effects of an absolute, imposed order, a rule that alienates desire by seeking to appropriate it.

It is of course clear in the poem that Tzingal's consuming ardor in the poem is tantamount to poetic desire itself: the desire for total knowledge, truth, and the union of these two in an absolute expression. The fulminating regent seeks to fulfill this desire through the creation of the Homunculus, a miniature man made to order by the court Astrologer. Properly named Flyting but called Tweak throughout the poem, the Homunculus is the monarch's eyes and ears, a creature small enough to inhabit the undetected recesses of the castle walls and to accumulate the secrets of its denizens. Moreover, the tiny spy's loyalty to King Tzingal is unswerving:

> —Ah no, I can't be bribed to speak. Whatever
> Could you bribe me with?

The things I dream of are forever
Beyond my reach, sunk deep in earth
Or at a human height.

(p. 2)

PAPER, SCISSORS, ROCK: THE GO-BETWEENS

King Tzingal thus maintains control of his gloomy kingdom through the invasive scrutiny of his subjects' desires. To this end, Tweak is his most perfectly accomplished agent: in accordance with the King's command, the Homunculus spies upon the castle inhabitants, then reports the politics and gossip gleaned through his undetected surveillance. In the text, Tweak is a pure sign of the economy of knowledge—knowledge construed here in terms of plans for political rupture or as the secrets of personal desire. As the poem suggests, Tweak is tightly bound to the King in a relation of profound specularity: this "minim" man (and it is noteworthy that the adjective reads the same forward and backward) owes the debt of his existence to the King and thus reports the findings of his wily espionage only to the mad monarch:

> I'm silent in a dusty nook
> But in the Council Chamber I speak
> My mind straight out and am respected.
> No one can trust me but the King
> Who caused me to be made.
> That's my safety from the murderous boot
> And poison marmalade.

(p. 2)

The Homunculus serves all the deranged King's possessive designs: the order, agent, and reflection of political scheming and secret desire, Tweak stands within the poem as the perfectly efficient instrument of King Tzingal's complete dominion. By transmitting information to the King, he furnishes his sovereign's desire for absolute rule with the substance of knowledge.

But perhaps Tweak's most startling feature is his avowed immunity to the seduction of being loved:

> I have no love of being loved; a minim man
> Prefers to flourish by means of fear,
> To cast beyond his stature giant shade.
>
> (p. 2)

What insures the miniature man's perfect efficacity in this role is his *lack* of affective need, and consequently, his insouciance regarding recognition for his services. Much as his name suggests, Tweak inhabits the elusive wrinkles of the text, and within them, gathers, witholds, and betrays all secrets. His omniscience is implied not only in the economy of his function in the poem but also in the circumstances of his creation. "Conceived with purpose" and "drawn up to plan" (p. 3), this minuscule model of a man represents the final achievement of the magic arts, the result of an elaborate alchemical rite:

> My father was a mage, my mother a pour
> Of mystery chemicals. I was born
> On a table bright with flame and glassware,
> And had no childhood except an ignorance
> Of politics and gossip.
>
> (p. 1)

Tweak's omniscience in the poem may be allied to his fleeting omnipresence. Unlike the other figures in the realm who have distinctly ascribed private chambers in the castle, the little spy's only abode is a bottle through which he has perceptual access to all of the castle's hidden places—its nooks and crannies, cracks and crevices:

> I'm hardly the first man to live in a bottle
> And see the world through a different size.
> I'm the King's most privy counselor,
> And know the secrets lisped at midnight
> By love-performing ministers
> And cunning courtesans. I spy the spies
> Who never seek beneath their beds
> Or in the arras-folds hard by the banisters
> Of the shadowed gallery.
>
> (p. 1)

Omniscient and omnipresent, exempt from the desire for personal recognition and betraying no human or tangible need, Tweak symbolizes the infallible alliance of knowledge and power. He stands in the text as the King's agent of authority, secure in his allegiance because of his unconcern for otherness or material gratification.

Yet there is something in the poem that ultimately overturns this rigid economy in which all knowledge is submitted to King Tzingal's glowering, intransigent rule. In the introductory stanzas of the poem, Tweak explains his own origins and privileged status in the castle to a strangely silent interlocutor. Much in the same way that he stirs anxiety and suspicion among the other figures in the text, the dwarf "tweaks" us as readers with a curious innuendo at the end of the first monologue:

> I was conceived with purpose, drawn up to plan
> And have a surer measure than a man.
> It's s [sic] rarefied temptation
> Could smudge my honesty,
> And as for what *you* offer . . .
> > Well, we'll see.
> > > (p. 3)

Who is this "you" in the passage? Is the miniature man suggesting that his unwavering loyalty to the King might be swayed? If so, what possibly could decide this "minim man"—along with all the absolute inferences of his poetic form and function—to switch allegiance? And to what place or political group would his newfound allegiance be directed?

As the poem progresses, we are gradually led to assimilate this mysterious "you" in Tweak's introductory monologue with Petrus, King Reynal's Master Envoy. Paradoxically, Petrus's mission is similar to Tweak's because he has been engaged to discover the whereabouts of the poem's emblem of desire, the poet/harpist Marco. But unlike Tweak, for whom the royal command to gather information (especially the knowledge of hidden desire) has no purpose or compensatory value beyond the fulfillment of the task, Petrus is both personally and politically implicated in his fictional quest. What Petrus seeks is knowledge with a view toward restitution of desire's lost object; what the Homunculus seeks is knowledge of desire with a view toward its submission to Tzingal's absolute control. Marco's absence represents in both courts the pretext of all speech and activity; knowledge of his whereabouts is thus the subject and object of all quests in the poem.

Petrus's inquiry leads him into dialogue with several of the poem's characters, one of which is the Astrologer's Page, Pollio. Prior to Petrus's interview with the Astrologer, the Page introduces himself to the emissary and seizes the opportunity to engage in private conversation. He questions Petrus about the outside world, and finally recommends that the emissary purchase his debenture. To embellish the proposal Pollio enumerates some of the qualities that make him worthy as a servant:

> —Oh no, sir, I'm not unhappy here,
> But adventurous to roam the wider world:
> It's the youth blood in me, and curiosity.
> But I'm no featherwit, as soon you'd see,
> Were you my master. For I have a clever
> Way with secrets, how to weasel them out
> And noise them all abroad,
> Or how to keep them quiet as a shroud
>
> .   .   .   .
>
> You'd find me, Master-Envoy, quicksilver-deft
> At any use or task, in bedchamber or in foyer.
>
> For there are matters, both of word and deed,
> That here have taken shape and would have value,
> If ever they be known outside these walls
> To rival principates; and all you
> Could ever desire to know is in my head.
>
> (p. 10)

Like Tzingal's "minim man," the Page claims to withold the quiet power of knowledge as well as the awareness of how and when to use that knowledge. Again like Tweak, Pollio's secrets and abilities are not limited to any one particular cognitive area: his services useful "in bedchamber or in foyer," the Page hints that his knowledge spans the official arena of politics as well as the private sphere of desire. But unlike the Homunculus, Pollio announces that his competence and loyalty may be had for the mere price of his debenture.

The successive interviews between Petrus, Tweak, and the Page not only lead to the eclipse of King Tzingal's mad designs, but also imply the dilemmas inherent to any attempt at poetic writing. If the poetic enterprise is the search for a totalizing linguistic form, for the perfect expression of man's experience and condition, then the three figures named above play major roles in demonstrating the seduction and pitfalls of that undertaking.

As go-betweens or intermediaries, these three figures occupy a privileged status in the poetic circuits of knowledge and desire; because of their access to both inner and outer worlds, they enjoy a certain immunity to the authorities whom they encounter or serve. Tweak, for example, operates in a circuit between King Tzingal and the deranged monarch's underlings or foes; through him, secrets and knowledge of the other are transformed into an armament of absolute control. Yet, the miniature man has no titular role or defined place in the oppressive government that he so effectively reinforces. Omnipresent, evanescent, and omniscient, combining in his poetic presence the inferences of authority, the fundamental elements of nature, and the highest achievement of the magic arts, Tweak informs and supersedes the hierarchy that he serves. As the mirror of the mad King's realm, he dwells in the fissures of the castle walls, ferreting out the frenzied desires of Tzingal's subjects. His rigorous economy and function within the text remain secure because of his imperviousness to the desires he detects and because of his professed resistance to the lure of recompense.

Pollio, too, is a liminal figure in the poem since he serves both the official and erotic interests of the court's Astrologer. Unlike Tweak, however, the Page is initially subservient to the bloodless lust and dead erudition of his master. The young servant claims to withold a "nether history / Of Castle Tzingal" (p. 10) but will divulge his information to Petrus if the emissary assumes his debenture. Knowing how to dislodge and retain the secrets of their poetic world, Tweak and the Page suggest similar cognitive acuities. But their knowledge can be had only at a price, a price which for each reflects the specificity of his function and desire in the poem. Pollio's desire, openly claimed in the text, is for the experience of otherness or difference, for change from the withering stagnation and servitude that he lives with the Astrologer. Upon taking leave from his master, the Page decries the Astrologer's interpretive practices, strategies that wholly submit the signs of nature to the transient political ploys of men:

> How often have the stars said right
> As you interpret them?
> I have no fear to grapple whatever fate
> You foretell mine. I go to seek a saner home,
> Petrus my mentor and I no catamite.
> I hear no stars speak politics at night.

> (p. 10)

Despite Tweak's claim that his services cannot be bought, Petrus finally comes up with the offer that causes the tiny spy to reveal the circumstances of Marco's disappearance. But what sort of leverage can be used with this minim man who symbolically combines the forces of nature, culture, knowledge, and art and who seems to lack nothing? What sort of promise could be made to Tweak that would cause him to divulge the required information and switch allegiance? Though the dilemma permits no facile solutions, King Reynal's Master-Envoy strikes an imaginative bargain that buys the information he's seeking:

> Do you bear a more imaginative bribe
> Than that you offered me when
> You first approached me? I hope
> You've racked your brain for— . . .
>   You say
> That under King Reynal I'd have a duchy?
> There's a thought might cause my fealty to slip.

(p. 25)

Thus, this miniature man, this inscription of omniscience and omnipotence, will reveal his secrets in exchange for property—for the legitimacy implicit to the status of landowner in King Reynal's realm. Unlike the Page, who seeks a way out of the conditions of his servitude, Tweak is swayed by the prospect of having a place within a hierarchical structure.

Though accurate, the knowledge that Petrus's offer procures from Tweak comprises no glad tidings. The Homunculus tells Reynal's emissary that:

> King Tzingal conceived a jealousy of the poet;
> Gave orders for his murder
> And then with his own hand chopped off his head.
> He ordered my father Astrologer to do it
> With a burning poison, but reserved the harder
> Pleasure for his own royal sword.
> He fancied you see that Marco and the Queen . . .
> Well, you need no pictures drawn.
> And there was no truth in it, not the least,
> But King Tzingal never inquires for proof.

(p. 25)

Nevertheless, the mission that King Reynal delegated to Petrus has been carried out, since the emissary was instructed to discover either Marco's whereabouts or the circumstances of his absence. With the news of the poet/harpist's decapitation at the hands of King Reynal, Petrus hastens to recommend retaliatory measures to his own regent.

Before scrutinizing the consequences of Petrus's retaliatory decision, let us examine a bit further this remarkable interlude between the Master-Envoy and King Tzingal's tiny spy. This scene between two of the poem's middle men is a pivotal interval in the text because it assembles the poem's major themes; moreover, this passage speaks with outstanding clarity to the wider-ranging questions of poetic production outlined in the beginning pages of this essay. Of the numerous clues to reading contained in this scene, three features are especially noteworthy.

The first of these concerns Petrus's formal status in the poem. Like Tweak and the Page, Petrus is a go-between, a messenger whose quest leads him to cross the boundary between distinct but neighboring orders. Unlike these two figures, however, Petrus maintains a balanced or harmonious relation to the titular authority he serves. Tweak ultimately controls and overrules King Tzingal through a canny manipulation of the mad monarch's desires. Though Tzingal may use the secrets that Tweak confides to enforce obedience and terror among his subjects, the King himself is not humanly immune to the effects of the miniature man's information. Apprised of the Queen's fancy for Marco, Tzingal conceives a jealousy so overwhelming that he breaks his own rule by murdering the poet. The King's secret infraction then places him in an ambiguous relation to Tweak, because Tweak's knowledge of the murder carries a potential threat to the royal order. On the other hand, Pollio's persona suggests the subjugation of vital desire to a statically imposed order. Conformable with Tzingal's allegations, the master Astrologer has lost desire's creative impulse, and has reduced his magic art to a sterile formula of signs. The knowledge he imposes upon Pollio, along with the domestic and erotic services he exacts from the Page, betrays a disregard for the vitality apparent in the servant's competence and desire for knowledge.

By now it is evident that the order of authority examined here and represented in *Castle Tzingal* by various monarchs, magicians, and middle men is in a more extended sense a synonym for poetic language in its quest for universal signification. Considering that the poetic project is an attempt to express the pure note of meaning, the articulation of ultimate truth, we must recognize the profound ambivalence of that enterprise. How can one express that which is eternal, universal, and absolute through writing—a form of representation that has its own force, form, laws, and hierarchy? How can the poet express universal oneness through a medium that establishes and enforces difference? If Tweak and Pollio's verse performances in relation to their own masters remind us of the unstable and ultimately failed relation between language (hierarchy, order) and the expression of human desire, then Petrus's presence in the text ingeniously hypothesizes the possibility of that relation.

As the representative of this text's "other" kingdom, a realm in which political organization, family structure, and the forces of desire have apparently achieved a functional balance, Petrus stands forth in the poem as the missing link between Tzingal's dark, fractured regency and a nearly idyllic peace. Implied in his figure is the equilibrium of social hierarchy, kinship, and desire that is so sorely wanting inside Tzingal's court. But this balance, this strength that Petrus symbolizes is strangely conveyed in the language of the poem by his absence from all direct modes of speech. Petrus exists in the poem only as the silent interlocutor of a dialogue or as the origin of the various letters addressed to King Reynal. Always implied but never explicit, Petrus's agency in Tzingal's land is a silent one. This is the first significant feature of the dialogue between Petrus and Tweak.

Second, this passage is of foremost importance because of its place in the overall organization of the poem. Like most of Chappell's poetry, *Castle Tzingal* has a classically precise organization; a careful look at the dialogue between Petrus and Tweak shows us that it is the twelfth of twenty-three poetic segments. This versified conversation between two middle men thus constitutes, in the most literal and graphic sense, the absolute middle of the poem.

Finally, this dialogue is notable for the multiple ways that it alludes to absence as a vehicle of meaning. Through this dialogue, we will remember, Petrus learns of Marco's death at the hands of King Tzingal. Much like an attempt to enforce and control desire itself, the deranged monarch's act in killing the poet is similar to one of the aspects of poetic writing. By decapitating Marco, the monarch imposes the absence of ruptured loss and death upon his kingdom, thereby stirring the very frenzy of desire that he had hoped to deflect or quell. The song that then haunts the castle and points to Marco's absence mirrors the King's murderous act because it rends the continuity of sleep and evokes the schismatic pain of memory. The tale that Tweak tells is one of a tearing and murderous difference, a void signifying exclusion, dismemberment, loss, separation, and death. But Petrus's absence from all forms of direct speech in this passage (and throughout the poem) is an absence of a completely different nature. Petrus's exclusion from all direct forms of speech in the poem is a silence that unifies instead of one that divides and destroys. The knowledge he acquires from Tweak represents fulfillment and loss at the same time: fulfillment because in gathering the news of Marco's death, Petrus accomplishes the mission delegated to him, and loss because the news of Marco's death signifies a dolorous blow for all of King Reynal's realm. This dual signification of life and death implicit to Petrus's silence is repeated in the strategies he employs to gain Tweak's allegiance. By promising Tweak a place and property in Reynal's kingdom, Petrus manages to break the spy's ties of loyalty to Tzingal and to establish a new bond to Reynal. Though the nearly idyllic unity of Reynal's kingdom has been destroyed by the news of Marco's death, a reformulated, though slightly less pure, unity is hinted in the triple alliance of Petrus, Tweak, and the Page.

SOME OTHER PLACE, THE RIGHT PLACE

If I have dwelled at length on the roles of Petrus, Tweak, and the Page, it is because these are the only three figures of the poem to escape the murderous touch of Tzingal and the destruction of his kingdom by any means other than death. Tzingal's Admiral seeks the peace of death by hanging himself in his bedchamber, whereas Queen Frynna, more and more haunted by the ghostly melody that she hears during sleep, drinks a potion that induces death's slumber. Finally, at Petrus's behest, Tweak serves the King a blood-searing elixir that brings on the monarch's own demise. Before he draws his final breath, Tzingal sees Tweak put a torch to his chamber's tapestries:

> I take the flambeau here
> And flame the curtain, and now the tapestry
> That celebrates your coronation we see flare
> Like the glory of holy martyrs.

(p. 45)

Thus, in a highly symbolic gesture, Tweak burns the tapestry depicting Tzingal's coronation before the dying King's eyes. In much the same way that Tzingal's murder of Marco placed the monarch at the mercy of the dwarf's whim, the image of Tzingal's coronation is here submitted to the consuming flames. The only remaining words of the poem are those of the Song for a Disembodied Voice.

The image of a burning edifice is a prominent motif in some of Chappell's other poetry,[11] and is often accompanied by a chaotic dispersion of voices. But if fire is a dominant motif in Chappell's writing, it is still only one of many elements that he uses to dramatize his largest concern: the ontological implications of poetry. In his poem "A Prayer for Truth,"[12] Chappell's hope is that his verse "find the solid places," that it not be abandoned to the more savage and unstable regions of earth. Is this not the foremost allusion of *Castle Tzingal* as well?

I have pointed out that Tweak, Petrus, and the Page are the only ones to escape unscathed from Tzingal's murderous rule and the ultimate devastation of his castle. But what remains to be emphasized is the very inviting relation between these three figures' names or titles and the components—material and cognitive—of poetic writing. As his name suggests, Tweak is that pinch of consciousness representative of the omniscience, skill, and perceptual infallibility necessary for the supreme articulation. The Page, on the other hand, is the one begging exposure to otherness and desire, similar to the blank page of writing that beckons to the poet's inscription. And finally, Petrus as a figure in the poem comes to signify the balance and solidity implied by the phonic and etymological resonances of his name. The name "Petrus" is phonically and graphically similar to the term "petrous," which as an adjective means "stony, hard, solid." As a noun, however, the petrous is a bone behind the temple that supports the inner ear, which is the physiological site of hearing and equilibrium. Both as an adjective and as a noun, the term derives from the Greek *petra*, "a rock." So with a little onomastic liberty, we may see in the threesome who are freed from Castle Tzingal's walls allegories of poetic creation: Tweak and Pollio, symbolizing omniscience, skill, desire, and the locus of writing, find a place with Petrus, the solid figure who assures their solidarity in another land. The scheme seems nearly perfect.

I say "nearly perfect" because, after the gloomy sojourn through Castle Tzingal, the prospect of renewed solidarity suggested by the silent withdrawal of Petrus, Tweak, and the Page must remain conjectural and slightly impure. As the Song for a Disembodied Voice so poignantly reminds us, "The happy season of the world has left no mark" (p. 31). In fact, if the possibility of restored unity obtains in the survivors' departure to the "other" place, that possibility is transmitted to the reader only by or as an absence. The text of *Castle Tzingal* emerges from an instance of origi-nary loss or fractured perfection; throughout the text, the poem's writ-ing consistently echoes that loss and postpones all possible restitution. The spectre of ruptured perfection revealed in Marco's disappearance and death will always taint the possibility of paradise regained. The decapi-tation of the poet/harpist is thus a nearly paradigmatic illustration of writing's ambivalence as invoked by Blanchot: in the language of *Castle Tzingal,* the perfection of truth is implied only by the graphic figures of its destruction or deferral.

Paradoxically, it is perhaps through these figures of loss or absence that we may best consider *Castle Tzingal* (or any of Chappell's poetry) exem-plary of a southern literary tradition. In what may be termed a bifurcated concept of community, many writers of the American South since Faulk-ner have posited that the region's identity is rooted in a loss of faith in the redemptive potential of history and in a profoundly isolated view of the individual in society. Robert Penn Warren's novel *Flood,* for example, shows us a protagonist, Brad Tolliver, returning to his native town in Ten-nessee in an attempt to discover the connections between his adulthood and a more general, locatable notion of culture. Accompanied by a friend who will direct the movie of his script in the making, Brad visits a ceme-tery where he hopes to find the grave of a figure alive in his childhood memories. Recalling the impressive individuality of the deceased character, Brad turns his own memory into a larger reflection upon the South: "Hell, no Southerner believes that there is any South. He just believes that if he keeps on saying the word he will lose some of the angry lonesomeness." Further along, Brad remarks that southerners do not believe in God, but pray because they believe in "the black hole in the sky God left when He went away." Lewis Simpson's discussion of this and other works of south-ern literature after the First World War suggests that the sense of place so clearly discernible in much contemporary southern writing is a place of mourning and dream instead of a strictly mimetic representation. [13]

On both internal and external levels, *Castle Tzingal* stands as a spar-kling demonstration of this premise: forever seeking restoration of its own lost wholeness, the writing of the text constitutes that differential inter-val between the moment of solidarity's failure and the fervent, but silent intimation of its renewed possibility.

NOTES

1. For the specific passages alluded to here, see Mark Morrow, *Images of the Southern Writer* (Athens: University of Georgia Press, 1985). The comments of Chappell, Percy, Welty, and Price appear respectively on pp. 8, 60, 86, and 62.

2. See in particular *L'Écriture et la différence* (Paris: Editions du Seuil, 1967) and for Plato, *La dissémination* (Paris: Editions du Seuil, 1972). Derrida's most notable discussion of Rousseau may be found in *De la grammatologie* (Paris: Editions de Minuit, 1967).

3. See in particular pp. 237–322, 401–36, 493–530, 685–96 in *Les Écrits* (Paris: Editions du Seuil, 1966).

4. See *L'espace littéraire* (Paris: Editions Gallimard, 1955).

5. In the introduction to his volume, Morrow mentions that nearly 450 southern writers published novels between 1940 and 1983. See *Images of the Southern Writer*, x.

6. Lewis Simpson, *The Dispossessed Garden: Pastoral and History in Southern Literature* (Baton Rouge: Louisiana State University Press, 1983). See especially chap. 3, "The Southern Recovery of Memory and History," pp. 65–100.

7. Percy has, of course, given us a provocative view on the impact of the camera image in his novel *The Movie Goer* (New York: Avon Books, 1960).

8. Fred Chappell, *Castle Tzingal* (Baton Rouge: Louisiana State University Press, 1984).

9. *Midquest: A Poem* (Baton Rouge: Louisiana State University Press, 1981) and *Source* (Baton Rouge: Louisiana State University Press, 1985).

10. This and all subsequent quotations of the poem are taken from the edition cited in note 8 above.

11. See his lyric rendition of a burning church, "My Grandfather's Church Goes Up," in *Midquest: A Poem*, pp. 74–77.

12. *Source*, p. 7.

13. Robert Penn Warren, *Flood: A Romance of Our Time* (New York: New American Library, 1965), pp. 143–44. I am indebted to Lewis Simpson for alluding to this work; see his discussion in *The Dispossessed Garden*, pp. 91–94.

Critical Creolization:

Grace King and Writing on

French in the American South

JOAN DeJEAN

"Creole: a person of the white race, born in the French or Spanish tropical colonies" (*Robert Dictionary*). This is the only definition of the term admitted in modern French dictionaries. According to twentieth-century French lexicography, therefore, Creoleness is a simple phenomenon, a product of racial purity, and Creoles differ from those known as French only by virtue of their foreign birth. However, the modern dictionary, when it gives the history of "creole," sends us back to the time when the word entered the French language. This origin reveals that in the beginning the word was not seen as ideologically neutral: "*Criole:* a term of relations. It's the name that the Spanish give to their children born in the Indies. The Spanish who come from Spain are great enemies of the *crioles,* and stop them from being promoted to important positions" (*Furetière Dictionary,* 1690).

Furetière brings the word into French as what he calls "a term of relations," in this case, political relations of power and dependency, and exposes "creole" as a word displaying the sense of greater ethnic purity possessed by those born in the motherland with regard to those of their own nationality born in the motherland's territories across the sea. It should be noted that the first officially authorized French dictionary, the French Academy's 1694 volume, does not admit *criole.* The French Academy's exclusion of *criole* may have resulted from a desire to maintain a vision of linguistic purity, that is, linguistic neutrality, to avoid any word that might suggest language's complicity in "relations" of power. This same desire may still inspire the image of uncomplicated racial and ethnic "relations" conveyed by modern French lexicography.

Furetière took his cue from Spanish reflections on the derivation of "creole." According to Garcilaso de la Vega's history of the Incas the term originated in a Carib word, assimilated by the Spanish conquerors of the West Indies: "The children of Spaniards are called *criollo* or *criolla;* the negroes gave this name to the children born to them in the Indies, in order to distinguish them from those born in Guinea, their homeland. . . . The Spanish borrowed this name from them."[1] In de la Vega's reconstruction —and I realize that there is not universal agreement on the derivation of "creole," although all linguists see it as the product of some sort of linguistic cross-fertilization—*criollo* entered Spanish as the result of a double theft. Negro slaves took a word from the native inhabitants of the Indies, and the Spanish conquerors of the islands in turn appropriated the term.[2]

All these borrowings, as Furetière alone in the history of lexicography points out, are bound up with the desire to establish one's racial and ethnic purity. Each race and ethnic group appropriates the term from a group it considers less powerful and socially inferior. It then uses the term to designate its own children's birth outside the country to which they trace their ethnic origin. Each group initially turns to "creole" to proclaim its primacy: the Creole child may have been born in the colonies but he or she is of pure Spanish or French stock and therefore superior to the indigenes. However, this self-appropriated badge of ethnic purity implicates the Creoles in a parallel (and undoubtedly unforeseen) political "relation." The native-born French and Spanish repay the Creoles for their contempt for the indigenes by scorning them as socially inferior, by implication as ethnically less pure.

Such hypersensitivity to ethnic purity can be explained only by the menace of racial impurity, the fear on the part of the native-born that through the Creoles the racial diversity of the colonies might enter unadulterated blood lines, contaminate them, and render their legitimacy suspect. Hence the evolution in the Creoles' usage of the term from a word originally signaling ethnic purity to, as twentieth-century definitions make clear, a word now primarily indicating *racial* purity: "white man, white woman born in the colonies" (*Littré Dictionary*). Yet French dictionaries or elite English dictionaries like the *Oxford English Dictionary* do not explicitly recognize the specter of racial blending any more than the complex relations of power designated by Creoleness. The final usage of the term I will evoke is one never admitted in French, and in English admitted only in popular lexicons. In the latter case, the word is generally written no longer with a capital but with a lowercase *c*—as though to use orthography to reinforce its message of democratization: "creole: any person of mixed Creole and Negro ancestry speaking a form of French or Spanish" (*American Heritage Dictionary*). The ultimate threat of and for Creoleness is creolization, for creolization admits the possibility of race "relations," of miscegenation.

In the years that followed the Civil War, New Orleans was one of the last stages on which the drama of Creoleness was played out in all its complexity. At that time, the heretofore insulated Creole microcosm that had dominated Louisiana life for generations was invaded by modern conquistadors, known to the Creoles as "the Americans." It was into this world in full ethnic crisis that Grace King was born. She has traditionally been praised as chronicler of the disappearing rites of Creole gentility, but it is as critical observer of the politics of Creoleness that she may be of interest today.

Grace King's literary reputation is still alive today only in her native city, New Orleans. And even there, she is only faintly remembered as a writer who contributed somehow to the memorialization of southern glories past and in particular of the Golden Age of French New Orleans. This state of affairs would not have surprised the author herself, who repeatedly denounced the inadequacy of the southern reading public: "Books are of no account in the South, I am sorry to say. The Macmillans do not count upon New Orleans at all in the estimated sale of my books."[3] It is perhaps just as well that southerners, and New Orleanians in particular, have never examined King's writings too closely, for her oeuvre proposes a vision of the French presence in America that works subtly to subvert some of the ideals most cherished by the Louisiana French, notably the rigidly unbending social, ethnic, and racial hierarchy that is the backbone of all their self-definitions. King's vision can be seen as a commentary on the role of the outsider with respect to the French tradition, a commentary that at the same time defines King's own ambiguous place in American letters. Moreover, I will suggest in conclusion, King's staging of the relation between French and Other in the New World at the turn of the century can today be read as a cautionary tale about the equally ambiguous place in criticism reserved for those of us who write about French literature in America and in English.

Grace King presents a complex illustration of an uncommon phenomenon that I will call literary translingualism. By this I mean to denote works that seem somehow simultaneously written in two languages, works whose ideal reader would respond to the challenge of keeping two syntaxes constantly in mind. I came to reflect on this phenomenon while studying Charlotte Brontë's *Villette* in the bilingual context of a course taught with a colleague from the English department. To our repeated amazement, we would read key words, key phrases, and therefore key scenes of the novel differently because we assimilated these elements into the particular national linguistic and literary tradition with which we were individually most familiar. My "French" *Villette* was not completely different from my colleague's "English" Brontë; rather our readings confirmed each other in unexpected ways. Consider, for example, the theatrical performance described in the chapter entitled "The Fête." In French the scene becomes a reenactment of the configuration in *The Misanthrope,* in which the male lead's sobriquet, Ours, is intended to translate the bearishness that Brontë's "sincere lovers" have in common with Molière's; whereas in English "ours" refers pronominally to the struggle in *Villette* between antagonistic heroines, each fighting for the male lead's heart.

The translingual reading I am proposing goes beyond familiar questions of literary influence: Brontë's syntax in *Villette* exploits the Gallic potential in English to the extent that the bilingual reader experiences the unsettling sensation of having his or her instincts as a French reader activated while reading a work in English—until the reader recognizes only "bear" and not the familiar possessive pronoun in "ours." Similarly, Brontë's equivocalness can be seen as a translation of a position more complex than the author's alleged hostility to the alien language in which she was immersed during her Belgian sojourn. For *Villette* blends overt criticism of French ways with an impressive mastery of the French tongue, a mastery that functions as an act of camouflaged homage by making *Villette* either in some sense a French novel written in English, or an English novel imbued with its author's struggle to suppress her desire to have written it in French.

A similar, but far more politically intricate, kind of linguistic sidestepping on the threshold between two cultures and two languages characterizes Grace King's most original fiction. Whereas the intention of Brontë's liminality remains finally ambiguous, King elects a vantage point on a linguistic and cultural margin in order to offer a redefinition of the tradition to which she allegedly belonged. King's pronounced ideological bent reflects the increased complexity of the collision between Anglo and Gallic in turn-of-the-century New Orleans. On the southern scene, the connotations of Frenchness were not only social and literary. King also confronted the phenomenon of Creoleness in all its complexity, so that her fiction forces the reader to examine translingualism in a context in which linguistic identity was inextricably bound to the explicit issue of ethnic purity and the implicit question of racial purity.

Just as Brontë's attitude toward the French tradition has been interpreted as unalloyed hostility, so King's has been characterized as unquestioning allegiance. Indeed, few writers in America would seem to have been more closely bound by sympathy and education to the continuation of France in the New World than she. According to her own description in her autobiography, *Memories of a Southern Woman of Letters,* she belonged to a family unabashedly pro-Creole, in the sense in which that term has traditionally been used by the inhabitants of Louisiana, that is, to refer exclusively to those born in Louisiana of pure French or Spanish stock. Her education, in true Creole fashion, had very little to do with the English and American traditions. She was trained in a French-speaking school, whose curriculum was undoubtedly as resolutely modeled on that of French schools in France as that of the Creole school described in her novel *The Pleasant Ways of St. Médard.*[4] In the 1898 short story "Destiny" the aging heroine, reflecting on just such an education, provides what seems to be an apt characterization of its hypercorrect and outdated orthodoxy: "Oh, the dignity, the reserve, the seriousness, the implacable correctness, of our life [in the Creole school]! and for studies, an unceasing marmottage of grammar, catechism, French history, and etiquette. . . . I used to say, we are being prepared for a heaven presided over by Louis XIV as God" (Bush, 187). Yet even as King's cultural universe was being formed, she saw its foundations threatened when, at the age of nine, she witnessed the federal occupation of New Orleans and saw her family obliged to abandon its life and possessions in the city and take up residence on its plantation whose name, "L'Embarras," must have seemed ironically appropriate to those newly introduced to financial hardship.

However, King's relation to Creoleness could not have been as uncomplicated as critics have maintained. If her family's sympathies were Creole, her family itself was not. The first detailed evocation in her memoirs is of her maternal heritage: Anglo-Saxon (her maternal grandmother was born in Georgia), Huguenot, and undoubtedly—since King, who never failed to note the contribution of such factors, was silent on this score—of neither exceptional wealth nor privilege. Upon her arrival, King's grandmother experienced the stereotypical Anglo-Saxon reaction to French license and was scandalized by "the sinfulness of New Orleans."[5] Nor was King's paternal heritage more in harmony with the French microcosm: "The home in which memory began to make these first gatherings was a plain dwelling of the usual prosperous American lawyer" (MSW, 2–3). King, in other words, begins her autobiography with what would be read by any Creole as a confession of difference: in the Catholic, pseudo-French world of late nineteenth-century New Orleans, she was born Protestant, English-speaking, American, totally and unredeemably an outsider. Even her name, ringing brashly Anglophonic, set her apart in the Gallic microcosm in which her life and her literary existence were to be played out.

King's mother initiated the family's assimilation into the world of Creoleness. King describes her mother as "the only Protestant in her day school where she was a day boarder, picking up French as she went along, conforming in everything to her Creole and Catholic mates, even to allowing herself to be prepared for her first communion, when at last she felt forced to acknowledge the truth. 'But, mon père, I am a Protestant.' 'What a pity,' said the good priest placidly, and dropped her from the class" (MSW, 2). King recounts the incident without commentary, but its placement at the outset of her mother's portrait implicitly indicts the authority figures in the transplanted French universe as unable to assimilate even the Other completely dedicated to the desire to be reborn into Sameness. King's mother could immerse herself in a foreign language and foreign customs but, as soon as her difference was made known, the representative of the Creole paternal law "dropped her from the class" and ostracized her from the social order to which she was thereby forbidden to aspire. King's mother responded with the strategy that, according to her daughter, she maintained all her life: "She drank wine for breakfast and practiced her piano as though she too were a good little Creole" (MSW, 2). She refused to acknowledge her nonexistence in the paternal order, pretending instead that she had received baptism into Creole legitimacy.

King's maternal legacy was thus one of Sameness feigned: she recreated the Creole world that was itself already a duplicitous reenactment of recipes for Frenchness devised on distant shores and for ever more distant times. In her fiction, King seems on the surface always the dutiful daughter, celebrating the rites and the rights of Creoleness and in the process resolutely estranging herself from the "foreign" American culture that surrounded the Gallic microcosm.[6] When it is examined more closely, however, King's oeuvre indicates a redefinition of Creoleness that is at the same time a prescription for its survival in the Reconstruction era during which old boundaries could no longer be rigidly maintained—a redefinition of Creoleness as permeable to Otherness.

King's fiction constantly stages a deep-seated ambivalence toward the facile distinction between Same and Other that serves as the basis for traditional definitions of "Creole." Nowhere perhaps is this ambivalence displayed with more complexity than in the short story with which she made her literary debut, "Monsieur Motte." King is so powerfully attracted to French culture that the story provides an extreme illustration of the phenomenon Jefferson Humphries has referred to as the "recurring symbiosis between French and southern writers."[7] Like Brontë in *Villette,* King goes far beyond the simple borrowing of French literary models to create a translingual relation with the linguistic, cultural, and literary phenomenon of Frenchness. Indeed, King may well have been indebted to Brontë for the plot of "Monsieur Motte." Like *Villette,* her story is set in a French-speaking *pensionnat de demoiselles* in which the central pedagogical event is the history examination by the professor most feared by the students because of what King calls his "diabolical temper."[8] In King's version, the professor is named Monsieur Mignot and the school, here called the Institute St. Denis, is identified as eminently Creole. Despite the fact that in 1874 New Orleans was, legally, an American city, history for that year's graduating class was limited to *L'histoire de France par D. Lévi Alvares, père.*

The story's most salient feature is its flamboyant linguistic Gallicism. An early French reviewer, undoubtedly attracted to it on account of its evident affinities with the codes of Frenchness, said of its author: "She isn't really purely and simply Anglo-Saxon, . . . because she loves France, she understands it, she seeks out and foregrounds all that survives [of France] in a land that has remained strongly marked [by France]."[9] American commentators like King's recent editor Bush, on the other hand, criticize these same features as flaws: "One of the defects of the story in its original version . . . was an excessive use of French phrases intended to give the illusion that the characters were speaking French" (Bush, 53). Indeed, the tale presents a blatant challenge to the non-Creole reader. Nearly every paragraph in "Monsieur Motte" contains words or phrases, often key ones, in French. Moreover, the elements given in French are rarely cognates easily decipherable by the non-French-speaking reader. King does not use French to provide a veneer of local color, as the American reader might expect. Instead, she creates true linguistic local color, that is, an accurate representation of a sociolect firmly posed on the frontier between two languages. The inhabitants of King's school are incapable of any communication in one language alone; their ambivalent politico-geographic status is doubled by their linguistic dialogism: they function independently —that is, without a detour via the other language—neither in English nor in French.

Moreover, for King's Creole schoolgirls French is operative not merely as a linguistic system, but at the same time as a complex historico-cultural system in which they have been immersed but which remains nevertheless in major ways incomprehensible to them. For example, the description of the private quarters of the institute's headmistress, Eugénie Lareveillère, is centered on the massive four-poster bed, which so impressed the students that they "felt a tremor of awe at the sight of it, and understood instinctively . . . that here, indeed, was one of those *lits de justice* which caused such dismay in the pages of French history" ("MM," 108). Even the Anglophone reader who understands *lit* might not be familiar with the expression referring to the sofa upon which the king of France sat when holding formal sessions of Parliament.

And even the reader who grasps the scene's linguistic import would, unless that reader also shared to some degree the schoolgirls' exposure to the French educational system, be unable fully to understand the irony of this confrontation between brute reality and a code devised to govern a reality far removed from the Creole microcosm. The schoolgirls have learned by rote memory the facts of an extraterritorial legal system. It is only when a central term of that system can be translated into the surroundings of Creoleness that the phrase finally transmits its metaphorical meaning of irrevocable justice laid down from an awe-inspiring site of judgment to these Others raised as French. Neither Bentzon's nor Bush's evaluation of the place of French in "Monsieur Motte" is sensitive to this liminality. King's English is not merely "decorated with the affection of French phrases"; at the same time it is more than an attempt to "foreground all that remains of France" in Louisiana. King portrays the process by which these Creole schoolgirls come to language only in and through a collision between two linguistic and cultural systems, a clash that indicates the new meanings acquired by French in America, the semantic liminality of Creole French.

"Monsieur Motte" appeared in the first issue of the *New Princeton Review*. The lead article of the journal's inaugural number was by Charles Dudley Warner, King's first literary benefactor and the man who had made her debut in those pages possible. Entitled "Society in the New South," Warner's essay attempts to account to northern readers for the extraordinary state of turmoil in which the South then found itself. From his initial premise—"The American Revolution made less social change in the South than in the North" (1)—Warner paints a portrait of southern society as relatively stable until the Civil War but radically changed since the war. Warner's meditation on social upheaval sets the tone for "Monsieur Motte," which concludes with previously unthinkable intrusions of a new sociocultural order into a society its members had always considered immune to change.

The students at the Institute St. Denis have been well prepared to see their world turned on end by, ironically, the history lessons of Monsieur Mignot. The price of the attempted assimilation of the Creole schoolgirls into the official French cultural system is their complete failure to grasp *L'histoire de France* as an organized progression endowed with higher meaning. They face their final history examination with the fatalism of the outsider observing from a distance the creation of a geographical empire: "If experience proved anything, if the study of the history of France itself made one point clear, it was the dependence of great events on trifles, the unfailing interposition of the *inattendu,* and, consequently, the utter futility of preparation" ("MM," 91). This moral serves the central characters in "Monsieur Motte" in good stead when, at the tale's ending, the foundation of the well-ordered Creole society is suddenly threatened by the "interposition of the *inattendu,*" a fracturing event of the kind analyzed by Charles Dudley Warner.

King's ending is constructed around what might be seen as a southern Reconstruction variant on the final movement of Brontë's *Villette.* Brontë's novel, you will remember, has a fairy-tale ending in which her heroine, Lucy Snowe, is endowed with financial independence and a schoolhouse of her own by the pension's most feared teacher, M. Paul Emanuel, who takes on the combined role of foster father and husband-to-be. The foster parenting that brings "Monsieur Motte" to an end is, however, hardly the wish-fulfilling stuff of fairy tales, to which Brontë's conclusion is often compared. King's heroine, the budding young Creole beauty Marie Modeste,[10] orphaned during the Civil War at the age of four, believes that she will at last meet, on the occasion of the *fête* that closes the school year, the enigmatic rich uncle, Monsieur Motte who, for as long as she can remember, has paid for her education and provided her with the most elaborate *toilettes* ever seen by the young belles of the institute. Marie Modeste has never set eyes on Monsieur Motte, everyone believes, because he is so old and so ill that he is unable to stand the agitation of a youthful presence in his home. His niece has therefore, unlike any other student, been obliged to spend all her vacations inside the hermetically sealed French microcosm of the institute. But she is certain that the mysterious Monsieur Motte will at last enter her life for the *distribution de prix,* at which she is to receive the coveted prize for French history. However, on that momentous occasion when Marie Modeste is rewarded for her acquisition of the intellectual foundation of Frenchness, Monsieur Motte is nowhere to be found.

It is only the next day that Marie Modeste learns the truth about the legitimacy of her personal French history. The tale's final twist is delivered as quietly as the translingual ambiguity of Brontë's *fête* scene—although it is hard to imagine that it could have been read as anything but explosive in Reconstruction New Orleans. In Louisiana in 1886 King's message must surely have justified the careful precautions she took to hide her authorship of "Monsieur Motte" (*MSW,* 65). As an early American literary historian pointed out, her ending removed her story from its "distinctively French atmosphere" and made it "originally and particularly American." [11] Her ending portrays King as an American and reveals her understanding that Creoleness, explicitly a purely linguistic and ethnic phenomenon, cannot be divorced from its political and racial implications. The young Creole belle learns that Monsieur Motte was only a fiction, invented and kept alive by Marcélite, the quadroon *coiffeuse,* to protect Marie Modeste from the knowledge that Marcélite, a former slave, was her sole source of support. Moreover, Marcélite is also the closest thing to a blood tie left to Marie Modeste: when Marcélite's mother was sold to the owner of a distant plantation, Marie Modeste's grandmother had taken the abandoned baby, had her sleep in her own bed, even nursed her along with her own baby daughter. Marcélite thus became the foster sister (*soeur de lait*) of Marie Modeste's mother and, upon the death of her parents, she stepped in to take her white sister's place and raise her child in the style and in the culture for which she had been destined.

Once her heritage has been revealed to her, Marie Modeste is prepared to go and live with the real "Monsieur Motte," even though the *coiffeuse* is certain that New Orleans is not ready for such race "relations": "Go to my home! A white young lady like you go live with a nigger like me! . . . What! You don't think you ain't white! Oh, God! Strike me dead!" ("MM," 131–32). She is saved from the "destruction" Marcélite fears when more typical foster parents present themselves: Eugénie Lare-veillère and her confidant, the notary Monsieur Goupilleau, offer to act as parents for her. However, the story's convenient (and conventional) final twist should not be allowed to obscure the daring call for miscegenation that was King's inaugural literary gesture.

"Monsieur Motte" 's final words are reserved for the notary Goupilleau, who takes the headmistress's hands in his to sound a note of southern pride: "And they say, . . . Eugénie, that the days of heroism are past, and they laugh at our chivalry" ("MM," 133). "They" refers here to the standard villain in Reconstruction New Orleans, the northerners who had overthrown the city's traditional power structure, but Goupilleau's use of "our" is less traditional. Marcélite is responsible for the only "heroism" and "chivalry" the story relates. The final "our" of "Monsieur Motte" welcomes, therefore, the quadroon born a slave into the camp of the south-erners who, even in defeat, are still confident of their moral superiority. In addition, King even baptizes Marcélite an official member of the ethnic group whose blood flows in the quadroon's veins and on whose milk she was suckled: the *coiffeuse*'s last name, Gaulois, identifies her as a partici-pant in the origins of Frenchness—"nos ancêtres les Gaulois"—hence, as onomastically destined to provide the Creole baby with the education that will enable her to claim her birthright.

By making a quadroon the mother of the French race in the New World, the paradigmatic Gallic matrix, King in effect suggests that, in order for the Creoles to survive in the newly Americanized world then being cre-ated in Reconstruction New Orleans,[12] they should admit a crucial new definition of "Creole," one rarely avowed, even by current lexicography: "creole" (with a lowercase *c*) used to refer to an individual of mixed Creole and Negro ancestry who speaks Creole French or Spanish. With the new type of C/creole heroine she proposes, King recalls the derivation Garcilaso de la Vega proposed for "Creole," as a native word appropriated by foreign conquerors. King thus reverses the trajectory of "Creole" by replacing the word in a context that suggests the primacy of black inven-tion and the ease with which that originality, like Marcélite's "heroism," is appropriated by the dominant European elite.

In her literary debut, King's relation to southernness seems a far cry from the unproblematic conservative stance Robert Bush has attributed to her, that of "a symbol of the embattled patrician in the post-Reconstruction era."[13] Nor is the vision of the current state of Creoleness transmitted by her later works any less complicated. In subsequent fiction, King devises less blatant strategies to challenge the ethnic and cultural purity of the French presence in the New World. Most strikingly, in a number of works she suggests that the French origin that is the foundation of the Creole sense of superiority was already contaminated, that, even before the threat of the intermingling of the colonial experience, the French blood that flowed in Creole veins was somehow impure. This question subtends many of the scenes of marriage and childbirth that are a prominent feature of King's fiction.

For example, "La Grande Demoiselle" recounts the rise and fall in Creole society of the archetypal southern belle, Idalie Sainte Foy Mortemart des Islets. La Grande Demoiselle, as she is known to everyone, finds her "career" abruptly cut off by the Civil War. Abandoned by the crowd of *preux chevaliers* who had previously been in constant attendance, she ends her life in a position of obscurity and humility once unthinkable for the proudest representative of one of the proudest Louisiana families. After the war, the Grande Demoiselle is touched by racial contamination when she is reduced to the condition of teacher in "the colored public school" (Bush, 137). Her social humiliation is completed with her marriage to another of the class of *nouveaux pauvres,* Old Champigny, a ridiculous figure known as "Champignon."

But La Grande Demoiselle's loss of status is not endemic to the Creole experience. Her title identifies her as a reincarnation of a figure prominent in French history, an individual also known to posterity by a sobriquet, La Grande *Mademoiselle,* the cousin whose rebellious spirit was slowly annihilated by the king for whom Louisiana was named, Louis XIV. La Grande Mademoiselle was one of the prominent aristocrats who led the Fronde, an abortive revolution against the young Sun King. To punish her, the monarch persistently thwarted every marriage proposed to her and banished her for years to an estate whose name, Champigny, Grace King borrows for the husband of her heroine.[14] The implicit comparison in King's story between the plots of these female victims of ill-fated revolutions insinuates that the Creole elite of Louisiana was descended at least spiritually from French bloodlines already subjected to the humiliation of defeat.

This proposed origin for Louisiana history is clearly enunciated in King's late historical novel, *La Dame de Sainte Hermine.* The novel explores the creation of New France from what would be, for any project but King's, a skewed perspective. The reader is introduced to Bienville and other familiar figures, but at the center of attention are two fictional women, neither of whom is introduced as a source of heroic action. King's heroines—the aristocratic Marie Alorge, Dame de Sainte Hermine, and the peasant Annette—are central to her entire fictional project because she grants them exemplary status with regard to the three crucial moments in the establishment of racial purity: inheritance, marriage, and childbirth. Marie Alorge, an orphan destined to inherit a vast estate, is tricked out of her birthright by an unscrupulous uncle who marries her off to his son and then implicates her in a plot against his son's life carried out by a man the uncle had encouraged to become her suitor. The uncle is then able to obtain a *lettre de cachet* against the wealthy heiress, a decree permanently exiling her to Louisiana "where all sorts of criminal women were being sent and kept there unable to get away."[15] The decree also allows the uncle to appropriate the family title and estate for his ne'er-do-well son. In Louisiana, Marie Alorge, technically nameless, finds a new life with the chevalier de Loubois, but she is never able to establish the legality of any aspect of her new family status. She is never legally free of her first marriage, so both her second union and the daughter born from it are illegitimate.

Marie Alorge's fall from legitimacy is reenacted in the story of the servant girl Annette. She is shipped off to Louisiana by her father. There, she is forced to marry a poor carpenter so disappointed with his new bride that he spends his wedding night in a drunken stupor. She fails to fulfill an important part of the function intended for her in the New World by not helping to populate the new colony: her only child is a foundling. Jointly, King's two heroines thus reinforce the vision of the transfer of French blood lines to Louisiana already sketched in "La Grande Demoiselle." The French arrive there in exile, disinherited by their families in France. Once there, fate conspires with the fathers who have already repudiated them, and they are unable to pass on their birthright. In King's fiction, this scenario is enacted time and again: the French arriving in Louisiana either have no heirs or they leave adopted or illegitimate offspring.

Like the ending of "Monsieur Motte," the final message of *La Dame de Sainte Hermine* is transmitted by a notary, an individual entrusted with the power to legitimate all rites of inheritance. King's fiction of the founding of Louisiana ends with a will, drawn up by "Garic, Notary," that distributes the only worldly goods left to the disowned Dame de Sainte Hermine. The will is composed of two documents. In the first place, Marie Alorge, by leaving her goods to the "obscure poor" and describing herself as "having no legitimate heirs in this colony," closes off her lineage in the New World. Then, in a codicil attached to the first document the woman cut off from her life in the Old World provides for the future of the New France: "She so wills, that the mulatto, named François, son of her slave Marie, aged twelve, should be freed and given all the privileges of the freed" (296). *La Dame de Sainte Hermine* echoes the message of "Monsieur Motte": those of mixed blood, mulatto or quadroons, are designated by their names—François, Gaulois—as the legitimate heirs of the French legacy in America.

That King was not blind to the difficulties of this illegitimate cultural and ethnic transmission is evident from another early story, "The Little Convent Girl," a tale of reentry into the Creole microcosm of New Orleans. An eighteen-year-old girl—she is never referred to as anything but "the little convent girl"—is returning to her birthplace on a steamboat from Cincinnati, where she had been taken as an infant by her father. Her father has just died, so she is going home to the mother whom she does not remember and with whom, on her father's orders, she has been denied all contact. In fact, she could not have known her father well either for, like Marie Modeste in "Monsieur Motte," all her life has been spent inside a convent school, so that she has become "the beau-ideal of the little convent girl" (Bush, 150). Most of the story recounts her timid liberation, in the course of the journey, from total passivity and repression.

At the end of this lighthearted narrative of a shy awakening to pleasure, King takes the reader by surprise with a revelation as unexpected as the disclosure with which she brings "Monsieur Motte" to a close. In Cincinnati, the little convent girl is placed under the captain's care by sisters who leave him with a letter from the mother superior and instructions to hand the child over in New Orleans to her mother, whom he will know when she presents him with a facsimile of the letter. At the end of the journey, the exchange takes place as planned. The first shock King has in store for the reader is registered only as the couple is leaving the boat: "All wanted to say good-by to the little convent girl, to see the mother who had been deprived of her so long. Some expressed surprise in a whistle; some in other ways. All exclaimed audibly, or to themselves, 'Colored!' " (Bush, 155).

But whereas in "Monsieur Motte" King's initial proposal for the future of creolization ends on a heroic note, "The Little Convent Girl" does not cloak its subversion of Creole racial purity with optimism. When the steamboat next docks in New Orleans, the mother brings her daughter for a visit, in the hope of cheering her up. The little convent girl has no apparent reaction, but as they are leaving, she jumps from the gangway and drowns. King offers no explanation for the suicide of this child of miscegenation who could pass for white, and could therefore have initiated a new process of creolization: she simply allows the little Creole to disappear into "that vast, hidden, dark Mississippi that flows beneath the one we see" (Bush, 156).

Because King's presentation of the phenomenon of creolization is consistently elliptical, initially it seems difficult to make claims about the ideological situation of her fiction. However, it is possible to understand the ambiguity she favors as the essence of her reckoning with the French presence in Louisiana. King writes not as a politico-cultural insider, a Creole, but rather as someone who speaks a creolized language and participates in the French heritage *outre mer* only as an ethnic half-breed, a *creole*. King foregrounds the weakening of racial and ethnic purity and undermines thereby the very foundation of Creoleness, the conviction that one is of direct, legitimate French descent and enjoys privileged access to French culture. By adopting this focus in much of her fiction, King suggests that the most accurate commentary on the experience of Frenchness can be written by those who are in various ways of illegitimate lineage. I initially compared King's creolized language to Brontë's uncannily translingual English. Her meditation on the political implications of Creoleness suggests additional comparisons—the duchesse de Duras's *Ourika,* a tale of a creole's fate in revolutionary France; George Sand's *Indiana,* a novel that follows its two heroines, the Creole Indiana and the creole Noun, in France and the New World—comparisons that point to the possible existence of a tradition of creolized fiction.

In addition, the creolization of the critical viewing angle that King proposes can be suggestive for those who could be described as King's "legitimate" heirs, that is, all those engaged in the project Denis Hollier refers to as *francographia.* By this, Hollier means writing about France, French literature, and the French cultural experience from a position geographically ex-centric, that is, outside the French "geographical empire." [16] Hollier's concept best describes the situation of the native-born French writing as expatriates, as latter-day *émigrés.* I would like to propose an additional term modeled on Hollier's, *creolegraphia,* writing as a creole, to characterize the vantage point of those writing about the French literary and cultural experience from a position doubly that of the outsider, from outside the French geographic empire and with no legitimate claim to French blood.

Traditionally, would-be practitioners of *creolegraphia* have been at a considerable disadvantage. Native-born French critics, and especially those working within the French educational system, tend to assume on the one hand that they possess an insider's relation of privileged access to the phenomenon of immutable, absolutely pure Frenchness, and on the other that all outsiders are categorically denied sensitivity to the most intimate secrets of this ethnocultural heritage. For generations, American critics of French for the most part wrote as though they accepted this judgment and therefore considered themselves unworthy to criticize either the artisans or the ideology of Frenchness. Speaking from a position of implicit cultural inferiority, American critics of French literature have often tended to be more French than the French themselves and to reinforce in their criticism the readings and the canon on which is founded the French sense of cultural purity and superiority. In recent years, American critics have left this configuration behind and elected a variety of personally inflected voices that reflect their distance from the process of gallicization, their decision to break from rather than move closer to Frenchness.

Grace King's practice of *creolegraphia* suggests a compromise between these two traditions of outsiders writing about France from the outside, a compromise path that may merit exploration at a time when it seems increasingly difficult to identify new voices in which to articulate criticism about French literature. As King defines it, writing as a creole would involve a two-stage process. The first phase would resemble the criticism of French literature initially developed in this country, in that its objective would be to mimic as closely as possible the discourse and the ethics of Frenchness. The second phase would be similar in some way to the voices of dissent that have recently put into question the French cultural enterprise, the voices Hollier has in mind when he speaks of *francographia*. But *creolegraphia* would be a self-conscious attempt to take advantage of the unique situation of writing about French in America. It would turn the greatest potential weakness of any criticism written in this country that is devoted to a foreign language—that of being destined for only the most limited of publics—into its constitutive strength. The critic writing as a creole must maintain the precarious position of the outsider who might be able to pass for an insider but who chooses to retain his difference. Critical creoleness is a situation of permanent liminality, a threshold position and a sideways glance like those persistently attributed to the viewer figures in the canvases of Degas—who may have been helped to sidestep his own ethnic purity by his prolonged contact with his Creole relations in Louisiana. From that liminal position, King's fiction suggests, the critic would gain a heightened sensitivity to the "relations" of power essential to the preservation of Frenchness. The creolization of criticism would legitimate the contributions of those disinherited on the one hand by the French and on the other by the American critical traditions.

NOTES

I would like to thank Maria DiBattista, without whose collaboration I would never have enjoyed the quirky pleasures of "translingualism," and Jefferson Humphries, without whose gentle prodding I would never have explored my literary/critical roots.

1. *Histoire des Incas,* trans. J. Baudoin (Amsterdam, 1704), 2:460.

2. A similar borrowing from a native language is at the root of "Béké," the term by which whites born in the French Antilles designate themselves.

3. Letter to Warrington Dawson, 5 Aug. 1924, in *Grace King of New Orleans: A Selection of Her Writings,* ed. Robert Bush (Baton Rouge: Louisiana State University Press, 1973), 403. Quotations of Grace King's correspondence and, whenever possible, of her works are taken from this anthology, cited hereafter as Bush.

4. *The Pleasant Ways of St. Médard* (New York: Henry Holt, 1916), 163. To my knowledge, no one has studied the time lag between the establishment of educational curricula and practice in France and their re-creation outside France, in particular in a distant, and by the late nineteenth century only a former, French colony like Louisiana. By the time of King's education, for example, I would suspect that the educational model and standards adopted in Louisiana Creole schools were hopelessly out-of-date, reflecting the approximately century-old ideals of the apogee of French colonial rule there.

5. *Memories of a Southern Woman of Letters* (New York: Macmillan, 1932), 2; hereafter cited as *MSW*.

6. Bush refers to a letter to her sister from 1885 (the year she began her literary career) in which King declares that she will adopt French literary models to the exclusion of English or American ones (4–5).

7. Humphries, *Metamorphoses of the Raven: Literary Overdeterminedness in France and the South since Poe* (Baton Rouge: Louisiana State University Press, 1985), 10.

8. "Monsieur Motte," *New Princeton Review* 1 (Jan. 1886): 92, hereafter cited as "MM." I quote from the original version rather than the second edition that Bush reprints on account of Bush's claim that for its revised version King "improved the story by greatly reducing [the number of French phrases]" (53–54). I take this precaution even though my own comparison of the two editions does not substantiate Bush's claim. The only modification of the heavy use of French

I could find is the occasional substitution of "hairdresser" for *coiffeuse* (see, for example, *New Princeton Review*, 95, and Bush anthology, 58), although *coiffeuse* is still found on occasion in the revised version.

9. Th. Bentzon (Marie-Thérèse Blanc, a disciple of George Sand and eventually a personal friend of King), "Les romanciers du sud en Amérique," *Revue des Deux Mondes* 116 (Apr. 1893): 683.

10. The headmistress of Brontë's *pension* is named Modeste Maria.

11. Fred Lewis Pattee, *History of American Literature since 1870* (New York: Century, 1922), 362.

12. In "The Old Cabildo of New Orleans," King describes the Americanization of the city's French heart: "The old quarter was 'reborn' between 1830 and 1850; and reborn, it was fondly hoped and proclaimed, American; which then, as now, meant enterprising, progressive, rich" (Bush, 303).

13. Bush, "Grace King and Mark Twain," *American Literature* 44 (Mar. 1972): 52.

14. The Grande Mademoiselle's estate was Champigny-sur-Veude. King's interest in the Grande Mademoiselle did not end with this early story. In a 1906 letter she recommends highly a recent book, *Louis XIV and the Grande Mademoiselle,* saying "it is considered the strongest piece of historical work ever done by a French woman" (Bush, 393).

15. *La Dame de Sainte Hermine* (New York: Macmillan, 1924), 26.

16. Hollier, proposal for *The Harvard History of French Literature.*

Power, Sexuality, and Race

in *All the King's Men*

CARL FREEDMAN

All the King's Men is generally acknowledged to be Robert Penn Warren's masterpiece and probably the most important political novel in the entire range of American literature—indeed, perhaps the most important political novel, excepting several by Conrad, in the English language. But before it can be discussed intelligently, a couple of critical stumbling-blocks must be cleared out of the way. First, there is the popular notion (always repudiated by Warren himself) that the novel is "about" Huey P. Long.[1] Of course, Warren did live in Louisiana during Long's heyday, and it would be perverse to maintain that this matrix has left no traces in the text. But Warren has written both fiction and history and surely appreciates the difference between them; certainly, no one with a detailed knowledge of Long's career could mistake *All the King's Men* for a roman à clef. Second, there is the belief that it is necessary or possible to decide whether the novel is "for" or "against" Willie Stark. Even on the most manifest and self-conscious level, Warren (who, with his colleague Cleanth Brooks, holds ironic tension to be the essence of the poetic) takes a considerably more complex view.[2] Clearly, the novel is morally appalled by Willie while at the same time maintaining a certain sympathy for his genuinely populist impulses and considerable awe at his energy and personal magnetism. Marvell's Horatian ode on Cromwell, a poem which deeply impressed the New Critics in general, provides a pertinent analogy: Cromwell is imaged as a bolt of lightning, a natural force, and, at least to some degree, moral and even political judgments seem secondary to sheer bedazzlement. But Willie is not the center of Warren's novel in the same way that Cromwell is of Marvell's poem. The former's view of politics is even more complex than its view of Willie, and needs to be analyzed in some detail. My argument, however, will be that political power, though the overriding manifest theme of *All the King's Men,* ultimately functions as a code for a more basic concern with sexual relations; and that sexuality, in turn, encodes a still more fundamental preoccupation, one that the novel shares with most serious southern literature—namely, race, slavery, and the historic guilt of the South.

The point may be briefly put in the limited but suggestive terms of literary influence. The deep strategies and evasions of the text can be partly conceptualized as a contradiction between two mighty and antithetical precursors, Conrad and Faulkner. Conrad, especially the Conrad of *Nostromo,* is clearly Warren's conscious model of what political fiction ought to be: the Conradian device of refracting diverse political stances through the liberal prism of moral irony and political indeterminacy is strongly present throughout *All the King's Men.*[3] But the device is fully possible for Conrad because, as a Polish émigré and British Master Mariner, he is finally a free-floating intellectual, at home only in the watery spaces *between* concrete social formations. Warren, like almost every other southern novelist of the age, must also contend with the vastly different model of Faulkner, as *rooted* a novelist as has ever written, and one whose career was devoted to brooding over racial right and wrong and desperately attempting, in many ways, to decipher the meaning of southern history. Conrad is Warren's freely chosen predecessor, but Faulkner, so to speak, insists upon certain prior rights of eminent domain. Warren, one might say, wants to be Conrad but cannot help also being Faulkner.

Nonetheless, criticism above the level of a reductive hermeneutic essentialism—which would discard manifest layers of meaning like artichoke leaves—must first of all do justice to the novel's manifest theme of power politics. Here the Conrad in Warren is preeminent. So strong is Conrad's presence that several of the major characters in *All the King's Men* are even based, evidently, upon counterparts in *Nostromo.* Judge Irwin recalls Don José Avellanos, the conservative of high aristocratic honor, though not of completely unsmirched integrity, who is hopelessly archaic in the modern world. Willie Stark himself is a kind of Monterist figure, a "great man" and a populist demagogue (a type that was not, after all, invented by Huey Long). The narrator Jack Burden, a classically Lukácsian middle-of-the-road protagonist, is in a sense Warren's version of the Everyman or "our man" of Conrad's title: a man of certain considerable abilities but fundamentally weak, who is plunged into a complex world of power politics to which he is never really adequate. But Warren's discipleship to

Conrad is no slavish imitation, and *All the King's Men* makes significant revisions in the Conradian scheme—primarily by a certain shift to the left. Whereas Conrad dismisses the Montero brothers with sniffily genteel distaste, Warren is fascinated by Willie. The latter's appeal is not written off as the inexplicable but always vulgar taste of the masses; on the contrary, it is strongly registered in the text itself: "I would wait for the roar. You can't help it. I knew it would come, but I would wait for it, and every time it would seem intolerably long before it came. . . . There is nothing like the roar of a crowd when it swells up, all of a sudden at the same time, out of the thing which is in every man in the crowd but is not himself. The roar would swell and rise and fall and swell again, with the Boss standing with his right arm raised straight to Heaven and his red eyes bulging."[4] Nor does the novel present Willie's humanitarian projects (such as the building of the great medical complex, an undertaking that indirectly leads Willie to his death) as mere hypocrisy. Certainly they are intended for the aggrandizement of his own ego: but his identification of himself and the people is ultimately a sincere one (despite the many ruses necessary to give this identification political efficacy), so that Willie cannot be reduced to a case of simple egoism. There is here an understanding of popular politics that is wholly absent in Conrad. Similarly, Warren's attitude toward Jack is different from Conrad's toward Nostromo. Whereas the latter is for his creator not only inadequate but finally uninteresting— an apparent hero who turns out to be "common" in the most pejorative sense—there is in Warren's portrayal of Jack an almost Joycean insistence on the extraordinariness of the ordinary man, so that, by the end of the novel, Jack Burden is the closest thing to a hero that the text can offer. The Jeffersonian tradition, after all, has had an impact on most southern literary and intellectual figures, and Warren is no exception. Insofar as either novel can be read as politically programmatic, both correspond fairly well to the public personae of the authors: on the one hand, an elitist European tory; on the other, a moderate southern Democrat.

But, of course, neither *Nostromo* nor *All the King's Men* ultimately presents itself as partisan; and it is in the deliberate attempt to *avoid* partisanship that Warren's deepest affinity with Conrad lies. All the available political stances in the text—the outdated conservatism of an Irwin, the amoral populism of a Willie, not to mention the murderously cynical opportunism of a Duffy, who by the end is the most powerful politician in the state—are shown to be unacceptable.[5] Jack Burden, like the novel itself, is never able or willing to choose decisively among them; and the only choice Jack makes which the novel really endorses is his decision to leave politics altogether and instead to cultivate a private life of moral values, wedded happiness, and academic scholarship. This retreat is necessary in order to resolve a contradiction generated by the way the text frames the nature of political choice in the first place. Irwin and Willie are the essential political poles, and since neither is ultimately adequate, though both have their attractions, the only viable option is to seek some alternative "above" politics entirely. What is operative here is an ideologically determinate failure of imagination: namely, the text's almost complete inability to imagine a fundamentally different kind of politics, a revolutionary or even radically reformist politics which would be popular and not manipulative, honest and not hidebound. Southern history does not lack examples of such political projects. But, in the southern context, the core and sine qua non of such a politics is necessarily the issue of race—an issue which the novel wants to evade but, as we shall see, finally cannot. As in much of Conrad, this ostensibly "political" novel is in fact programmed *against* politics from the start.[6]

Again as with Conrad, Warren's antipolitical thrust is enforced primarily by a reduction of the political to the personal. Jack Burden's retreat to private life is seen not as an abdication of social responsibility (as a different sort of novelist might see it) but as the only feasible means of personal salvation. The central questions surrounding Willie concern not his place in the sociopolitical history of his state (which bears some resemblances to Louisiana but, significantly, is never given even a fictional name) but the complexities of his character and his effects on those closest to him. Even a comparatively minor character like Sugar-Boy is explicable only in terms of the text's personalist stress: wholly nonpolitical, inarticulate, and, indeed, nearly imbecilic save for his remarkable skills with automobiles and firearms, he is finally of interest because of his absolute personal loyalty to Willie Stark. But the chief point to be made here is that the text's reduction of the political to the personal depends upon a logically prior *severance* of the two categories. In this sense, Warren writes from squarely within the classical liberal tradition, according to which the political is but a particular and autonomous sphere of existence, with which one may or may not choose to become involved. There is nothing here of the Marxist principle that putatively private life is actually a highly specialized department of material social reality; or of the feminist insistence that apparently contingent or "natural" details of daily living have political sources and effects; or of the Foucauldian insight that power does not merely repress or distort personal subjectivity, but constitutes it, from the ground up as it were. Yet, though an individualistic liberalism may be the official ideology of the text, it is by no means all that the text has to offer. In order to justify this statement, it is now necessary to examine one of the precise ways in which the novel reduces politics to individual character, a way which breaks sharply with the Conradian model and which provides a mediating term between manifest individualism and the ultimately racial-historical concerns of *All the King's Men:* for Warren, unlike Conrad, is deeply sensitive to and interested in the matter of sexuality.

Indeed, a sexual connotation is obliquely operative in the novel's title and famous opening paragraphs, which evoke a dry, desolate countryside, burning and lethal. Such a landscape inevitably recalls—especially in view of Warren's literary generation and general critical allegiances—*The Waste Land* of Eliot, where the sterility of the land is figured in the sexual incompetence of its monarch, the Fisher-King. Warren thus suggests a correlation between this Eliotic image and the Mother Goose rhyme in which all the resources and power of the king are helpless to reconstruct the great egg, a trope of fertility and generation; and an additional, more incidental layer of allusion is no doubt contributed by the fortunate coincidence of Huey Long's nickname, "the Kingfish." In the first few paragraphs, then, the text has not only suggested the reducibility of power to sex—in the sense that sexual failure is, at least metaphorically, the basic determinant of political failure—but also the incommensurability of the two terms, in the sense that no quantum of political power is capable of refructifying erotic quality.

This gestural and figurative scheme, suggesting erotic character to be a more basic and actual category than public power, is concretized at great length in the narrative structure of *All the King's Men,* which may be read as an account of the sexual careers of its joint protagonists, Willie and Jack. Both come more manifestly to our attention for their connected roles in the power story, but it will be convenient to begin by considering them separately, since, although they to some degree mirror one another and their lives are complexly intertwined through most of the novel, they are basically asymmetrical. Jack is an observer, an outrider, an aide-de-camp of power, but not a figure of power in his own right. Willie, of course, is.

If Willie is, for the political world of the novel, the king—or, in secular American terms, "the Boss"—he is also the irrevocably shattered egg of sexual hope. His general high-spirited promiscuity is no doubt to be taken as a symptom of some basic dysfunction, but the latter is more crucially expressed in the two most important erotic ties of his life, that with his wife, Lucy, and that with his secretary-mistress, Sadie Burke. The two women are themselves antithetical—Lucy the conventionally submissive and dutiful helpmeet, at home only within the traditional perimeters of domesticity; Sadie the cynical and ruthlessly efficient careerist, thoroughly conversant with the intricacies of power politics—but both relationships end in disaster. Sadie is a driving force behind the mightily self-driven Willie (it is worth recalling that she was already a skilled and experienced politician when Boss Stark was still the feckless Cousin Willie), but the heights of political grandeur to which they together climb cannot, for Sadie, compensate for Willie's inability to make a decisive erotic commitment to her. Their liaison becomes increasingly tense and problematic, and Sadie eventually makes an indispensable contribution to Duffy's murderous plot after she discovers that in Willie's liaison with Anne Stanton she may have to contend with a rival more than a match for her own charms: the result is Willie's death and the shattering of Sadie's psyche. Sadie, the mistress and accomplice of power, finally stands for Thanatos.

As for Lucy, she has long ago been all but nominally cast aside by Willie, as his political horizons have expanded and he has found the puritanical schoolteacher decreasingly adequate to his taste. But their marriage remains vital in the form of its issue, Tom Stark, the collegiate football hero. Whereas the illicit affair with Sadie can generate only power and finally death, the marriage does bear legitimate fruit—but not in the long run. Despite Lucy's worried maternal cautions, Willie encourages and glories in Tom's athletic prowess and general rowdiness: for in Tom's attainment of the big-man-on-campus role there is both the reflection in miniature of Willie's own statewide dominance and, at the same time, the *kind* of achievement which Willie's impoverished rural background made impossible for himself but which his political success enables for Tom. Tom follows not in his father's footsteps but in the footsteps which the Boss would *like* to have had, and this path leads directly to Tom's fatal injury on the football field; dying, Tom leaves behind only the bastard product of a reckless undergraduate libido, and the hospital vigil for him prefigures Willie's own fate. Again, political power and personal failure are not only closely linked; the latter term remains the more fundamental and important.

Jack Burden's women are perhaps more interesting than Willie's—his reward, so to speak, for being less directly involved with politics—but they are contrasted along similar axes. Lois, Jack's wife for a time, is, like Lucy, a wife of the conventional domestic sort, but her domesticity is of a far more glamorous and erotically charged sort—the domesticity, as it were, of the bedroom rather than the kitchen or parlor. Jack eventually considers her merely insipid (as Willie considers Lucy), but there is in his shrinking from her—in his gratuitous rudeness and his nearly pathological devotion to sleep while still living with her—an inadequacy that belongs to him as much as to her, a kind of sexual paralysis. This, indeed, is the chief contrast between the sexual failures of Willie and Jack. Whereas Willie, the representative of power, fails through a hyperactivity that results in death and dishonor, Jack, who serves and observes power but wields none, fails through an incapacity to act. The term of sexual incapacity, however, brings us to the most prominent female character in the novel, Anne Stanton.

In Jack's personal history Anne plays the Virgin to Lois's Whore, while at the same time recalling Sadie Burke in the sense that she is interested in Jack's ideas and public role, rather than only in private household matters. First and foremost, she is Jack's partner in sexual paralysis. What ought to be the consummation of their youthful summer courtship ends in opaque anticlimax—"I couldn't any more have touched her than if she had been my little sister" (296), Jack recounts—and from this point, apparently, there can be no turning back. Jack proceeds to a life of weary restlessness and inability to make erotic connection, while Anne becomes a spinster devoted to charitable good works (charity, one may note, being the individualistic substitute for politics). The friendship between them endures, after a fashion, and becomes a weird, shadowy caricature of a love affair, at once unhappily celibate and permeated with intense sexual tension. The relationship seems inherently unstable, and it is, indeed, one crucial and unexpected move by Anne which ultimately topples the entire precarious structure of political power and erotic bleakness that has been organized around Jack and Willie. When Anne becomes Willie's mistress, she not only implicitly renounces her role as (nominally) secular Virgin (hence provoking her brother Adam's homicidal and suicidal fury), but, in more strictly narrative terms, she switches from the locus of near-power and paralysis defined by Jack to the alternative locus of power and amoral energy defined by Willie—thus violating the erotic-characterological organization of the novel. Like a chess piece which has inexplicably moved in a way contrary to the rules, Anne brings the game to a close, ushering in the novel's tragic catastrophe in which all public and private failures are sealed. Anne, like any genuine type of the Virgin, is invested with enormous suppressed sexual energy; what is most noteworthy here is that, when this energy is finally liberated to explosive effect, it not only brings down the curtain on the private lives of the individual characters but also on the whole project of insurgent populism that had been led by Willie Stark. Nowhere more than in its catastrophe does the novel insist upon the epiphenomenal status of the sociopolitical dimension in comparison to personal, especially sexual, destiny.

But—it will surely be pointed out—the novel does have a resolution *beyond* catastrophe. Willie's political aims have ended in defeat, and such of his organization as has survived is inherited by his murderer. Willie himself is dead by violence, as are Tom Stark, Adam Stanton, and Judge Irwin. Sadie Burke has retreated to a sanatorium, and Sugar-Boy is a broken man without purpose. Yet in the novel's final pages (which, especially toward the very end, become curiously oracular and laconic, and so somewhat different in style and tone from the main body of the text) we are told, in significantly casual phrasing, that Jack and Anne, whose lives one would have guessed to be permanently shattered by intimate tragedy, are in fact happily married; and we also learn that Lucy Stark—and thus even, in a sense, the marriage of Lucy and Willie—has attained a new vitality and purpose as she adopts and nurtures her illegitimate grandchild. Jack Burden and the novel itself affect a new, unexpected energy, and, in the final phrase of *All the King's Men,* Jack announces his brave, lucid, existential acceptance of "the awful responsibility of Time." Many readers have felt this resolution to be tacked-on, gratuitous, heterogeneous to the essentially tragic vision of the novel as a whole.[7] But it seems to me that the ending, however inappropriate, is also the logical effect of an instability in the deep structure of the text. The use of the political to code the erotic —the way in which the novel has all along subordinated its manifest public theme to its more latent private theme—has functioned throughout as a strategy to avoid the most fundamental issues of the political, and, as such, amounts to an individualistic reductionism, a conjuring trick in the service of liberal ideology. The weakness of the ending in comparison to the power of the main body of the novel—the descent into a wholly conventional moralism and domesticity—is the price ultimately exacted for this brilliantly executed but fundamentally illegitimate illusionism. For the tenor of erotic characterology has come to depend so heavily on its political vehicle that, when the latter is finally obliterated—when the political world of the novel disappears in the catastrophic climax and the antipolitical reductionism of the text thus reaches its logical culmination—

the erotic characterology is itself maimed, having lost its primary mode of expression. It is in this way convenient that so many of the more important characters simply die. But not all of them do (total slaughter would suggest a parody of a Jacobean tragedy), and, having lost the language in which to express its Eliotic theme of sexual sterility and disaster, the text is forced to employ the unmotivated rescue-device of domestic love in order to achieve any resolution at all. In the end, the text's reduction of the political compels it to retreat from its most powerful and complex investigations of the personal itself.

I am tempted to say that the foregoing analysis of the novel, in terms of an asymmetric intercoding between the political and the erotic, might be essentially complete, if *All the King's Men* were not a *southern* novel; if, in other words, the literary influence of Faulkner and the social pressure of a guilty racial history were not inescapable factors with which to be reckoned; or if, to put it in terms more specific to the text itself, it were not for the presence of the apparently incidental but actually fundamental chapter 4, the story of Cass Mastern. Very tenuously connected to the main plot of the novel by virtue of being (apparently) an ancestor of Jack Burden's and the subject of his abandoned doctoral dissertation in American history, Cass Mastern is in some ways the most important character in *All the King's Men*. His story too is a sexual and personal one, but it is a good deal more than that as well.

In the most obvious narrative terms, of course, the Mastern story stands in analogic relation to the twentieth-century plot organized around Jack and Willie, and some of the operative analogies are obvious enough. Gilbert Mastern, a slaveholding pillar of the antebellum regime who rapidly rebuilds his fortune in the postwar era, displays energy and brutal efficiency in a way somewhat similar to that of Willie Stark, while his brother Cass resembles Jack Burden in being quieter, more introspective, and more intellectually oriented. Jack himself, as historical researcher, is rather bored by Gilbert but fascinated by the sensitive, guilty, doomed Cass, and he credits Cass with his own version of moral wisdom: "Cass Mastern lived for a few years and in that time he learned that the world is all of one piece. He learned that the world is like an enormous spider web and if you touch it, however lightly, at any point, the vibration ripples to the remotest perimeter and the drowsy spider feels the tingle and is drowsy no more but springs out to fling the gossamer coils about you who have touched the web and then inject the black, numbing poison under your hide" (188–89). The elaborate biologistic metaphor—containing no hint of any concrete social situation—makes clear that this homily, though supposedly about human connectedness, is cast in asocial, meta-physical terms which (because void of any actual content of collectivity) must logically resolve into a liberal and moralistic individualism; as such, the passage is of course at one with the official ideology of the novel itself, and it is in this way that the text offers to establish a profound connec-tion between the Mastern story and the larger narrative in which it is embedded. What is remarkable, however, is that Jack's (or the novel's) arachnoid wisdom is an utterly inadequate and misleading gloss on what the life history of Cass Mastern actually reveals. If *All the King's Men* insists upon analogizing Cass to Jack, the most interesting, if unconscious, effect of this analogy is to highlight the *differences* between their stories, and, in so doing, to acknowledge social perspectives which the novel for the most part attempts to foreclose.

Cass's character, like Jack's, is defined in largely sexual terms, but their erotic histories are quite different. Jack, who grows up in the relatively free-and-easy home of his coquettish mother, and who seldom seems to lack sexual opportunities, suffers from erotic inertness until mysteriously rescued by the deus ex machina of married love. Cass, reared in a monastic Calvinism, comes to disaster through a chain of events initiated by what he himself calls "the illicit sweetness of the flesh" (164). The guilt pro-voked by his affair with Annabelle Trice and the consequent suicide of her husband (and Cass's friend) Duncan is intolerable enough; but the disas-ter spreads far beyond the perimeter of this conventional moral fable. As Faulkner knew so well, sex in the Old South is seldom far removed from racial crime, and the most completely innocent victim of Cass's transgres-sion turns out to be Annabelle's slave Phebe, who is literally sold down the river when Annabelle can no longer endure Phebe's probable knowledge of her secret. In larger terms, however, the "secret" is not merely the em-pirical fact of the illicit liason but the entire system of racial injustice; one might say that Cass's sin is in a sense not simple adultery but miscegena-tional rape, for, though he goes to bed with Annabelle, it is Phebe whom he (unwittingly but determinately) violates. Indeed, Cass comes to under-stand the racial infrastructure not only of his specific act but of his entire society and way of life when he attempts (unsuccessfully) to find and res-cue Phebe. His journey includes, most chillingly, the witnessing of a slave sale, in which the typical southern condensation of warped sexual desire, the cash nexus, and brutal racial exploitation is displayed with almost un-bearable force; Cass, while failing to find Phebe, is moved to free his own slaves and to adopt Abolitionist sympathies (both acts without parallel in the life of Jack Burden).[8] More than that even, he becomes able, in a passage that resonates both with the Sartrean (and Fanonian) concept of the remorse-producing *look* of the oppressed, and with the less systematic insight of Faulkner,[9] to articulate how the slaveholding system necessarily poisons all life, sexual and otherwise, in the South: "Then, much later, I began to understand. I understood that Mrs. Turner flogged her Negroes for the same reason that the wife of my friend sold Phebe down the river: she could not bear their eyes upon her. I understand, for I can no longer bear their eyes upon me" (184). Cass Mastern dies during the Civil War, in which he marches alongside his compatriots while declining to accept a rank higher than private, to fire his gun, or to take any enthusiasm in the Confederate cause.

In chapter 4, then, sexuality functions in a mode fundamentally different from that of the rest of the novel. Far from serving an individualist stress that largely occludes the sociopolitical dimension, the exploration of sex and personality functions in the Mastern story to open up a radically social perspective on issues of infinitely greater political significance than the local, temporary battle between the populist movement of Willie Stark and the conservative plutocracy of Judge Irwin and his colleagues. Jack Burden's figure of the spider web may mark the limits of his own understanding, but it is hopelessly too abstract and metaphysical to convey the historical depth and specificity which chapter 4 enforces. If Cass remains the formal analogue to Jack, he also functions as an implicit critique of the latter's relative shallowness and isolation. But the critique is far more than a characterological one. What may seem true on the most superficial level of linear plot—that chapter 4 does not really belong in *All the King's Men*—is actually true in a much more important sense, namely, that the embedded narrative of the slaveholding South is radically out of synchronization with the ideology of liberal individualism which the remainder of the novel attempts to uphold. As such, it works to undermine or explode the strategies of ideological containment which the main text tries to implement. The fact that sex, as the Mastern story shows, involves not a metaphysical but a *concrete* human connectedness, and thus can signify the fundamentally racial basis of southern social history, inevitably problematizes its use, in the story of Jack Burden and Willie Stark, as a merely individual category and the signified of a tale of power politics. More generally, the Mastern story, which, as the (pseudo)genealogical links remind us, is set in a society not at all far removed from that of the main text—the Mastern brothers are the maternal uncles of the man thought to be Jack Burden's father—implies a searching criticism of a narrative which can deal at length with southern personal and political relations while failing ever to consider the system of racial oppression on which virtually everything else southern rests. Actually, the exclusion is not quite total: the opening paragraph of *All the King's Men* describes an imagined car crash as being witnessed with wise indifference by several "niggers" working in the fields, and early in his political career (*before* becoming amoral and manipulative) Willie Stark has to contend with the charge of "nigger-lover" from his opponents. But these are extremely minor points, tiny chinks through which something of racial reality filters in, and their significance would be obscure were it not for the intense searchlight of the Mastern story.[10] The nineteenth- and twentieth-century narratives are fundamentally at odds with one another, and the result is to give to the text as a whole a richness and complexity—and political decency—which it would otherwise lack. Even the deceptive placidity of the ending cannot remain undisturbed by the harrowing memory of chapter 4.

My essential claim, then, is that *All the King's Men* is an ideologically fissured text, the most fundamental and compelling concerns of which emerge only athwart its official ideology; or, in more colloquial language, that the novel knows better than it knows. But I will, in conclusion, make one further point: that the novel does *not* necessarily know better than Robert Penn Warren himself came to know. Widely considered second only to Faulkner among modern southern writers—author of a career that has included high distinction in fiction, poetry, literary criticism, drama, historiography, editing, and teaching—Warren has a noteworthy place in the social as well as the literary history of his native region. In 1930, Warren was a frankly segregationist contributor to the collective Agrarian manifesto *I'll Take My Stand:* though his essay on the race issue, "The Briar Patch," seems in some respects enlightened—Warren supports legal equality between the races and, more tentatively, the unionization of black labor—his tone is irredeemably paternalistic, and his opposition to *social* equality is clear. Yet, however unacceptable the essay may be, it is surely worth noting that, in a volume exclusively devoted to the history, character, and destiny of the South, Warren, alone among the Agrarians, chose as his topic the overwhelmingly most important matter facing the South. By the 1950s his concern with race remained as strong as ever, but his standpoint had undergone radical revision. He became—and was to remain through the 1960s—the most prominent literary voice among white southerners to speak for racial justice (and, specifically, for the crucial Supreme Court decision of 1954), and to announce to his fellow whites that the old order of segregation and oppression (to which so many southern intellectuals of his generation remained attached) was and deserved to be finished.[11] Warren, who began in company with Donald Davidson and Allen Tate, went on to earn the respect of James Baldwin and to begin a friendship with Malcolm X shortly before the latter's assassination. It is in the context of this record, at least as much as in terms of any more strictly literary-formal development, that *All the King's Men* must be understood. Published in 1946, it is something of a transitional work, in which one can locate both the pressure of the old order—which so generally tried to render the Afro-American into Ralph Ellison's Invisible Man—and a nascent awareness that the construction of a healthy southern culture requires the white South squarely to confront its evil racial history.[12] In this way, the novel is a watershed not only for Warren but also, perhaps, for southern culture as a whole.[13] Though it is perilously easy to sentimentalize the racial changes that have taken place in the South since 1946—to forget the violence of the opposition against which they were achieved, or to underestimate continuing economic inequality and the persistence of a bitter, if generally less vocal, white racism—yet no reasonable analysis can count those changes as anything less than momentous. In this history, *All the King's Men* has a noteworthy place.

NOTES

1. See, for instance, Warren's introduction to the Modern Library edition of *All the King's Men* (New York: Random House, 1953), i–vi.
2. See Warren, "Pure and Impure Poetry," in *Selected Essays* (New York: Random House, 1958), 29: "The poet . . . proves his vision by submitting it to the fires of irony—to the drama of his structure—in the hope that the fires will refine it. In other words, the poet wishes to indicate that his vision has been earned, that it can survive reference to the complexities and contradictions of experience." "Pure and Impure Poetry," which is sometimes considered the most important single essay in the entirety of the New Criticism, adumbrates a doctrine developed at greater length by Cleanth Brooks in such works as *The Well-Wrought Urn*.
3. Warren himself describes *Nostromo* as "one of the few mastering visions of our historical moment and our human lot" (Warren, " 'The Great Mirage': Conrad and *Nostromo*," in *Selected Essays*, 58).
4. Robert Penn Warren, *All the King's Men* (San Diego: Harcourt Brace Jovano-

vich, 1982), 146. Further references to the novel will be to this edition, and page numbers will be given parenthetically in the text.

5. An exception may be made for Hugh Miller, Willie Stark's scrupulous and cultivated attorney general, who approves of Willie's radical populism but resigns when he can no longer stomach the Boss's methods. But, as a character, Miller is minor almost to the point of invisibility, and I think that his (extremely weak) presence in the novel tends rather to strengthen than to weaken my argument. The point is that the text, although, strictly speaking, not absolutely incapable of conceiving of a Hugh Miller, is driven to marginalize him drastically. If Miller were as prominent a character even as Duffy or Sugar-Boy, the political story of *All the King's Men* would be very different.

6. Warren has been quite candid on this point. See his Modern Library introduction, vi: "The book, however, was never intended to be a book about politics. Politics merely provided the framework story in which the deeper concerns, whatever their final significance, might work themselves out." The notion of concerns "deeper" than politics is of course revealing.

7. See, for instance, Richard H. King, *A Southern Renaissance: The Cultural Awakening of the American South, 1930–1955* (New York: Oxford University Press, 1980), 285: "Indeed this confusion of the psychological and moral lies at the root of Warren's entire literary project and the world-view informing it. Jack Burden's problem seems so elusive because, though his symptoms are psychological—the lack of affect and an inability to feel, withdrawal from involvement with others, a willingness to be used—Warren 'solves' the problem through a moral conversion, a (William) Jamesian willing to will. Love serves as the *deus ex machina;* it is at once a psychological and morally informing force."

8. It is worth remembering that such parallels *do* exist in the life of Faulkner's Ike McCaslin.

9. It is relevant to quote Faulkner's own judgment of *All the King's Men:* the "Cass Mastern story is a beautiful and moving piece. That was his novel. The rest of it I would throw away" (quoted in Joseph Blotner, *William Faulkner* [New York: Random House, 1974], 2:1214). This comment, though obviously unfair and hyperbolic, is also genuinely penetrating. Not only does Faulkner recognize the particular affinity between the Mastern story and his own work; he also seems to appreciate the essential *disjunction* (which I discuss below) between the Mastern story and the main text, and the superior social insight of the former.

10. The departure from Louisiana history is worth mentioning here, for the impact of Huey Long on black citizens, and the general racial character of his movement, are among the most interesting aspects of the Long story.

11. Faulkner perhaps deserves to be mentioned here, but his record was far more mixed than Warren's. During the era of the civil rights movement, some of Faulkner's public statements on race were progressive and insightful, while on other occasions he was capable of descending to a banal and vicious racism which

is directly challenged by the most searching elements of his own fiction. It is of course significant that his literary influence has weighed so heavily on many of the best and most radical Afro-American novelists, from James Baldwin to Alice Walker.

12. Warren's essay on Faulkner, which is almost exactly contemporary with *All the King's Men,* displays a similarly divided consciousness: "The fact of slavery itself was not a single, willed act. It was a natural historical growth. But it was an evil, and all its human and humane mitigations and all its historical necessity could not quiet the bad conscience it engendered" (Warren, "William Faulkner," *Selected Essays,* 63). Here an unflinching condemnation of slavery as evil coexists with a reluctance to assign responsibility and a curiously revealing oxymoron which holds chattel slavery in the South to be at once "natural" and "historical."

13. It is quite appropriate that Walter Sullivan (in *A Requiem for the Renascence*) should view *All the King's Men* as marking the *end* of a vital southern culture. Sullivan's attachment to the old segregated South is perhaps too well known to require any special comment; but for a useful, if somewhat overgenerous, consideration of the Sullivanian perspective, see Lewis P. Simpson, *The Brazen Face of History: Studies in the Literary Consciousness in America* (Baton Rouge: Louisiana State University Press, 1980), 255–76.

Zora Neale Hurston and

the Speakerly Text

HENRY LOUIS GATES

Zora Neale Hurston, a black southerner, is the first writer that
our generation of black and feminist critics has brought into the canon, or
perhaps I should say "the canons." For Hurston is now a cardinal figure in
the Afro-American canon, the feminist canon, and the canon of American
fiction, especially as our readings of her work become increasingly close
readings, readings which Hurston's texts sustain, delightfully. The curious aspect of the widespread critical attention being shown to Hurston's
texts is that so many critics who embrace such a diversity of theoretical
approaches seem to find something new at which to marvel in her texts.

My own method of reading *Their Eyes Were Watching God* stems fundamentally from the debates over modes of representation, over theories of
mimesis, which form such a crucial part of the history of Afro-American
literature and its theory. Mimetic principles can be both implicitly and
explicitly ideological, and the explication of Hurston's rhetorical strategy,
which I shall attempt below, is no exception. I wish to read *Their Eyes* in
such a way as to move from the broadest notion of *that which* it thematizes through an ever-tighter spiral of the *ways in which* it thematizes—
that is, its rhetorical strategies. I shall attempt to show that Hurston's text
not only cleared a rhetorical space for the narrative strategies that Ralph
Ellison would render so deftly in *Invisible Man*, but also that Hurston's
text is the first example in our tradition of "The Speakerly Text." By this
term I mean a text whose rhetorical strategy is designed to represent an
oral literary tradition, designed "to emulate the phonetic, grammatical,
and lexical patterns of actual speech and produce the 'illusion of oral narration.'"[1] "The speakerly text" is that text in which all other structural
elements seem to be devalued, as important as they remain to the telling

of the tale, because the narrative strategy signals attention to its own importance, an importance which would seem to be the privileging of oral speech and its inherent linguistic features. Whereas Jean Toomer's *Cane* draws upon the black oral voice essentially as a different voice from the narrator's, as a repository of socially distinct, countrapuntal meanings and beliefs, a "speakerly text" would seem primarily to be oriented toward imitating one of the numerous forms of oral narration found in classical Afro-American vernacular literature.

Obviously, I am concerned with what we traditionally think of as matters of voice. "Voice," here, connotes not only traditional definitions of "point of view," a crucial matter in the reading of *Their Eyes,* but also the linguistic presence of a literary tradition that exists for us as written text essentially because of the work of socio-linguists and anthropologists such as Zora Neale Hurston. In this essay I want to discuss the representation of what we might think of as "the voice of the black oral tradition"—represented here as direct speech. I concern myself as well with Hurston's use of free indirect discourse as the rhetorical analogue to the text's metaphors of "inside" and "outside," so fundamental to the depiction of Janie's quest for consciousness, her very quest to become a speaking black subject.

Zora Neale Hurston rather self-consciously defined her theory of the novel against that received practice of realism which Richard Wright would attempt to revitalize in *Native Son* (1940). Hurston thought that Wright stood at the center of "the sobbing school of Negrohood who hold that nature somehow has given them a low down dirty deal."[2] Against Wright's idea of psychological destruction and chaos, Hurston framed a counternotion which the repressed and conservative maternal figure of *Their Eyes* articulates: "It wasn't for me to fulfill my dreams of what a woman oughta be and to do. Dat's one of de hold-backs of slavery. But nothing can't stop you from wishin'. You can't beat nobody down so low till you can rob 'em of they will." The sign of this transcendent self would be the shaping of a strong, self-reflective voice: "Ah wanted to preach a great sermon about colored women sittin' on high, but they wasn't no pulpit for me. Freedom found me with a baby daughter in mah arms, so ah said ah'd take a broom and a cook-pot and throw up a highway through de wilderness for her. She would expound what ah felt. But somehow she got lost offa de highway and next thing ah knowed here you was in de world. So whilst I was tendin' you of nights ah said ah'd save de text for you."[3] Hurston re-voices this notion of the articulating subject in her autobiography, *Dust Tracks on the Road* (1942), in a curious account of her mother's few moments before death: "Her mouth was slightly open, but her breathing took up so much of her strength that she could not talk. But she looked at me, or so I felt, to speak for her. She depended on me for a voice."[4]

We can begin to understand how far apart Hurston and Wright stand in the tradition if we compare Hurston's passage about her mother with the following passage from Wright's *Black Boy,* a "death-bed" revision of Hurston's passage: "Once, in the night, my mother called me to her bed and told me that she could not endure the pain, that she wanted to die. I held her hand and begged her to be quiet. That night I ceased to react to my mother; feelings were frozen."[5] Wright said that this event, and his mother's extended suffering, "grew into a symbol in [his] mind, gathering to itself all the poverty, the ignorance, the helplessness. . . ." Wright explains: "Her life set the emotional tone of my life, colored the men and women I was to meet in the future, conditioned my relation to events that had not happened, determined my attitude to situations and circumstances I had yet to face." If Hurston figures her final moments with her mother in terms of the search for a voice, then Wright three years later, figures the significance of a similar scene as responsible for a certain "somberness of spirit [he] was never to lose." No two authors in the tradition are more dissimilar than Zora Neale Hurston and Richard Wright.

The narrative voice Hurston created, and her legacy to Afro-American fiction, is a lyrical and disembodied yet individual voice from which emerges a singular longing and utterance, a transcendent, ultimately racial, self, extending far beyond the merely individual. Hurston realized a resonant and authentic narrative voice that echoes and aspires to the status of the impersonality, anonymity, and authority of the black vernacular tradition—a nameless, "self-less" tradition, at once collective and compelling, true, somehow, to the unwritten text of a common "blackness." For Hurston, the search for a "telling" form of language, indeed the search for a black literary language itself, defines the search for the self.

For Richard Wright, nature was ruthless, irreducible, and ineffable. Unlike Hurston, Wright sees fiction not as a model of reality, but as a representative bit of it, a literal report of "the real." Art, for Wright, always remains referential. His blackness, therefore, can never be a mere sign; it is, rather, the text of his great and terrible subject. Accordingly, Wright draws upon the voice of the third-person, past-tense authorial mode, and various tools of empirical social science and naturalism to blend public with private experience, inner with outer history. Rarely does he relinquish the "proprietary consciousness," the constant sign of his presence and of some larger context, which the third-person voice inevitably entails. Rather predictably, Wright found Hurston's great novel to be "counter-revolutionary," and Hurston replied that she wrote novels "and not treatises on sociology."

Hurston and Wright's divergent theories of narrative structure and voice, the cardinal points of a triangle of influence, with the attendant ramifications on the ideology of form and its relation to knowledge and power, comprise a matrix of issues to which subsequent black fictions, by definition, must respond. The rhetorical question that subsequent texts must answer remains the question which the structure of *Their Eyes* answered for Hurston: "In what voice would the Negro speak for her or himself in the language of fiction?" By discussing *Their Eyes*'s topoi and tropes, its depiction of the relations between character, consciousness, and setting, and its engagement of shifting points of view, we can begin to understand how primary remain Hurston's rhetorical strategies in this compelling text.

On the broadest level, *Their Eyes* depicts the search for identity and self-understanding of an Afro-American woman. This quest for self-knowledge, which the text thematizes through an opposition between the "inside" and the "outside" of things, directs attention to itself as a central theme of the novel by certain narrative strategies. I am thinking here especially of the use of the narrative "frame" and of a special form of plot negation. The tale of Janie Crawford-Killicks-Starks-Woods is narrated to her best friend, Phoeby, while the two sit together on Janie's back porch. We, the reader, "overhear" the tale that Janie narrates to her author, whose name we recall signifies the poet. Phoeby, as we might suspect, is an ideal listener: to seduce Janie into narrating her story, Phoeby confesses to her friend, "It's hard for me to understand what you mean, de way you tell it. And then again Ah'm hard of understandin' at times" (p. 19). Phoeby speaks as the true pupil; Janie responds as the true pedagogue: " 'Naw, 'tain't nothin' lak you might think. So 'tain't no use in me telling you somethin' unless Ah give you de understandin' to go 'long wid it. Unless you see de fur, a mink skin ain't no different from a coon hide. Looka heah, Phoeby, is Sam waitin' on you for his supper?' " (p. 19).

At the end of the telling of Janie's tale, an interruption which the text signifies by ellipses and a broad white space, Phoeby, always the perfect pupil, responds to her teacher as each of us wishes the student to respond: " 'Lawd!' Phoeby breathed out heavily, 'Ah done growed ten feet higher from jus' listenin' tuh you, Janie. Ah ain't satisfied wid maself no mo'. Ah means tuh make Sam take me fishin' wid him after this. Nobody better not criticize yuh in mah hearin' ' " (p. 284). Such a powerfully transforming tale has effected an enhanced awareness even in Janie's transfixed pupil. And to narrate this tale, Hurston draws upon the framing device, which serves on the order of plot to interrupt the received narrative flow of linear narration of the realistic novel, and which serves on the order of theme to enable Janie to recapitulate, control, and narrate her own story of becoming, the key sign of sophisticated understanding of the self. Indeed, Janie develops from a nameless child, known only as Alphabet, who cannot even recognize her own likeness as a "colored" person in a photograph, to the implied narrator of her own tale of self-consciousness. This is merely one of Hurston's devices to achieve thematic unity.

Hurston matches the use of the frame with the use of negation as a mode of narrating the separate elements of the plot. The text opens and ends in the third-person omniscient voice, which allows for a maximum of information giving. Its third paragraph commences: "So the beginning of this was a woman and she had come back from burying the dead" (p. 9). By introducing this evidence of the return from burying the dead, Hurston negates her text's themes of discovery, rebirth, and renewal, only to devote the remainder of her text to realizing these same themes. Hurston also draws upon negation to reveal, first, the series of self-images that Janie does not wish to be and, second, to define the matrix of obstacles that frustrate her desire to know herself. The *realization* of the full text of *Their Eyes* represents the fulfillment of the novel's positive potentialities, by which I mean Janie's discovery of self-knowledge.

How does this negated form of plot development unfold? Hurston rather cleverly develops her plot by depicting a series of intimate relationships in which Janie engages with a fantasy of sexual desire, then with her grandmother, with her first husband, Logan Killicks, her second husband, Joe Starks, and finally with her ideal lover, Verigible Woods, "Tea Cake." Her first three relationships are increasingly problematic and self-negating, complex matters which Hurston renders through an *inverse* relation between character, or consciousness, on one hand, and setting on the other. If we think about it, Janie comes to occupy progressively larger physical spaces—Nancy's cabin in the backyard of the Washburn's place; Logan Killicks's "often-mentioned" sixty acres; and ultimately Joe Starks's big white wooden house, replete with bannisters, and his centrally located general store. Indeed, it is fair to say that Mayor Starks owns the town. With each successive move to a larger physical space, however, her housemate seeks to confine Janie's consciousness inversely, seemingly, by just as much. It is only when she eschews that which her Grandmother had named the "protection" (p. 30), both of material possessions and of rituals of entitlement (i.e., bourgeois marriage), and moves to the swamp, to "the muck," with Verigible "Tea Cake" *Woods* that she, at last, gains control of her understanding of herself. We can, in fact, conclude that the text opposes bourgeois notions of "progress" (Killicks owns the only organ "amongst colored folks"; Joe Starks is a man of "positions and possessions") and of the Protestant work ethic, to more creative and lyrical notions of unity. Tea Cake's only possession is a guitar. The relation between character and setting, then, is an ideal one for the pedagogical purpose of revealing that "character" and "setting" are merely aspects of narrative strategy and not "things" in the ordinary sense that we understand a "thing."

Their Eyes consists of a complex mode of narration. This mode of narration consists, at either extreme, of narrative commentary (rendered in third-person omniscient and third-person restricted voices) and of character's discourse (which manifests itself as a direct speech in what Hurston called "dialect"). Hurston's innovation is to be found in the middle spaces between these two extremes of narration and discourse, in what we might think of as represented discourse, which, as I am defining it, includes both indirect discourse and free indirect discourse. It was Hurston who introduced free indirect discourse into Afro-American narration. It is this innovation, as I hope to demonstrate, which enables her to represent various traditional modes of Afro-American rhetorical play while simultaneously representing her protagonist's growth in self-consciousness through free indirect discourse. Even more curious, Hurston's narrative strategy depends upon the blending of the text's two most extreme and seemingly opposed modes of narration—that is, narrative commentary, which begins at least in the diction of standard English, and character's discourse, which is always foregrounded by quotation marks and by its "black" diction. As the protagonist approaches self-consciousness, however, not only does the text use free indirect discourse to represent her development, but the *diction* of the black character's discourse comes to *inform* the diction of the voice of narrative commentary such that, in several passages, it is extraordinarily difficult to distinguish the narrator's voice from the protagonist's. In other words, through the use of what Hurston called a highly "adorned" free indirect discourse, which we might think of as a third or mediating term between narrative commentary and direct discourse, *Their Eyes Were Watching God* resolves that implicit tension between standard English and black dialect, the two voices that function as verbal counterpoints in the text's opening paragraphs.

Let us return briefly to the triangle of influence that I have drawn to connect *Native Son* and *Their Eyes Were Watching God*. As I argued earlier, for Zora Neale Hurston the search for a form of narration and discourse, indeed the search for a black formal language itself, defines both the search for the self and is its rhetorical or textual analogue. Not only would Ralph Ellison concur, but he would go farther. Ellison's is a literal "morality" of narration. As he writes in *Invisible Man*, "To remain unaware of one's form is to live death," an idea that Hurston prefigures in *Their Eyes*, from the moment when the child, Janie (Alphabet), fails to recognize her own image in a group photograph to the moment in the text when, first, Janie learns to distinguish between her "inside" and her "outside," and second, when the diction of the black character's dialect comes to inform heavily the diction of the narrative commentary. We might think of Hurston's formal relation to Wright and Ellison in this way: whereas the narrative strategy of *Native Son* consists primarily of a disembodied, omniscient narrative commentary similar to the voice that introduces *Their Eyes*, Ellison's first-person narrative strategy in *Invisible Man* revises the possibilities of representing the development of consciousness that Hurston chose to render through a dialect-informed free indirect discourse. Wright uses free indirect discourse to some extent in *Native Son*, but its diction is not informed by Gibber's *speech*, only by his *thoughts*. The distinction between figures of speech and figures of thought is one useful way to distinguish between Wright and Hurston's narrative strategies. The narrative strategies of *Native Son* and *Invisible Man* represent, then, the extremes of narrative mode in the tradition; the narrative strategy of *Their Eyes* partakes of both these as well as of a subtle blend of the two. Rhetorically, at least, *Native Son* and *Invisible Man* Signify upon the strategies of *Their Eyes Were Watching God*. There can be little doubt that this sort of narration, so concerned to represent the sheer multiplicity of American oral narrative forms and voices, is more closely related to the "speakerly" strategies of *Their Eyes* than it is to most other texts in the Afro-American canon. These are rather large claims to make, but they are firmly supported by the Signifyin(g) strategies of the text itself.

Hurston, whose definition of "signify" in *Mules and Men* is one of the earliest in the linguistic literature, had made *Their Eyes Were Watching*

God into a paradigmatic Signifyin(g) text. Its narrative strategies resolve the implicit tension between the literal and the figurative, between the semantic and the rhetorical, contained in standard usages of the term "signifying." *Their Eyes* draws upon the trope of Signifyin(g) both as thematic matter and as a rhetorical strategy. Janie gains her voice, as it were, within her husband's store not only by daring to speak aloud where others might hear, but by engaging in that ritual of Signifyin(g) (which her husband had expressly disallowed) and by openly Signifyin(g) upon the impotency of her husband, Joe, Mayor, "I-God," himself. Janie kills her husband rhetorically by naming his impotence (with her voice) in a public ritual of Signifyin(g). His image fatally wounded, he soon succumbs to a displaced "kidney" failure.

Their Eyes Signifies upon *Cane* in several ways. First, its plot reverses the movement of *Cane*'s plot. Whereas the settings of *Cane* move from broad open fields through ever-diminishing physical spaces to a circle of light in a dark and damp cellar (corresponding to the level of self-consciousness of the central characters), *Their Eyes*'s settings within its embedded narrative move from the confines of Granny's tiny cabin in the Washburn's backyard through increasingly larger physical structures, finally ending "on the Muck" in the Everglades, where she and her lover, Tea Cake, realize the male-female relationship for which Janie had longed so very urgently. Similarly, whereas *Cane* represents painfully unconsummated relationships, the agony of which seems to intensify in direct proportion to the diminishment of physical setting, true consummation occurs in *Their Eyes* once Janie eschews the values implied by material possessions (such as middle-class houses, especially those in which sit idle women who rock their lives away), learns to play with Tea Cake, and moves to the swamp. Furthermore, the trope of the swamp in *Their Eyes* signifies exactly the opposite of that in W. E. B. Du Bois's *Quest for the Silver Fleece*. Whereas the swamp in Du Bois's text figures as an uncontrolled chaos that must be plowed under and controlled, for Hurston the swamp is the trope of the freedom of erotic love, the antithesis of the bourgeois life and order that her protagonist flees but to which Du Bois's protagonists aspire. Du Bois's characters gain economic security by ploughing up and cultivating cotton in the swamp; Janie flees the bourgeois life that Du Bois's characters realize, precisely by abandoning traditional values for the uncertainties and potential chaos of the uncultivated, untamed swamp, where love and death linger side by side. We recall Du Bois's shadowy figure who seems to dwell in the swamp is, oddly enough, named "Zora."

But *Their Eyes* is also a paradigmatic Signifyin(g) text because of its representations, through several subtexts or embedded narratives presented as the characters's discourse, of traditional black rhetorical games or rituals. It is the text's *imitation* of these examples of traditionally black rhetorical rituals and modes of storytelling that allows us to think of it as a "speakerly text." For in a speakerly text, certain rhetorical structures seem to exist primarily as *representations of oral narration,* rather than as integral aspects of plot or character development. These verbal rituals signify the sheer play of black language which *Their Eyes* seems to celebrate. These virtuoso displays of verbal play constitute Hurston's complex response to the New Negro Poets's strictures of the use of dialect as a poetic diction. *Their Eyes Were Watching God*'s narrative *Signifies upon* James Weldon Johnson's arguments against dialect just as surely as Sterling A. Brown's *Southern Road* does. Indeed, we are free to think of these two texts as discursive analogues. Moreover, Hurston's masterful use of free indirect discourse (*style indirect libre*) allows her to Signify upon the tension between the two voices of Jean Toomer's *Cane* by adding to direct and indirect speech a strategy through which she can privilege the black oral tradition, which Toomer found to be problematical and dying.

Figures of play are the dominant repeated figures in the second half of *Their Eyes.* After Janie meets Tea Cake, figures of play supplant those floral figures that appeared each time Janie dreamed of consummated love. Moreover, it is the rhetorical play that occurs regularly on the porch of his store that Janie's husband, Jody, prevents Janie from enjoying. As the text reads,

> Janie loved conversation and sometimes she thought up good stories on the mule, but Joe had forbidden her to indulge. He didn't want her talking after such trashy people. "You'se Mrs. Mayor Starks, Janie. I god, Ah can't see what uh woman uh yo' sability would want tuh be treasurin' all dat gum-grease from folks dat don'e teven own de house dey sleep in. 'Tain't no earthly use. They's jus some puny humans playin' round de toes uh Time." (p. 85)

When the Signifyin(g) rituals commence—rituals that the text describes as created by "big picture talkers [who] were using a side of the world for a canvas"—Jody forces Janie to retreat inside of the store, much against her will.

Eventually, however, this friction ignites a heated argument between the two, the key terms of which are repeated, in reverse, when Janie later falls in love with Tea Cake. Their exchange follows:

> "Ah had tuh laugh at de people out dere in de woods dis mornin', Janie. You can't help but laugh at de capers they cuts. But all the same, ah wish mah people would git mo' business in 'em and not spend so much time on foolishness."
>
> "Everybody can't be lak you, Jody. Somebody is bound tuh want tuh laugh and play."
>
> "Who don't love tuh laugh and play?"
>
> "You make out like you don't, anyhow." (p. 98)

It is this tension between work and play, between maintaining appearances of respectability and control against the seemingly idle, nonquantifiable verbal maneuvers that "produce" nothing, which becomes the central sign of the distance between Janie's unarticulated aspirations and the material aspirations signified by Jody's desire to "be a big voice," a self-designation that Jody repeats with alacrity almost as much as he repeats his favorite parenthetical, "I-god."

"Play" is also the text's word for the Signifyin(g) rituals that imitate "courtship," such as the symbolic action executed by Sam Watson, Lige Moss, and Charlie Jones, which the text describes in this way: "They know it's not courtship. It's acting out courtship and everybody is in the play" (p. 105). Play, finally, is the irresistible love potion that Tea Cake administers to Janie. Tea Cake, an apparently unlikely suitor of Joe Stark's widow, since he is a drifter and is generally thought to be "irresponsible," seduces Janie by teaching her to play checkers. When Janie responds to his challenge of a game with "Ah can't play uh lick," Tea Cake proceeds to set up the board and teach her the rules. Janie "found herself glowing inside. Somebody wanted her to play. Somebody thought it natural for her to play. That was even nice. She looked him over and got little thrills from every one of his good points" (p. 146). No one had taught her to play in her adulthood. Joe's prohibition the text repeats as Tea Cake's perceptive mode of seduction. As Tea Cake concludes prophetically, "You gointuh be uh good player too, after while." And "after while," Janie and Tea Cake teach each other to become "good players" in what the text depicts as a game of love.

This repeated figure of play is only the thematic analogue to the text's rhetorical play, plays of language that seem to be present essentially to reveal the complexity of black oral forms of narration. For *Their Eyes Were Watching God* is replete with storytellers, or "signifiers," as the black tradition has named them. These signifiers are granted a remarkable amount of space in this text to reveal their talents. These imitations of oral narrations, it is crucial to recall, unfold within what the text represents as Janie's framed tale, the tale of her quests with Tea Cake to the far horizon and her lonely return home. This "oral" narrative commences in Chapter Two, while Janie and her friend, Phoeby, sit on Janie's back-porch and "the kissing, young darkness became a monstropolous old thing while Janie talked" (p. 19). Then follow almost three full pages of Janie's direct speech, "while all around the house, the night time put on flesh and blackness" (p. 23). Two paragraphs of narrative commentary follow Janie's narration; then, curiously, the narrative "fades" into "a spring-time afternoon in West Florida," the springtime of Janie's adolescence.

Without ever releasing its proprietary consciousness, the disembodied narrative voice reassumes control over the telling of Janie's story after nine paragraphs of direct discourse. This narrative shift is from third-person to "no-person" (that is, the seemingly unmediated representation of Janie's direct speech), back to the third-person of an embedded or framed narrative. This device we encounter most frequently in the story-telling devices of film, in which a first-person narrative "yields," as it were, to the form of narration that we associate with the cinema. ("Kabnis," we remember, "imitates the drama.") *Their Eyes Were Watching God* would seem to be imitating this mode of narration, with this fundamental difference: the bracketed tale in the novel is "told" by an omniscient, third-person narrator who "reports" thoughts, feelings, and events that Janie could not possibly have heard or seen. This framed narrative continues for the next eighteen chapters, until in chapter 20 the text indicates the end of Janie's story-telling to Phoeby, which we have "overheard" by the broad white spaces and a series of widely spaced ellipses that I mentioned earlier.

This rather unusual form of narration of the tale within a tale has been the subject of some controversy about the "success" or "failure" of Janie's depiction as a dynamic character who comes to know herself. Rather than retread that fruitless terrain, I would suggest that the subtleness of this narrative strategy allows for, as would no other mode of narration, the representation of the forms of *oral narration* that *Their Eyes* imitates so often. So often, in fact, that the very subject of this text would appear to be not Janie's quest, but the emulation of the phonetic, grammatical, and lexical structures of actual speech, an emulation designed to produce the illusion of oral narration. Indeed, each of the oral rhetorical structures emulated within Janie's bracketed tale functions to remind the reader that she or he is "overhearing" Janie's narrative to Phoeby, which unfolds on her porch, that crucial place of storytelling both in this text and in the black community. Each of these playful narratives are, by definition, tales within the bracketed tale, and most exist as significations of rhetorical play rather than as events that develop the text's plot. Indeed, these embedded narratives, consisting as they do of long exchanges of direct discourse, often serve as plot impediments but simultaneously enable a multiplicity of narrative voices to assume control of the text.

Zora Neale Hurston seems to be not only the first scholar to have defined the trope of Signifyin(g), but the first to represent the ritual itself. Hurston represents a Signifyin(g) ritual in *Mules and Men,* then glosses the word "signify" as a means of "showing off," rhetorically. The exchange is an appropriate one to repeat, because it demonstrates that women most certainly can, and do, Signify upon men, and because it prefigures the scene of Signification in *Their Eyes* that proves to be a verbal sign of such importance to Janie's quest for consciousness. The text reads:

> "Talkin' 'bout dogs," put in Gene Oliver, "they got plenty sense. Nobody can't fool dogs much."
>
> "And speakin' 'bout hams," cut in Big Sweet meaningly, "if Joe Willard don't stay out of dat bunk he was in last night, Ah'm gonter sprinkle some salt down his back and sugar-cure *his* hams."
>
> Joe snatched his pole out of the water with a jerk and glared at Big Sweet, who stood sidewise looking at him most pointedly.
>
> "Aw, woman, quit tryin' to signify."
>
> "Ah kin signify all Ah please, Mr. Nappy-Chin, so long as Ah know what Ah'm talkin' about."[6]

This is a classic Signification, an exchange of meaning and intention between two lovers of some urgency.

I use the word "exchange" here to echo Hurston's use in her essay "Characteristics of Negro Expression." Hurston in this essay argues that "language is like money," and its development can be equated metaphorically with the development in the marketplace of the means of exchange from bartered "actual goods," which "evolve into coin" (coins symbolizing wealth). Coins evolve into legal tender, and legal tender evolves into "cheques for certain usages." Hurston's illustrations are especially instructive. People "with highly developed languages," she writes, "have words for detached ideas. That is legal tender." The linguistic equivalent of "legal tender" consists of words such as "chair," which comes to stand for "that-which-we-squat-on." "Groan-causers" evolves into "spear," and so on. "Cheque words" include those such as "ideation" and "pleonastic." *Paradise Lost* and *Sartor Resartus,* she continues, "are written in cheque words!" But "the primitive man," she argues, eschews legal tender and cheque words; he "exchanges descriptive words," describing "one act . . . in terms of another." More specifically, she concludes, black expression turns upon both the "interpretation of the English language in terms of pictures" as well as upon the supplement of what she calls "action words," such as "chop-axe," "sitting-chair," and "cook pot." It is the supplement of action, she maintains, which underscores her use of the word "exchange."

Such an exchange is that between Big Sweet and Joe Willard. As the exchange continues, not only does the characters' language exemplify Hurston's theory, but the definitions of Signifyin(g) that I have been drawing upon throughout this essay are also exemplified. Let us continue the exchange:

> "See dat?" Joe appealed to the other men. "We git a day off and figger we kin ketch some fish and enjoy ourselves, but naw, some wimmins got to drag behind us, even to de lake."
>
> "You didn't figger Ah was draggin' behind you when you was bringin' dat Sears and Roebuck catalogue over to my house and beggin' me to choose my ruthers. Lemme tell *you* something, *any* time Ah shack up wid any man Ah gives myself de privilege to go whereever he might be, night or day. Ah got de law in my mouth."
>
> "Lawd, ain't she specifyin'!" sniggered Wiley.
>
> "Oh, Big Sweet does dat," agreed Richardson. "Ah knowed she had somethin' up her sleeve when she got Lucy and come along."
>
> "Lawd," Willard said bitterly. " 'My people, my people,' as de monkey said. You fool with Aunt Hagar's chillun and they'll sho discriminate you and put you' name in de streets." (pp. 161–62)

Specifying, putting one's name in the streets, and "as de monkey said" are all figures for Signifyin(g). In *Dust Tracks on a Road,* she even defines "specifying" as "giving a reading" in the following passage:

> The bookless may have difficulty in reading a paragraph in a newspaper, but when they get down to "playing the dozens" [Signifyin(g)] they have no equal in America, and, I'd risk a sizable bet, in the whole

world. Starting off in the first by calling you a seven-sided son-of-a-
bitch, and pausing to name the sides, they proceed to "specify" until
the tip-top branch of your family tree has been "given a reading."
(p. 225)

The sort of close reading that I am attempting here is also an act of Specifying.

Let me return briefly to Hurston's theory of "Negro Expression" before turning to explicate rhetorical strategies at work in *Their Eyes Were
Watching God*. Her typology of black oral narration, in addition to "picture" and "action" words, consists of what she calls "the will to adorn,"
by which she means the use of densely figurative language, the presence
of "revision," which she defines as "[making] over a great part of the
[English] tongue," and the use of "metaphor and simile," "the double-
descriptive," and "verbal nouns." It is Hurston's sense of revision, defined
as "originality [in] the modification of ideas" and "of language," as well
as "reinterpretation," which is the ultimate meaning of the trope of Sig-
nifyin(g). By "revision," she also means "imitation" and "mimicry," for
which she says "the Negro, the world over, is famous," and which she
defines as "an art in itself." The Negro, she claims, imitates and revises,
not "from a feeling of inferiority," but rather "for the love of it." This notion of imitation, repetition, and revision, she maintains, is fundamental
to "all art," indeed is the nature of art itself, even Shakespeare's.

Near the end of her compelling essay, Hurston argues that "dialect" is
"Negro speech," and Negro speech, she contends throughout the essay,
is quite capable of expressing the most subtle nuances of meaning, despite "the majority of writers of Negro dialect and the burnt-cork artists."
"Fortunately," she concludes, "we don't have to believe them. We may go
directly to the Negro and let him speak for himself." Using in large part
Hurston's own theory of black oral narration, we can gain some understanding of the modes of narration at work in *Their Eyes* and thereby
demonstrate why I have chosen to call it a "speakerly text." I derive this
term both from Roland Barthes's opposition between the "readerly" and
the "writerly" texts—the binarism of which I am here *Signifyin(g)* upon—
as well as from the trope of "the talking book," which is not only the Afro-
American tradition's fundamental repeated trope but also a phrase used
by Zora Neale Hurston and Ishmael Reed to define their own narrative
strategies.

It is a fairly straightforward matter to list just a few of what we might think of as Hurston's "figures of adornment," the specifically black examples of figurative language that Hurston labels "simile and metaphor," "double-descriptives," and "verbal-nouns." These follow, as expressed in *Their Eyes:*

1 An envious heart makes a treacherous ear.
2 Us colored folks is branches without roots.
3 They's a lost ball in high grass.
4 She . . . left her wintertime wid me.
5 Ah wanted yuh to pick from a higher bush.
6 You got uh williy' mind, but youse too light behind.
7 . . . he's de wind and we'se de grass.
8 He was a man wid salt in him.
9 . . . what dat multiplied cockroach told you.
10 still-bait
11 big-bellies
12 gentlemanfied man
13 cemetery-dead
14 black-dark
15 duskin-down-dark[7]

This list certainly could be extended. Suffice it to say that the diction of both the character's discourse and the free indirect discourse are replete with the three types of adornment that Hurston argued were fundamental to black oral narration.

In addition to these sorts of figures of adornment, *Their Eyes* is comprised of several long exchanges of direct discourse, which seem to be present in the text more for their own sake than to develop the plot. *Their Eyes* consists of a remarkable percentage of direct speech, rendered in black dialect, as if to display the capacity of black language to convey an extraordinarily wide variety of ideas and feelings. Frequently, these exchanges between characters extend for two or three pages, with little or no interruption from the text's narrator. When such narrative commentary does surface, it often serves to function as stage directions rather than as a traditional onmiscient voice, as if to underscore Hurston's contention that it is drama that "permeates [the Negro's] entire self" and the dramatic to which black oral narration aspires. Because, as Hurston writes, "an audience is a necessary part of any drama," these Signifyin(g) rituals tend to occur out-of-doors at the communal scene of oral instruction, on the porches of homes and stores.

The representation of modes of black narration begins, as we have seen, with Janie's narration of her story to Phoeby, the framed tale in which most of the novel's action unfolds. Throughout this narrative, the word "voice" recurs with great frequency. Who *speaks,* indeed, proves to be of crucial import to Janie's quest for freedom, but who *sees* and who *hears* at all points in the text remain fundamental as well. We recall that Phoeby's "hungry listening helped Janie to tell her story." Almost as soon as Janie's narrative begins, however, Nanny assumes control of the text and narrates the story of Janie's genealogy from slavery to the present as Janie listens painfully. This quasi-slave narrative, rendered as a tale within a tale, is one of the few instances of direct speech that serves as a function of the plot. Subsequent "speaking" narrators assume control of the narrative primarily to demonstrate forms of traditional oral narration.

The repeated metaphors of inside and outside begin in the text's first chapter. Janie narrates her tale, as Phoeby listens outside her back porch. Janie's metaphorical and densely lyrical "outside observations," the narrator tells us, "buried themselves in her flesh." After she experiences her first orgasm, then kisses Johnny Taylor, she extends herself "outside of her dream" and goes "inside of the house." It is inside houses in which a series of people (first her grandmother, Nanny; then her first husband, Logan Killicks; then her second husband, Joe Starks) attempt to oppress her and prevent her from speaking and asserting herself. Janie dreams out of doors, in metaphors of flowering springtime, often under pear trees. When Logan insults her, the narrator says that "she turned wrongside out just standing there and feeling." Jody seduces her with dreams of "far horizons," "under the tree" and outdoors "in the scrub oaks." That which Jody speaks *out loud* and that which Janie thinks *inside* come to represent an opposition of such dimensions that we are not at all surprised when their final confrontation occurs. Janie is forced to retreat inside the store when the storytelling rituals commence.

Janie's crucial, if ironic, scene of self-discovery is represented rather subtly in this figurative framework of inside and outside. This coming to consciousness is not represented by a speaking scene, however; it is represented in these inside-outside figures. When she finally does speak, therefore, by Signifyin(g) in the store upon Jody's impotence, the gaining of her own voice is a sign of her authority, but *not* a sign of a newly found *unified* identity. Janie's speaking voice, rather, is an outcome of her *consciousness of division.*[8] Here is a rhetoric of division.

The text represents this consciousness of division in two scenes that transpire in the chapter preceding the one in which she Signifies upon Jody. The text reads: "The spirit of the marriage left the bedroom and took to living in the parlor. It was there to shake hands whenever company came to visit, but it never went back inside the bedroom again. So she put something in there to represent the spirit like a Virgin Mary image in a church. The bed was no longer a daisyfield for her and Joe to play in. It was a place where she went and laid down when she was sleepy and tired" (p. 111). In this passage, Janie's inner feelings, "the spirit of the marriage," are projected onto outer contiguous physical spaces (the bedroom and the parlor). Her *inside*, in other words, is figured as an *outside*, in the rooms. Her bed, moreover, ceases to be a place for lovemaking, as signified by both the daisy-field metaphor and the metaphor of play (reminding us, through the repetition, of her central metaphors of dream and aspiration that repeat so often in the novel's first half). The contiguous relation of the bedroom and the parlor, both physical spaces through which the metaphorical "spirit of the marriage" now moves, reveals two modes of figuration overlapping in Janie's indirectly reported thoughts for the first time—that is, one mode dependent upon substitution, the other on contiguity.[9] Clearly, the rhetorical relations between "sex" and "spirit of marriage," and "spirit of the marriage," "bedroom," and "parlor" are complex.

Until this moment in the text, Janie's "literacy" was represented only as a metaphorical literacy. Janie's "conscious life," the text tells us, "had commenced at Nanny's gate," across which she had kissed Johnny Taylor just after experiencing her first orgasm under her "blossoming pear trees in the back-yard." In the moving passage that precedes the event but prepares us for it by describing her increasing awareness of her own sexuality, rendered in free indirect discourse, Janie names her feelings in her first metaphor: "The rose of the world was breathing out smell. It followed her through all her waking moments and caressed her in her sleep" (pp. 23–24). Janie's first language, the language of her own desire, is registered in a lyrical and metaphorical diction found in these passages of free indirect discourse.

One paragraph later, as a sign that she can name her division, the direction of her figuration reverses itself. Whereas in the first scene she projects her inner feelings onto outer physical space, in this scene she *internalizes* an outer physical space, her scene of oppression, the store: "Janie stood where he left her for unmeasured time and thought. She stood there until something fell off the shelf inside her. Then she went inside there to see what it was. It was her image of Jody tumbled down and shattered. But looking at it she saw that it never was the flesh and blood figure of her dreams. Just something she had grabbed up to drape her dreams over" (p. 112). Janie has "internalized" the store through the synechdoche on the shelf. As Barbara Johnson summarizes the rhetorical import of this scene: "These two figural mini-narratives [represent] a kind of chiasmus, or crossover, in which the first paragraph presents an externalization of the inner, a metaphorically grounded metonymy, while the second paragraph presents an internalization of the outer, or a metonymically grounded metaphor. . . . The reversals operated by the chiasmus map out a reversal of the power relations between Janie and Joe." [10] When she speaks aloud in public against Jody and thereby redefines their relationship, it is the awareness of this willed figurative division of which her speaking voice is the sign. As the text reads, Janie "found that she had a host of thoughts she had never expressed to him, and numerous emotions that she had never let Jody know about. Things packed up and put away in parts of her heart where he could never find them" (p. 112).

Janie is now truly fluent in the language of the figurative: "She had an inside and an outside now and suddenly knew how not to mix them." The text represents this fluency in this way: "Then one day she sat and watched the shadow of herself going about tending the store and prostrating itself before Jody, while all the time she herself sat under a shady tree with the wind blowing through her hair and her clothes. Somebody near about making summertime out of lonesomeness" (p. 119). Janie's discovery of an ability to name her own division and move the parts simultaneously through contiguous spaces, her newly found and apparently exhilarating double-consciousness, is that crucial event that enables her to speak and assert herself after decades of being defined almost exclusively by others.

The text prefigures this event. The sign that this consciousness of her own division liberates her speaking voice is Janie's first instance of voicing her feelings within the store, which occurs in the text midway between the "slapping" scene in which she first internally "names" her outside and inside (p. 112) and the scene in which she so tellingly Signifies upon Joe (pp. 121–22). Janie speaks after listening in a painful silence as Coker and Joe Lindsay discuss the merits of beating women:

". . . Tony love her too good," said Coker. "Ah could break her if she wuz mine. Ah'd break her or kill her. Makin' uh fool outa me in front of everybody."

"Tony won't never hit her. He says beatin' women is just like steppin' on baby chickens. He claims 'tain't no place on uh woman tuh hit," Joe Lindsay said with scornful disapproval, "but Ah'd kill uh baby just born dis mawnin' fuh uh thing like dat. 'Tain't nothin' but low-down spitefulness 'ginst her husband make her do it." (p. 116)

This exchange, of course, refigures the crucial scene in which Joe slaps Janie because her meal was not well prepared. Joe Lindsay's comparison in this passage of "beatin' women" and "steppin' on baby chickens" echoes Joe's proclamation to Janie that "somebody got to think for women and chickens and cows" made during their argument about who has the right "to tell" (pp. 110–11). After Joe Lindsay finishes speaking and after his sexist remarks are affirmed as Gospel by Jim Stone, Janie—for the first time—speaks out against the men's opinion about the merits of beatings. As the text states, "Janie did what she had never done before, that is, thrust herself into the conversation":

"Sometimes God gits familiar wid us women-folks too and talks his inside business. He told me how surprised He was 'bout y'all turn- ing out so smart after Him makin' yuh different; and how surprised y'all is goin' tuh be if you ever find out you don't know half as much 'bout us as you think you do. It's so easy to make yo'self out God Almighty when you ain't got nothin' tuh strain against but *women and* chickens." (p. 117, emphasis added)

Janie reveals God's "inside business" to the superficial store-talkers, warn- ing all who can hear her voice that a "surprise" lies in waiting for those who see only appearances and never penetrate to the tenor of things. Joe, we learn just four pages later, is in for the surprise of his life: the killing timbre of Janie's true, inner voice. Joe's only response to this first scene of speaking is to tell his wife, "You gettin' too moufy, Janie," a veritable literalizing of the metaphor of "mouth." He then issues an order, the ulti- mate sign of ignoring and circumventing Janie's domain: "Go fetch me de checker-board *and* de checkers." Joe's turn to the male world of play at Janie's expense leads Janie to "play the dozens" on his sexuality and thus to his death. These metaphorical echoes and exchanges are deadly serious in Hurston's text.

Earlier in the narrative, Hicks defined the metaphorical as "co-talkin'," and says that his is "too deep" for women to understand. He explains, "Dey love to hear me talk because dey can't understand it. . . . Too much co to it" (p. 59). At the same time that Janie learns to name her inside and outside and to move between them, Jody argues that women "need tellin' " because "somebody got to think for women and chillen and chickens and cows" because a man sees "one thing" and "understands ten," while a woman sees "ten things and don't understand one" (pp. 110–11). Jody ironically accuses Janie of failing to understand how one thing can imply or be substituted for ten, thereby arguing that Janie does not understand metaphor, whereas Janie is a master of metaphor whose self-liberation awaits only the knowledge of how to "narrate" her figures contiguously. It is Jody who has failed to read the situation properly. As a character in *Mules and Men* argues, most people do not understand the nature of the figurative, which he characterizes as an expression that has "a hidden meaning', jus' like de Bible. Everybody can't understand what they mean," he continues. "Most people is thin-brained. They's born wid they feet under the moon. Some folks is born wid they feet on de sun and they kin seek out de inside meanin' of words" (pp. 162–63). Jody, it turns out, is both thin-brained and thin-skinned and proves to have been born with his feet under the moon. He is all vehicle, no tenor. The "inside meanings of words," of course, we think of as the tenor, or the "inside" meaning of a rhetorical figure, while the "outside" corresponds to its "vehicle." Janie, as the text repeats again and again in its central metaphor for her character, is a child of the sun.

Hurston's use of free indirect discourse is central to her larger strategy of critiquing what we might think of as a "male writing." Joe Starks, we remember, fondly and unconsciously refers to himself as "I-God." During the lamp-lighting ceremony (pp. 71–74), Joe is represented as the creator (or at least the purchaser) of light. Joe is the text's figure of authority and voice, indeed the authority of voice:

> "Naw, Jody, it jus' looks lak it keeps us in some way we ain't natu-
> ral wid one 'nother. You'se always off talkin' and fixin' things, and
> Ah feels lak Ah'm jus' markin' time. Hope it soon gits over."
> "Over, Janie? I god, Ah ain't even started good. Ah told you in de
> very first beginnin' dat Ah aimed tuh be uh big voice. You oughta be
> glad, 'cause dat makes uh big woman outa you." (p. 74)

Joe says that "in de very first beginnin' " he "aimed tuh be uh big voice," an echo of the first verse of The Gospel According to St. John: "In the beginning was the Word, and the Word was with God, and the Word was God." Joe, we know, sees himself and wishes to be seen as the God-figure of his community. The text tells us that when speakers on formal occasions prefaced their remarks with the phrase "our beloved Mayor," the phrase was equivalent to "one of those statements that everybody says but nobody believes like 'God is everywhere'" (p. 77). Joe is the figure of the male author, he who has "authored" both Eatonville and Janie's existences. We remember that when Joe lights the town's newly acquired lamp, Mrs. Bogle's alto voice sings "Jesus, the light of the world":

> We walk in de light, de beautiful light
> Come where the dew drops of mercy shine bright.
> Shine all around us by day and by night
> Jesus, the light of the world.
>
> (p. 73)

So, when Janie Signifies upon Joe, telling him that he not only is nothing but a man, but an *impotent* man at that, the revelation of the truth *kills* him. Janie, in effect, has *rewritten* Joe's text of himself and liberated herself in the process. Janie "writes" herself into being by *naming*, by speaking herself free.

It is prefigured, perhaps, in Hurston's subtle revision of Douglass's well-known apostrophe in the opening two paragraphs of *Their Eyes*. Hurston underscores her revision of Douglass's canonical text by using two chiasmuses in her open paragraphs. The subject of the second paragraph of *Their Eyes* (women) reverses the subject of the first (men) and figures the nature of their respective desire in opposite terms: a man's desire becomes reified into a disappearing ship, and he is transformed from a human being into "a Watcher," his desire personified onto an object, beyond his grasp or control, external to himself. Nanny, significantly, uses this "male" figure ("Ah could see uh big ship at a distance" [p. 35]) as does Tea Cake, whose use *reverses* Douglass's by indicating Tea Cake's claim of control of his fate and capacity to satisfy Janie's desire: "Can't no ole man stop me from gittin' no ship for yuh if dat's what you want. Ah'd git dat ship out from under him so slick til he'd be walkin' de water lak ole Peter befo' he knowed it" (p. 154).

A woman, by contrast, represents desire metaphorically, rather than metonymically, by controlling the process of *memory*, an active subjective process figured in the pun on (re)membering. Such is the process of narration which Janie will share with her friend, Phoeby, which we shall "overhear." For a woman, "the dream is the truth," the truth is her dream.

Janie is thought to be (and is maintained) "inarticulate" by her first two husbands, but is a master of metaphorical narration; Joe Starks, her most oppressive husband, by contrast, is a master of metonym, an opposition through which Janie must navigate her selves to achieve self-knowledge. The first sentence of the text ("Now, women forget all those things they don't want to remember, and remember everything they don't want to forget") is itself a chiasmus (women/remember//remember/forget) similar in structure to Douglass's famous chiasmus ("You have seen how a man became a slave, you will see how a slave became a man.") Indeed, Douglass's major contribution to the slaves's narrative was to make chiasmus the central trope of the slave narration, in which a slave-object makes him- or herself into a human-subject through the act of writing. The overarching rhetorical strategy of the slave narratives written after 1845 can be represented as a chiasmus, as repetition and reversal. Hurston, in these enigmatic opening paragraphs, Signifies upon Douglass through formal revision, and creates a well-defined space for a woman's narrative voice in a male-determined tradition.

If *Their Eyes* makes impressive use of the figures of outside and inside, as well as the metaphor of double-consciousness as the prerequisite to becoming a speaking subject, then the text's mode of narration, especially "speakerlyness," serves as the rhetorical analogue to this theme. I use the word "double" here intentionally, both to echo W. E. B. Du Bois's metaphor for the Afro-American's peculiar psychology of citizenship and to avoid the limited description of free indirect discourse as a "dual voice," Roy Pascal's term.[11] Rather than a "dual voice," free indirect discourse as manifested in *Their Eyes* is a dramatic way of expressing a *divided* self. Janie's self, as we have seen, is a divided self. Long before she becomes aware of her division, of her "inside" and "outside," free indirect discourse communicates this division to the reader. After she becomes aware of her own division, free indirect discourse represents, rhetorically, her *interrupted* passage from "outside" to "inside." Free indirect discourse in *Their Eyes* reflects both the text's theme of the doubling of Janie's self and that of the problematic relation between Janie as a speaking subject and her relation to spoken language. Free indirect discourse, furthermore, is a central aspect of the rhetoric of the text and serves to disrupt the reader's expectation of the necessity of the shift in point of view from third-person to first with Janie's framed narrative. Free indirect discourse is not the "voice" of *both* a character *and* a narrator; rather, it is a bi-vocal utterance containing elements of both direct and indirect speech. It is an "utterance" that no one could have spoken, yet which we recognize because of its characteristic "speakerlyness," its paradoxically *written* manifestation of aspiration to the *oral*. For Hurston, free indirect discourse is an equation: direct speech equals narrative commentary; representation of an action equals repetition of that action; therefore, narrative commentary aspires to the immediacy of the drama. Janie's quest for consciousness, however, always remains that of the consciousness of her own division, which the dialogical rhetoric of the text—especially as expressed in free indirect discourse—underscores, preserves, and seems to celebrate. It is this theme and this rhetoric of division which together comprise the "modernism" of this text.

But Hurston allows us to rename free indirect discourse; near the beginning of her book, the narrator describes the communal, undifferentiated voice of "the porch" as "a mood come alive. Words walking without masters; walking together like harmony in a song." Because the narrator attributes these words to "the bander log" (p. 11), or the place where Kipling's monkey sits, Hurston here gives one more, coded, reference to Signifyin(g): that which "the porch" (monkeys) has just done is to Signify upon Janie. If Signifyin(g) is "a mood come alive," "words walking without masters," then we can also think of free indirect discourse in this way.

There are numerous indices whereby we identify free indirect discourse in general, among these grammar, intonation, context, idiom, register, content; it is naturalized in a text by stream-of-consciousness, irony, empathy and polyvocality.[12] The principal indices of free indirect discourse in *Their Eyes* include those which "evoke a 'voice' or presence" that supplements the narrator's, especially when one or more sentences of free indirect discourse follow a sentence of indirect discourse. Idiom and register, particularly, Hurston uses as markers of black colloquialism, of the quality of the "speakerly" informed by the dialect of the direct discourse of the characters. In *Their Eyes*, naturalization would seem to function as part of the theme of the developing, but discontinuous, self. This function is naturalized primarily by irony, empathy, and polyvocality. When it is used in conjunction with Joe Starks, irony obtains and distancing results; when it is used in conjunction with Janie, empathy obtains, and an illusory identification results, an identity that we call "lyric fusion" between the narrator and Janie. Bivocalism, or the "double-voiced" utterance, in which two voices co-occur, is this text's central device of naturalization, again serving to reinforce Janie.

Their Eyes employs three modes of narration to render the words or thoughts of a character. The first is direct discourse:

> "Jody," she smiled up at him, "but s'posin—"
> "Leave de s'posin' and everything else to me."

The next is indirect discourse:

> "The vision of Logan Killicks was desecrating the pear tree, but Janie didn't know how to tell Nanny that."

The third example is free indirect discourse. Significantly, this example occurs when Joe Starks enters the narrative:

> Joe Starks was the name, yeah Joe Starks from in and through Georgy. Been workin' for white folks all his life. Saved up some money—round three hundred dollars, yes indeed, right here in his pocket. Kept hearin' 'bout them buildin' a new state down heah in Floridy and sort of wanted to come. But he was makin' money where he was. But when he heard all about 'em makin' a town all outa colored folks, he knowed dat was de place he wanted to be. He had always wanted to be a big voice, but de white folks had all de sayso where he come from and everywhere else, exceptin' dis place dat colored folks was buildin' theirselves. Dat was right too. De man dat built things oughta boss it. Let colored folks build things too if dey wants to crow over somethin'. He was glad he had his money all saved up. He meant to git here whilst de town wus yet a baby. He meant to buy in big. (pp. 47–48)

I selected this example because it includes a number of standard indices of free indirect speech. Although when read aloud, it sounds as if entire sections are in, or should be in, direct quotation, none of the sentences in this paragraph are direct discourse. There are no quotation marks here. The character's idiom, interspersed and contrasted colorfully with the narrator's voice, indicates nevertheless that this is an account of the words that Joe spoke to Janie. The sentences imitating dialect clearly are not those of the narrator alone; they are those of Joe Starks *and* the narrator. Moreover, the presence of the adverb *here* ("yes indeed, right here in his pocket") as opposed to "there," which would be required in normal indirect speech because one source would be describing another, informs us that the assertion originates within and reflects the character's sensibilities, not the narrator's. The interspersion of indirect discourse with free indirect discourse, even in the same sentence, serves as another index to its presence, precisely by underscoring Joe's characteristic idiom, whereas the indirect discourse obliterates it. Despite the third person and the past tense, of which both indirect and free indirect discourse consist, several sentences in this paragraph appear to *report* Joe's speech, without the text's resorting to either dialogue or direct discourse. The principal indices of free indirect discourse direct the reader to the subjective source of the statement, rendered through a fusion of narrator and a "silent"-but-"speaking" character.

This difference between the representation of the level of diction of Janie's discourse and the free indirect discourse that the text asks us to accept as the figure of Janie's thoughts, reinforces for the reader both Janie's divided consciousness as well as the double-voiced nature of free indirect discourse. It is as if the narrative commentary cannot relinquish its proprietary consciousness over Janie as freely as it does for other characters. Nevertheless, after Janie falls in love with Tea Cake, we learn of her feelings through a remarkable amount of free indirect discourse almost always rendered in what I wish to call "idiomatic," but standard, English.

It is because of these dramatic shifts in the idiom in which the voice of the narrator appears that we might think of *Their Eyes* as a *speakerly* text. For it is clear that the resonant dialect of the character's discourse has come to "color" the narrator's idiom such that it resembles rather closely the idiom in which Janie's free indirect discourse is rendered. But *Their Eyes* would seem to be a speakerly text for still another reason. Hurston uses free indirect discourse not only to represent an individual character's speech and thought but also to represent the *collective* black community's speech and thoughts, as in the hurricane passage above. This sort of anonymous, collective, free indirect discourse is not only unusual, but quite possibly was Hurston's innovation, as if to emphasize both the immense potential of this literary diction, one "dialect-informed," for the tradition, as well as the text's apparent aspiration to imitate oral narration. One example follows:

> Most of the flame-throwers were there and naturally, handling Big John de Conquer and his works. How he had done everything big on earth, then went up tuh heben without dying atall. Went up there picking a guitar and got all de angels doing the ring-shout round and round de throne. . . . That brought them back to Tea Cake. How

come he couldn't hit that box a lick or two? Well, all right now, make us know it. (p. 232)

Still another example is even more telling:

> Everybody was talking about it that night. But nobody was worried. The fire dance kept up till nearly dawn. The next day, more Indians moved east, unhurried but steady. Still a blue sky and fair weather. Beans running fine and prices good, so the Indians could be, *must* be, wrong. You couldn't have a hurricane when you're making seven and eight dollars a day picking beans. Indians are dumb anyhow, always were. Another night of Stew Beef making dynamic subtleties with his drum and living, sculptural, grotesques in the dance. . . . (p. 229)

These instances of free indirect discourse are followed in the text by straight diegesis, which retains the dialect-informed echoes of the previous passage:

> Morning came without motion. The winds, to the tiniest, lisping baby breath had left the earth. Even before the sun gave light, dead day was creeping from bush to bush watching man. (p. 229)

There are many other examples of this curious voice (see pp. 75–78 and 276). Hurston in this innovation is asserting that an entire narration could be rendered if not in "dialect" then in a dialect-informed discourse. This form of collective, impersonal free indirect discourse echoes Hurston's definition of "a mood come alive. Words walking without masters; walking together like harmony in a song." The ultimate sign of the dignity and strength of the black voice is this use of a dialect-informed free indirect discourse as narrative commentary beyond that which represents Janie's thoughts and feelings alone.

There are paradoxes and ironies in speakerly texts. The irony of this dialect-informed diction, of course, is that it is not a repetition of a language that anyone speaks; indeed, it can never be spoken. As several other scholars of free indirect discourse have argued, free indirect discourse is "speakerless," by which they mean "the presentation of perspective outside the normal communication paradigm that usually characterizes language." [13] It is literary language meant to be read in a text. Its paradox is that it comes into use by Hurston so that discourse rendered through direct, indirect, or free indirect means may partake of Hurston's "word-pictures," and "thought-pictures," as we recall she defined the nature of

Afro-American spoken language. "The white man thinks in a written language," she argued, "and the Negro thinks in hieroglyphics." The speakerly diction of *Their Eyes* attempts to render these pictures through the imitation of the extensively metaphorical medium of black speech, in an oxymoronic "oral hieroglyphic" that is meant only for the printed page. Its obvious oral base, nevertheless, suggests that Hurston conceived of it as a third language, as a mediating third term that aspires to resolve the tension between standard English and black vernacular, just as the narrative device of free indirect discourse aspires to define the traditional opposition between *mimesis* and *diegesis* as a false opposition. And perhaps this dialogical diction, and this dialogical narrative device, can serve as a metaphor for the critic of black comparative literature whose theoretical endeavor is intentionally double-voiced as well.

NOTES

1. I cite a definition of *skaz* deliberately, for this concept of Russian Formalism is similar to that which I am calling "the speakerly." See Victor Erlich, *Russian Formalism: History-Doctrine* (Mouton: The Hague, 1969), p. 238.

2. Zora Neale Hurston, "How It Feels to Be Colored Me," *The World Tomorrow* (1928).

3. Zora Neale Hurston, *Their Eyes Were Watching God* (1937; Urbana: University of Illinois, 1978), pp. 31–32. All subsequent references are to this edition, and shall be given parenthetically in the text.

4. Zora Neale Hurston, *Dust Tracks on a Road: An Autobiography* (Philadelphia: J. D. Lippincott, 1942), pp. 94–95.

5. Richard Wright, *Black Boy* (1945; New York: Harper & Row, 1966), p. 111.

6. Zora Neale Hurston, *Mules and Men: Negro Folktales and Voodoo Practices in the South* (1935; New York: Harper & Row, 1970), p. 161. All subsequent references to this text shall be given parenthetically.

7. The best discussion of the representation of black speech in Hurston's writing is Karla Francesca Holloway, *A Critical Investigation of Literary and Linguistic Structures in the Fiction of Zora Neale Hurston*, Ph.D. Dissertation, Michigan State University, 1978. See especially pp. 93–94.

8. I wish to thank Barbara Johnson of Harvard University for calling my attention to this ironic mode of self-consciousness.

9. In a brilliant analysis of this scene of the novel, Barbara Johnson writes that "the entire paragraph is an externalization of Janie's feelings onto the outer surroundings in the form of a narrative of movement from private to public space. While the whole figure relates metaphorically, analogically, to the marital situa-

tion it is designed to express, it reveals the marriage space to be metonymical, a movement through a series of contiguous rooms. It is narrative not of union but of separation centered on an image of conjugality but of virginity." See her "Metaphor, Metonymy, and Voice in Zora Neale Hurston's *Their Eyes Were Watching God,*" in *Black Literature and Literary Theory,* ed. H. L. Gates, Jr. (New York: Methuen, 1984), pp. 205–21.

10. Cf. Johnson: "Janie's 'inside' is here represented as a store that she then goes in to inspect. While the former paragraph was an externalization of the inner, here we find an internalization of the outer; Janie's inner self *resembles* a store. The material for this metaphor is drawn from the narrative world of contiguity; the store is the place where Joe has set himself up as lord, master, and proprietor. But here, Jody's image is broken, and reveals itself never to have been a metaphor, but only a metonymy, of Janie's dream: 'Looking at it she saw that it never was the flesh and blood *figure* of her dreams. Just something to drape her dreams over.' " Johnson, ibid.

11. See Roy Pascal, *The Dual Voice: Free Indirect Discourse and Its Functioning in the Nineteenth-Century European Novel* (Totowa, N.J.: Rowman and Littlefield, 1977), pp. 1–33.

12. Brian McHale, "Free Indirect Discourse," *PTL* 3 (1978), pp. 264–80.

13. Janet Holmgren McKay, *Narration and Discourse in American Realistic Fiction* (Philadelphia: University of Pennsylvania Press, 1982), p. 19.

Remus Redux, or French Classicism

on the Old Plantation:

La Fontaine and J. C. Harris

JEFFERSON HUMPHRIES

It will appear crazy to some, and offensive to just as many, to mention Joel Chandler Harris, creator of Uncle Remus, in the same breath with the French poet and fabulist Jean de La Fontaine—Harris, apologist for the antebellum South, for slavery, patentee of the ultimate white fantasy of the adoring, passive, blissful-in-abjection black man who recounts tales of "Brer Rabbit" in pathetically endearing, illiterate dialect, alongside one of the great masters of French classicism and all its resources of irony, paradox, and every manner of literary subterfuge. But to justify such a comparison, the two need have no more in common than the genre of fable.

While a great deal of critical attention has been lavished on the resources of fable in La Fontaine's literary practice, no comparable scrutiny of rhetoric and genre in Harris's work has ever been attempted. Harris's undertaking in the Uncle Remus tales is conditioned at least as much by properties innate to the genre of fable as it is by a pseudoanthropological and apologist intention and a particular set of circumstances in American history. Illuminated by insights gleaned from La Fontaine, Harris's work appears more complex but also more clear. His differences from La Fontaine are all the more instructive because of what the two bodies of work have in common. What becomes apparent is a much more paradoxical view of the black man than anyone has realized, and a much more complicated attitude toward literature on the part of nostalgia-stricken white southerners like Harris.

Fable is, generically, a particular kind of allegory, one in which animals, plants, and sometimes even inanimate objects speak and act as though human. This is a classic illustration of the dictionary definition of allegory: "speaking otherwise than one seems to speak." And allegory, as Angus Fletcher has pointed out, is awfully close to the meaning of irony: "saying one thing and meaning another." The irony is in the service of a moral, or maxim, with which every fable is supposed to conclude, and for which it serves as an illustration. From the outset, the genre is a kind of trickery. Its message pertains to men but is conveyed through the "acts" and "speech" of animals which cannot in reality speak or walk upright. The maxim, raison d'être of every fable, does not apply to animals but to men. This is very far from a direct imitation of reality, and it ought to be reserved for moments of extreme subtlety, when there is an imperative to expression which cannot declare its meaning, or its source, or its intention, directly. The genre of the maxim itself, incorporated if only by implication in that of the fable, enacts a similar self-contradiction: it must be particular, grounded in detail, and yet reflect the most universal truth; it must be original (clever), inventive, and yet create the sense in a reader of having always been true. *Maxima sententia:* the greatest truth in the smallest space. So, as we have seen, maxim is always paradox, an algebra of oppositions (universal/particular, commonplace/original, Truth/fragment) in which the essence is neither of the terms opposed but the tension of their very fine discrepancy. If that noncoincidence disappears, the maxim becomes a cliché, and loses its force. The goal of every maxim, as an *original* statement, must not be to eliminate this tension but rather to increase it. So fable, from beginning to end, from animals speaking and wearing clothes to the kernel of wisdom at the end, is nothing but irony and paradox.

It is not at all accidental that in France the fable and the maxim reached the highest point of their development at the same time, during the reign of Louis XIV, in the works of La Fontaine and La Rochefoucauld. The indirection of both genres served both to lure and to foil the scrutiny of a repressive political regime. To lure, by the possibility of commentary or even advice to the monarch being concealed under the inscrutable lamination of allegory, which would of course excite the keenest attention, reading and rereading, by those in power. To foil, because handled properly, irony and allegory will never stop leaping back and forth across the gap of their ambiguousness, never deliver plainly in a neat package the "content" occulted by the same rhetorical gestures which sustain the illusion of its presence and its *virtual* accessibility. The idea is to convince the reader that there really is a "content" there, just out of reach, which one more careful reading might reveal, while making sure that such a resolution of ambiguities is impossible. This is not true only for the purposes of avoiding censorship and purloining some measure of power (that of seduction, the power of the story to command a furrowing of brows among the truly powerful), but for the literary quality of fable or maxim. The greater, the more subtle the irony, the better, the more effective, the more original, these are seen to be. Louis Marin has written in *Le récit est un piège:*

> In its desire for power, power will always listen to the fable as if it controlled the secret of knowing (end, code, meaning), of Truth which would make power absolute—that is, without any left over, without exteriority. And the storyteller—if he is clever—will always allow to appear a residue that must be guessed at, invented, which makes all knowledge (and truth) uncertain. That means this, but also that, and maybe even something else. Thus power—and the knowledge of power—disperses itself by its very desire for power in fables and stories. Thus does it lose its time in appearances; thus is it diverted by amusement; thus does it play like a child. "Why should one wonder / That the soundest reasoning / Fatigued often from lack of sleep / Should take pleasure in nodding, cleverly rocked / By tales of Ogre and Fairy?" (33–34, my translation)

Joan DeJean, another recent reader of La Fontaine, has said: "The dazzling surfaces of Classicism constitute a brilliant machine for controlling all readers, for keeping them in the dark, for discouraging them from asking questions about the identity of the master artist who surrounds them with '*dorures*' and who caresses them when the lights are out" (109). One would have trouble finding a more precise metaphor for the fabulist's position, for his power is conditioned on his disappearance, his invisibility. The identity of La Fontaine exists only in what he says, and so is subjected to the same play of irony, paradox, and allegory. Like a puppeteer, dressed entirely in *black,* his presence is only known by its erasure, the illusion of its absence, the mirage of these animals talking and acting like men, these sentences which throw back the reader's scrutiny like polished metal surfaces. This disappearance *is* power, the only real power accessible within a realm of absolutism to anyone but the monarch. Even the king's underlings have no power of their own but only what he lends them. The fabulist's power comes from his respect for language, for its unreliability, its power to deceive even the most powerful and the most astute. It is not a power purchased by linguistic pragmatism, except insofar as words must be *used* to seduce a reader's attention, but by a wariness of the traps within language—the possibility of being misunderstood (understood positively) in a dangerous fashion, of being caught in a seditious gesture of rhetoric, intended or not. This wariness appears to the audience/reader as an inscrutability, a purposeful concealment of some valuable, positive thing to be known—a secret. Some readers of La Fontaine would have it that such a secret is actually delivered, whole, by each fable. This can be true only if one admits with the critic Ross Chambers (in contradiction with his own reading of La Fontaine) that "there are no secrets." The "secret" is part of the allegorical illusion of the fable, and does not exist. As the maxim, or "point," of each fable, it is of course "delivered"—but as what? Ironic paradox, a statement which calls itself into question, erases its positiveness even as it is disclosed. So the " 'interest' of the fable" cannot be pedagogical, as Chambers calls it, unless one conceives of and espouses the teaching of ignorance, something not reflected in his conclusion. The "secret" which he sees being disclosed in a fable about secrecy is the most severe irony, pure oxymoron: "Et je sais même sur ce fait / Bon nombre d'hommes qui sont femmes [And I even know of, on this matter / A good number of men who are women]." It is difficult for me at least to agree with Chambers's construal of such a facetious paradox as liberationist polemic.

All of this calls for illustration. Here is a well-known short fable of La Fontaine. Marianne Moore's translation gives a good sense of the original's ironically lapidary language.

> Certain Renard gascon, d'autres disent normand,
> Mourant presque de faim, vit au haut d'une treille
>   Des raisins murs apparemment,
>   Et couverts d'une peau vermeille.
> Le galant en eut fait volontiers un repas;
>   Mais comme il n'y pouvait atteindre:
> "Ils sont trop verts, dit-il, et bons pour des goujats."
>   Fit-il pas mieux que de se plaindre?
> [A fox of Gascon, though some say of Norman descent,
> When starved till faint gazed up at a trellis to which grapes
> were tied—
>   Matured till they glowed with a purplish tint

As though there were gems inside.
Now grapes were what our adventurer on strained haunches chanced
to crave
But because he could not reach the vine
He said, "These grapes are sour; I'll leave them for some
knave." Better, I think, than an embittered whine.]

"Norman" and "Gascon" here are figures for two apparently quite contradictory attitudes toward language. The Norman, somewhat like the New Englander in American popular folklore, is always reluctant to commit himself; "répondre en norman [to reply as a norman]" means to reply equivocally: "maybe yes, maybe no." On the other hand, the Gascon uses language to assert himself with utmost fervor. Synonyms listed in the *Petit Robert* are *fanfaron* and *hableur,* "blusterer," "braggart." So, as I am indebted to Ross Chambers for pointing out, the fable is equivocating between, and extolling, both ambiguity in language ("Norman") and the outright, and deliberate, conflation of language with reality ("Gascon")—in the fox and in itself.

Even so, the crux of the matter is not the fox's provenance but *vision,* distorted by *hunger.* In the French, the word *apparemment* appears prominently in the description of the grapes. What is at stake here is perception, appearance, even if *apparemment* is understood to mean "obviously," "evidently," rather than "apparently," on account of the word's emphatic placement, after rather than (as usual) before the adjective *murs.* Either way, the mediation of perception is invoked. Because the fox is "starved till faint," and because the grapes are above him, with the light (one supposes) shining through, they look to him to be perfectly ripe. That perception may or may not be accurate. The attempt to reach the grapes fails, and the fox uses language to "change" the nature of the grapes, making them unworthy of his desire. Desire first embellishes an object visually and then, frustrated, denigrates it to diffuse the frustration. At both stages a drama of representation is enacted in which the object itself is not much more than pretext. Because of a physical imperative (hunger, a particular instance of desire) the fox first sees the grapes as desirable, and then because gratification is blocked, negates that first perception. Language is a response to the frustration of desire, of consumption. The fox will never know if the grapes were really ripe or not, and neither will the reader. His response to this suspension of knowledge is a commentary on the grapes, by which he achieves a certain mastery over his desire and over the circumstances. What follows—the "maxim" or "secret" of the fable—is only half given to us by the narrator. Just what is better than complaining, than an "embittered whine"? To denigrate the grapes, of course, but this conclusion is left to the reader. When one cannot verify supposition (are the grapes ripe?) grounded in desire, it is better to diffuse the desire by revising the supposition than to embrace and give voice to frustration. Yes, but this is too evident. What can the narrator be alluding to? The first line led us to suppose a specifically human, perhaps ethno-logic content. What might it be, beyond the two apparently contradictory attitudes toward language already alluded to? Isn't our situation, as read-ers, rather like the fox's? We have supposed something about the words of the fable because of our desire to know its meaning. At the end, there is no revelation save the banal assertion—which we are left to complete—that it is better to denigrate an object that is out of reach than to pursue it futilely. This is cliché, something we already knew. What greater meaning might be implied? The last line of the fable does not stop our wondering, as this reading demonstrates. As readers of the fable, we do not follow the fox's example, even though we see it as commonplace. Oughtn't we, if the wisdom here is so evident, to do as the fox does and denigrate the fable? Yet we do not. We continue to read fables and to be puzzled by this one. The narrator has enacted an allegory which shows his readers their own lack of wisdom in continuing to read him, in not diffusing their own desire to know what the allegory of the fable *means*, to confirm a sup-position about it. The clear implication, according to this reading, is that we, readers, are fools. But the narrator will not confirm this supposition either. He derives a power over us from two things: our hunger to know what he means, and his own absence from the fable, his refusal to declare himself, his intentions. His, like every literary voice, is without a subjec-tivity attached which we might interrogate about intentions and origins. Just as the fox's (and the fable's) origin and linguistic strategy are in doubt ("Gascon" or "Norman"?), so the fable is cut off from any sure intention, origin-ality, authorial authority. Could the real meaning of this fable be that men do not do what they ought to do, even when they know and rec-ognize the wisdom of the right action? Perhaps. In inventing new endings, commentaries, codas for the fable, we do follow the fox's example after a fashion, responding to the frustration of our desire to know with lan-guage, with *revised* suppositions, though these do not entirely negate the ones we began with. These revisions, instead of diffusing our desire completely, only defer it, master it for a moment and then give way to fresh wonderings, a more subtly directed desire to know. And of course the fox does not diffuse his hunger, either, by saying that the grapes are sour. He simply redirects it, frees it for new "suppositions," new objects. There is something both Norman and Gascon about this process, embracing as it does the ambiguousness of language (its "Norman" aspect) and its power to affect or overwhelm reality (its "Gascon" side).

What is illustrated here is just what astute readers of La Fontaine—Louis Marin most notably—have pointed out before: the *power* of the fabulist, the power of dissimulation, allegory, irony. That power is just as much at stake in the Uncle Remus tales as in La Fontaine, but perhaps even more interestingly, for the fabulist himself (Remus) has become part of the fable. He appears, and is visible, but within the framework of fable this appearance cannot be more than a veil, an illusion cloaking the "truth" of his character—a "truth" which the fable conceals and empowers by diffusion. That he should be black is not a matter of choice to Harris as his author, but still the fact is coincident with certain aspects of the fable, and of color, in a sufficiently pregnant way to have charged Harris's imagination, albeit unconsciously. Black is a color which by definition connotes both absence and surfeit of visible light, invisibility and overvisibility. The fabulist is just this sort of absent presence, cloaked in shadow to sustain the illusion of his allegorical voices and shapes. He "caresses" his audience "when the lights are out," as Joan DeJean puts it. What, and who, is the audience of Uncle Remus? A *white* boy. The fabulist here is a literal darkness, a shadow, at the opposite end of the visible spectrum from his listener. Yet white is also defined as both "achromatic" and "perceived to belong to objects that reflect diffusely nearly all incident energy throughout the visible spectrum," free from color and yet reflecting every color. So teller and listener are each a mirror image, a reversal, of the other, and the blackness of Remus reflects a certain "chromatic" potential for "blankness," for obscurity, disappearance, and *power* which is latent in the white child who listens to him. The boy's attention is compelled by something which, as a (chromatic) figure, reverses him, achieving in the process the power of the fabulist, maker of maxims. Harris's fable is thus an allegory of fable, a fable of fable itself, in which both teller and listener are engulfed in the ambiguous "lesson" of the tale. This lack of a clear distinction between the levels of representation within the story is established by Harris as something emanating from the "dark presence" of the black storyteller.

The old man [spoke] in a tone which implied that he was quite prepared to believe the dream was true. "Many's and many's de time,
deze long nights en deze rainy spells, dat I sets down dar in my house
over ag'in' de chimbly-jam'—I sets dar en I dozes, en it seem lak dat
ole Brer Rabbit, he'll stick he head in de crack er de do' en see my
eye 'periently shot, en den he'll beckon back at de yuther creeturs, en
den dey'll set dar en run over de ole times wid one er n'er, en crack
der jokes same ez dey useter. En den ag'in," continued the old man,
shutting his eyes and giving to his voice a gruesome intonation *quite
impossible to describe,*—"en den ag'in hit look lak dat Brer Rabbit'll
gin de wink all 'roun, en den dey'll tu'n in en git up a reg'lar juberlee.
Brer Rabbit, he'll retch up and take down de trivet, en Brer Fox, he'll
snatch up de griddle, en Brer B'ar, he'll lay holt er de pot-hooks, en
ole Brer Tarrypin, he'll grab up de fryin' pan, en dar dey'll have it, up
en down, en 'roun' en 'roun'. Hit seem lak ter me dat ef I kin git my
min' smoove down en ketch up some er dem ar chunes w'at dey sets
dar en plays, den I'd lean back yer in dish yer cheer en I'd intrance
you wid um, twel, by dis time termorrer night, you'd be settin' up
dar at de supper-table 'sputin' 'longer yo' little brer 'bout de 'lasses
pitcher. Dem creeturs dey sets dar," Uncle Remus went on, "en dey
plays dem kinder chunes w'at moves you fum 'way back yander; en
many's de time w'en I gits so lonesome kaze dey ain't nobody year
um ceppin' it's me. Dey ain't no tellin' de chunes dey is in dat trivet,
en in dat griddle, en in dat fryin'-pan er mine; dat dey ain't. W'en
dem creeturs walks in en snatches um down, dey lays Miss Sally's
pianner in de shade, en Mars John's flute, hit ain't nowhars."

"Do they play on them just like a band, Uncle Remus?" inquired
the little boy, *who was secretly in hopes that the illusion would not
be destroyed.*

"Dey comes des lak I tell you, honey. W'en I shets my eyes en dozes,
dey comes en dey plays, but w'en I opens my eyes dey ain't dar. Now,
den, w'en dat's de shape er marters, w'at duz I do? I des shets my eyes
en hol' um shot, en let um come en play dem ole times chunes twel
long atter bedtime done come en gone." (185–86, emphasis mine)

The most interesting difference from the fables of La Fontaine may be
the stance of Harris himself. He has projected the voice of the fabulist—
his own voice—into the fable and into the figure of a black man. Harris
tries, in his preface to the stories, to describe his role as that of an amateur

anthropologist, a folklorist, taking great pains to authenticate the tales as "African" in origin and to capture phonetically the dialect of the black storyteller. His relation to his fables, to literature, is thus highly ambiguous and represented as identical to his relation with the black man. The black storyteller *is* the narrative representation of that ambiguity toward the indeterminacy, the power of literature, which Harris is compelled to enact, but from a distance, to enact and deny at once. His purpose has always been assumed, by himself and his critics, to be the glorification of antebellum plantation society:

> If the reader not familiar with plantation life will imagine that the myth-stories of Uncle Remus are told night after night to a little boy by an old Negro who appears to be venerable enough to have lived during the period which he describes—who has nothing but pleasant memories of the discipline of slavery—and who has all the prejudices of caste and pride of family that were the natural results of the system; if the reader can imagine all this, he will find little difficulty in appreciating and sympathizing with the air of affectionate superiority which Uncle Remus assumes as he proceeds to unfold the mysteries of plantation lore to a little child who is the product of that practical reconstruction which has been going on to some extent since the war in spite of the politicians. (xxvi–xxvii)

He represents the black man as quaint, comical, endearing, but ignorant; the stories Remus tells, though sophisticatedly ironic, are phrased in the language of an illiterate, though charming, dialect. The power of literature is represented here as *illiterate,* and knowledge, education (whiteness), as incompatible with that power (blackness, literature) to which the white writer is drawn inexorably but which he is compelled to project outside of himself, into an otherness of obscurity and anachronism. Yet the act of Harris's writing, like the rapt attention of the little boy in the stories, confirms that power even as it thrusts it away in the guise of a specifically *racial* otherness. The heretofore ignored significance of these stories is that, in them, the mentality of nostalgic postbellum southerners like Harris is represented, and it turns out to be rather peculiar in ways one might not have expected. In every one of these tales is an allegory of the educated, conservative white southerner's view of race relations, and he appears to be less sure of his superiority than has been assumed. The same allegory represents the white southerner's relation to literature as equally complex:

as any publisher can attest, the region has always been the least hospitable to the best writing, even when it comes from the pens of natives. "Science," accuracy, a soberness with regard to fact and history, are embraced by Harris. These, at least, are of practical value. "Fable," literature, the word wielded for its own sake, for nothing but the pleasure it can give— and the power, but this is not so apparent—are projected into the black man's face and voice. Or rather, simply assumed to belong there. But it must always be remembered that, in this way, the black man is denigrated for the very same reason that the fox libelled his grapes—because of his distance, his status as the holder of a secret which he will not reveal, which makes him an object of *frustrated* desire and empowers him to dispense pleasure in small doses. He is disparaged for his power of words, a power of darkness latent in the white man, but which the white man alienates from himself so that he may have the pleasure of being seduced by it and of bludgeoning it with a disdain born of fear. For to wield that power directly is to embrace, to *disappear* into the power of the literary word, the indeterminacy of allegory.

In the Remus corpus there is a fox-and-grape story which serves perfectly as a point of comparison with La Fontaine. Entitled "How Brother Fox Failed to Get his Grapes," it begins with a wry evocation by the narrator of the black man's quaint suspicion, grounded in ignorance, of newfangled medical science.

One night the little boy failed to make his appearance at the accustomed hour, and the next morning the intelligence that the child was sick went forth from the "big house." Uncle Remus was told that it had been necessary during the night to call in two physicians. When this information was imparted to the old man, there was an expression upon his countenance of awe not unmixed with indignation. He gave vent to the latter:

"Dar now! Two un um! W'en dat chile riz up, ef rize up he do, he'll des nat'ally be a shadder. Yer I is, gwine on eighty year, en I ain't tuck none er dat ar doctor truck yit, 'ceppin' it's dish yer flas' er poke-root w'at ole Miss Favers fix up fer de stiffness in my j'ints. Dey'll come en dey'll go, en dey'll po' in der jollup yer en slap on der fly-plarster dar, en sprinkle der calomy yander, twel bimeby dat chile won't look like hisse'f. Dat's wat! En mo'n dat, hit's mighty kuse unter me dat ole folks kin go 'long en stan' up ter de rack en gobble up der 'lowance, en yit chilluns is got ter be stucken down. Ef Miss

Sally'll des tu'n dem doctor mens loose onter me, I lay I lick up der physic twel dey go off 'stonish." (177–78)

This demonstration of the old man's hopelessly primitive understanding is juxtaposed with a description of his slavish devotion to his "white folks," the Victorian mawkishness of which is impressive: "Every night after supper Uncle Remus would creep softly into the back piazza, place his hat carefully on the floor, rap gently on the door by way of announcement, and so pass into the nursery. How patient his vigils, how tender his ministrations, only the mother of the little boy knew; how comfortable and refreshing the change from the bed to the strong arms of Uncle Remus, only the little boy could say" (178). Uncle Remus's visits make the boy's "term of imprisonment . . . full of pleasure," the pleasure of blackness, of storytelling: "Almost the first manifestation of the child's convalescence was the renewal of his interest in the wonderful adventures of Brother Rabbit, Brother Fox, and the other brethren who flourished in that strange past over which this modern Aesop had thrown the veil of fable" (178). What is the strange past referred to here? Some antediluvian age of fantasm in which rabbit and fox wore clothes and spoke, in which the gap between myth and reality were closed and also, by implication, that between representation and Truth, literature and "science," black and white? That "strange past" is *created* by the "veil of fable" thrown by the black storyteller. Harris says in his introduction that the 'mythic' time alluded to is no more remote than the years before the Civil War: "the myth-stories . . . are told by an old Negro who appears . . . to have lived during the period which he describes" (xxvii). The prelapsarian age in question can be none other than the southern antebellum years. The old black man, "strong" yet quaintly ignorant, adept with words but fearful of science, is the only remaining link with that "age of fable." This gives him both his power and his weakness, the strength of myth and the frailty of obsolescence. It is as though no clock had begun to tick until the defeat of the South, no grim seconds counted till the gray uniform had been amply blood-spattered and ripped. Remus survives as a fading remnant of that magical age, the last of a race of wizards, whose powers are always fading but never disappearing, always ambiguous because his being is past, a discrepancy with the present and even with Time. Remus is a bit of the hypothetical "mythic" reality before there was Time, of a reality which never was (when slaves were happy and loved servitude and every white master was serenely benevolent), of untime, fallen into the dross of temporal existence. So he is always in danger of disappearing completely, of becoming invisible. His language, so archaic, so ungrammatical, incompatible with the "science" of grammar, risks becoming unintelligible. But this threat of disappearance *is* his power, as the only remaining bond with a past outside of time. Of course the little boy would rather float in the giddy firmament of darkness, no-time, that is, in the arms of the old black man, than on the clammy white sheets of his very real and medicinal bed.

As for the story itself, it deals with the power of words over perception, but in a more pointed, subtly aggressive way than La Fontaine's version. Brother Rabbit and Brother Fox find themselves rivals for the attention of the same gaggle of women in the neighborhood. Whether rabbit, fox, or some hybrid, the species of these females is never specified. We must understand them to partake of a golden age in which differences of genus did not count for nearly so much as nowadays. Brother Rabbit—perpetual underdog, with no weapon at his disposal but language—decides to humiliate his competitor in the only way he can. He tells Brother Fox about a bunch of grapes he has seen.

> "'I wuz takin' a walk day fo' yistiddy,' sezee, w'en de fus' news I know'd I run up 'g'in' de bigges' en de fattes' bunch er grapes dat I ever lay eyes on. Dey wuz dat fat en dat big,' sezee, 'dat de nat'al juice wuz des drappin' fum um, en de bees wuz a-swarmin' atter de honey, en little ole Jack Sparrer en all er his fambly conneckshun wuz skeetin' 'roun' dar dippin' in der bills,' sezee.
>
> "Right den en dar," Uncle Remus went on, "Brer Fox mouf 'gun ter water, en he look outer he eye like he de bes' frien' w'at Brer Rabbit got in de roun' worl'. . . .
>
> "'. . . Dey er dat ripe,' sez ole Brer Rabbit, sezee, 'dat dey look like dey er done melt tergedder, en I speck you'll fin' um full er bugs, but you kin take dat fine bushy tail er yone, Brer Fox,' sezee, 'en bresh dem bugs away.'
>
> "Brer Fox 'low he much 'blige, en den he put out atter de grapes in a han'-gallop." (179–80)

The rabbit has followed the example of La Fontaine's fox, but to manipulate the fox's desire, not his own. He has created, out of nothing but words and the slight resemblance between a bunch of grapes and another, less palatable, but very real object, a surrogate object of desire. He has, with words, made that object of desire "appear" so compelling that the fox chooses to pursue it rather than "Miss Meadows and the gals." The rabbit has even given hints of his deceitfulness, which, however, only serve to make the illusion, the Fox's error, more effective. He warns the fox that the "grapes" will be full of "bugs." In fact, "Dem ar grapes all so fine wuz needer mo' ner less dan a great big was'-nes', en dem bugs wuz deze yer red wassies." (181)

Remember that the black man and the little boy are just as much within the realm of fable as the fable itself. What the rabbit does with the larger, more dangerous fox is just what the black man does for the boy: to "invent" out of words an illusory object of desire, the story of the fox, the rabbit, and the grapes. That story demonstrates the power of language to deceive, to manipulate, and to humiliate even an adversary who has every apparent advantage of force. And the old black man, though he does not subject the white audience to humiliation, certainly does manipulate, "deceive" him—deception and verbal manipulation being the very essence of successful storytelling. The latent possibility of humiliation is sketched very graphically, however, with the implication that it could be used, if necessary. The boy submits to this control because, like La Fontaine's reader, he wants the secret of knowledge, to feel the mythical wholeness before the fall into defeat and Time, which for him and for Harris is represented by the pre–Civil War South.

That the Old South of Harris and many other postbellum white southerners' nostalgia should be fable, a sort of prelapsarian myth, is not as surprising as that the guardian of that myth should be a black man. Still, one might object, that black man is a white fantasy, the most flaccid of Uncle Toms. But reading him alongside La Fontaine shows at least that Uncle Remus is not the helpless, doting Negro that even his author tries to make him into. If the black man is to sustain the fable of the Old South—by dissimulation, irony, all the resources of the fabulist—he must have the fabulist's power. This is a power which is not granted. It must be acquired by anyone who would wield it, and it can be achieved only through verbal elusiveness. If the white child, or Harris, takes pleasure in the black man's wielding this power of narration over their greater resources of force, this does not mean that he is their creature, any more than La Fontaine can be called the creature of Louis XIV and his minions. It is by appearing to gratify a need to *know*, a nostalgia for Pure Knowledge, Fabulous Origin, in the only way that these can be gratified—by trickery, deferment, an endless series of supplements and substitutions for the absence of any such knowledge, the infinite invention of new, always ephemeral objects of desire—that the black man in the South of Harris's childhood, or the man of letters in seventeenth-century France, compel a superior political force to respect them. If Remus is a white fantasy, he is not one which disparages the black man. Very much the contrary. Remus is the embodiment of literature. The white southerner, with his condescension to literature and blackness (the former prejudice has perhaps survived intact to a greater degree than the latter), his confusion of the two, is the one who appears in a bad light, sitting raptly, open-mouthed, at the feet of an uneducated black man, begging for another tale.

The consequence of white positivism, of expecting a real, definitive answer to all questions, is illustrated in the story of the tar baby. Because the tar baby (man- or fox-made simulacrum of Negro) will not speak to him, the rabbit strikes it, trapping himself, losing all freedom of movement. Of course the tar baby was a trap set by the fox to catch the rabbit. To entrap his tormentor, the fox makes a false "fabulist," a "black man." This tar baby inspires a compulsion to know, to hear words spoken, on the part of the rabbit. Because the tar baby cannot give the rabbit what he demands (respond to his greeting), appearing to withhold it, the rabbit becomes frantic, finally surrendering all privilege of unencumbered motion, all dignity of superior intellect, stuck in the gooey obscurity of an "Uncle Remus," a made-up fable-spinner. He regains his power only by realizing his error and playing tar baby to the fox. He tells his captor that the torture he most fears is to be thrown into a briar patch. Hearing this, the fox throws him right away into the nearest one. The rabbit, to whom there is no friendlier element than briars, sashays off home. The dark power of words can only be escaped by embracing it, something which Harris will do only at a distance, in the persona of Remus, fantasy though he may be.

There is considerable evidence, though, that Harris's depiction of the black is not fantasy, beyond assertions by nostalgia-struck simpletons delerious with age that "why yes, the niggers was just like that in the old days, back on the plantation." Many prominent blacks have embraced old Remus, among them the critic Henry Louis Gates. Uncle Remus is nothing but a white man's translation of the black figure of the "signifying monkey."

The Signifying Monkey is a trickster figure, of the order of the trickster figure of Yoruba mythology, Esù-Elégbára in Nigeria, and Legba among the Fon in Dahomey, whose New World figurations—Exú in Brazil, Echu-Elegua in Cuba, Papa Legba in the pantheon of the *loa* of Vaudou in Haiti, and Papa La Bas in the *loa* of Hoodoo in the United States—speak eloquently of the unbroken arc of metaphysical presuppositions and patterns of figuration shared through space and time among black cultures in West Africa, South America, the Caribbean, and the United States. These trickster figures, aspects of Esù, are primarily *mediators:* as tricksters they are mediators and their mediations are tricks.

The versions of Esù are all messengers of the gods: he interprets the will of the gods to man; he carries the desires of man to the gods. He is known as the divine linguist, the keeper of *àse* ("logos") with which Olódùmarè created the universe. Esù is guardian of the crossroads, master of style and the stylus, phallic god of generation and fecundity, master of the mystical barrier that separates the divine from the profane world. In Yoruba, Esù always limps, because his legs are of different lengths: one is anchored in the realm of the gods, the other rests in the human world. The closest Western relative of Esù is Hermes, of course; and, just as Hermes' role as interpreter lent his name readily to "hermeneutics," the study of the process of interpretation, so too the figure of Esù can stand, for the critic of comparative black literature, as our metaphor for the act of interpretation itself. . . .

Unlike his Pan-African Esù cousins, the Signifying Monkey exists in the discourse of mythology not primarily as a character in a narrative but rather as a vehicle for narration itself. It is from this corpus of mythological narratives that signifying derives. The Afro-American rhetorical strategy of signifying is a rhetorical practice unengaged in information giving. Signifying turns on the play and chain of signifiers, and not on some supposedly transcendent signified. Alan Dundes suggests that the origins of signifying could "lie in African rhetoric." As anthropologists demonstrate, the Signifying Monkey is often called "the signifier," he who wreaks havoc upon "the signified." One is "signified upon" by the signifier. (Gates, 687–89)

To "signify" can mean, in Afro-American usage, to make fun of someone or simply to display great verbal virtuosity, talking a great deal and never saying anything identifiable as a "content." This is just what Uncle Remus does. Even if Remus is a white fantasy, a tar baby set up by Harris for the pleasure of "signifying" on himself, he is still a surprise. Who would have thought the myth of the Old South depended above all else on the figure of a black man? It may be going too far, but one might wonder, with the real changes that have occurred in the way the black man is seen by the white South, and a concurrent decline of zeal for the age of southern glory, if we might not expect such literature to find more widespread and profound acceptance in the region.

WORKS CITED

Chambers, Ross. "Histoire D'Oeuf: Secrets and Secrecy in a La Fontaine Fable." *Sub-stance,* no. 32 (1981): 65–74.
DeJean, Joan. "La Fontaine's *Psyche:* The Reflecting Pool of Classicism." *L'Esprit Createur* 21, no. 4, 99–109.
Gates, Henry Louis, Jr. "The 'Blackness of Blackness': A Critique of the Sign and the Signifying Monkey." *Critical Inquiry* 9 (1983): 685–724.
Harris, Joel Chandler. *The Complete Tales of Uncle Remus.* Boston: Houghton Mifflin, 1955.
La Fontaine, Jean de. *The Fables of La Fontaine.* Trans. Marianne Moore. New York: Viking Press, 1954.
Marin, Louis. *Le récit est un piège.* Paris: Editions de Minuit, 1978.

The Fathers:

A Postsouthern

Narrative Reading

MICHAEL KREYLING

*And we do all so desire, to avoid
knowing about history!*
—Fredric Jameson,
The Political Unconscious

Since Lewis Simpson gave us "postsouthern" as an enabling word we have been lax in implementing it in our critical vocabulary.[1] Our delay might be because we see, perhaps only dimly, that "postsouthern" necessitates a reordering of our familiar vocabulary, the one by which we know and are known. We still, for the most part, follow the formalist piper; even though we have known for a long time that the New Critical method is more useful on poems and short stories than on the novel or narrative in general, we continue to apply it to our readings of southern narrative. Too often our historical studies are marred by the methodological flaw that Fredric Jameson describes in *Marxism and Form:* the dead, schematic application of sociology to literature.[2] Based on a reading of so many literary-works-as-case-studies we derive a definition of southern literature that we then apply to still more supposed southern works. Not surprisingly we find that they usually qualify as southern. As Jameson points out, however, the fallacy in this circular approach is that the schematic critic always takes out only what he or she has just put in (*MF*, 398). This is a pantomime of historical criticism, reassuring and seemingly positive, but done with mirrors. Both the formalist and the circular critical habits satisfy the desire not to know history, or to avoid dealing with narrative on its own shifting, complex ground—which is the same thing.

But Simpson has shown, for the literary consciousness in America and more specifically in the South, that the familiar approaches are unsafe. History always cohabits with narrative, begetting the condition of existence and experience, and confronting us with its brazen face in spite of our strategies of evasion and containment.

This is not scandalous news. Even such a traditionalist as Cleanth Brooks, in *Modern Poetry and the Tradition* (1939), foretold perhaps more than he intended of this potential trap for the idealist critic. Writing of southern poets (Warren, Ransom, Tate), Brooks argued that "the Old South cannot exist in the mind of the modern Southerner apart from its nonexistence in the present. . . . Consequently, the Southern poet who is unwilling to sentimentalize the past or to limit himself to objective descriptions of the local color of the present, must of necessity mediate his account of the Old South through a consciousness of the present; that is, of its present nonexistence." We seem to have heard only the Brooksian resolution which follows this admission of history: "his real test as a poet will be his ability to bring the two sorts into a unity."[3] As critics of southern narrative, we have begun with the presumption of unity under the aegis "South" and have neglected the tense coexistence of two antithetical forms of consciousness: formalist and historical. It is not the fashion of criticism today to believe much in unity; as postsouthern critics we might do our vocation a good service by returning to the "two sorts" of historical experience—the past as nonexistent and the past recovered in a work claiming formalist unity. We ought to forget the present as a gallery in which selected elements of the past are exhibited, as if real. This alteration in critical outlook would estrange us from many works we had thought familiar. It would also deny "South" and the canon of southern literary works the stability of closed interpretation. We would make ourselves orphans.

The postsouthern critic is not, however, as fatherless (or motherless) as he or she might seem. The New Criticism—which has almost certainly shaped our critical sense and practice—has proven as fully historical as any human work. A narrative criticism cognizant of Jameson's dialectical model seems now to be called for, a criticism of "widening fields" rather than the exclusive assertions of inner logic and formal unity, of the conditions of historical genesis rather than the traditional orthodoxy of southern myth, of attention to the "disguised expression" and alienating of reality (*MF*, 415). We have to reconcile the absolutism of southern myth (its exclusively inner referentiality) with the relational, diachronic nature of history in which "southern" has had its meaning. We stand to lose some fixity of meaning in the process.

We have had a partial model for this sort of critical work in our midst for some time. Not surprisingly it is the work of the South's most formidable intellect: Allen Tate. His works stand behind a fluid postsouthern criticism just as they stood behind the stable southern renascence. And the one work that affords us the widest scope for re-vision is *The Fathers*.[4]

Tate's present, the moment or juncture in which *The Fathers* has its genesis, was the interwar period of American and European history. Tate often used dates such as 1918–40, middle to late modern. His novel's referential core is there, not in the Old South, historical or mythic. We have construed his provocative, compact phrase—"the past in the present"— only one way: there was a classical, southern culture of tradition, stasis, unity, and art that existed in time, was invaded and overwhelmed by a barbaric nonculture of industrial, bourgeois, competitive capitalism, and passed from active existence in the minds and artifacts and institutions of men to take up a symbolic existence in the metaphysical realm. We are impoverished for its passing; but the works in which the departed reality is returned, and the acts of interpretation that restructure it for critical homage and consideration, constitute a vital lifeline. Without both we are marooned, dissociated—as the aging Lacy Buchan whom Tate had the prescience to see as the figure of the modern critic—in a diversity from which only confusion flows.

We have not misread *The Fathers* so much as we have underread it. We have, to borrow and tinker with a term from Jameson again, stayed mostly inside the first horizon of interpretation.[5] This is inadequate for a reading of *The Fathers* (and for anything Tate wrote), for Tate worked from an immensely subtle historical consciousness that encompassed, though it probably did not accept, Jameson's sense of the relational nature of all consciousness. In this sense Tate himself is our first qualified postsouthern critic. A reading of his only novel along lines suggested jointly by himself and Jameson and Simpson argues the usefulness of re-presenting individual works of southern narrative in interpretive settings that simultaneously destabilize the premises of the southern canon and broaden it. This double and precarious act, it seems to me, is called for in our postsouthern moment.

The thought of Allen Tate is clearly very important in Simpson's *The*

Brazen Face of History. Tate's is perhaps the only southern intellect capable first of formulating the southern dilemma in a wide-ranging philosophical and cultural setting that would, in Simpson's words, "take the form of a heroic attempt at an inquiry into the epistemological meaning of the South and of an attempted recovery of the limits and validity of the historical and mythic South as the ground of, the source of, a unified sensibility—of 'a knowledge carried to the heart'" (172–73). We mistake both Tate and Simpson, I think, if we search either's writing for the positive content of this "knowledge"; both assess the conditions of the epistemological case (limits and validity), not the content. This is where the postsouthern critic must find his or her beginning and rules of engagement, and where Jameson's model first becomes handy.

Jameson's rereading in the canons of Western literature and criticism from a dialectical perspective is a macrocosm into which we can accommodate postsouthern critical work on narrative. We must, first, avoid the southern myth by trying to historicize the text. "There is," Jameson writes, "a kind of antinomy for the mind in the notion that a book 'comes into being' at a fixed date" (*MF*, 312), and many of us in the criticism of southern texts have resisted (actively and passively) the imperative to account for the works we interpret, in their respective historical conditions. This, as Jameson explains in *The Political Unconscious,* is more complex an operation than the constructing of a context (*P*, 81). But it begins there. Second, there is the obligation of commentary on other critical rereadings of the subject work—metacommentary (208–209). The literary text is never single or finished, no matter how devoutly we would wish both; "the work is precisely not complete in itself but is handed down to us as a kind of gesture or verbal thrust incomprehensible unless we are able to understand the situation in which the gesture was first made, and the interlocutors to whom it was a reply" (*MF*, 377).

There is also, for Jameson, and ought to be as well for the postsouthern critic, a more rigorous rereading of the work, a reading that takes into account such unfamiliar and willfully skeptical concepts as "strategies of containment" and alienation of the real. Unless we are willing to abandon the canon of southern works to the rigor mortis of repeated formalist rereadings, we must break the spell of "southern" and entertain the possibility of postsouthern.

There is not, nor should there be, much surprise that Tate has been on this ground—or at least has surveyed it from a wary distance. The strong intellectual and emotional claims of southern history, a decided position on the regional "imagination," a firm political and literary ideology—these Tate possessed. *The Fathers* is, for the present purpose, the most useful single work in his achievement. It "came into being" at a certain time crucial both to Tate's own writing career and to the modern age with which he knew himself to be engaged. It has generated a respectable body of critical commentary over the five decades of its transmission to us—enough time to make possible some attempt at metacommentary. And it rewards rereading with new possibilities for reconstructing.

A postrenascent Tate wrote, in "A Southern Mode of the Imagination" (1959), that the southern mode of the imagination was (is) rhetorical.[6] "The traditional Southern mode of discourse presupposes somebody at the other end silently listening: it is the rhetorical mode. Its historical rival is the dialectical mode, or the give and take between two minds, even if one mind, like the mind of Socrates, prevail at the end" (583). We make a subtle mistake when we assume ourselves to be the only "somebody at the other end," or when we construct a hypothetical or ideal listener-reader. *The Fathers* is, in many neglected ways, dialectically engaged with its own time, not the nonexistent past. We need to consider its historical circumstances in this light in order to become aware of its diversity.

When *The Fathers* has been moved back into history, however, it has been into the questionable history of the Old South. Critics point to mention of Hinton Helper, the off-stage battles, the Lincoln-Douglas debates, or the cameo appearance of President James Buchanan, and conclude that Tate's fiction does indeed acknowledge history. But a list of historical bits no matter how extensive cannot amount to historical consciousness. Tate knew this; he is fluent in more than one vocabulary.

Tate uses the vocabulary of the Civil War and the Old South civilization of myth as characters in his debate with the issues of the 1930s: the strong sense of the impending doom of civilization as victim to "emotional naturalism," Rousseauistic restlessness and disunity, and the mass, machine society dedicated to efficiency and utility rather than the controls of a traditional ethical culture with metaphysical dimensions. This is the emerging catastrophe to which Irving Babbitt, among others, reacted in *Rousseau and Romanticism* (1919), a book with which Tate was familiar at first hand and at second through the mediation of Eliot.[7] *The Fathers* can be read as operating in a dialectical relationship with Babbitt's work on certain issues. When we put the two into conversation we can better understand the present to which Tate addressed *The Fathers,* its first "interlocutor."

Babbitt's civilization was in severe danger of dissolution but was not, in his opinion, hopeless: "If, then, one is to be a sound individualist, an individualist with human standards—and in an age like this that has cut loose from its traditional moorings, the very survival of civilization would seem to hinge on its power to produce such a type of individualist—one must grapple with what Plato terms the problem of the One and the Many." Babbitt quickly adds that his formulation is not to be construed as a crude and simplistic either-or. "Life does not give here an element of oneness and there an element of change. It gives a *oneness that is always changing*" (xiii). Having squared the circle, Babbitt goes on with his diagnosis and prescription. "My effort in this present work is to show that this failure [of the civilization at large to reconcile One and Many] can be retrieved only by a deeper insight into the imagination and its all important role in both literature and life. Man is cut off from immediate contact with anything abiding and therefore worthy to be called real, and condemned to live in an element of fiction and illusion, but he may, I have tried to show, lay hold with the aid of the imagination on the element of oneness that is inextricably blended with the manifoldness and change and to just that extent may build up a sound model for imitation" (xv).

Tate attacked Babbitt's position in "Humanism and Naturalism" (1929), an essay that T. S. Eliot published first in *The Criterion* under the title "The Fallacy of Humanism." Babbitt's damning flaw, Tate argued, was his eclecticism; the truce Babbitt proposed between imagination and oneness Tate would not admit. No center, he held, could come from within the flawed system itself—in this case the human self. "Until this center [a "living center of judgment and feeling"] is found," Tate wrote, "and not pieced together eclectically at the surface, humanism is an attempt to do mechanically—that is, naturalistically—what should be done morally."[8] Tate reacted negatively to the scale of values behind the part of Babbitt's case that calls for the impetus toward oneness to come from within the diseased imagination itself. The center that Tate wanted could come only from beyond the human sphere, and from beyond history. Human substitutes were, by definition, natural and originated in the troubled self. "Control" of the problem, Tate charged, was not the same as solution: "unity." Tate had found a symbol for this cultural and personal unity this "anything abiding" and therefore real, in the Old South—its people, institutions, forms of property. The nonexistence of the South in the present paled under its power as a symbol of the One. Obviously, I have abbreviated Tate's symbolizing poetics; but just as obviously this is a selective poetics. Some aspects of the Many must be excluded if the One is to be achieved. Traces show up in *The Fathers;* we will get to them in time. The humanist doctrine "of restraint does not look to unity, but to abstract and external control—not to solution of the moral problem, but to an attempt to get the moral results of unity by main force, by a kind of moral fascism" (171).

The Fathers is Tate's riposte to the humanist thrust, and the original condition of its transmission to us. He and the humanists had agreed on the threatening specter. Babbitt's vision of the horror might serve, for example, as a thematic portrait of the character of George Posey. "It is right here," Babbitt wrote, "that the failure of the incomplete positivist, the man who is positive only according to the natural law, is most conspicuous. What prevails in the region of the natural law is endless change and relativity; therefore the naturalist positivist attacks all the traditional creeds and dogmas for the very reason that they aspire to fixity" (xii). George Posey is visible elsewhere in Babbitt's modern tableau: "It was pointed out long ago that the characteristic of the half-educated man is that he is incurably restless; that he is filled with every manner of desire. In contrast with him the uncultivated man, the peasant, let us say, and the man of high cultivation have few and simple desires" (194–95). In this framework George Posey moves, buying and selling for the sheer need to try to quell his restlessness; becoming by turns tournament champion, peddler, private, smuggler, murderer, and in Lacy's older eyes, hero; he is unpredictability in the flesh, now fleeing his mother-in-law's funeral, now returning. The character of George Posey, then, is not simply Tate's conjuration of the mythic, evil protocapitalist in the southern myth. He is to be construed first as a symbol of Tate's version of the humanist image of the romantic naturalist become machine-age man. His "fable," as Tate allowed *The Fathers* to be called, is not first and only a fable of North and South—"the novel *Gone with the Wind* ought to have been";[9] it is a fable of humanism and religion, history and dogma, vying for power in and over the present.

Tate's Major Buchan and the order he represents, moreover, are not first and only a rendering of the actual Old South man. In them Tate explored the classical alternative to the romantic naturalist. Babbitt's classical man insisted on "restraint and proportion" (16), on decorum that was more than mere etiquette (23), on the imitation of a model that was genuinely universal, "set above [the] ordinary self" (22), and capable of subsuming it within a larger whole (166). To Babbitt this was sound imagination, but to Tate that alternative was chaos in disguise. In "Humanism and Naturalism" he had written as much; in *The Fathers* he dramatized the mutual destructivity of these wrongly conceived alternatives. He did not design *The Fathers* to recover southern history, in the simple sense of returning it for contemplation in the present, so much as he structured it to refute history itself.

The Fathers is, then, an elaborate evasion of history, for its central historical fact, the War Between the States, is actually de-realized, made into part of the master symbol. In Brooks's words this is a mediation of the Old South through the consciousness of its nonexistence in the present, Tate uses the southern version of the past as a sort of objective correlative for his sense of history in its present moment. The conflagration of 1861–65 foretells and confirms a return to apocalypse unless there is a change in the present order. Babbitt had prepared the way to see the Civil War as symbol:

> What leads the man of to-day to work with such energy according to the natural law and to be idle according to the human law is his intoxication with material success. A consideration that should therefore touch him is that in the long run not merely spiritual success or happiness, but material prosperity depend on an entirely different working. Let me revert here for a moment to my previous analysis: to work according to the human law is simply to rein in one's impulses. Now the strongest of all impulses is the will to power. The man who does not rein in his will to power and is at the same time very active according to the natural law is in a fair way to become an efficient megalomaniac. Efficient megalomania, whether developed in individuals of the same group or in whole national groups in their relations with one another, must lead sooner than later to war. (366)

The events of 1861–65 Tate recovers from history the only way he can —as symbols of the present emergency. This instance of unity stands for Unity itself. History is thus used to abolish history.

In this feat of establishing symbol over history Tate was urged on by, among others, Cleanth Brooks, who parallelled Tate's operations in his (Brooks's) literary recovery of tradition. In 1939, one year after the publication of *The Fathers*, Brooks dedicated *Modern Poetry and the Tradition* to Allen Tate. Tate had become, by that time, a major focal point in the widening cultural battle between tradition and, as the antagonists were variously named, humanism or naturalism. Brooks had seen the specter of dissolution in modern poetry, and enlisted Tate as poet and as dissenter from the modern surrender of the metaphysical.

Brooks's original preface to *Modern Poetry and the Tradition* claims that the Romantic movement initiated by the early Wordsworth and continued by Shelley and Keats made a radical break in the tradition of English poetry. Following Eliot, Brooks sees poetry as a continuum; "every poet that we read alters to some degree our total conception of poetry" (xxix). The mark of the antagonist to history and early New Critic is evident in the assumption that a "total conception of poetry" does, in fact, exist. Such a totalizing conception can only exist outside time in a metaphysical universe beyond history and constituted by the order and unity clearly lacking in the world of "the irrational, of experience as experience" (78). The Romantic poets, according to Brooks, disturbed the "total conception" by willfully courting the irrational. The modern poets, whom Brooks takes as his chief subject matter, have done so once again. And the return of movement to the stillness of the total conception reawakens the traditional critic to the defense of poetry.

Brooks's argument requires an example of a mind that could find and use a master image, a totalizing symbol under which separate, even contradictory, elements could be brought into unity and totality. He had found that mind in Tate and that image in the South Tate had transformed. In a rather long passage, part of which has already been quoted, Brooks refines his argument by focusing on southern poets who have chosen the South as their subject matter. For those familiar with thematic interpretations of *The Fathers*, Brooks seems almost to be glossing it: "The problem presented by an attempt to hold on to a tradition is, thus, ultimately a problem of sincerity or integrity. . . . the Old South cannot exist in the mind of the modern Southerner apart from its nonexistence in the present. The sentimentalist can, of course, dwell upon the Old South exclusively, giving a romantic construct which has no connection with the actual South of the past. (It is not even a paradox to say that we cannot know the past without knowing the present.)" (75). The present indigestibility of Brooks's thinking lurks in his insistence upon unifying the past and present above history. To bring the past into unity with the present (to "weld past with present" [75]) means inescapably to realize the past and to abolish time. Brooks's position does not merely call for a lifelike rendering of the past; it requires us to temporize the past, to see it as different from the present yet connected by the metaphysical One, the total conception. He rejected theories of history as logical or causal sequences (96–98) because that thinking translated in his mind into the dread "scientific civilization," a view that shifted the guarantee of cultural unity into the human mind. Tradition then became the opposite of logic, the sign of coherence or agreement over time but outside the human mind: in something larger than the self. Tate's Major Buchan occupies this paradoxical role, consistent in a logic of tradition that is embarrassingly foolish (Lacy is embarrassed by his father's chatting with the spa room clerk, with his father's antiquated flirtation with his wife) and ultimately feeble under attack by the new man George Posey and his deputies the threshing machine and profit-and-loss ledger. In other words, *The Fathers* is a symbol of Brooks's cultural criticism seen as a whole program in *Modern Poetry and the Tradition*.

For Brooks and others Tate had taken on the deep disjunctions in history and had emerged with unity. A modern, nonsouthern poet such as Carl Sandburg makes the error Tate had avoided: he contemporizes the past by imposing his own present mind upon it. Sandburg's immersion in the scientific civilization of the present had paved the way to error. First, the scientific present convinces the mind of its primacy: narcissism. Second, the modern view of history as logical (causal) series culminating in the present and the personal transforms time into a point, a vortex. Tate's figure for this transformation is "the abyss," a space with only depth. The central action of the second section of *The Fathers* symbolizes this process of personal-cultural disintegration: George, Semmes, Lacy, and Yellow Jim—a motley kin group—relentlessly pass lower and lower into darkness and confusion, the terrible present to which George is leading them without knowing what he is about to do.

Tate could correct Sandburg, and did. His poems on the past, Brooks points out, especially the "Ode to the Confederate Dead," explore the reality and meaning of the past for the modern mind. "One cannot find a living relation," Brooks argues, "between the present and the past without being honest to the present—and that involves taking into account the anti-historical character of our present" (102). Tate knew this to be his territory: whether to realize history in time, or to realize it as an image outside of time. The "Ode" deals with the latter, a preference for form over history. The former, because of the narrative necessity of *The Fathers*, however, puts the image into motion, puts Tate in the foe's territory. It is not the Old South civilization Tate was after in his novel, but history itself in its own language, the language of narrative.

Here is a point of crucial distinction. Brooks, in *Modern Poetry and the Tradition*, seems to read Tate's version of the modern dilemma as static.

Those living then functioned in a society that guaranteed intelligibility of motive and unity of emotion and intellect. Thus the Confederate charge to death undertaken in a spirit beyond anything Tate's abstracted modern mind could possibly know. In "A Retrospective Introduction" to the 1967 reissue of his book, Brooks allows that he might make certain "qualifications" thirty years after his original readings. Perhaps here is a spot to make one, for most criticism of Tate tends to place Tate's alternatives in a static, ahistorical balance. Present moments of human consciousness in the South of venerated myth were qualitatively different from present moments of consciousness now—whenever *now* might be. The critic is to point to this dissociation in time and consciousness, affirm the ideality and unity of the past, transfer those qualities to the work under scrutiny, and extract a message that propels us on to a once and future state of completeness and unity. In this program the southern renascence finds its texts and commentary. And yet this critical operation omits the narrative dynamics of *The Fathers*. As an excursion into the text suggests, the unity of a completed network of exclusively internal relationships is not possible in narrative without evasions and "strategies of containment" by both author and critic, and sustained over time.

The Fathers must be read in the historical condition of its composition, not within the quasi-historical frame of its imagined action. The modernism-tradition debates of the 1930s, to which Brooks, Tate, Babbit, Eliot, and many others contributed, give *The Fathers* its first referential community of texts. We have neglected this grounding for a quasi-historical grounding in the history of the Old South regime. Jameson's program of interpretive horizons and historical skepticism helps us to see our way out of the problem.

The first horizon, as Jameson denominates it, is the arena of formal analysis: "the individual narrative, or the individual formal structure, is to be grasped as the imaginary resolution of a real contradiction" (77). In this horizon an application to *The Fathers,* and to the body of commentary that has grown to depend upon it, seems fairly clear, although not simple. The "real contradiction" that Tate's narrative purports to resolve is not the problem of the Civil War but of the vast repercussions in the American society of the interwar years of the economic changes conveniently called by the agrarian-industrial labels. As I have tried to show, Tate's novel reads his own "age" at least as plausibly as the age of the past of the Old South. References to actual history are not central to the conflict of the novel, and their mention only emphasizes Jameson's point that "history is inaccessible to us except in textual form, or in other words, that it can be approached only by way of prior (re)textualization" (82). Jameson also warns us not to devote undivided attention to history in the text; we cannot know history except as a version of our own present. Brooks and Tate were well aware of this trap too, yet considered it the modern problem, not the necessary ground of consciousness in time: "The situation is peculiarly the modern situation: we are obsessed with a consciousness of the past which drives us back upon history in search for meanings. [Those of the present are unacceptable.] The absolutes are gone—are dissolved, indeed, by our consciousness of the past—by our consciousness of a plurality of histories and meanings" (86). So far the agreement with Jameson might hold. Bringing an inherent unity out of this contingency in this anti-historicist alternative, Tate made the essence of Jameson's second horizon the field of his novel. We are never allowed off the ground of the divided attention, never allowed to deal with *The Fathers* without balancing relational aspects, past and present, North and South, kin by blood and kin by marriage. Jameson's second horizon is, he says, social and concerned with viewing reality as the field of class conflicts or relations—to see what is real as a function of the instruments (social and economic) of what does the seeing. Tate was no stranger to this concept, and his novel cannot be read without this sort of attention, but he proposed to resolve all pairs of relations into a unity. The novel resists his efforts at unity as much as it accepts them.

Schematic interpretation of *The Fathers* as meaning the how and why of the annihilation by modern industrial capitalism of the stable order of tradition is undermined when we see how the narrative evades the economic grounding of the traditional order itself. The defining of some human beings as commodities is usually attributed to George Posey. Lionel Trilling might have been the first to notice that George rides into the tournament on the back of Yellow Jim. But we can only preserve this neat schematic reading by ignoring Lacy's own evasion of the economic facts of Pleasant Hill. In what functions as patterned action in *The Fathers,* Lacy makes his gaze follow another's, only to skip the crucial facts of the scene he is led to behold. In one instance his gaze follows that of his brother Semmes.

I followed, and looking down on the brick walk between the house and the garden I saw Henry Jackson going round the end of the house with an armful of wood.

"He's carrying it to the front door," I said.

Semmes seemed not to hear me but followed the Negro with his eyes. "It don't make any difference where he totes it." He turned away from the window. "Twenty Negroes are too many for this place."

That was the beginning of my introduction to the world where people counted and added things, the first intrusion of change into my consciousness, and I only dimly knew what it meant. (19)

Lacy's evasion is keyed to the phrase "counted . . . things"; Semmes counts *people*. Counting and adding people as commodities is, Lacy knows, an introduction to change. And he only "dimly" recognizes the presence of history (change) in his enclave of tradition because full recognition would be the acknowledgment of the abyss.

Lacy looks out over the Buchan estate more than once, glancing each time toward and then away from the evidence that the work of the farm is done by others, and the more important fact that work itself, not an idea, is the means of keeping Pleasant Hill in existence. In another early scene Lacy remembers the bearing of George Posey just before he (George) fled the funeral. George greets Lacy, then looks away, perhaps assessing the cash value of the Buchan holdings. Lacy also makes an inventory. "He resumed his gaze. I too looked up at the gallery sagging at one end, the cracked paint on the weatherboarding, at the wisps of smoke struggling out of the big red end-chimneys, then off up the ridge towards the Negro cabins, a pink brick row, and towards the stables and, back of them, near the woods, the big unpainted tobacco barn" (7). Lacy looks back to George, whose eyes seem to concentrate on the dead woman's garden with its (to him) mocking "first shoots of April green." Then Lacy again trails George's gaze and is taken away with it to the horseblock, the cedar-lined drive leading away from Pleasant Hill to "the 'big road' that led into the great world—Fairfax, Occoquan, Pohick, Alexandria, then down the Potomac by salt water to the cities beyond the main!" (7).

The gazing scenes tell us much, for Lacy's attention skips from the Negro cabins, the hard actuality of work and history, to the escape signified by the salt water of the main and punctuated by the exclamation point. If the restless, romantic venture capitalist George Posey can translate his half-brother into cash for the purchase of a mare, Lacy can evade the clear signs of his economic exploitation of those who do the work and produce the life of Pleasant Hill. He moves smoothly from the order of history and economics, where things and people are counted up, to the magic realm of romance—the cities of the main.

Nor is this an isolated instance of Lacy's evasion. Scarcely two pages later a similar incident occurs. Lacy has gone to order Coriolanus to saddle George's horse, and after giving the old man the peremptory order, he turns to look at the back of the house that images his own fledgling authority over his elder: "One of the Negro girls was hanging a red quilt over the rail of the upper back gallery: it had come from my mother's bed. Over to the right beyond the out-kitchen, by the smokehouse, Henry Jackson, the yard boy, now that the severe old Coriolanus was out of sight, was whistling; one of the young wenches passed and he laughed and slapped her; she giggled. I felt an almost uncontrollable desire to laugh. I looked down at the pawed earth. There was a piece of old strap" (9). Behind the facade of Buchan ritual material life continues. Work resists the timeless mode that ritual enforces. The red quilt is the same red quilt beneath which Lacy's mother lay dying; only the black servant can deal with its staleness and mortality. Kitchen and smokehouse continue. So does the daily activity of lust and power: he slaps, she giggles. There is no such play when Lacy fondles Jane. The visual inventory is completed by another token of escape. Lacy picks up a bit of strap to commemorate his moment of close encounter with the material grounding of his life. When he exits the real to pursue Jane Posey in a heroic quest, he gets rid of the strap, the "indecorous thing" (88–89). After the burial and the ominous quasi-betrothal to Jane at the coffin of his mother, Lacy rushes to retrieve the strap (106). The last time he recalls it is triggered by his farewell note to his father just before leaving with George for the war (290). The strap appears each time Lacy moves away from ritual and toward history, signifying that the two orders, far from being separate, are coextensive.

This pattern is repeated throughout the first section in larger and smaller narrative segments. Lacy remembers the tournament where George triumphed over John Langton. Lacy saw most of it from the underside of the ladies pavilion where Squire Broadacre's son offered him "some of it"—"it" being Sis, a mulatto girl with "a pretty Caucasian face" (60). Almost all critiques omit this episode from their exhibits. Mizener does cite it, yet evades its import by turning to a literary comparison of Wink Broadacre, the young man who offers Lacy the use of Sis, as an "almost humorous" Tom Sawyer (xiv). Who can think of Tom Sawyer implicated in fornication and possibly incest? When the aesthetic unity of the work is the objective of the critic, as it is in Mizener's critique, certain aspects of the narrative must be contained.

Striving critically to argue the aesthetic absolute in form takes Tate at (one of) his words. In his reply to Trilling's review he states his own belief in an absolute; by denying that it is political or social, Tate leaves us free to assume the aesthetic. But by revising the ending to *The Fathers* Tate shows us how to subdivide the absolute—in fact, to qualify it. If Lacy can "partly represent" the old traditions, does that mean they can be selectively considered? The unity and coherence of the Old South fabric begins to fray.

Our habit of seeing *The Fathers,* and through it the genre of southern narrative, as fixed in the fields of meaning by an overarching truth—as the Old South was presumably fixed in history by possession of land, by veneration of place and family, by a unity of sensibility reflected in ritual —cannot be fully accounted for by the text alone. In fact, *The Fathers,* by its frequent return to scenes and figures of escape and evasion, continually advances the qualification or negation of unity and meaning. Lacy, being led by his father to his appointed place in the ritual funeral procession, "sees" the nonexistent truth all around him in spite of "the agreement, slowly arrived at, to let the abyss alone" (186): "There was of course no one moment that it was all leading up to, and that piece of knowledge about life, learned that day, has permitted me to survive the disasters that overwhelmed other and better men, and to tell their story" (101). Survival and narrating are identical. Better men cannot tell their stories because, like Major Buchan, they cannot bear the knowledge that narrative leads up to "no one moment" above any other, just to the next.

Jameson's third horizon renders narrative form self-conscious. This self-consciousness is detectable in Tate's handling of narrative in *The Fathers,* and is inferable from the fact that Tate seldom if ever returned to narrative. Narrative, because by its form it leads to no one moment, defeats the striving for unity. Part of the formal self-consciousness in Tate's novel is that the story itself denies its hoped-for resolution. Except for an early instance, critical readings have argued the unity.

In the history of critical commentary on *The Fathers,* the original skirmish pitted history versus unity, the Many versus the One. Since the late 1930s, however, critics of formal unity have controlled the rereading of the novel. Lionel Trilling, whose *Partisan Review* notice of *The Fathers* appeared in 1938, was involved in the controversy of his age on the side of history.[10] Trilling is also the original source for calling Tate's novel a fable. He sensed that Tate's relation to history in *The Fathers* was less like that of Balzac and more like that of the Grimm brothers or Joseph Ernest Renan. Trilling's review drew Tate temporarily out of the rhetorical mode, in which one expects one's readers to perform silently, and into the dialectical: Tate replied to his reviewer with a letter to the editor. Trilling's review, Tate's rejoinder, and a one-paragraph rebuttal signed, "The Editors," constitute a discreet segment of a critical dialectic, a tiny example of what Jameson calls "the relationship between the artistic fact as such and the larger social and historical reality to which it corresponds" (*MF*, 331).

Trilling's review acknowledges a central tension in *The Fathers*. The reality of history conflicts with the ideality of myth, the content of Tate's narrative (violent and disruptive) with the flawless evenness of time. Trilling ventures beyond the work itself and suggests that Tate himself might suffer from a version of this tension, clinging to tradition yet repulsed by its actual deeds.

Tate replied in time for the following issue, complimenting Trilling for his diligent awareness of his (Tate's) work, but taking issue with the reviewer's placement of *The Fathers* in the same arena with "a Marxian position" on human history. Tate denies Trilling's judgment that *The Fathers* is an "indictment of the Old South," by proposing it as "an indictment of the necessary limitation of human nature." "Any highly organized society," Tate continues, "Marxian or any other sort, could develop the tensions that give the dynamic force to my fable" (125). In other words, Tate prefers to see his novel ahistorically, as part of the debate over the culturally organizing dogmas vying for privilege in a world apparently facing the disintegration of civilization, but uncontaminated by any social or historical circumstances. Tate is very clear in saying that he finds no "political absolute" (125) only "the necessary limitations of human nature" considered apolitically. "The Editors" rebut Tate briefly, clarifying their historicist view that "the decay of the Old Smith [*sic*] which Mr. Tate's novel describes was the product of historical factors rather than of any 'necessary limitations of human nature'" (126). The line is drawn—history opposes dogma.

This brief exchange emphasizes the immediate conditions of the production of *The Fathers* in a politicized arena in which it, through its author, proposed to take no part. Thrust into an age debating the meaning of civilization and of form, *The Fathers* proposed to uphold the traditional view of form as immune from "historical factors" and from history itself. Companion works such as those by Babbitt and Brooks serve as coordinates to locate *The Fathers,* and Trilling's review is evidence of one other side's refusal to accept its premises.

The subsequent history of commentary on *The Fathers* illustrates that formalists have made it their own; its dogmatic nature is stressed at the expense of the historical. After reviews in the late 1930s, Arthur Mizener's 1947 essay in formalist criticism set the standard for interpretation. Mizener's essay, partially reprinted as the introduction to the 1960 reissue of the novel, stresses the resolution of the novel's tension through formal unity. *The Fathers,* Mizener argues, is unusual among American novels for its "remarkable unity of idea and form" (ix). Mizener sees a version of the tension Trilling pointed out but is less willing to indict the violent Old South. Even allowing for the evil in that vanished civilization, Mizener wants us to admit that "it was civilized in a way our life is not" (xii). Evil, even the "savage ideal" motivating John Langston, "is the unintended and limited evil of an otherwise ordered world" (xiv). The critic's final critical judgment is that, regardless of the evil in the political system, and regardless of the "unbounded evil" potential in George Posey (who is seen in his costume of Rousseauistic naturalist), *The Fathers* is "a sustained, particularized, and unified symbol" (xix).

Frank Kermode, reviewing the English edition in 1960, was perhaps even more impressed by the coherence and unity of *The Fathers.* "The dignity and power of this book depend upon the power of a central image presented with concreteness and profundity, and not upon one's acceptance of Mr. Tate's history."[11] The "central image" Kermode refers to is the whole, completed novel itself, its various subsidiary images having fully accreted across the temporal duration of the narrative. This mystical, time-and-history-abolishing process comes about through the power of the artist's concentration and intelligence. "To be obsessed by the chosen historical moment, as a theologian might meditate the Incarnation, so that one shares it with everybody yet avoids all contamination from less worthy and less austere intelligences—that is the basic qualification" (72). Kermode's review is tantalizing; more than Mizener he invests *The Fathers* with a unity for which the dogma of the theologian provides an appropriate simile. And Kermode also stresses the reduction of history to a moment, in fact an act of single and private will over actuality and material reality rather than an act of engagement with history. The particular dogma Kermode chooses is the Incarnation—perhaps the theological mystery that challenges the historical sense most seriously. Kermode sees how thoroughly Tate's meditation has escaped history. In Kermode's view the

Civil War is crucially significant to Tate, but not as history. "What the English Civil War meant to Mr. Eliot, the American means to Mr. Tate; the moment when the modern chaos began, though it cast its shadow before" (73). The American Civil War, Kermode rightly argues, is not an event but a symbol guaranteed from beyond time; part of a habit of seeing history not as human beings living with material concerns and circumstances, but as a design or pattern that is vouchsafed those of worthy and austere intelligence.

This is essentially the record of rereadings of *The Fathers* into the post-southern phase. Critics have either attempted to find unity in the novel by differing ways and means (a unified point of view, a redefinition or rediscovery of the central symbol, a reaffirmation of the southern tradition) or they have returned to the theme of tension, seeing George Posey as the modern man and Major Buchan as the civilized man of doomed tradition.[12] The trouble with clinging to either approach is of Tate's own making: the ending, of which there are now three versions, scrambles the order.

The problem of the three endings—the original, the revised ending of 1977, and Tate's "Note" to the revised edition in which he rereads both endings—is simply that Tate's revision acknowledges the coexistence of two readings, not the dogmatic unity of one. The original ending finds George and Lacy, at night, saying a cryptic farewell amid the ashes of Pleasant Hill. The chimneys are a dim and shaking blur (306) symbolically charging the scene with phallic retreat. George goes back to Georgetown and Lacy off to the Confederate Army, to "finish it," perhaps the last formal gesture of the traditional mode of life. "If I am killed," Lacy closes, "it will be because I love him more than I love any man" (306). There *The Fathers* originally ended, and Kermode thought that final sentence "as rich a sentence as ever ended a novel" (74). Lacy, of course, survives "it" and narrates the novel, but George is left in a pretty deep limbo. Resolution, if any, must be wrung from the aesthetic elements of the work, and one tradition of commentary has done that.

But Tate tinkered with the ending, in fact chose to write two additional endings. For the uninitiated, "it" in the 1977 version is glossed "until Appomattox four years later." George does not go out ambiguously, shedding identities as he does suits, but goes on to perform "important things" that Lacy could not know or tell. Lacy himself is brought back to George's grave to testify to George's restoration of Susan and their daughter, and to "what he did for me" (307). "What he became in himself I shall never forget. Because of this I venerate his memory more than the memory of any other man" (307).

What George Posey became in himself Lacy shall never forget and we shall never know. The relative spareness and clarity of the original final sentence is obscured by the 1977 revision. To what does "this" refer, if not to "what he became in himself"? Tate asks us to clarify one indeterminacy with another. His "Note" to the revised edition further muddles the case. Here are the final two sentences of the "Note": "He [Lacy] affirms the principles that George scorns, and in a sense, as his surrogate, attributes them to George. George will permit Lacy to survive in a new world in which not all the old traditions, which Lacy partly represents, are dead" (314). This is yet a third rewriting of the ending, more qualified and equivocal and evasive than the second. Tate clearly rethought his novel from its end, from its purported closure, from the punctuation of its presumed unity. He is the novel's most deconstructive critic. But he only acknowledges an evasion pattern discernible from the outset. He must have known, through Lacy the survivor, that narrative catches all striving for unity and foils it: "there was of course no one moment it was all leading up to."

NOTES

1. Lewis P. Simpson, *The Brazen Face of History* (Baton Rouge: Louisiana State University Press, 1980), esp. chap. 13.

2. Fredric Jameson, *Marxism and Form* (Princeton: Princeton University Press, 1971). References hereafter cited parenthetically in text as *MF*.

3. Cleanth Brooks, *Modern Poetry and the Tradition* (1939; repr. Chapel Hill: University of North Carolina Press, 1967), 75–76.

4. There are two versions of Allen Tate's *The Fathers:* the first was published in 1938 (repr., intro. by Arthur Mizener, Denver: Allen Swallow, 1960), and a revised edition was published in 1977, with an introduction by Thomas Daniel Young (Baton Rouge: Louisiana State University Press).

5. Fredric Jameson, *The Political Unconscious* (Ithaca: Cornell University Press, 1981), 76–93; hereafter cited parenthetically in text as *P*.

6. Allen Tate, "A Southern Mode of the Imagination," in *Essays of Four Decades* (Chicago: Swallow Press, 1986), 577–92.

7. Irving Babbitt, *Rousseau and Romanticism* (Boston: Houghton Mifflin, 1919).

8. Allen Tate, "Humanism and Naturalism," in *Memoirs and Opinions, 1926–*

1974 (Chicago: Swallow Press, 1975), 180; see Tate's preface to this volume, p. xi, for information on first publication of this essay by Eliot.

9. Arthur Mizener, introduction to Tate, *The Fathers*.

10. Lionel Trilling, "Allen Tate as Novelist," *Partisan Review* 6 (Fall 1938): 111–13. For Tate's letter to the *Partisan Review* and the editorial rebuttal, see 7 (Winter 1939): 125–26.

11. Frank Kermode, "Old Orders Changing," *Encounter* 15 (Aug. 1960): 74.

12. These critical views would be fairly represented by the following: Ferman Bishop, *Allen Tate* (New York: Twayne, 1967); Lynette Carpenter, "The Battle Within: The Beleaguered Consciousness in Allen Tate's *The Fathers*," *Southern Literary Journal* 8 (Spring 1976): 3–24 (unified by point of view); Thomas Daniel Young, introduction to Tate, *The Fathers* (Baton Rouge: Louisiana State University Press, 1977) (the novel seen as affirmation of southern myth belatedly over the conquering North); Robert J. Brinkmeyer, *Three Catholic Writers of the Modern South* (Jackson: University Press of Mississippi, 1985) (Tate's quest for dogmatic unity successful in *The Fathers*); Robert S. Dupree, *Allen Tate and the Augustinian Imagination* (Baton Rouge: Louisiana State University Press, 1983) (primarily a study of the poetry, but organized around the idea of Tate's resolution of the contradictions of the tradition-history dilemma: the narrator of *The Fathers* "intuits that history has some kind of direction, even if it is not usefully knowable" [126]); and Richard Law, "'Active Faith' and Ritual in *The Fathers*," *American Literature* 55 (Oct. 1983): 345–66 (one of the first critical essays to suggest that the novel does not end on a resolved note; Tate, Law says, set out to prove the hypothesis that tradition creates a useful human civilization but actually illustrates the contradictions better than the hypothesis [348]).

Edgar Allan Poe:

The Error of Reading and

the Reading of Error

JOSEPH G. KRONICK

In a famous letter to Evert A. Duyckink, Melville expresses his grudging admiration for Emerson, who, despite his "oracular gibberish," can be counted as one of the "thought-divers": "I love all men who *dive*. Any fish can swim near the surface, but it takes a great whale to go down stairs five miles or more; & if he dont attain the bottom, why, all the lead in Galena can't fashion the plumet that will. I'm not talking of Mr. Emerson now—but of the whole corps of thought-divers, that have been diving & coming up again with blood-shot eyes since the world began."[1] Although "blood-shot eyes" may have figured in contemporary portraits of a haggard Edgar Allan Poe, he never, so he tells us, chose to search the depths for truth: "As regards the greater truths, men oftener err by seeking them at the bottom than at the top; the depth lies in the huge abysses where wisdom is sought—not in the palpable palaces where she is found."[2] For Melville, we discover truth only by diving deep, but for Poe, deep leads unto deep and not to truth. This contrast between depth and surface may serve as some indication of what distinguishes Poe from his northern contemporaries, but critical discussion of symbolism and, more recently, of the hieroglyphic has erased this difference.[3]

Poe has long been the other of American literature—he is either the protosymbolist who has returned to us via the translations of Baudelaire, Mallarmé, and Valéry, or the poet of the unconscious who has anatomized that part of the psyche few writers ever admitted existed. Roy Harvey

Pearce aptly describes Poe as "a kind of cultural hero of the imagination."[4] When he is not being defended as a founder of modernism or as the dark genius of American literature, he is attacked for the crudity of both his style and thought. The vigor of Poe's defenders and detractors has assured his status as a major writer, but it has taken poststructuralists to secure for Poe a place in the American renaissance. The way for this revision, however, was prepared by F. O. Matthiessen's and Charles Feidelson's theories of symbolism. Although Matthiessen hardly mentions Poe in *The American Renaissance,* he says that Poe is closer to his American contemporaries than to Baudelaire precisely because he shared with Emerson and Hawthorne the "loosely Platonic" concept that in poetry the word is to the idea as the body is to the soul.[5] Feidelson, who gives a little more attention to Poe in his *Symbolism and American Literature,* also says Poe's idea of literature was basically the same as Emerson's, Hawthorne's, and Melville's, but whereas transcendentalism is a kind of "materialistic idealism," Poe sought to rarefy or idealize matter, instead of beginning with the Christian concept of spirit.[6]

Following Matthiessen's and Feidelson's pioneering work, John Irwin's *American Hieroglyphics* succeeds in assimilating Poe into the American renaissance by substituting the Saussurian concept of the sign for Matthiessen's Coleridgean notion of the symbol. Poe now joins Emerson, Whitman, Melville, and Hawthorne in their attempts to discover the origin of man by deciphering the origin of language. The hieroglyph is central to Irwin's study "because in pictographic writing the shape of a sign is in a sense a double of the physical shape of the object it represents."[7] Irwin's examination of the mirroring of the self in the hieroglyph reorients us toward a semiological reading of nineteenth-century American literature.

We have come more and more to think of the writers of nineteenth-century America as telling us that the self is a product of language. The self has been dislodged from its principal place as the origin of the work or as that which we can identify as consciousness and is now seen as a product of the play of signifiers in a text without a determinable signified. If we reject the phenomenological description of consciousness as the self-presence of the speaking subject, then in the writerly text, we may conclude that the self becomes an activity of writing, and the pure auto-affection of consciousness is opened to the temporal and spatial play of signs that function in the total absence of the subject.[8] The play of signifiers opens a space in writing wherein the author declares his absence.[9]

And we confirm his absence whenever we read his tales: "Ye who read are still among the living; but I who write shall have long since gone my way into the region of shadows" (1:218).

The receptivity of Poe's texts to poststructuralist readings may rest largely on his insistence on their textuality. Poe's love of cryptography, literary hoaxes, and puzzles opens his texts to pyrotechnical displays of interpretive skills, for Poe remains a writer who draws many of his readers not because they like or admire him but because his texts are so malleable for the close interpreter. This quality may explain the hold Poe's texts have exerted on his French readers from Baudelaire to Lacan and Derrida. Barbara Johnson has investigated the triad of Poe, Lacan, and Derrida within the framework of psychoanalysis and has argued that the disagreement over the meaning of "The Purloined Letter" reveals that the meaning of a message is so "traversed by its own otherness to itself" that any reading must be in a sense narcissistic—the reader can find only the message that he or she sends.[10] The intensity of these readers, however, makes them liable to blindness, as was that other Parisian interpreter, the prefect of police in the Dupin tales: " 'He impaired his vision by holding the object too close. He might see perhaps, one or two points with unusual clearness, but in so doing he, necessarily, lost sight of the matter as a whole' " (1:412). Poe offers a sure remedy for this failing—be superficial. If critics have not heeded this advice to seek for clues in obvious places, it is not because they have been inattentive to the surface of Poe's texts.

Various psychoanalytic and poststructuralist readings have focused almost entirely on the interrelationship of signifiers in Poe's text to the exclusion of any signified content. This transformation of Poe's works into texts, to borrow Roland Barthes's distinction,[11] has produced readings striking not only for their theoretical insights but also for their avoidance of those questions that have plagued Poe criticism, that is, the uncertainty of his intentions and his so-called execrable style. The questions of style and intention would seem to throw us back into the uncertain theoretical position of pre–New Critical interpretation, but Shoshana Felman has suggested that "the critical discourse surrounding Poe, is indeed one of the most visible ('self-evident') *effects* of Poe's poetic signifier, of his text." Felman rightly points out that the question of effects is a question of the place of the analyst or interpreter in the text: "the very position of the interpreter—of the analyst—turns out to be not *outside,* but *inside* the text."[12] Felman's essay is a subtle and valuable one, but it may be said that she reaches conclusions not only shared by many of Poe's critics but, as she argues so well, one already anticipated by Poe, even down to the unreadability of the analytical.

There are certain mysteries, Poe says, that are like "a certain German book . . . 'er lasst sich nicht lesen'—it does not permit itself to be read" (1:388). The question of the unreadability of the Poe text is a question of superficiality. It is the superficiality, the very overdeterminedness, of his tales that renders them opaque. For the psychoanalytic critic, this unreadability is the negative moment wherein depth is restored to the text as a projection of the reader. In making the interpretation, rather than the text, the object of analysis, the critic beats Poe at his own game—the critic now asserts that all interpretations of Poe err by being superficial, but in their very superficiality they register the effects of Poe's signifiers. Depth now is shifted from the text to the reader, who in turn ascribes it to the text. The psychoanalytic critic reinscribes the interpretation and returns it to its source: the reader. We discover in Poe's texts and their scenes of misreading that error makes interpretation possible: "Deprived of ordinary resources, the analyst throws himself into the spirit of his opponent, identifies himself therewith, and not unfrequently sees thus, at a glance, the sole methods (sometimes indeed absurdly simple ones) by which he may seduce into error or hurry into miscalculation" (1:398). By identifying the interpretation with the text, the reader is seduced into the error of profundity. The text that generates the interpretation is only known by the effects it produces. The reader, however, identifies the effect with the author and ultimately errs by his ingenuity: "The analytical power should not be confounded with simple ingenuity; for while the analyst is necessarily ingenious, the ingenious man is often remarkably incapable of analysis" (1:399).

Error in Poe is always an error of intentionality—either the critic attacks Poe for failing to achieve the effects he seems to have intended, such as humor or horror, or the critic defends Poe for having anticipated the interpretations his texts have elicited. In one case, the reader confounds Poe's texts with their effects, and in the other, the reader confounds the effects with his own ingenious interpretation. In both cases, the effect is an interpretation, and this interpretation is a product of the error of profundity, the confusion of significance with depth. But in erring, the interpreter confirms the truth of Poe's texts—understanding is not only impossible but also unproductive, for misreading alone generates textuality. The reader errs by his or her ingenuity because Poe's texts are analytical, not ingenious. To analyze is not to uncover or bring to light what is hidden;

it means to expose what lies in plain view—that is, the impenetrability of the familiar. To read Poe, then, is to confound the familiar with the hidden.

Poe's tales are filled with clues that reflect both upon himself as writer and on the reader as well. In tale after tale, Poe incorporates within his stories their own misreading. As Patrick Quinn has pointed out, much of "The Fall of the House of Usher" concerns the narrator's failure to interpret the clues laid out before him in this doppelgänger. The doubling in this story extends beyond the incestuous pairing of Roderick and Madeline Usher to the narrator, who "is at the same time both the author of the story and, as spectator of its events, the audience as well." [13] Unlike Roderick, whose desire for his sister reflects a desire for self-possession, the narrator is incapable of reflection—that is, the story he tells escapes him or passes beyond his vision.

The image of this failure of vision comes in the beginning when he admits he cannot explain the horror he feels upon seeing the House of Usher: "I was forced to fall back upon the unsatisfactory conclusion, that while, beyond doubt, there *are* combinations of very simple natural objects which have the power of thus affecting us, still the analysis of this power lies among considerations beyond our depth" (1:317). The very familiarity of this arrangement places the scene beyond the understanding, but, the narrator goes on to say, an aesthetic rearrangement brings the natural within the realm of understanding: "It was possible, I reflected, that a mere different arrangement of the particulars of the scene, of the details of the picture, would be sufficient to modify, or perhaps to annihilate its capacity for sorrowful impression" (1:317–18). Only by disordering the scene through aesthetic representation can the narrator control its effects. This reflection on the affective properties of a "scene" or "picture" leads to a reflection to the second degree—the narrator proceeds to the tarn and looks down into the reflection in the water and gazes "with a shudder even more thrilling than before—upon the remodelled and inverted images of the grey sedge, and the ghostly tree-stems, and the vacant eye-like windows" (1:318). Reflection leads to reflection, but the narrator's blindness produces no insight; his eyes, like those of the windows, are vacant. Distinctly missing from this image, however, is the face of the narrator, which we can expect is reflected in the water. The text is certainly overdetermined. The narrator enters upon a highly artificial scene only to call it natural and then transforms this artifice into a second artifice.

The inverted image found in the tarn foreshadows the inverted relation between the House and its inhabitants and between the incestuous twins as well. Finally, we get further doublings in the inclusion of the previously published poem, "The Haunted Palace," which is said to be an impromptu composition, and in the "Mad Trist" of Sir Launcelot Canning, a nonexistent book from which the narrator reads only to hear echoes in the house of the ludicrous tale before him.

Lost in this seemingly unending series of reflections, the narrator can never resolve the events into a discernible meaning. Nor can we agree with Quinn that the reader can decipher the clues that escape the frightened narrator, for whatever naturalistic or symbolic reading we can come up with, the tale's multiple scenes of reflection are tropes for the very misreading it attributes to the narrator. The readers participate in the deception when they attempt to fix the tale within one of the several perspectives offered in the text.

The scene of reading receives its most explicit treatment in "The Purloined Letter" and the passage on the game of odd and even. The game, we will recall, consists of guessing whether an opponent has an odd or even number of marbles hidden in his hand. This guessing game is perfected by a boy who invariably succeeds by identifying himself with his opponent. As the narrator says, " 'It is merely . . . an identification of the reasoner's intellect with that of the opponent.' " The narrator, being a man of average intellect—he is smarter than the prefect of police but not as smart as Dupin—has not quite fathomed the significance of Dupin's story. The identification is not strictly with the intellect but with the expression of the opponent. Dupin quotes the boy himself: " 'When I wish to find out how wise, or how stupid, or how good, or how wicked is any one, or what are his thoughts at the moment, I fashion the expression of my face, as accurately as possible, in accordance with the expression of his, and then wait to see what thoughts or sentiments arise in my mind or heart, as if to match or correspond with the expression' " (1:689–90). It is by imitating the expression of the other that the boy achieves understanding. By means of his wholly superficial imitation, thoughts and sentiments lying within or behind the expression spontaneously arise within the imitator.

The process would seem to be a paradigmatic example of the hermeneutic principle that understanding means understanding the expression, not some hypostasized interior that exists independent of the expression. This promise of complete understanding, however, exceeds anything the hermeneutician would claim as possible. Richard Wilbur correctly remarks that Dupin, despite his "analytical genius," really bases his solutions on "poetic intuition." [14] But applying the boy's description of his method to Dupin's solution of the mystery, we might say that his intuition is more properly phenomenological—he intuits the intention of his opponent in a wholly sensuous way.

The importance of the superficiality of this method underlies Dupin's explanation of the prefect's failure to discover the letter: "For its practical value it [the boy's method] depends upon this . . . and the Prefect and his cohort fail so frequently, first, by default of this identification, and, secondly, by ill-admeasurement, or rather through non-admeasurement, of the intellect with which they are engaged. They consider only their *own* ideas of ingenuity; and, in searching for anything hidden, advert only to the modes in which *they* would have hidden it" (1:690). Failure to identify is a failure to imitate. The prefect can identify only with what resembles him; the other or the different escapes the range of his understanding because he has not learned the art of mimicry. It is, of course, tempting to see in this passage on identification with the other a metaphor for various models of psychoanalytic reading. I would, however, agree with Bloom that such "Freudian translations are in his case merely redundant." [15] (We might note that in dismissing Freudian readings of Poe as redundant, Bloom at once hits upon a feature of Derrida's reading of Poe—all interpretation is redundant or a repetition of a pre-text—and yet fails to grasp it.) But the question of identification can be put within a hermeneutic framework as well, and in light of Poe's penchant for cryptography and the various tropes for reading in "The Purloined Letter," this approach seems to have a certain "authorization."

The failure of the prefect, therefore, is a failure to "read" his opponent. He has been too ingenious and not analytical enough. Confronted with a text, he projects an understanding that he possesses but which does not correspond to that of the text. The Minister D., of course, has anticipated how the police will act and so is able to circumvent their efforts to recover the letter. We are within the hermeneutic circle. All efforts to understand a text, according to Heidegger, involve an act of projecting a meaning onto the text, and this meaning is revised through the course of time. Gadamer describes the hermeneutic circle succinctly: "The process that Heidegger describes is that every revision of the fore-project is capable of projecting before itself a new project of meaning, that rival projects can emerge side by side until it becomes clearer what the unity of meaning is, that interpretation begins with fore-conceptions that are replaced by more suitable ones." [16] The police project upon the minister a certain mode of behavior that corresponds with what experience has taught them to expect. But having made this projection, they do not revise it when their interpretation fails. Indeed, they simply repeat the error, assuming that their theory must be right and that the error lies in the execution. The police fail, not because they offer the wrong interpretation, but because they fail to understand what is being interpreted. Heidegger writes, "Any interpretation which is to contribute understanding, must already have understood what is to be interpreted." [17] The police believe that they are confronted by an intellect that is no different from theirs: "They consider only their *own* ideas of ingenuity; and, in searching for anything hidden, advert only to the modes in which *they* would have hidden it" (1:690). Their error lies in their ingenuity; they fail because they are confronted with an intellect that is either above *or below* their own. The prefect says, the minister is "a poet, which I take to be only one remove from a fool" (1:684). The prefect's error is to think the minister is only one remove from a fool, for, as we shall see, if he recognized that D. is a fool, he could have solved the case himself.

Dupin explains his success in retrieving the letter by referring back to his joke that the truth is " 'A little *too* self-evident' " (1:681). As self-evident truth, the mystery bears its solution in its face, so to speak—it is the evidence of its own truth or solution. The prefect insists that the surface hides a mystery that he must explore to the depths. Dupin corrects this mistake by describing another scene of misreading. In a passage where Dupin begins to sound like Emerson, he elaborates his own theory of correspondence: " 'The material world . . . abounds with very strict analogies to the immaterial; and thus some color of truth has been given to the rhetorical dogma, that metaphor, or simile, may be made to strengthen an argument, as well as to embellish a description' " (1:694). Metaphor is here defined in quite traditional terms as the material embodiment of the intellectual or nonmaterial idea. What is curious, however, is Dupin's second illustrative example. Following an analysis of the principle of the *vis inertia* in physics and metaphysics, he speaks of a " 'game of puzzles . . . which is played upon a map.' " The object of this game is to find a given word on a map that an opponent has selected from the various names of countries, cities, rivers, mountains, and so on. The novice invariably chooses an obscure or minutely printed name, whereas the experienced player chooses names so large as to stretch across the map and thereby escape the notice of the opponent. Dupin next proceeds to explicate this metaphor: " 'the physical oversight is precisely analogous with the moral inapprehension by which the intellect suffers to pass unnoticed those considerations which are too obtrusively and too palpably self-evident. But this is a point, it appears, somewhat above or beneath the understanding of the Prefect' " (1:694). The misreading of the map proves analogous to a moral misreading. The moralist, like the novice, believes truth is found in some *recherché* corner. Dupin confirms that this is the source of the prefect's error when he says that the prefect fails to entertain the possibility that the " 'Minister had deposited the letter immediately beneath the nose of the whole world, by way of best preventing any portion of the world from perceiving it' " (1:694–95).

Let us return to the game of odd and even, the foolishness of poets, and the problem of expression. The boy, we will recall, adopts his expression to the expression of his opponents. He says that the simpleton behaves in the most obvious fashion. If the boy guesses even, the simpleton, Dupin says, possesses the " 'amount of cunning . . . just sufficient to make him have them odd upon the second' " (1:689). A simpleton of a degree above the first would reason his opponent would anticipate this and keep the number even. If we turn now to the minister, we find he is said to be extremely clever. The scene of the crime is another scene of reading, but this one yields knowledge. Caught off guard by her husband and then by the minister, the personage leaves a letter on a table with only the address showing. The prefect says, the minister's " 'lynx eye immediately perceives the paper, recognizes the handwriting of the address, observes the confusion of the personage addressed, and fathoms the secret' " (1:682). The personage, unlike Dupin and the minister, betrays herself because she believes that what lies in plain sight will be discovered. On the basis of the handwriting and the expression of the personage, the minister discovers the letter's contents.

The minister, as is well known, foils the police's search by leaving the letter exposed in a card-rack. The prefect errs, according to Dupin, " 'by being too deep or too shallow, for the matter in hand' " (1:689). It is at this point in the story that Dupin tells of the game of odd and even. The boy succeeds by being as deep or as shallow as his opponent. But his method itself is shallow or superficial, even if it produces deep thoughts. The prefect knows D. to be a poet and one remove from a fool, and had he been willing to think like a fool, as I have said, he would have succeeded. Dupin knows D. to be both a poet and a mathematician, and being both poet and something of a mathematician himself, he knows how D. thinks.

I would like to turn now to Dupin's spotting of the letter in the card-rack. What stands out in this scene is that D. has, after all, made an attempt to hide the letter. Spotting the card-rack with a solitary letter, Dupin sees " 'This last was much soiled and crumpled. It was torn nearly in two, across the middle—as if a design, in the first instance, to tear it entirely up as worthless, had been altered, or stayed, in the second. It had a large black seal, bearing the D—— cipher very conspicuously, and was addressed, in a diminutive female hand, to D——, the minister, himself. It was thrust carelessly, and even, as it seemed, contemptuously, into one of the upper divisions of the rack' " (1:695). Dupin has no trouble recognizing this as the letter by virtue of the "radicalness" of its differences from the original description of the stolen letter. The first letter had a red seal " 'with the decal of the S—— family.' " It was also addressed to the personage and was written in a large, bold hand. Finally, the soiled appearance of the minister's letter seems a little too deliberate because its condition is " 'so inconsistent with the *true* methodical habits of D——' " (1:696). I describe this scene at length because it is significant for a few basic reasons. First, the minister attempts to disguise the letter. Second, Dupin recognizes the letter by virtue of its difference—he recognizes its identity because the letter no longer resembles itself. Finally, the soiled appearance of the letter betrays the minister because he, we might say, no longer resembles himself, since his habits are methodical, not slovenly. Dupin's analytical skills are like those of the boy's, but only up to a certain point. He knows in principle how the minister's genius will work and suspects the letter will be in the open. If we think of Dupin as identifying with the expression of D., then we might conclude that he recognizes the letter when he sees that it is hidden differently from the way he—that is, Dupin as the double of the minister—would have hidden it. It is the moment when identity confronts radical difference within itself that recognition emerges. If the minister were true to his genius, he would not have made any alteration in the letter and would have left it as he first found it for all to see. He fails, in other words, not because he suffers a lapse in ingenuity but for not being, if I may say so, stupid enough, for only a complete idiot or a genius would leave the letter for all to see. And if this is the case, then according to "The Purloined Letter," there is nothing to distinguish a genius from an idiot. If he had been a better poet and, therefore, a bigger fool, the minister would have succeeded. But Dupin, who a number of critics have identified as D.'s double, perhaps D.'s brother or even D. himself, cannot be duped.[18] By identifying himself with D., he thinks whatever

D. thinks. The question here concerns the identity between subject and object. That Dupin succeeds in his investigation by uncovering difference within identity subverts the speculative ideal of absolute identity between subject and object.

Gadamer describes this ideal in a discussion of Hegel and self-conscious-ness: "Everything that is alive nourishes itself on what is alien to it. The fundamental fact of being alive is assimilation. Differentiation, then, is at the same time non-differentiation. The alien is appropriated. . . . this struc-ture of what is alive has its correlative in the nature of self-consciousness. Its being consists in its being able to make everything the object of its knowledge, and yet in everything that it knows, it knows itself. Thus as knowledge it is a differentiation from itself and, at the same time, as self-consciousness, it is an overlapping of and return to self." [19] Since D. H. Lawrence, readers have been quick to point out the vampirish elements in Poe—his characters frequently are described as nourishing themselves by assimilating, and destroying, others. The appropriation of the alien —that is, the negative moment of knowledge wherein perception of the alien leads to the perception of oneself as differentiated from the other— is the origin of self-consciousness. The negative moment of differentiation, says Gadamer, is overcome by self-consciousness and the return of the dif-ferentiated self to its self. Poe's debt to the German Romantics, so well documented by Henry A. Pochmann and G. R. Thompson, makes him a good candidate for employing a reflective model of self-consciousness.[20] But Poe seems at various points to deny that such a return to the self is possible. Although Dupin discovers the letter in D.'s possession and re-turns it to the personage, he fails to possess his other, D., and thereby fails to possess himself. In recognizing the letter, Dupin comes to recognize that he is not himself—he is neither Dupin nor D. but the reader whose identity is determined by the radical difference of the letter. He thus signs the letter "Atreus": "—un dessein si funeste, / S'il n'est digne d'Atree, est digne de Thyeste" (1:698). It was Thyestes who seduced the wife of Atreus, who then slew Thyestes' sons and served them to their father for a meal. If we can assume that Dupin plays Atreus to D.'s Thyestes, then D.'s design is worthy of Thyestes, but Dupin's is worthy of Atreus, for he has the final revenge.[21]

This reading of "The Purloined Letter" can make no claim to complete-ness, and this is hardly the first reading to suggest the tale is an allegory of reading. In various ways, the truth is taken to function at a performative level—the reader, as Barbara Johnson says, "is in fact one of its effects.

The text's 'truth' is what puts the status of the reader in question." [22] The letter dictates whatever can be said about it. Perhaps the ultimate power of the tale is that its control over theoretical discourse remains hidden behind the rather pyrotechnical displays of reading of which the tale has been the occasion. Allen Tate has warned, "All readers of Poe, of the work or of the life, and the rare reader of both, are peculiarly liable to the vanity of discovery." [23] Readers of Poe are frequently guilty of believing themselves not only to have discovered what previous readers have passed over but also things Poe himself hardly foresaw. This can hold true of the critic who admires Poe, such as Irwin, and the critic who does not, such as Bloom. Two questions remain: is Poe conscious of the effects his stories produce? and have his critics been too profound?

The most egregious error of missing what lies in plain view occurs in *Arthur Gordon Pym*. On the island of Tsalal, Pym and his companion, Peters, discover themselves wandering in chasms that Peters says resemble an alphabetic script, but Pym takes the chips of marl that precisely fit the indentures as proof they were naturally produced (1:1167). The self-evident sign of human labor—the very sign that the indentures were chipped out of the rocks—leads Pym into error. He errs by being literally too deep—he wanders in the chasms of writing and, therefore, cannot perceive the traces of language all around him. This error remains unsolved by Pym and Peters, but an interpretation is offered by an unnamed person, whom we are directed to identify with Poe, since he has been mentioned in Pym's preface as the author of the first chapters of the narrative. Poe, then, corrects Pym's error by deciphering the mysterious writing he identifies as a conglomeration of Ethiopian, Arabic, and Egyptian words. He translates the figures as "To be shady," "To be white," and "The region of the south" (1:1181). Tsalal is the shady region where nothing white is found, and the south is the region of white. Although this may be a coded allegory of antebellum America, it is but another of Poe's puzzles created for the express purpose of being deciphered. Pym's error generates another text, the interpretive note. Poe posits the mystery beneath our noses so that he may interpret it. The error, then, lies in attributing profundity to the author who deciphers a mystery he himself has created.

In an early Dupin tale, "The Murders in the Rue Morgue," Dupin says, " 'Thus there is such a thing as being too profound. Truth is not always in a well. In fact, as regards the more important knowledge, I do believe she is invariably superficial. . . . By undue profundity we perplex and enfeeble thought' " (1:412). Poe repeatedly returns to this concept not only in the tales of ratiocination but also in such pieces as "The Poetic Principle," which begins with the declaration, "I have no design to be either thorough or profound" (2:71). The question of profundity is also a question of effects; Poe claims in several places, including a review he wrote of his *Tales* in 1845, that his first aim "is for a novel effect" (2:873). He explains this aim at greater length in the famous essays "The Poetic Principle" and "The Philosophy of Composition."

"The Murders in the Rue Morgue" is an illustration of a series of propositions on the nature of analysis. The solution to the murder is offered as an illustration of Dupin's analytical skills, but we are told that analytical mental features are "little susceptible of analysis. We appreciate them only in their effects" (1:397). The explanation of Dupin's method, which the prologue tells us appears as if it were intuition and not analysis, can be found in Poe's "A Few Words on Secret Writing": "The reader should bear in mind that the basis of the whole art of solution, as far as regards these matters, is found in the general principles of the formation of language itself, and this is altogether independent of the particular laws which govern any cipher, or the construction of its key. The difficulty of reading a cryptographical puzzle is by no means always in accordance with the labor or ingenuity with which it has been constructed. . . . this complexity is only in shadow. It has no substance whatever. It appertains merely to the formation, and has no bearing upon the solution, of the cipher" (2:1280). The best of cryptograms would not be recognized as such: "Experience shows that the most cunningly constructed cryptography, if suspected, can and will be unriddled" (2:1283). The difficulty of the cryptogram ultimately rests on its appearance as something other than a cryptogram. It is not at all a matter of the ingenuity with which the cryptogram has been constructed. The solution of the cipher, then, rests upon the recognition of it as a cipher. The most difficult cipher is one that is taken to be something other than a cipher. This conforms to the logic of "The Purloined Letter." The prefect errs by being too profound—he thinks the letter has been ingeniously hidden and that, in order to find it, he must expend an equal amount of ingenuity. But the expenditure is unequal—the minister uses nearly no ingenuity at all. The little he does use leads to his downfall. Dupin recognizes the letter because he can see from its appearance that it is cunningly disguised; in other words, he sees it is a cipher. His replacement perfectly resembles the disguised letter and will, therefore, escape the attention of D., who will eventually find that his letter has been replaced by a riddle, one whose manuscript provides the solution.

The crucial advice, however, is to base the solution on the "general principles of the formation of language itself" and not on any "particular laws which govern any cipher, or the construction of its key." Poe's advice is quite sound and fits in rather neatly with hermeneutical principles. If the cipher is a language, it must be understandable and, as Poe says, a certain order must be agreed upon between those communicating by the cipher. There must, therefore, be rules governing the cipher's construction but *not* for its solution: there are not rules for the solution of cipher, and anyone in search of them "will find nothing upon record which he does not in his own intellect possess" (2:1291). The cipher would be worthless if each message required an individual key for its solution—the cipher would be no cipher at all. The cipher, consequently, must conform to a general rule of customary usage, which means, says Gadamer, "that we cannot arbitrarily change the meaning of words if there is to be language."[24] And the cipher, like a made-up language, must follow some order in its renaming of words so that understanding remains possible. "Language," Gadamer writes, "has no independent life apart from the world that comes to language within it."[25] The world is available to us in language, and language, in turn, has no life apart from the world that is re-presented in it. Language, according to Gadamer, is in its very essence human. Turning back to Poe on ciphers, we find that he applies this principle to secret writing: "it may be roundly asserted that human ingenuity cannot concoct a cipher which human ingenuity cannot resolve" (2:1278). Although Poe never says so explicitly, his comments on the solving of ciphers rest upon the principle that language, because it is by definition human, is always understandable, and because ciphers must conform to the general principle of the formation of language, they will always be solved. This also explains why Dupin has no trouble solving the mystery concerning the language spoken by the murderer of Madame and Mademoiselle L'Espanaye: the fact that no one could understand it meant it was spoken by an animal, not a person.

Poe's skill as a cryptographer comes into play in many, if not all, of his tales. Ever since Baudelaire, readers have said all of Poe's writings are autobiographical, and critics have attempted to decode Poe's "secret autobiography."[26] Testing the analytical skills of his readers in these cryptograms, Poe inscribes his name or those of his contemporaries in various tales, or readers exercise their ingenuity looking for meanings hidden behind the signifiers of the text. Yet as many readers note, Poe's texts appear so willfully overdetermined that he seems to be declaring that his tales are ciphers, which, according to his principle, would be as good as giving the solution away at the start of the game.

"The Gold-Bug" is a curious and, yet, obvious case in point. Louis Renza has discussed how the second part of the story, wherein the code is deciphered, displaces the first narrative concerning the gold-bug. This displacement, he says, mimics a critical reading of the first part and forces the "reader to adopt a reflective relation to the narrative as a whole." Legrand's pretended illness is a further doubling of this reflective relation in which the "aesthetic effect has become retroactively and irrecoverably, lost or sabotaged by its production of the reader's self-conscious relation to it." [27] The doubling of the interpreter's self-conscious relation to the text can be found in most romantic literature, from Shelley's *Triumph of Life* to Melville's *Confidence Man*. Renza, like so many of Poe's readers restores depth to Poe's superficial texts by applying a self-reflexive model of reading. Once again, the buried meaning becomes the reflective consciousness produced by the text: "this lost aesthetic relation to the narrative becomes the tale's *still* buried treasure." [28]

Poe's use of cryptography and the transformation of a narrative into a critical explication of a code makes "The Gold-Bug" one of the more heavy-handed examples of the romantic allegory of reading. The story opens with Legrand telling of his discovery of a gold-bug that he has temporarily lent to someone. In place of showing the bug to the narrator, he draws it. He is insulted when the narrator says he sees the picture of a skull, not of an insect. The scene is one of either a misreading or a misrepresentation. When later in the story we discover the paper is a parchment containing a picture of a skull, we realize that the first misreading resulted from a substitution of one image for another. As the story deals with cryptography, it is not out of place to note how the tale turns upon the relation of signifier to signified. The connection of the two signifiers—the bug and the skull—is metonymic or simply contingent. After Legrand had been bitten by the bug, the freed slave, Jupiter, picked it up with the parchment he had found on the shore where the bug was discovered. The bug, then, serves as a false sign for the narrator-interpreter. We look for meaning in the bug and seek some connection between the bug and the skull, expecting a signifier to point toward a signified. The connection, however, is at best metonymic. The bug that bites Legrand is the occasion for the discovery of the parchment with the drawing of the skull. Legrand plays a game and transforms the metonymy into a metaphor. Having been bitten by what Jupiter insists is a gold-bug, he pretends to be struck mad with desire for some gold he believes is hidden.

The narrator-interpreter seeks, according to the principle of cryptography, a signifier that would translate the encoded signifier. Because he finds no relation between the gold-bug and the skull, he believes Legrand is mad. Legrand, however, recognizes the arbitrary relation between the signifiers and proceeds to create the interpretable story of the gold-bug by pretending to be mad. The fiction, then, is a double—there is Legrand's pretended madness and the double signifier. The signifier, consequently, is a fiction or, perhaps more accurately, a trope. The gold-bug has an interpretable meaning only by virtue of Legrand's providing the metaphor of being bitten by a gold-bug.

Legrand discovers that the parchment, when held to heat, has a secret writing. This invisible writing is the perfect cipher because it does not appear to be a message at all, not even a coded one. It is discovered by accident, and once the discovery is made, Legrand easily deciphers the secret.

The fiction of the signifier is repeated at the level of the narrative. Just as there is no connection between the two signifiers, there is also a disjunction between the story proper and the decipherment of the code. The latter usurps the place of the former. The narrator proves to have failed in his interpretation. The double signifier and the superfluous mysteries point to the ultimate fictionality of any interpretation. Understanding rests upon the substitution of metaphor for metonymy. No one would accuse the narrator of undue profundity—the conclusion he draws from Legrand's behavior is quite sensible. The deception is deliberate and passes unnoticed because the narrator has no reason to suspect Legrand. The narrator cannot solve this mystery because it rests not on contingency but upon an error—Legrand is insulted when he believes the narrator has mistaken his drawing of the bug for that of a skull. The error is Legrand's and not the narrator's, but this error leads to Legrand's chance discovery of the parchment and the decipherment of the code.

The question still remains concerning Poe's crypts—do they lie in the plays on names and the hidden details in the story or are they in the scene of misreading? The source lies in errors. The paper with a drawing of a bug turns out to be a parchment with a drawing of a skull. The metamorphosis takes place for the purpose of the story. In "The Purloined Letter,"

Dupin recognizes the disguised letter and describes both sides, which is impossible without actually turning it over himself. Julian Symons cites Laura Riding's objection to Dupin's solution in "The Murders in the Rue Morgue": the ape could not possibly climb out of the window and fasten it by the secret catch.[29] The errors seem to be gratuitous. Poe aims at one level at a purely mechanical analysis of evidence leading to the solution of the puzzle or mystery. To make the solution work, however, he must either reconstruct the mystery, which he literally does with the newspaper accounts in "The Mystery of Marie Roget," or introduce discrepancies, as in "The Murders in the Rue Morgue" and "The Purloined Letter," or finally, join two systematic narratives by an implausible series of accidents, as in "The Gold-Bug." Are we left with concluding that Poe is a careless artist, as bad in the construction of his plots as he is in his various styles? Harold Bloom has been the most recent of a number of critics who say "yes."

Those who praise Poe are those who find him an ingenious writer who anticipates any possible interpretation. Those who condemn him point to the sloppy construction of plots and his execrable style. I would suggest that the former have been too profound to understand Poe, while the latter, if not superficial, have focused on the apparent deficiencies of Poe's surface. Poe characterizes these readings in his *Marginalia:* "In reading some books we occupy ourselves chiefly with the thoughts of the author; in perusing others, exclusively with our own. . . . there are two classes of suggestive books—the positively and the negatively suggestive. The former suggest by what they say; the latter by what they might and should have said. It makes little difference, after all. In either case the true book-purpose is answered" (2:1338). Poe's detractors have occupied themselves with Poe's thoughts. Yvor Winters, for instance, criticizes him for his "childish view of intellectuality, on the one hand, and the unoriented emotionalism of the tale of effect on the other."[30] His defenders have been preoccupied with their own thoughts. Hence, they are forever finding in the tales the doubling of the reader or the narrator. John Irwin finds "the indeterminate status of nature's script" in *Arthur Gordon Pym* acted out by the interpreter who attributes to the author his ingenious archaeological uncovering of "resemblance between *tkl* and *Tekeli-li*": "Such an interpretation may simply be a self-projection that creates the illusion of depth, a shadow mistaken for a body."[31] Even if it is an illusion, depth has been restored to the text as a function of the interpretive act.

In a letter about "The Murders in the Rue Morgue," Poe suggests a third mode of reading: "You are right about the hair-splitting of my French Friend:—that is all done for effect. These tales of ratiocination owe most of their popularity to being something in a new key. I do not mean to say that they are not ingenious—but people think them more ingenious than they are—on account of their method and *air* of method. In the 'Murders in the Rue Morgue,' for instance, where is the ingenuity of unravelling a web which you yourself (the author) have woven for the express purpose of unravelling? The reader is made to confound the ingenuity of the suppositious Dupin with that of the writer of the story."[32] The tales are, in fact, ciphers—they are mechanically constructed to appear as ingenious webs of mystery so that the reader will attribute the ingenuity of the character to the author. Because of their "*air* of method," the reader thinks them more ingenious than they are, but the ingenuity does not lie in the complexity of the puzzle to be solved but in their effect.

When Poe tells his correspondent that there is no ingenuity at all; he merely follows his own rules for composition laid out for all to see in "The Philosophy of Composition": "Nothing is more clear than that every plot, worth the name, must be elaborated to its *dénouement* before any thing be attempted with the pen. It is only with the *dénouement* constantly in view that we can give a plot its indispensable air of consequence, or causation, by making the incidents, and especially the tone at all points, tend to the development of the intention" (2:13). The denouement of the tale of ratiocination is the effect of attributing ingenuity to the author. To achieve this end, he tells his tale in order that the reader will mistake Dupin's ingenuity for Poe's. But there is no trick to Poe at all. He merely follows the rules for constructing a cryptograph. And if we recall that no rule is necessary for solving a cryptograph—whatever the reader needs, he already possesses —then we may conclude that not only is the author's ingenuity an illusion but so is the reader's, for the answer lies in any reader's mind because the rules for the solution are grounded in language. The error, then, consists in attributing ingenuity to anyone, whether it be the author, the text, or the reader. Interpretation requires no thought, for even language does not think for us—thought is an effect of language, and this is why error alone produces interpretation. Error opens up the identity of language and thought to the radical difference between signifier and signified that alone makes reading a forever erring task.

224 JOSEPH G. KRONICK

NOTES

1. Herman Melville, *The Confidence-Man: His Masquerade,* ed. Hershel Parker (New York: Norton, 1971), 257.

2. Edgar Allan Poe, *Essays and Reviews,* ed. G. R. Thompson (New York: Library of America, 1984), 2:8. Hereafter this volume will be cited in the text, as will volume 1, *Poetry and Tales,* ed. Patrick Quinn (New York: Library of America, 1984).

3. The figure of the hieroglyphic in Poe has received its most extensive treatment in John T. Irwin, *American Hieroglyphics: The Symbol of the Egyptian Hieroglyphics in the American Renaissance* (New Haven: Yale University Press, 1980).

4. Roy Harvey Pearce, *The Continuity of American Poetry* (Princeton: Princeton University Press, 1961), 142.

5. F. O. Matthiessen, *The American Renaissance: Art and Expression in the Age of Emerson and Whitman* (London: Oxford University Press, 1941), 242–43.

6. Charles Feidelson, Jr., *Symbolism and American Literature* (Chicago: University of Chicago Press, 1953), 36.

7. Irwin, *American Hieroglyphics,* 61.

8. I refer to Jacques Derrida's critique of Husserl in *Speech and Phenomena,* trans. David B. Allison (Evanston, Ill.: Northwestern University Press, 1973), 78.

9. The concept of the absence of the author has been treated in various ways by Derrida, Roland Barthes, and Michel Foucault. See, for instance, Jacques Derrida, "Signature Event Context," in *Margins of Philosophy,* trans. Alan Bass (Chicago: University of Chicago Press, 1982), 307–30. See also Michel Foucault, "What Is an Author?" and Roland Barthes, "From Work to Text," in *Textual Strategies: Perspectives in Post-Structuralist Criticism,* ed. and trans. Josué V. Harari (Ithaca: Cornell University Press, 1979), 73–81 and 141–60.

10. Barbara Johnson, "The Frame of Reference: Poe, Lacan, Derrida," *Yale French Studies* 55/56 (1977): 503.

11. Barthes, "From Work to Text."

12. Shoshana Felman, "On Reading Poetry: Reflections on the Limits and Possibilities of Psychoanalytic Approaches," in *The Literary Freud: Mechanisms of Defense and the Poetic Will,* ed. Joseph M. Smith (New Haven: Yale University Press, 1980), 147, 145.

13. Patrick F. Quinn, *The French Face of Edgar Poe* (Carbondale: Southern Illinois University Press, 1957), 237.

14. Richard Wilbur, "The Poe Mystery Case," in *Responses, Prose Pieces: 1953–1976* (New York: Harcourt Brace Jovanovich, 1976), 134.

15. Harold Bloom, "Inescapable Poe," *New York Review of Books,* Oct. 11, 1984, 24.

16. Hans-Georg Gadamer, *Truth and Method,* trans. Garrett Barden and John Cumming (New York: Crossroad, 1982), 236.

17. Martin Heidegger, *Being and Time,* trans. John Macquarrie and Edward Robinson (New York: Harper and Row, 1962), 194.

18. See, for instance, Wilbur, "The Poe Mystery Case," 135–37. David Ketterer suggests that Dupin and D. are brothers in *The Rationale of Deception in Poe* (Baton Rouge: Louisiana State University Press, 1979), 252–54.

19. Gadamer, *Truth and Method,* 223.

20. See Henry A. Pochmann, *German Culture in America: 1600–1900* (Madison: University of Wisconsin Press, 1957), 388–408, and G. R. Thompson, *Poe's Fiction: Romantic Irony in the Gothic Tales* (Madison: University of Wisconsin Press, 1973).

21. For a discussion of the doublings of the signature in "The Purloined Letter," see Joseph N. Riddel, "The 'Crypt' of Edgar Poe," *Boundary* 2 7 (Spring 1979): 139–40.

22. For essays on "The Purloined Letter" as an allegory of reading, see Johnson, "The Frame of Reference"; Felman, "On Reading Poetry"; and Riddel, "The 'Crypt' of Edgar Poe."

23. Allen Tate, "The Angelic Imagination: Poe as God," *Essays of Four Decades* (Chicago: Swallow Press, 1968), 433.

24. Gadamer, *Truth and Method,* 367.

25. Ibid., 401.

26. The phrase "secret autobiography" comes from Louis A. Renza, "Poe's Secret Autobiography," in *The American Renaissance Reconsidered,* ed. Walter Benn Michaels and Donald E. Pease (Baltimore: Johns Hopkins University Press, 1985), 58–89.

27. Ibid., 66.

28. Ibid.

29. Julian Symons, *The Tell-Tale Heart: The Life and Works of Edgar Allan Poe* (1978; repr. New York: Penguin Books, 1981), 224.

30. Yvor Winters, *In Defense of Reason* (Chicago: Swallow Press, 1947), 255.

31. Irwin, *American Hieroglyphics,* 234.

32. John Ward Ostrom, ed., *The Letters of Edgar Allan Poe,* new ed., 2 vols. (New York: Gordian Press, 1966), 2:328.

Absalom, Absalom!:

The Outrage of Writing

ALEXANDRE LEUPIN

And I speculated on time and death and wondered if I had in-
vented the world to which I should give life or if it had invented
me, giving me an illusion of greatness.
—Joseph Blotner,
    William Faulkner's Essay on the Composition of Sartoris

I think a writer is a perfect case of split personality. That he is
one thing when he is a writer and is something else while he is a
denizen of the world.
—Faulkner, in *Faulkner in the University*

In *Absalom, Absalom!* narrative transmission of the central fiction (Thomas Sutpen's "design") operates according to an itinerary in
which all of the nodal points and metonymical connections are established with extreme precision. This itinerary includes two places: Jefferson
(where chapters 1 to 5 are told) and Boston (chapters 6 to 9); there are
at least six narrators and, symmetrically, that many narratees: Rosa Coldfield to Quentin Compson (chapter 1); Mr. Compson, Quentin's father,
to his son (chapters 2 to 4); Rosa, once again, to Quentin (chapter 5);
Quentin to Shreve McCannon, a fellow student of his at Harvard (chapters 6 and following); Thomas Sutpen to General Compson, Quentin's
grandfather (the story told to Quentin by his father in chapter 7).

At the first reading of the text, one thing becomes obvious: as much as
or even more so than Thomas Sutpen, Faulkner the writer seems to want to
establish firmly the genealogy of his metaphorical child (the novel), so that
it could at any instant present its own birth certificate and proof of its fictitious filial relationship. What can this indicate, if not that the genealogical

obsession of the characters of the novel is a generalized metaphor for the transmission of the story itself? For the narrative methodically follows the family tree of the Compson family.[1] Fictitious genealogy problematizes the paternity (or maternity) of the text itself, as well as the questions of writing's signature and its title to property or propriety.[2]

As Faulkner emphasizes, Quentin Compson is the stitch which binds the threads of the story, the seam which sets the fabric of the text and holds it together: "Quentin Compson, of the *Sound and the Fury,* tells it, or ties it together; he is the protagonist so that it is not complete apocrypha."[3] Without this necessary link, the structure which distills the narrative would collapse, and the story would be unauthentic, fictitious, even deceitful (such are the connotations of the word "apocrypha"): unsigned, stripped of all truthfulness. But Faulkner's declaration contains in itself a contradiction. For the one who formally guarantees that the fiction is not a counterfeit is himself a fictitious character, from another Faulkner text: a character, that is to say, an effect of verisimilitude. This is a fact that the author himself would never dispute (how could he?). Therefore, in spite of his insistence upon preserving the referential dimension of his characters, their "living" and almost independent natures, Faulkner ascribes the entirety of his work—characters as well as "events," chronology, geography, to a literal, generalized apocrypha: "my apocrypha," as he rightly calls his texts.[4]

Thus, Faulkner would have his name inscribed in the place of all narrative voices, in spite of the referential weight that the text seems to accord them. This self-evident fact, however, conflicts in *Absalom, Absalom!* (and elsewhere) with the constant obsession for tracing the genealogical grounding of the text within his fiction. Why this immense and detailed work if Faulkner, a priori, as signer is always assured of his presence and textual property rights?

Because writing is, in principle, that which undoes the very possibility of signature and ownership of the text, that which makes any authentification of the apocrypha always impossible—in spite of, and against the evidence of signed manuscripts or covers bearing the name of the author (which, incidentally, cannot constitute or institute a signature): the agency of fiction is what reabsorbs authority in the detours of textuality.

Faulkner's name is no more adequate than Quentin's when it comes to authenticating the narrative, a fact which he foresaw in its fullest implications: the map of Yoknapatawpha County, which is a part of the very text of *Absalom, Absalom!,* and which gives it the effect of verisimilitude, is without a doubt the ironic extreme of that effect itself. What does it mean after all to inscribe oneself as "sole owner and proprietor" of an imaginary land? First of all, it is to evict all fictive possessors, all of the genealogies claiming authority or property rights, even unto the right of the living word (including Quentin's). But also, and in the same stroke, to designate oneself as proprietor of this fictitious territory corresponds to a radical disappropriation, since it is to deprive oneself of all real possession, except for the domain of words. The famous map thus shows that by wanting to sign the text as its master, Faulkner is forced to transform himself into a *fiction of the master*.

Consequently, the truth of the text cannot be seen as a reproduction of nature, of laws (psychological, biological, social, historical, etc.), or as an expression of a "deepest self" which would be the secret but definitive source of the work; this truth is more the reflection of another law (language's own) and another territory (that of fiction). Though a truism, it is important to emphasize this to critics who are concerned with "facts," "characters," "social reality," "history," and so on: in Faulkner's, as in Balzac's works, which have in common the trait of reappearing characters, the more fiction seems realistic, the more its apocryphal nature is revealed.[5] Not even Quentin Compson can secure the text against this drift.

In the same way that it does not assure the "authenticity" of the narrative, Faulkner's genealogical fiction (or the signature for which it serves as metaphor) does not succeed in creating a hierarchy for the narrative transmission according to a hereditary line that would clearly differentiate roles and places (of father and son, brother and sister, man and wife). On the contrary, it subverts these relationships by a calculated indeterminacy which transgresses all rigorously sexualized family structure in the story; an indeterminacy which must be considered in the light of the signer's disappearance. For example, the Boston narration not only erases the distinction between one and the other (Shreve and Quentin, in turn narrators and narratees) but also confuses father and son: the very act of narrating is what calls this differentiation into question: "He sounds just like father," Quentin thinks. And later: "Yes, Shreve sounds almost exactly like father: that letter." And again: "Maybe we are both Father."[6]

In the same manner, the place or the name of the grandfather repeats this confusion: "And I reckon grandfather was saying 'Wait, wait for God's sake wait' about like you are," Quentin says to Shreve (203). In *Absalom, Absalom!* (and perhaps in a more generalized sense, in literature), to become the father of the tale is to question the name of the father and fatherhood, the possibility of its inscription, and even beyond this, the possibility of any fictional genealogy. Moreover, the text offers the space in which the son can ascend to the father's place across a supplement of knowledge which gives him a certain superiority; Shreve explains this to Quentin: "And your old man wouldn't know about that too [. . .]. But I know. And you know too" (295). This passage exactly echoes the following:

> "He didn't know it then. Grandfather didn't tell him all of it either, like Sutpen never told Grandfather quite all of it."
> "Then who did tell him?"
> "I did." Quentin did not move. (219)

In a parallel manner, and according to a logic of which we only begin to perceive the necessity, narrator and narratee are never, with perhaps only one exception, strictly separated roles. Except for Thomas Sutpen, the only pure narrator, all of the other vectors of the narration become listeners at one moment or another. Briefly, the acts of narrating (a metaphor for writing) and of listening (an emblem of reading and interpretation) are linked in a profound solidarity, representing two sides of a single activity. In one passage, Faulkner describes the complicity of listening and recitation as a happy marriage: "That was why it did not matter to either of them [Quentin or Shreve] which one did the talking, since it was not the talking alone which did it, performed and accomplished the overpassing, but some happy marriage of speaking and hearing wherein each before the demand, the requirement, forgave condoned and forgot the faulting of the other" (261). Everything takes place as if some power of fiction (an unnameable force for which the desire to narrate would be the hypostasis) overtakes all of the narratees, and forces them to metamorphose into narrators.

In the passage I have just quoted what must be questioned is the "happiness" of that metaphorical marriage which covers the failures of Quentin and Shreve's reconstruction of the past, the perilous reconstitution of events that never "happened," in the strictest sense of the word. First of all let us note that in the exchange between narrators and narratees, the story does not cease to interpret itself, and, due to a rift that is both slight and immense, the narrator, whoever it is, always hears the echo of his or her voice, in the return of a division which always deprives him or her of possession of the enunciative act, which makes the original site of recitation vacillate. From this perspective then, does not the *mise en abyme* of writing and reading have more to do with a profound horror than with happiness?

The liaison, repetition, and mirror have nothing cheerful about them: the confusion of roles also permits the (dead) father of the story to take his vengeance upon the wiser son, to precede and survive him in a repetition which totally abolishes the supplemental knowledge of the son. All that can be read is an insistent reiteration, in which the answer always repeats the question: "*Am I going to have to hear it all again* he [Quentin] thought *I am going to have to hear it all over again I am already hearing it all over again I am listening to it all over again I shall have to never listen to anything else but this again forever so apparently not only a man never outlives his father but not even his friends and acquaintances do*" (228). The infinite repetition obliterates the very possibility for that which "happens" ever really to begin, and so never really to end: the very notion of "event" becomes unthinkable. "*Maybe nothing ever happens once and is finished*" (215). The paternal word, continually returning, thus empties the son's survival of any sort of uniquely appropriable content, or of any individually assumable narration. But on the other hand, its repetition obliterates in the same stroke the name of the father, because the paternal word assumes all generation, even the most original. That our pleasure as readers comes from a repetition which is itself an intolerable dispossession is not the least of the paradoxes that Faulknerian writing imposes.

From the beginning then, fiction destabilizes all strict notions of identity. On the border of the text, Faulkner makes it clear: Quentin is the prey of a dialogical division that suspends him between a death which has already preceded him and a life that tries vainly to escape this antecedence: "Then hearing would reconcile and he would seem to listen to two separate Quentins now—the Quentin Compson preparing for Harvard in the South [. . .]; and the Quentin Compson who was still too young to deserve yet to be a ghost, but nevertheless having to be one for all that, since he was born and bred in the deep South" (6).

The deadliness of the narration will have already captured any possible narrator (and any writer for whom it is the metonym—never representing him, as we shall see, in *entirety*). It would be futile to couch this observation in historic or geographic terms, because the deep South is here the symbol of a generalizable phenomenon: the text, in every instance, redistributes the distinction between life and death. It *is,* and it *produces* at the same time a phantom space, neither truly alive nor truly dead.

The ambiguity of this difference subsumes all possible distinction between fiction and reality as well as between truth and falsehood. The two principal narrators of *Absalom, Absalom!,* Shreve and Quentin, furnish the paradigm of this ambiguity: here as elsewhere we must follow Faulkner literally. In fact, the equivocal, mortal nature of this textual space permits the two narrators to identify themselves with characters of the fictive past who are (always) absent: it allows them to take the place of the dead. Quentin is not only duplicated and divided by Shreve, but also, and in turn, they cannot distinguish themselves from the characters of their narration, Henry Sutpen and Charles Bon. The glacial bedroom of the dormitory at Harvard is a tomb ("The room was indeed tomblike: a quality stale and static and moribund beyond any mere vivid and living cold" (284), the place predestined for identification with the dead: "In the cold room, where there was now not two of them but four" (242). Now, as it turns out, the narrative, far from giving an appearance of depth and life to its characters (speaking or spoken about) produces a disincarnation that permits their circulation outside the limits of time and space: "It did not matter to them (Quentin and Shreve) anyway, who could without moving, as free now of flesh as the father who decreed and forbade [. . .] who could be already clattering over the frozen ruts of that December night" (243). We see that this disincarnation effaces narrative categories: the notions of exterior and interior (of narrating and narrated) have collapsed because of it. It is not sufficient to interpret this transgression in the light of a simple sleight-of-hand, due to some "artistic magic" and, as such, void of significance: what Faulkner truly underscores is that the force of fiction reveals the inanity of any attempt to escape its grasp. The deadly power of the text is to show how illusory any reassuring delimitation between its interiority and exteriority is: always, whether one likes it or not, the author and the reader (since they are practically brothers) have already submitted to the expropriation of identification where boundaries continue to be elusive.

The voice (or rather its simulacrum, immediately wrought by writing) is not the only mode in which the fictitious narration circulates. Prefatorily to the text, Rosa Coldfield insists on delegating the responsibility of writing to Quentin: "You will be married then I expect and perhaps your wife will want a new gown or a new chair for the house and you can write this and submit it to the magazines" (7). Her insistent deferral of putting the voice into writing—sound that becomes mute, silent —indicates Rosa's mistrust of the written (should we say her horror?): for she herself possesses all the credentials which would permit her to write the fable of Thomas Sutpen: "Then almost immediately he decided that neither was this the reason why she had sent the note,[7] and sending it, why to him, since if she had merely wanted it told, written, and even printed, she would not have needed to call in anybody—a woman who even in his (Quentin's) father's youth had already established herself as the town's and county's poetess laureate" (8).

This refusal of writing, according to Mr. Compson, is explained by two hypotheses (again it would be useless to distinguish between conjecture and "fact" here, since both come from a narrative differentiation within the text). First, Quentin was chosen as privileged listener because of his youth and gender: "It's because she will need someone to go with her—a man, a gentleman, yet one still young enough to do what she wants, do it the way she wants it done" (9). The second reason is a family reason, so to speak: "And she chose you because your grandfather was the nearest thing to a friend Sutpen ever had in this country, and she probably believes that Sutpen may have told your grandfather something about himself and her [. . .]. And so, in a sense, the affair, no matter what happens out there tonight, will still be in the family; the skeleton (if it be a skeleton) still in the closet" (9–10). For Rosa, it is a question of making sure that the story is not haphazardly channeled: in the first place, the listener is young enough to receive her narrative vision without modifying it—a naive hope, destined to be shattered; next, the story will only be told in a family setting which will guarantee that the dirty laundry is washed at home.

Rosa's cautiousness is, without a doubt, justified. For in one way, as the text itself proclaims, the writing of *Absalom, Absalom!* aims to dismiss the priority of any one central vision, any privileged point of view in which one of the speakers or the author would be the unique bearer of truth; this instability is one of the goals explicitly avowed by Faulkner himself.[8] Concurrently, the activity of the letter in the text abolishes the very essence of linear continuous time, of a temporal mode which is necessary to the establishment of chronological hierarchies and genealogies. If the story has the characteristics of a will (we will return to this idea) or funeral wake, it does not permit the institution of a patriarch or first testator.

On the other hand, the story's tomblike earnestness works upon the voice in such a way as to introduce the interval of death. One can see that the act of Faulknerian writing dismisses Rosa's reasons, and that it poses itself diametrically opposite her denial. For by its very nature, writing cannot attain the life of the voice, the affirmation of presence, or the preservation of a family novel closed upon itself. On the contrary: we know that Quentin, among other examples, crushed by the narrative of *Absalom, Absalom!* (which is the deforming mirror of his own textual avatar in *The Sound and the Fury*) will kill himself at Harvard after putting the final point to the fiction of the text's narrative transmission.

Except for the message which summons Quentin to Rosa Coldfield, the first manifestation of writing in the strict sense of the word appears in the fourth chapter. Quentin receives from his father a letter written by Charles Bon to Judity Sutpen, which she once gave to Quentin's grandmother—we must also note the transference of the letter from one sex to the other. In its complexity, this epistolary transmission traces the oral delivery of the story, or vice versa: both are emblems of each other.

As it turns out, this "first" missive can be read (or interpreted) as a living sign only in the space of an "original" evanescence or disappearance, invoked here by the absence of the signer (and, of course, his voice). This space is similarly connoted by a "fading" which affects the materiality of signs. The white, which pierces and recovers the living linearity of time (the black of the characters) *is* the origin, infinitely problematical: "Quentin hearing without having to listen as he read the faint spidery scripts not like something impressed upon the paper by a once-living hand but like a shadow cast upon it which had resolved on the paper the instant before he looked at it and which might fade, vanish, at any instant while he still read: the dead tongue speaking after four years and then after almost fifty more, gentle sardonic whimsical and incurably pessimistic, without date or salutation or signature" (107). Writing is therefore always menaced by that sense of absence which permits its ghostly manifestation: it is the object of cuts, quotes, repetitions, but also the subject of these same operations; this is because the very possibility of such scriptural activities derives from the coupling of white and black.

There is yet another occurrence of scriptural metaphor which illustrates the dynamics proper to writing: the announcement of Rosa Coldfield's death, in a letter from Mr. Compson to his son (I shall not enlarge upon the epitaphic characteristics of the contents of this letter). In fact, this poetic and funerary notification is deliberately cut by the narrative. The citation, started on page 143, will not be taken up and completed (if we dare to write the word, since we are beginning to see that there is not, in this domain, any possible completion) until page 310.

But let us return to Charles Bon's letter: for its transmission is accompanied by pseudocircumstantial details that are of foremost significance. In the first place, for Judith, who is the original receiver and initial reader, what becomes of the letter is unimportant: "And your grandmother saying 'Me? You want me to keep it?' 'Yes,' Judith said. 'Or destroy it. As you like. Read it if you like it or don't read it if you like'" (105).

The receiver's indifference regarding the circulation of the missive indicates assuredly that, contrary to what Rosa would have wished, writing cannot be contained within the family, and the story cannot be reduced to a genealogical reading.

But there is more: for Judith as well as for her father, Thomas Sutpen, the concern here is with the *impression* (in every sense of the word), the *trace* or the *mark* with the stamp and its imprint, with the stripe and its thread. How can the individual, as prisoner of a fate which supersedes and abolishes him, make a mark (even if only as testator) and add his own thread to the tapestry of society? How can he have a tombstone erected with a distinguished inscription, when the job of textualizing produces such confusion and when the epitaph is doomed to fade?

> You get born and you try this and you don't know why only you keep trying it and you are born at the same time with a lot of other people, all mixed up with them, like trying to, having to, move your arms and legs with strings only the same strings are hitched to all the other arms and legs and the others all trying to make a rug on the same loom only each one wants to weave his own pattern into the rug; and it can't matter, you know that, or the Ones that set up the loom would have arranged things a little better, and yet it must matter because you keep on trying and then all of a sudden it's all over and all you have left is a block of stone with scratches on it provided there was someone to remember to have the marble scratched and set up or had time to, and it rains on it and the sun shines on it and after a while they don't even remember the name and what the scratches were trying to tell, and it doesn't matter. (105)

Here it is futile to attempt a commentary of this passage that would give justice to its marvelous richness, just as it seems impossible to me to exhaust the significance of *Absalom, Absalom!* and, a fortiori, of the entire

Faulknerian work; at times, commentators are forced to avow such humility. I shall limit myself therefore to the examination of certain aspects. Judith's response to the fading of the individual trace—to the origin and end of the mark—is that of the purest exteriority: in this particular respect, she is situated in an inverse relation to her father's solution. In fact, only the maximal distancing between the author and the receiver, only the unknown stranger can guarantee the truth of the letter. And this guarantee insures not the perpetuity of the inscription (its meaning), but rather, the life that an unlimited circulation gives it, *without regard to its meaning*. What counts here, for the survival of the letter—and, we might add, of the text in general, is the circuit of its transmission (a remark that is obviously applicable to the narrative structure of the text itself): "And so maybe if you could go to someone, the stranger the better, and give them something—a scrap of paper—something, anything, it not to mean anything in itself and them not even to read it or keep it, not even bother to throw it away or destroy it, at least it would be something just because it would have happened, be remembered even if only from passing from one hand to another, one mind to another, and it would be at least a scratch, something" (105). But in order for the imprint to make sense (once again, let us hastily generalize: in order for literature to be readable) the letter must have put aside in its circulation among unknown strangers not only individuals, authors, and addressees, but also the very mainspring of meaning. It must put into question the verb *to be* itself, and this very questioning will confer upon it its own paradoxical being, in suspension, from one hand and mind to another: "something that might make a mark on something that *was* once for the reason that it can die someday, while the block of stone can't be *is* because it never can become *was* because it can't ever die or perish" (106).

Now, as it turns out, the text cannot escape its funereal or epitaphic aspect, and the blankness which is the death of meaning and being (but this blankness will also be, as we shall see, the condition of its survival in reading). In this sense, the transmission of the text to the reader guarantees its being and its possibility of being *something,* but at the same time this transmission must concede to an initial effacement.

The funerary steles which are strewn throughout Sutpen's Hundred and the text bear witness to this. For whatever sort of desire eternity may direct upon it (a desire to reconstitute or to reassemble its scattered members), the tombstone is nothing but the vestige of a ghostly corpse, unfinished and incompletable by any certainty of being, caught in an unlimited passion and patience that nothing can conclude—not even a reading which claims to be exhaustive (see 155 and following).

In order to be effective, then, the transmission of the text must surrender to the demand and logic of the incision. Nothing shows this better than the first page of the story, where an anonymous narrator appears (*out of nowhere*, like Thomas Sutpen); as readers we must be careful not to confuse this narrator with one of the story's characters, and above all, with Faulkner himself. This narrator, without voice, signature, or presence in the story's system of recitative delivery, nonetheless has an important role: providing the two frames (descriptive but also functional) where the story is to unfold. These two locations—Jefferson and Harvard—are thus anonymously and paradoxically homogenized.

But this uniformity is also a revealing yet discreet sign of the fissure which cuts the narrative diffusion. The systematics of heredity in the story are therefore dependent upon a blank, one which is repeated everywhere and metaphorically, in the deaths of all the narrators and narratees: Rosa Coldfield, "dead" in 1910 in *Absalom, Absalom!*, Jason Richmond Compson, "dead" in 1912 in *The Sound and the Fury*, his son Quentin, "dead" on the second of June 1910, in the same text. This leaves only Shrevlin McCannon, who disappeared in Alberta, "now a practicing surgeon" (316), a professional at cutting and sewing the body, who vanishes without leaving any trace—not even a manuscript. The lesson furnished by these fictitious disappearances must be applied to the text itself, literally, or almost literally, once again. The story delivers itself to us only by inscribing the death of its transmission: this is the most profound sign of its *textual* nature and reality. The text must be severed so that, by an imperceptible yet immense leap, it may begin, in the solidarity of reading and writing. Death and its configuration are thus to be read as a trope of inversion, as the inaugural and incontrovertible possibility of the phantom life of fiction. We cannot read, and this is always the case, except by acknowledging a space which erases its own origin and by recognizing a primordial incision (modifying the concepts of time and being, permitting insertion, repetitions, and a confusion of the continuum of memory and life); this is the very possibility of any reading.

At the heart of the story, the ambition and project of that "demon" Thomas Sutpen could be considered, at a first reading, the perfect analogues of those of the writer: to create a dynasty as well as a world that bears and retains his name for eternity.[9] And all of this, to be done ex nihilo: "Then in the long unamaze Quentin seemed to watch them overrun suddenly the hundred square miles of tranquil and astonished earth and drag house and formal gardens violently out of the soundless Nothing and clap them down like cards upon a table beneath the up-palm immobile and pontific, creating the Sutpen's Hundred [. . .] like the oldentime *Be Light*" (6).[10]

The biblical reference lends to Sutpen's *design* an almost divine, and therefore, sacrilegious dimension, one which can be seen as well in its baptismal aspect. Like Adam in Genesis, or like even the biblical Logos, which departs from the word to create, Thomas Sutpen is above all the one who names and decrees, the one who desires to assure the continuity of his land and lineage on the sole basis of his name. Mr. Compson explains this to Quentin: "Yes, he names Clytie and he named them all (. . .) with that same robust and sardonic temerity, naming with his own mouth his own ironic fecundity of dragon's teeth" (50).

The demonic analogy (luciferian ambition) of surpassing the divinity applies as well to his marriage with Rosa Coldfield: "He will decree this marriage for tonight and perform his own ceremony, himself both groom and minister; pronounce his own wild benediction on it with the very bedward candle in his hand" (136). In this respect, Sutpen is the metaphorical equivalent of Faulkner himself, baptizing, ex nihilo, his characters and cutting up, ex nihilo (but where?) the imaginary map of Yoknapatawpha County, which seems to include Sutpen's Hundred. His entire textual performance is aimed at establishing a firm and irrevocable claim to the territory of fiction. However, there is madness in this *design,* as Rosa points out: "If he was mad, it was only his compelling dream which was insane and not his methods" (137).

Faulkner confides to the reader the task of determining the essence of this madness, the enigma masked by the different rationalizations of the characters. This task is fundamental, for it is around the concept of madness that Faulkner differentiates himself from his character, and that the character no longer seems to be a globalizing metaphor of the writer; rather, Sutpen becomes the writer's synecdoche who fails where Faulkner succeeds.

This madness, the blind spot of the story which neither the demonic explanation nor any fictive narrator is able to pin down, is nothing else but the wish to inscribe the name of the father—in the sense of the law, origin, foundation of all genealogy and all difference—not recognizing that difference itself is absolutely "original." Sutpen's desire constitutes his name as an absolute, as a beginning which excludes difference both in its racial avatars (his denial of *miscegenation*) and in its sexual representations, since woman is for Sutpen only a means of reaffirming the patriarchal and phallocentric name as the origin of all difference.[11]

What must be emphasized in this respect is that the symbolic order that Sutpen wants to found does not differ at all from the symbolic order of the society in which Sutpen wants to inscribe it: his project is merely an exaggeration, a caricature. Jefferson and Sutpen share the same racist and phallocentric law: the only difference is that the planters of Jefferson justify their outrageous privileges in the name of an "aristocratic" genealogy whose function is to mask nobly the arbitrariness of their injustice. Sutpen, on the other hand, "who came out of nowhere and without warning upon the land" (as Rosa complains [7]), disdains this kind of ideological justification and out of this disdain he brutally lays bare the frailty and inconsistency of their system. It is the evidence of their fault and not the fault itself that the people of Jefferson condemn, for they are all accomplices.

They share with Sutpen the same unjust truth: "Or maybe Father and I are both Shreve, maybe it took Father and me both to make Shreve or Shreve and me both to make Father or *maybe Thomas Sutpen to make all of us*" (215, my emphasis), Quentin thinks. It is thus that he identifies Sutpen as the great revealer of an arbitrariness on which all of the white characters of the story depend. May we therefore say that the novel as a whole, in its writing and composition, proceeds from an identical arbitrariness, denial, or exclusion? The answer here can be nothing but a categorical no. Thomas Sutpen is the emblem of the writer only in the consideration of one point which radically separates them. The fictional character is to be read as a synecdoche of the scriptural work only in a topical inversion: the refusal of difference (or its production as originary and absolute principle, which amounts to the same thing), which brings the death of the *design,* is the exact antithesis of the project of writing. But in order to justify this response, we must necessarily examine the question of the blackness: as a race, as a sign, as difference.

Blackness as a general category is radically excluded from the genealogy of recitative transmission which I have sketched in general terms above. Black men and women *do not* narrate anything in *Absalom, Absalom!:* a strange silence which demands interpretation.

At first glance, it would seem that Faulkner espouses in this exclusion the same prejudices exhibited by the white characters in the novel; the transmission from white man to white man (and white woman to white woman) bars racial difference from his system. However, upon closer scrutiny, we may note that interracial mingling permeates even the most prominent genealogical pattern of the text, the lineage which is the very paradigm of white heritage: Thomas Sutpen's. The *ideological* refusal of racial mixture (what Faulkner calls miscegenation) brings about the end of the Sutpen line and catalyzes the failure of his lineage plan. Further, this refusal brings not only the South, but also any community that refuses difference, to its death. However, sexual *practice* belies ideology here and produces a remnant, the only fictional trace of the story's past: Jim Bond. As the half-black, half-white great-grandson of Thomas Sutpen, Jim Bond is the only one to survive the general catastrophe which strikes all of the fictional lineages, and it is upon him that the story closes:

> "You've got one nigger left. One nigger Sutpen left. Of course you can't catch him and you don't even always see him and you never will be able to use him. But you've got him there still. You still hear him at night sometimes. Don't you?"
> "Yes." Quentin said. (311)

This irreducible remainder, who at the end of the narrative escapes the clutches of genealogical obsession (while still being, paradoxically, its "accidental" product) cannot be interpreted merely in the light of the opposition between the ideology of whiteness and the practice of sexual relations. For this elusive remnant, this trace of blackness and whiteness together, is the only thing to survive the narrative hemorrhage; and he survives as the narrative's supplement, marked by the sign of the phantom and the night.

In this role as supplement, he adds a little something to the name of the father, or more precisely, a *d*, to which Faulkner draws our attention in a pun made by the black man Luster (introducing, by the way, a difference between the words of law and the words of reading, which would deserve an extensive commentary): "'And you said "Spell it" and Luster said, "Dat's a lawyer word. Whut dey puts you under when de Law ketches you. I des spells readin' words'" (177). The *d* added to the name of Bon, who because of his mixed blood cannot be Thomas Sutpen's heritor, invokes meanings strangely resonant with the character's role in the text. For Jim Bond is the equivalent of (1) that which removes itself from, but still recognizes or remarks, the law (bond: bail); (2) that which sustains and ties the novel together (bond: link); and (3) that which stands as the reminder of slavery (bond-age). [12]

If the only remainder of the text (which is fictitious, phantasmal) is the product of a mixture of blood, we are therefore forced to reconsider the function of blackness and whiteness and their mutual relation to the project of writing. For, even though Jim Bon(d) is excluded from the turns and detours of narrative transmission, he plays a central role on another level: he symbolizes disruption, survival, and the affirmation of difference in a system which seems to exclude him a priori; in the last analysis, he is the symbol of what is redeemed from the novel.

It is clear that the problem is not to be limited to an empirical or historical aspect: these are only the effects of a more essential problematic, a problematic through which *Absalom, Absalom!* transcends its referential dimension and assumes a promise of eternity for itself. If the white characters/narrators/listeners refuse difference in its historical or empirical manifestation, writing and the text know that in order to be produced, they must acknowledge difference and mix their blood on a more essential level. The novel is written therefore *against* a discourse of racial purity; the elusive vestige of writing produced by the novel finds its origin *in miscegenation* itself.

And this commingling is discernible even on the most literal and graphic plane: the black/white opposition is the "original" dyad from which the black characters of writing come upon the virgin page. Without this difference and opposition, there would not be a text, but only black or white alone, illegible.

The questions of race (the mixing of blood) and sexual difference are linked by a necessary solidarity, which, once again, is of the symbolic order (the historical or biological manifestation of the problem being but the effect, and not the cause, of the question). By the same principle that puts a discourse of racial purity into question, sexual identity is never absolutely defined in *Absalom, Absalom!* The exception to this is Thomas Sutpen, who attempts (and this is his madness) the irreducible and real affirmation of the phallic principle, and thus destines the principle to dissolution and death. Yet examples of sexual indeterminacy abound. Rosa Coldfield appears for the first time "a breathing indictment, ubiquitous and even transferable, of the entire male principle" (48), but she subsequently becomes a hermaphrodite: "I became all polymath love's androgynous advocate" (121). [13] It is the same for her aunt, Rosa's virginal double in the procreation that precedes: "that strong vindictive consistent woman who seems to have been twice the man that Mr. Coldfield was and who in very truth was not only Miss Rosa's mother but her father too" (51). The same is true of Henry Sutpen and Judith, whose common blood erases sexual difference: "The two of them, brother and sister, curiously alike as if the difference in sex had merely sharpened the common blood to a terrific, an almost unbearable similarity" (142). Similarly, Shreve and Quentin (and by extension Charles Bon and Henry Sutpen, in whatever order) are never clearly situated on one side of the line of sexual demarcation: "There was something curious in the way they looked at one another, curious and quiet and profoundly intent, not at all as two young men might look at each other but almost as youth and a very young girl might out of virginity itself" (246).

The love of Charles and Judith is without doubt the foremost example where the sexual difference is confused (complicated also with the question of race, since Charles Bon is of mixed blood). Henry's identification with his sister's future husband reduces the difference of the sexes to nothingness, by qualifying the name of the ultimate prohibition, incest: "In fact, perhaps this is the pure and perfect incest: the brother realizing that the sister's virginity must be destroyed in order to have existed at all, taking that virginity in the brother-in-law, the man whom he would be if he could become, metamorphose into the lover, the husband" (79). This infraction of the law of the brother and father is immediately echoed in Charles Bon himself: "Perhaps in his fatalism (Charles) loved Henry the better of the two, seeing perhaps in the sister merely the shadow, the woman vessel with which to consummate the love whose actual object was the youth" (89). As it turns out, incest in this novel never actually "happens," just as with the case of Quentin and Caddy in *The Sound and the Fury*. But simply because it does not manifest itself fictively does not mean that this paradigm of all *miscegenation* is not taken up and secretly assumed on the level of writing. A justification of this reading implies a detour to one of Faulkner's own remarks concerning *The Sound and the Fury* in *Faulkner in the University;* [14] Caddy is presented in this work as the feminine origin of the "theme of the book," at once a symbol of novelistic discourse and a filial creation of the Faulknerian imagination: "To me she was the beautiful one she was my heart's darling. *That's what I wrote the book about* and I used the tools which seemed to me the proper tools to try to tell, try to draw the picture of Caddy" (6). Like Pygmalion, Faulkner has not done anything but (he never ceases to do anything but) fall in love with the daughter of his works. Between the writer and his text there is an affair which puts into question both sexual difference and all genealogical distinction: the birth of the novel comes from an amorous confusion between the author and the character, an incest which goes so far as to make Faulkner, in his turn, the product of his own writing (see the epigraphs at the beginning of this article).

If this applies to *Absalom, Absalom!* as well (and we have no reason to doubt it) then incest is the very motivation of writing. Happening yet not happening, incest suggests the necessity of bypassing all difference (between black and white, between father and daughter, between brother and sister) and of blending all difference into a general mixture, so that a remnant can be produced. This is the outrage of writing: it must put itself outside the law, secretly paying its bail (bond), in order to have the chance of *happening*.

In the case of Henry and Judith Sutpen, incest (the metaphor of all possibility) is itself enabled only by a prohibition which seems to precede it: the prohibition of virginity. In the same way, the identification between Henry and Charles depends on a law which taboos any carnal relations between them.[15] As the obsession with an impalpable barrier, not only between sexes but also between individuals, virginity has numerous symbolic distillations in *Absalom, Absalom!*: Rosa Coldfield, her aunt, Quentin Compson, and even Thomas Sutpen. In fact, the association between Sutpen and virginity is repeatedly emphasized: coming from West *Virgin*ia (18), a virgin until the age of twenty-five (204), "clearing *virgin* land" (13), his own offspring (Judith and Clytie) are posed in the novel as untouched feminine principles.

At a first reading, virginity appears to be that which is exempt from all mixing and compromise in relation to otherness and difference: it solitarily affirms the impossibility of principles (male/female, black/white) ever coming together. In this sense, virginity is intimately linked with death and with the incapacity of regeneration. Thus, in *The Sound and the Fury:* "In the South, you are ashamed of being a virgin. Boys. Men. They lie about it. Because it means less to women, Father said. He said it was men who invented virginity not women. Father said it's like death" (June 2).[16]

But in *Absalom, Absalom!* Rosa Coldfield seems to see, on Sutpen's tombstone, even when the date of death has not yet been engraved, a virginal hope: "Miss Coldfield possibly (maybe doubtless) looked at it every day, as though it were his portrait possibly (maybe doubtless here too) reading among the lettering more of maiden hope than she ever told Quentin about" (156).

The blankness of the funerary inscription, the still virgin stone is thus also the promise of a future that Rosa keeps silent, but which is unveiled by writing, between the lines. In this respect, virginity does not put our reading of mingling (racial and sexual) into question, but rather confirms it, since virginity is its condition. Thus, for Henry Sutpen, his sister's virginity is meaningless, or better, has a double meaning—it is something which only has meaning when taken away: "Henry was the provincial [. . .] who may have been conscious that his fierce provincial's pride in his sister's virginity was a false quantity which must incorporate in itself an inability to endure in order to be precious, to exist, and so must depend upon its loss, absence, to have existed at all. In fact this is the pure and perfect incest" (79). Now, as it turns out, this white space, in the loss of which everything begins (descendance, meaning: sense), is exactly what gives birth to its own transgression by incest, and in extension, by writing. Virginity is that which the text simultaneously approaches and flees with all of its forces: to rejoin its immaculate origin would mean silence; in the same way, the denial of this original absence would be the death of the narrative (of any narrative). Faulkner's writing must therefore inscribe itself—and this is an absolute necessity—*between* virginity and loss of virginity: "Yes, Judith, Bon, Henry, Sutpen: all of them. They are here, but something is missing; they are like a chemical formula exhumed along with the letters from that forgotten chest, the paper old and faded and falling to pieces, the writing faded, almost indecipherable, yet meaningful, familiar in shape and sense, the name and presence of volatile and sentient forces" (83).

From this point, the reader cannot help but negotiate with the initial white blankness that only exists in and because of its transgression, its erasure (its covering by the remnant and by blackness). For the blankness is in the geometrical space where his reading comes to supplement the text: "You bring them in the proportions called for, but nothing happens; you re-read, tedious and intent, poring, making sure that you have forgotten nothing, made no miscalculation; you bring them together again and again: just the words, the symbols, the shapes themselves, shadowy inscrutable and serene, against that turgid background of an horrible and bloody mischancing of human affairs" (83). In the chemical precipitation of reading, nothing actually happens: there are the letters and symbols, the calculation and weight of their difference, measures always retaken because always missing something (a silence that is absolutely unyielding), a struggle for and against erasure, founded upon "human affairs." Thus, nothing happens if not this—that in reading and writing, in their scandal, a certain power surfaces: the power of fiction.

NOTES

"*Absalom, Absalom!*: The Outrage of Writing" is translated from the French by Douglas Saylor.

This text acknowledges its debt to the following books and articles: Thadious M. Davis, *Faulkner's "Negro"* (Baton Rouge: Louisiana University Press, 1983); John T. Irwin, *Doubling and Incest, Repetition and Revenge: A Speculative Reading of Faulkner* (Baltimore: Johns Hopkins University Press, 1975); Lee Jenkins, *Faulkner and Black-White Relations: A Psychoanalytic Approach* (New York: Columbia University Press, 1981); François Pitavy, "The Narrative Voice and Function of Shreve: Remarks on the Production of Meaning in *Absalom, Absalom!*," in Elisabeth Muhlenfeld, ed., *William Faulkner's Absalom, Absalom! A Critical Casebook* (New York: Garland, 1984); Olga W. Vickery, *The Novels of William Faulkner: A Critical Interpretation* (Baton Rouge: Louisiana State University Press, 1964).

For questions of theoretical or critical vocabulary used in this study, I refer the reader to the following texts: J. Derrida, *Of Grammatology* (Paris, 1967), for the question of difference and supplement; J. Derrida, *La double séance*, in *La dissémination* (Paris, 1972), for the hymen and virginity; J. Lacan, *La signification du phallus*, in *Ecrits* (Paris, 1966); *La grand'route et le significant "être père,"* in *Le Séminaire III, Les psychoses*, Paris 1981.

1. Rosa Coldfield and Shrevlin McCannon cannot be exempted from this familial system.

2. The French word *propriété* contains this dual significance. —TRANS.

3. *Selected Letters of William Faulkner*, ed. J. Blotner (New York: Random House, 1977), 79.

4. F. L. Gwynn and J. L. Blotner, eds., *Faulkner in the University* (Charlottesville: University of Virginia Press, 1959), 285; see this work for each time the author speaks of his characters. Faulkner enjoyed creating the illusion of referential depth of characters in the minds of his listeners, and not without a certain bemused wit.

5. Thus Cleanth Brooks, in his polished and informed book *William Faulkner: The Yoknapatawpha Country* (New Haven: Yale University Press, 1963), distin-

guishes in *Absalom, Absalom!* between "facts" and "conjectures made by narrators" (429–36). Such a dichotomy must be completely reexamined with respect to apocrypha, where the very meaning of the word "fact" opens itself to a great margin of uncertainty.

6. William Faulkner, *Absalom, Absalom!* (1936; New York: Random House, 1964), 149, 171, 215. Further references are to this edition and page numbers will be given in parentheses in the text.

7. The story departs in this way from a form of writing, so modest and apparently insignificant, and not from the speaking voice.

8. See the commentary on the narrators of *Absalom, Absalom!:* "But taken all together, the truth is in what they saw though nobody saw the truth intact. . . . It was, as you say, thirteen ways of looking at a blackbird" (Gwynn and Blotner, *Faulkner in the University,* 273).

9. Let us here emphasize that the "demonizing" of Sutpen by Rosa and Shreve cannot be read uniquely in a negative way. According to Faulkner, the demon is in fact the ineffable point from which the force of writing appears: "I think that if you have the demon, you're going to write anyway, nothing is going to stop you, and it may be you don't want things too easy" (ibid., 204). And again: "Well, I think there is a limitless supply of demons just like germs that hang around maybe just looking for lodgement in anyone that shows any aptitude for ink. That—that's, as I said, it's a vice and it's a virulent sort of vice too. If you ain't careful it'll get you" (ibid.). These are metaphors of the habitation, multiplication, and lethalness of germs that one could attribute almost directly to Thomas Sutpen.

10. The metaphor of constructor, architect and carpenter, well represented in the *design* of Sutpen, are also metaphors of writing: see, for example, Gwynn and Blotner, *Faulkner in the University,* 49–50.

11. Thus, the feminine inheritors do not count in genealogical transmission, since they can erase the name of the father (and origin) by marriage; when Sutpen envisions his descendants, it is only to the "masculine principle" that he confers the privilege of his dynastic heritage: "And, even after he would become dead, still watching the fine grandsons and great grandsons as far as eye can see" (223). It is also his refusal to recognize his last daughter that will bring about his assassination by Wash Jones (235–36).

12. Faulkner himself added a little *u* to his name, which appears with the added letter on the front cover of his first book-length literary attempt (*The Marble Faun* [Boston: Four Seas, 1924]).

13. Also see her remark in the same vein: "I lived out not as a woman, a girl, but rather as the man I perhaps should have been" (119).

14. The obvious question to pose here bears upon the status which should be granted to the author's letters, statements, and interviews concerning his work. I will not address the issue at great length here, since, from a certain perspective, all

documents become part of the literary *monument,* a pawn in the game of writing and fiction.

15. Cf. "the knowledge of the insurmountable barrier which the similarity of gender hopelessly intervened" (78).

16. *The Sound and the Fury* (New York: Random House, 1984), 78.

The Autograph of Violence

in Faulkner's *Pylon*

JOHN T. MATTHEWS

"It's not the money" / *"It was the money"*

Readers of *Pylon* have grown used to accepting Faulkner's legend about the circumstances of its composition and its significance to him. Caught in the toils of confronting the central questions of southern history and identity as he drafted *Absalom, Absalom!*, arrested by the technical tension between shifting perspectives and narrative coherence, Faulkner confesses his need to find release in simpler work. In *Pylon*, he says, he concentrated on characters who, unlike Sutpen and his tortured descendants, "had escaped the compulsion of accepting a past and a future[;] . . . they had no past." Faulkner "had to get away" from *Absalom* by writing about barnstorming aviators, who had "no place . . . in the culture, in the economy" (Gwynn and Blotner, 36). By then treating the narrative through a single focalization (the reporter), *Pylon* seeks to reduce effort, subject, and effect. Did this "holiday" clear Faulkner's head because his topic and approach were so purely different from *Absalom*'s, as he implies? Or might *Pylon* not have forced Faulkner to realize one of the main empowering principles of his greatest novel: that all individuals are radically conditioned by the historical and material realities of their eras, and that no writer can afford to believe his characters have no places in their cultures or economies.

Faulkner's insistence that the flyers are historically and socially anomalous accords with the reporter's dreamy view of these homeless gladiators of the air. In his efforts both to appreciate the flyers and also to facilitate their passage through New Valois, the reporter emphasizes their differences from the rest of the human race. Describing the improbable lives of

Roger Shumann, his wife, Laverne, and Jack Holmes to his editor, the reporter marvels at their inconceivable freedom, at their unearthly exploits:

> "and then the other guy, the parachute guy, dropping in, falling the couple or three miles with his sack of flour before pulling the ripcord. They aint human, you see. No ties; no place where you were born and have to go back to it now and then even if it's just only to hate the damn place good and comfortable for a day or two. . . . Because they dont need money; it aint money they are after anymore than it's glory because the glory cant only last until the next race and so maybe it aint even until tomorrow. And they dont need money except only now and then when they come in contact with the human race like in a hotel to sleep or eat now and then." (805–806)[1]

Neither money nor places of their own; neither jack nor homes: Faulkner lets the name of the parachute jumper squint at the reporter's sentimental idealization of the aviators' freedom.

The more the reporter insists on the flyers' otherworldliness, of course, the more we may wonder what such denial defends against. The reporter works tirelessly to shelter the aviators from the degradations of wage earning and class conflict. They are not, he contends, like "a gang of men hired to go down into a mine," who would surely strike if one day "the bigbellied guys that own the mine would tell them that everybody's pay had been cut two and a half percent . . . to print a notice how the elevator or something had fell on one of them the night before" (890). In the reporter's eyes, the flyers "submit" to the race organizers' tariff on their prize pool because money is less important to them than the exhilaration of flight.

Because he wants to champion the aviators' defiance of economic and social determinants, the reporter refuses to see their deep indebtedness to those who hold money and power. The flyers talk of virtually nothing but money, yet the reporter is so busy denying its importance to them that he never hears what they say. *Pylon* begins with a vivid account of Jiggs's effort to buy new boots. The narrative records the profound commodification of desire represented by the mechanic's fancy.[2] His eyes gorge on the boots in the store window, displayed as seductively as those in "the posed countrylife photographs in the magazine advertisements" (779)— the real source, we suspect, of Jiggs's longing, and perhaps the real destination of his gaze. But whatever bourgeois dream of gentrification his boots may betoken (and their purchase both stimulates and deflects that deeper desire to rise), Jiggs can plot his acquisition only in terms of the money he has and the money he will make. The opening pages disclose —in grotesque slow-motion—the relation between wages, credit, labor, and time upon which the aviators' world is inescapably founded. Like his fellow workers, Jiggs wholly depends on others for his means of survival. Though they are nomadic, the aviators are little different from the miners the reporter contrasts them to; the clerk in the store sniffs the stink of an "incorrigible insolvency" (780) on Jiggs.

The question of whether insolvency was indeed incorrigible was being confronted by both Faulkner (in his sharpening crisis in personal finances in 1933 and 1934) and by the country at large (in the renewed doubt about the efficacy of Roosevelt's New Deal).[3] Given these superimposed pre-occupations with economy, it is all the more significant that *Pylon* should need to establish its concern with money *against* the grain of the reporter's attitude. The reporter's contact with the aviators immediately adds to his expenses; he volunteers food, liquor, transportation, even cash advances against their prize winnings; and he obsessively justifies to his editor every penny he spends on their behalf. Yet he dismisses their indebtedness to him as nothing. The appearance of the aviators endangers the reporter's unexamined accommodation of economic injustice. He insists on his availability so emphatically that they borrow to the point of theft from him, a discovery that provokes in the reporter a renewed effort to deny that money might be the issue. If only Laverne will acknowledge to him that they took his cash as he lay asleep outside his own doorway, then the reporter's faith in an ethics beyond economics will remain unshaken. The reporter's hostship lets him seize the provision of money from the aviators and take it on himself, as if he chooses to degrade himself in order to keep them free. This relation involves an arrangement of mutual benefit and injury between the host and his guests. As Holmes observes, "maybe you never sent for us to come here, and maybe we never asked you to move in on us" (952).

That each party has moved in on the other to establish a parasitical relation may also suggest that the failure of communication between them involves a special kind of suppression or denial. Michel Serres has elaborated the coincidence between several senses of "parasite," a word which in French also denotes static: noisy interference. The reporter cannot hear the involvement of the aviators in questions of money because his own involvement requires and furnishes that interference. If he were not so deafened, the reporter would notice that the flyers share Jiggs's concentration on earnings. To them the prize winnings are a payday, to be converted instantly into life's necessities and scant pleasures.

The harsh constraints of the aviators' lives are summarized by Jiggs when he hears of a fellow pilot's fatal crash: "Burn to death on Thursday night or starve to death on Friday morning" (813). Shumann's unexpected victory in an early race means just one thing to the mechanic: "Yair, we're jake now. We can eat and sleep again tonight" (798). Why must Shumann place? "Jesus, he better had come in on somebody's money or we'd a all set up in the depot tonight with our bellies thinking our throats was cut" (796). The aviators constantly calculate money against risk as the quotient of their livelihoods: Shumann, for example, considers army pursuit planes "oversouped," liable "to kill you if you dont watch them. I wouldn't want to do that for two-fifty-six a month" (880).

Pylon gestures toward the money motive because the novel cannot contradict the reporter openly until the end. One of the gestures in its repertoire is punning, in which language can be made to point to one meaning while mouthing another. *Pylon* plays on the slang term for money —"jack"—so extensively that it forms a subliminal insistence on money's importance. There are the repeated references to getting and spending "jack," including the reporter's closing words to his editor, *"and when you come bring some jack because I am on a credit"* (992). Both objects and characters take on its name. From a jackstaff, the Hotel Terrebone displays a placard designating it as headquarters of the Aeronautical Association (814); Jiggs searches for his bootjack; death becomes "the old blackjack" (807). Jiggs calls the anonymous busdriver "Jack" (801); the child Jack is named in part for Jack Holmes; Jiggs jokes with him about his father-lessness, prompting a flurry of fists and the reporter's joke about another Jack, Dempsey; and after Shumann's death Jiggs throws in his lot with Art Jackson.[4] On the eve of Shumann's race in the plane that will kill him, he discovers Laverne already in bed, waiting naked for him with the child beside her. The tangled relation of passion, loyalty, risk, and money seems summarized in Shumann's laconic and perhaps innocent question as he enters the bed: "Want to move Jack to the middle?" (907).

At this point we might conclude that the struggle of interpretation in *Pylon* pits the reporter's sentimental idealization against a more realistic analysis. In one view, the aviators burn with the splendor of freedom, flight, fraternity, and honor; in another, they are workers struggling to maintain themselves against the exhaustions of southern history and economy. This interpretive contest might conclude with a colleague's contradiction of the reporter: "'And dont kid yourself,' the first said. 'It was the money. Those guys like money as well as you and me'" (976). This reporter goes on to predict correctly Laverne's decision to return her son to Shumann's parents; he sees that the economic motive must outweigh whatever sentiment is involved. Does this simple reversal of the reporter's position satisfactorily disclose the "truth" to be recovered from below the reporter's discourse of suppression? Can the novel—by finally articulating and at last acknowledging a contradictory view—come into possession of its own meaning?

If we grant that *Pylon*'s narrative furnishes more information about the aviators' situation than the reporter is willing to accommodate in his interpretive romance, then we must as well doubt that simply reversing his denials will correct all distortions. In both cases the reporter's account determines the range and terminology of the questions. Instead, I want to pursue registers of meaning that elude the reporter's control. The reporter's purposeful blindness to historical context—which frees him to concentrate on the aviators' perceived transcendence of historical embeddedness—is a blindness that the novel does not entirely share.

Deliberately between the lines, Faulkner invites us to consider the aviators' appearance at Mardi Gras as an event with historical, economic, and social significance—a significance that insinuates the revolutionary potential of the thirties. This potential for social transformation is not a subject often associated with Faulkner's fiction, and we shall have to admit the extent to which the reporter's will to trivialize the subversive energy of the economically oppressed is related to Faulkner's fear of that energy.[5] Whether it is or is not the money becomes a binary bracket that wards off a more profound question. The flyers neither transcend nor wholly accept their lot as wage earners; rather, they represent—however fleetingly—the very derangement of the order that prevails over them. The visualization of economic reversal, social equality, bodily indulgence, and collective intimacy is the essential thrust of the carnivalesque, and it is presented in *Pylon* as a thrust that may have to be reckoned with and not merely denied.

THE CARNIVAL

The thirties also stimulated one of the richest considerations of the carnival we have, Mikhail Bakhtin's *Rabelais and His World*.[6] Bakhtin's reading of Rabelais celebrates the revolutionary freedom of the carnivalesque and extols Rabelais's achievement in transmuting its street forms into novelistic ones. By concentrating on the power of the people to challenge all official truth through their practice of the carnival, Bakhtin also suggests the structural opposition in any society between the upper and lower strata, between authorized and unauthorized truth, between the designed work of reform and the heedless play of revolution. In the carnival, everything is at risk.

The sense of real risk, of pandemic jeopardy and unforeseeable transformation, agitates the period in which Faulkner is writing *Pylon* (and in which Bakhtin is writing *Rabelais*). The newspaper headlines reproduced in *Pylon* alone—cryptic and confused as they are—point to the desperation of the oppressed in the United States and abroad: "FARMERS REFUSE BANKERS DENY   STRIKERS DEMAND   PRESIDENT'S YACHT" (826). Amplified by the accounts that actually appeared in the New Orleans newspapers of early 1934, when the opening of the Shushan Airport was being covered by Faulkner's reporter friend, Hermann Deutsch, these stories chronicle the continued anguish of the unemployed worldwide, the hopes of socialistic reform, protests against fascism, and the rise of Hitler.[7]

Pylon rides on an interplay between this sense of imminent historical transformation and the celebration of the Mardi Gras carnival. The sober struggles of workers around the world to emancipate themselves may seem the very inverse of the narcotic revelry of carnival parades and air shows. Yet Bakhtin argues that the carnival—especially in its medieval roots—carries the threat of popular revolt and the promise of social betterment. Rather than sublimating and defusing such subversive impulses, the carnival actually stimulates them, in Bakhtin's view, and gives them material reality—for however brief a spell. The essential components of the carnivalesque include: (1) a charged sense in individuals of themselves as "the people," (2) the practice of parody and reversal, (3) an appreciation of the discrepancies between the upper and lower orders of society, (4) masked challenges to official truth, (5) exaltation of the body through its purposeful degradation, (6) celebration of physical renewal and reproduction, and (7) the fleeting materialization of utopian possibilities such as luxury, leisure, freedom, and equality.

Even the mention of these components will, I hope, resonate with the issues I have been emphasizing in *Pylon*. When the narrator describes Jiggs's rapturous face before the store window as having "hot brown eyes [that] seemed to snap and glare like a boy's approaching for the first time

the aerial wheels and stars and serpents of a nighttime carnival" (779),
I think we are meant to keep in mind a context often ignored by the reporter. In the novel, as in the events Faulkner witnessed in New Orleans
in February 1934, Mardi Gras and the air spectacle constitute a single phenomenon. The "aerial wheels" *are* the "nighttime carnival," and Faulkner
embodies the carnival mentality in the aviators and their fellow "revelers."
Yet as I go on to interpret Faulkner's use of the carnivalesque in *Pylon,*
I will observe that its original spirit appears deformed, though deformed
in instructive ways. Ultimately we shall notice the strain of translating a
medieval folk spectacle into the New Orleans of Roosevelt and Huey Long
through the idiom of Joyce's and Eliot's high modernism.

LAUGHTER

To Bakhtin's ears, the sound of the carnival is the sound of laughter. Laughter shakes what is established and shifts thoughts to its overthrow: "medieval laughter . . . is the social consciousness of all the people.
Man . . . in the carnival crowd . . . comes into contact with other bodies
of varying age and social caste. He is aware of being a member of a continually growing and renewed people. This is why festive folk laughter
presents an element of victory not only over supernatural awe, over the
sacred, over death; it also means the defeat of power, of earthly kings, of
the earthly upper classes, of all that oppresses and restricts" (92). "Carnival laughter" possesses a "complex nature" in that it is, "first of all,
a festive laughter. Therefore it is not an individual reaction to some isolated 'comic' event. Carnival laughter is the laughter of all the people.
Second, it is universal in scope; it is directed at all and everyone, including the carnival's participants. The entire world is seen in its droll aspect,
in its gay relativity. Third, this laughter is ambivalent: it is gay, triumphant, and at the same time mocking, deriding. It asserts and denies, it
buries and revives" (11–12). Bakhtin honors the purely corrosive, unbind-
ing forms of laughter in the carnival: the parodies of church liturgy and
ritual; the bawdy, playful language of the marketplace; the sport of mock
imprecation and naked hucksterism.

Faulkner acknowledges the force of such carnival laughter in *Pylon* even
as he refuses to give it space sufficient to its ends. The overwrought surface
of the novel teems with grotesquerie. "Laughing Boy in fit at Woishndon
Poik!" calls a newsboy (Laughing Boy in fifth at Washington Park). Here

language grows deformed in the mouth of the people. The dialect pronunciation produces an accidental but significant pun: the hawker's cry conjures up a laughter that might cause fits—uncontrollable social eruptions. The newsboy possesses "a new face, young, ageless, the teeth gaped raggedly as though he had found them one by one over a period of years about the streets" (813). This description conflates literary conceit and economic analysis: it looks *as if* the child has scavenged in the streets for his teeth, yet such a worker *is* no more than a scavenger unprovided for. In such subsidiary moments the novel expresses its subversive laughter. The newsboy's face holds the promise of "ageless" youth, and—like a laughing fit—holds the possibility of a new order to succeed the old.

Festive laughter, Bakhtin asserts, derides the powers that oppress. The mouthpiece for this kind of utterance is Jiggs. His own continuous punning and sarcasm eat away at the reporter's romantic interpretation of events, at the kind of incomprehension that masks the exploitation of the aviators. In the following exchange the reporter rails about the race organizers, who may be found at the hotel, paying at once for both lodging and sexual services:

> "Yair," the reporter cried, "they'll be here. Here's where to find guys that dont aim to sleep at the hotel. Yair; tiered identical cubicles of one thousand rented sleepings. And if you just got jack enough to last out the night you dont even have to go to bed."
>
> "Did what?" Jiggs said, already working over toward the wall beside the entrance. "Oh. Teared Q pickles. Yair; teared Q pickles of one thousand rented cunts if you got the jack too. I got the Q pickle all right. I got enough Q pickle for one thousand. And if I just had the jack too it wouldn't be teared." (814)

One must admit that Jiggs's response verges on unintelligibility, but it is the sort of wild unintelligibility that suggests semantic terrorism. The reporter simply envies those who have the cash to buy sex, but Jiggs's resentment exposes a more fundamental question begged by the reporter: his pun evokes both the stubborn misery of poverty ("teared") and the social stratification responsible for his plight (pushing the reporter's "tiered" to its metaphorical consequence). The potency of Jiggs's puns arises from the verbal violence they can perform. (Indeed, his other comment about his Q pickle being enough for a thousand cunts threatens the sexual and financial order that favors the Feinmans of this world.) Puns puncture the semantic precision of language, subverting univocal sense in the same way political subversion attacks authority.

Jiggs's laughter often ridicules his oppressors and defenders at the same time, suggesting their complicity. Explaining the meeting called to announce the cut in the prize purse, Jiggs mocks the reporter's belief that it's not the money: " 'Contestants' meeting. To strike, see? . . . Sure. For more jack. It aint the money: it's the principle of the thing. Jesus, what do we need with money?' Jiggs began to laugh again on that harsh note which stopped just as it became laughter and started before it was mirth" (875). This laughter cuts with the ambivalence of carnival laughter; it derides and triumphs at the same time.

Pylon allows for the performance of popular humor. Throughout the novel the aviators and revelers appear as comedians: Jiggs and the reporter resemble "the tall and the short man of the orthodox and unfailing comic team" (812); the reporter holds the flyers "immobile in a tableau reminiscent (save for his hat) of the cartoon pictures of city anarchists" (829); the barnstormers are said to disappear wherever "mules and vaudeville acts go" (975).[8] The carnival charges such humor with revolutionary potential.

DEATH, DESECRATION, REGENERATION

The carnival's celebration of the "contradictory world of becoming" (Bakhtin, 149) pays ambivalent tribute to carnal reproduction. Superimposed on the carnival's association with the lower orders of society is its association with the lower stratum of the body. Bakhtin describes the gestures and language of debasement characteristic of the carnival: they "are based on a literal debasement in terms of the topography of the body, that is, a reference to the bodily lower stratum, the zone of the genital organs. This signifies destruction, a grave for the one who is debased. But such debasing gestures and expressions are ambivalent, since the lower stratum is not only a bodily grave but also the area of the genital organs, the fertilizing and generating stratum. Therefore, in the images of urine and excrement is preserved the essential link with birth, fertility, renewal, welfare" (148). The imagery of desecration—of digestive and excremental befoulment—materializes the world and insists on the potency of all that is natural and carnal. *Pylon* presents a special case of Faulknerian scatology. The sexual, reproductive, and excremental become one, for instance, in Laverne's spectacular first parachute jump. Returning to the cockpit from the wing of Shumann's plane, Laverne straddles her pilot-lover. Roger realizes she is wearing nothing under her dress: "[s]he told him later that the reason was that she was afraid that from fear she might soil one of the few undergarments which she now possessed" (908). The modest seduction concluded, Laverne leaps overboard, settling to earth under the parachute, a vision of promise so naked that at least one on-looker falls into profoundest self-distraction. We should not be surprised that she is degraded in this same act; on the ground, "she now lay dressed from the waist down in dirt and parachute straps and stockings" (909). Roger refers to his startled erection as "the perennially undefeated, the victorious . . . the bereaved, the upthrust, the stalk: the annealed rapacious heartshaped crimson bud" (909). This description is a little less clinical than symbolic, and I suggest that its context is the grotesque exaltation of the phallus in carnival.

The same conflation of burial and resurrection—of both agricultural and coital sorts—may be seen in the reporter's gloss on the ménage à trois. Shumann and Holmes must lie in bed with Laverne so: " 'two farmers' boys, at least one from Ohio anyway she told me. And the ground they plow from Iowa; yair, two farmers' boys downbanked; yair, two buried pylons in the one Iowadrowsing womandrowsing pylondrowsing' " (849). Here the implanted pylon becomes the upthrust phallus, the buried plow, the triumphant "stalk." These images underpin the unified process of degradation, interment, and rebirth associated with the carnival. [9]

That life arises from the foulness of death is the miracle of the car-nival. "Folk culture organized the inferno according to its own fashion, opposing sterile eternity by pregnant and birth-giving death; preserving the past by giving birth to a new, better future," Bakhtin notes. "If the Christian hell devalued earth and drew men away from it, the carniva-lesque hell affirmed earth and its lower stratum as the fertile womb, where death meets birth and a new life springs forth. This is why the images of the material bodily lower stratum pervade the carnivalized underworld" (395). Lazarus figures this function in the medieval pageant, and it is no accident that Jiggs constantly refers to the cadaverous reporter by that name (797). Though he refuses to acknowledge its possibilities, moreover, the reporter does once approach the fundamental fusion of death and life achieved by the carnival, "confusing both the living and the dead without concern now, with profound conviction of the complete unimportance of either or of the confusion itself" (955).

Earlier the reporter has verged on the metamorphic possibility of the spectacle. Sickened by his deprivation and fatigue, he feels "the hot corrupted coffee gathering inside him like a big heavy bird beginning to fly as he plunged out the door and struck a lamppost and clinging to it surrendered as life, sense, all, seemed to burst out of his mouth as though his entire body were trying in one fierce orgasm to turn itself wrongsideout" (849). This is the stress of a new perception struggling toward birth, a perception represented in the carnival by grotesque imagery of the body's reversibility. In the carnival such reversal appears in "curses" that take the body and "burn it, hurl it to the ground, cripple the legs, cause diarrhea, and gripping; in other words, they turn the body inside out" (Bakhtin, 166).

In his unnatural height and thinness the reporter evokes the grotesque body of the carnival, a body that represents the prospect of the individual's merger with others through the transcendence of its limits. The carnival shows the body opening itself outward through "copulation, pregnancy, childbirth, the throes of death, eating, drinking, or defecation" (Bakhtin, 26). The reporter serves as host to the activities of "grotesque" physicality that he does not actually practice himself. Through them, the lower stratum insists on the recognition normally withheld by the official truth of reason, repression, sublimation, and individuality.

SUBVERSION, UTOPIA

On the eve of a Second World War, the dominant ideologies of the West were hardly threatened by folk carnivals. But the 1934 Mardi Gras in New Orleans must have represented to Faulkner's eyes an image for popular revolution and a suspension of the verities. During a time of continuing national and international crises, stymied by personal dilemmas in money and love, Faulkner explores in *Pylon* the complex relation between order and reform, power and resistance, stability and discontentment, entitlement and exclusion.

Those who possess power in New Valois remain concealed in *Pylon*. The signal of this situation is Colonel Feinman's absentee authority in the meeting with the aviators. Though the flyers are promised his appearance, Feinman exercises his right to summon and dismiss his employees, to rob them of their time, to make them deal with his representative rather than his person. Feinman's power increases according to this untouchability. The aviators glimpse his photograph, notice his name and initials all over the airport, and sense enviously his command of luxury (particularly women), but not until Matt Ord threatens to ground the plane Shumann wants to race does Feinman himself actually intervene. Feinman steps in to defend the integrity of capitalist entrepreneurialism: " 'Aint we promised these folks out there—' he made a jerking sweep with the cigar —'a series of races? Aint they paying their money in here to see them? And aint it the more airplanes they will have to look at the better they will think they got for the money? . . . Now, let's settle this business' " (929–30). Feinman wants to insure that there are no slips between production, advertisement, and consumption. Indeed, when Burnham crashes early in the races and his name must be deleted from the published program of subsequent events, the aviators are told that the "committee representing the business men of New Valois who have sponsored this meet and offered you the opportunity to win these cash prizes . . . feel that they are advertising something they cant produce" (879). In the tumultuous, irregular marketplace of the carnival, this kind of instability must be avoided at all costs. Any break in the smooth operation of the economic system may provide a point of puzzlement or dissent. The enfranchised protect their interests: the reporter and Jiggs drive through suburban New Valois on the way to the dump, hardly noticing that "even the sunlight seemed different, where it filtered among the ordered liveoaks and fell suavely upon parked expanses and vistas beyond which the homes of the rich oblivious and secure presided above clipped lawns and terraces, with a quality of having itself been passed by appointment through a walled gate by a watchman" (959).

At least part of the reason Feinman and the other members of the "committee" guard themselves so carefully involves the volatility of the working class in 1934. Against even his own sympathies, as Quentin's aghast disbelief reflects, Faulkner was well advanced toward an understanding of the sins of capitalism as he sorted out the economic and moral issues of slavery in *Absalom, Absalom!*.[10] In *Pylon,* the relative invisibility of those in power does not prevent the central question of their legitimacy from being raised. To the extent that a tiered economy and society depend on the violence of exploitation and oppression—certainly one of the truths *Absalom* comes to see—to that extent the carnival mentality represents trouble. Bakhtin notes that "[t]he serious aspects of class culture are official and authoritarian; they are combined with violence, prohibitions, limitations and always contain an element of fear and of intimidation" (90). The announcer of the air races attempts to mediate the conflict between worker and management, but he must occupy an impossible no-man's-land between parties that are quietly at war with each other: "the very slightness of the distance between him and the table postulated a gap more unbridgable even than that between the table and the second group" (877). Distracted by Laverne's departure, the reporter stands holding a wad of bills given him by Holmes for the return of Shumann's body; the warning to him should remind us of the violence of getting and keeping money: " 'Better put that stuff into your pocket, doc,' the soldier said. 'Some of these guys will be cutting your wrist off' " (954).

One strategy of the upper class is to concede a little to save a lot. Hagood, for example, feeds the reporter just enough money to secure him. Hagood's clothing and car, "which unmistakably represented money" (833; and cf. 834), link him to the authority of wealth. When Hagood agrees to lend the reporter more money for the flyers, Jiggs allegorizes the terms of the relation:

> "Write on my back if you want to, mister," [Jiggs] said, turning and stooping, presenting a broad skintight expanse of soiled shirt, apparently as hard as a section of concrete, to Hagood.
> "And get the hell kicked out of me and serve me right," Hagood thought viciously. He spread the blank on Jiggs' back and wrote the check. (961)

For a moment, Jiggs becomes the very stuff airports are made of, and adopts the very posture of the South's beast of burden.

Official culture retains its power throughout the New Valoisian Mardi Gras, even though we can occasionally glimpse openings for challenges to it. The organizers of the 1934 New Orleans carnival saw in the dedication of the Shushan Airport a chance to add novel thrills to the usual festivities. The air circus crowned a Mardi Gras that was to be the biggest and best in years. In an editorial appearing the day of the pageant, the *Times-Picayune* pointed out the historical significance of that year's Mardi Gras:

> The 1934 Carnival is the first in many years that has been free from certain hampering influences. The observance was suspended when America went into the World war, and scarcely was the war ended before prohibition came to cast a blight upon merriment. More recently the shadow of increasing economic trouble dampened all spirits and

checked even the most determined efforts to be entirely gay, if only for a period of a few days. The war is long gone, prohibition has ceased and industrial problems are being solved. . . . Those of us who refuse to believe in Santa Claus have to admit that the day has certain intangible values, certain qualities that help us get over the hump of existence. (Feb. 12, p. 6)

Official interpretations of the carnival, like this one, emphasize the merely cathartic benefits of the celebration; through temporary release and indulgence, the carnival sublimates and pacifies discontentment.

The carnival as staged in New Orleans in the thirties nervously protected the social status quo. The main activities were parades during the day and society balls at night. Although the carnival pretended to disguise—however briefly—the distinctions between classes and races, the arrangements actually reinscribed those divisions. Negroes paraded separately, for instance, "King Zulu" leading his "dusky" subjects costumed as African savages (*Times-Picayune*, Feb. 8, 1934, Mardi Gras supplement, p. 26). Masks could not be worn after sunset, and at this point even superficial egalitarianism dissolved; the balls were by invitation only and were thick with debutantes and the city's elite.

Against this official culture the carnival ought to protest. Yet that its force has become vestigial, domesticated by the very institutions it was meant to subvert, does not mean it has vanished. Faulkner identifies real threats in the carnival performers—particularly the aviators. Their form of relation strikes all of the novel's observers as scandalous, and strikes some of them as appealing too. The reporter's colleagues, for example, puzzle over the ménage à trois practiced by Laverne, Shumann, and Holmes. They wonder if Laverne is intimate with both men simultaneously, and cannot fathom the pilot's attitude: "But how about the fact that Shumann knew it too? Some of these mechanics that have known them for some time say they dont even know who the kid belongs to" (974). Jiggs's joke about the boy's paternity—"Who's your old man today, kid?" (787)—points to a radically alternate social order, one in which the bonds of fatherhood, ownership, and family are seriously revised. Laverne herself starts the joke after deciding on the boy's name by a roll of the dice; it is as if she wants to memorialize her nonconformism. [11]

Laverne's promiscuity protests the patriarchal authority of the nuclear family—the kind of family run by her brother-in-law. Faulkner associates the stability of such a unit with economic power: Laverne's brother-in-law profits from her dependence, since she cannot imagine being anything but a kept mistress or a neglected wife. That she comes to expect greater autonomy may be seen in her style of dress; her emphatic transvestism— those coveralls, walking shoes, and men's undershorts—converts practical necessity into social sign. Her cross-over signals a world of overturned gender roles, and evokes the association in Bakhtin between transvestism and revolution: "Men are transvested as women and vice versa, costumes are turned inside out, and outer garments replace underwear" (410). The reporters catch this note of self-reliance in Laverne, even though they think it's just risqué. Wondering what Laverne must have been thinking while Roger hung in the air before plunging to his death, one suggests she must have said to herself, "Thank God I carry a spare" (974). Holmes is a spare husband, but the joke's ambiguity also allows for references to both the phallus itself and to her child. In other words, Laverne has become custodian of the object of power; losing Shumann reconstitutes the authority she has sought to exercise from the moment she left her sister's and threw in with a barnstormer. Living with a kind of husband has settled her toward the bourgeois standards she's fled; at one point she even complains about not having a home like the Matt Ords' to which they can return Monday after Monday after Monday (887). Shumann's death forces Laverne once more to confront the economic realities of her life, to threaten the system with the "unnatural" solution of placing her son in sounder circumstances, and to expose to the reader's eyes the determination of the proletariat to escape the prisons designed for them.

The force of the carnival to unsettle economic and social structures will prevent this last formulation, I hope, from seeming too extreme. Barnstormers in Faulkner's fiction invariably appear as morally disruptive, from the curious ménage in "Honor" to the defiantly unlicensed clowns in "Death Drag." It is no wonder that Shumann should discover that his efforts to spring Laverne from the "dingy cadaver of the law" in one town should earn him the suspicion that he is spreading "criminal insinuations against the town's civil structure" (910).

The events of *Pylon* become more portentous in their indirect but sure reference to national and local politics. Faulkner could never have hoped to conceal Shushan Airport in New Orleans, Louisiana, behind Feinman Airport in New Valois, Franciana. He says as much in admitting that readers might recognize the originals through their thin disguises.[12] Since Abraham L. Shushan was Huey Long's chairman of the Levee Board, we might wonder exactly how the economic and political issues of the novel are inflected by the Long phenomenon, the enabling pretext of the novel's events. It is widely known that Faulkner modeled the novel's anonymous reporter on his friend, Hermann B. Deutsch, a writer for the *New Orleans Item-Tribune*. Deutsch wrote a number of by-line stories on the air show at Shushan Airport in 1934, and Faulkner's accounts incontestably reflect Deutsch's.

It is perhaps not as widely known that Deutsch also published a number of articles in national periodicals on the rise of Huey Long. The Shushan/ Feinman airport rises out of the waste-filled shores of Lake Pontchartrain as a monument to the Kingfish's reign. Like the reporter in *Pylon,* Deutsch shows himself oblivious to the profound questions raised by Long's popularity, avoiding them through the sardonic bemusement of his journalism. In an article for the *New Republic* called "Huey Long of Louisiana," for example, Deutsch recounts Long's capture of the governorship. Though he acknowledges Long's ambition, Deutsch lets Long's imperial style distract him from the popular demand for reform that empowered the Kingfish's flight: "how these drought-stricken farmers brought themselves to vote for the expenditure of five and a half million dollars for the building of a new state house remains a mystery to this day" (350). Deutsch sees Long as nothing but a buffoon playing to the vulgar masses, but he misses what the reporter in *Pylon* misses: irreverence is the first step in the serious performance of revolution.

Whether greeting official visitors in his bathrobe or trying to relieve himself between the legs of a predecessor at a crowded urinal, clown Long possessed a singular talent for inciting laughter that was deeply derisive of power and wealth.[13] Long's ability to convert derision into votes sustained his career. Long threatened serious economic reform both in his warfare with big business, especially the oil companies like Standard that had controlled Louisiana, and in his plan to redistribute personal wealth. The reversal of official order shoots through his slogan, "Every Man a King, No Man Wears a Crown." For all his demagoguery, Long must be given credit for understanding that the maldistribution of wealth was a central impediment to economic recovery. In agitating the oppressed, Long was willing to risk reform that was not orderly—at least in his rhetoric: "I tell you that if in any country I live in . . . I should see my children starving and my wife starving, its laws against robbing and against stealing and against bootlegging would not amount to any more to me than they would to any other man when it came to a matter of facing the time of starvation" (quoted in Brinkley, 44).

Long's nature was to be, or at least to seem, utterly uncontrollable. The sense of risk and revolution that he represented inevitably informs the conflict between the entitled and the oppressed in *Pylon*. When the air family steals the reporter's money, we can register the vibrations of the act all the way through the economic scale—down to the black maid, who picks the leavings, and up at least to Standard Oil, which posts the prize money so that Feinman can sell tickets so that Hagood can sell papers so that the reporter can borrow from the profits and open his pockets. The reporter in *Pylon* seeks to tone down the more subversive implications of the aviators' behavior. They do end up confessing to their crime, reaffirming a private code of ethics among thieves, and finally resigning themselves to domination by Feinman's will. This consoles the reporter, but it does not eradicate the novel's glimpse of lawless revolt.

The corporate sponsors of the air races firmly control the event. The pilots accept the cut in prize money in quarters that look like "a board room in a bank" (876). The local newspapers covering the dedication of the Shushan Airport ran several pictures of oil company officials posing with the winning pilots; these groupings underscore the forced cooperation of employee with employer. The more natural antagonism of the parties emerges not only in Faulkner's mild version of the pilots' near strike, but also in an incident upon which it is apparently based.[14] The Pan American Air Races had been plagued during Mardi Gras week by bad weather, and so the schedule of events had been extended several days. One gathers that many of the pilots had planned to move on to their next engagements, or to return to family between meets, but had agreed to stay in the hopes that all the races could be held. A week late, a few races still had not come off, and the pilots, growing restive, insisted that the one major remaining prize be split among the scheduled contestants. The organizers refused to dispense the prize unless the race took place. Finally the winds slackened the next day and Jimmy Wedell headed the list of those who competed and shared the $1,400 prize. At issue must have been contrary views of what the money constituted: was it wages or prize money? Feinman (like the actual organizers) wants to call it prize money and keep it under the control of its dispensers. The pilots, of course, see it as compensation for their time and labor, due them regardless of what the elements actually allow. The aviators' will to broach a hostile confrontation with their sponsors deepens the embeddedness of *Pylon* in the economic and social conflicts of its times.

THE AUTOGRAPH OF VIOLENCE

One kind of violence in *Pylon* involves the conflict of classes. This is the sort of conflict indicated by framing the novel's master question as whether it is or is not "the money"; the sort to be seized on by reductive Marxian analysis; the sort to emerge from comparing *Pylon* with proletarian novels of the thirties. But a novel as tonally complex, linguistically tortured, and helplessly unpolemical as *Pylon*, releases other kinds of violence from its central contradictions. The power of Faulkner's writing characteristically draws on the internal incoherence of the social, historical, and economic structures that condition the lives of his protagonists. The violence of these incoherencies frequently appears in the register of the narration, as well; the characters who are in positions to perceive such contradictions typically sheer away from the horror. This is one point of contact between the reporter and better-known Faulknerian protagonists like Horace Benbow, Gail Hightower, Quentin Compson, Ratliff, and Ike McCaslin, all of whom stare finally with empty eyes at the enormities of their heritage.

In my reading, *Pylon* revolves around the axis of declaring or suppressing, avowing or disavowing, the material reality of the South in the thirties. The reporter bears the marks of his interposition between the superficial conflicts of his world. When he tries to mix in with the flyers' "utopian" sexual arrangements, Holmes draws the line by slugging him. Next day the reporter sports a "bluish autograph of violence like tattooing upon his diplomacolored flesh" (914). But this is the kind of autograph that fades, that slips back into the gap between cause and sign. Later, after the reporter and Shumann have signed a promissory note for Ord's plane, a hearing must determine whether their signatures are valid. We are reminded that writing always leaves the province of the person proper. Even an autograph, the most intimate token of selfhood, is still open to avowal or disavowal. From this standpoint I think we can appreciate much more fully the phenomenal disembodiment of voice in *Pylon*.[15] It is not only that speech and writing—particularly in their impersonally technologized forms—are sundered from the body; this condition of language, even in its emphatically modern cast, figures in the specific suppression of the economic and political questions raised by *Pylon*.

With Quentin Compson in *Absalom, Absalom!* the reporter shares the sense of having seen too much and been blasted into solitude. The reporter has flirted with some of the enticements of the carnival, but any chance for real change subsides under the pressure of the official culture. Once Shumann is dead and Laverne has told her host to get lost, the reporter can listen to a colleague's advice to turn away: "Yair. I could vomit too. But what the hell? He aint our brother" (938–39). By the novel's end, the reporter denies anything but the sublimative function of the carnival: the masses disperse, the celebrants go "home now, knowing that they have got almost a whole year before they will have to get drunk and celebrate the fact that they will have more than eleven months before they will have to wear masks and get drunk and blow horns again" (968). The reporter's indifference to misery remains intact: the newspaper headlines wash over him, seeming nothing to him but "the identical from day to day—the bankers the farmers the strikers, the foolish the unlucky and the merely criminal" (917–18). By blocking out the clamor of this strife, the reporter countenances the status quo. He resigns his fortunes and his friends' to an incorrigible universal law: "Four hours ago they were out and I was in, and now it's turned around exactly backward. It's like there was a kind of cosmic rule for poverty like there is for water level, like there has to be a certain weight of bums on park benches or in railroad waitingrooms waiting for morning to come or the world will tilt up and spill all of us wild and shrieking and grabbing like so many shooting stars, off into nothing" (847).

In these passages Faulkner wants us to see the dynamic of avowal and disavowal at work in all writing. Literature worthy of the name for Faulkner must be writing that measures the ideological stakes of insight and blindness. This question empowers *Absalom, Absalom!*, the novel whose composition encases *Pylon,* and which struggles in kind over evading and acknowledging history. It is no accident that the language of one novel should well up in the other. The reporter, like a character in Mr. Compson's saga (or like his misfortunate son), sees himself as "the nebulous and quiet ragtag and bobend of touching and breath and experience without visible scars, the waiting incurious unbreathing and without impatience" (968).[16] By this point the scars—those autographs of violence—are no longer visible. The reporter has been carried on the tide of the carnival, but by its conclusion he falls back into isolation from the mass: taking a cab to the airport, he has "the sense of being suspended in a small airtight glass box clinging by two puny fingers of light in the silent and rushing immensity of space." Like Prufrock or the despairing Macbeth, the reporter looks into "tomorrow and tomorrow and tomorrow; not only not to hope, not even to wait: just to endure" (970).

On this note of self-parody (who has reserved greater import for the word *endure?*), Faulkner leaves his meditation on the carnival. Bakhtin observes that one of the signs of the degeneration of the folk carnival is its transformation into literary equivalents. The carnival's truly ambivalent, universal laughter decays into the reduced versions of literary parody or irony. *Pylon*'s peculiar resurrection of Joyce and Eliot at this point in Faulkner's career I attribute to the carnival material, which inevitably drives a modernist like Faulkner to the storehouse of literary parody.[17] Faulkner draws on the most potent forms of parody in his literary heritage, on Joyce's efforts to resuscitate the common imagination through a polylogic music, and on Eliot's early shorings of the fragments against ruin. These traces of the carnival spirit in literary parody are not adequate, however, to make a place for the activation of revolution. The carnival appears in *Pylon* as the image of *lost* possibilities for self-awareness, connection, and gaiety. Or as Jiggs puts it, and the narrator comments: " 'So this is Moddy Graw. Why aint I where I have been all my life.' " But the reporter continued to glare down at him in bright amazement (813).

NOTES

1. Page numbers cited parenthetically in the text refer to works in the Works Cited section at the end of this essay; quotations from *Pylon* are taken from the Library of America edition of Faulkner's novels. Citations of works from his *Collected Stories* are abbreviated *CS*.

2. Torchiana demonstrates the aviators' domination by the force of "finance capitalism" (297), arguing that they act self-sacrificially and heroically to resist the prevailing system of economic exploitation. Torchiana emphasizes the economic issues too often ignored in criticism of the novel (and of Faulkner in general). I depart from his reading by trying to understand how the reporter's kind of admiration actually smothers the potential for systemic change the novel almost glimpses; Torchiana follows the reporter—"the sensitive observer of the novel" (301)—in celebrating the flyers' alleged "disdain for money as such and their quixotic devotion to flying" (299).

3. See Blotner (324–26) on the details of Faulkner's mounting responsibilities after his father's death.

4. In two short stories also about barnstormers, "Death Drag" and "Honor," we find one pilot named Jock, another named Jack, and a driver called Jake.

5. Pearce identifies this potential for change in the novel as a vision of the apocalypse, "a minor but powerful current in the literature of the thirties" (131). My

aim is to show how the dread of such decentering has ideological implications, and that Faulkner sees how the oppressed hardly share the fear.

6. Since Bakhtin's work encountered official opposition in the Soviet Union, *Rabelais and His World* remained unpublished until the mid-sixties, when his thinking began to be taken up in the West as well.

7. The papers sympathetically tell the story of various workers' movements— from the coal miners' effort to negotiate a thirty-hour week to the New York City taxi drivers' strike against a Tammany Hall fare tariff. The National Recovery Administration is touted in a *New Orleans Times-Picayune* editorial as the "greatest legal instrument from the standpoint of human welfare since the emancipation proclamation" (Jan. 18, 1934, 24). A special series of articles in the *New Orleans Item-Tribune* by Ralph W. Page defends a strike by California cotton pickers, and denies that they are actually communists: "In Southern California they had just been shooting and jailing 'communist' strikers and agitators. But California's definition of a communist, anarchist and enemy of government is any workman who would strike for more pay. The strike was conducted by cotton pickers. Some called themselves communists. What they asked was more than 60¢ a hundred for picking cotton. Even a Negro can do this much, in Georgia, without offense" (Feb. 6, 1934, 5). Both dailies report the bloody riots by workers in Paris and Austria, the latter over the perceived softening of the aristocratic government to Nazi overtures. The *Item-Tribune* explicitly endorses Vienna's socialist reform: "There has been nothing wild or extreme about their measures. They have carried on much as progressive administrations in some American cities do, but more intelligently" (Feb. 16, 1934).

8. Faulkner refers to the vaudeville qualities of the barnstormers in "Death Drag" and to the flying circus in "Honor" (*CS*, 187, 559).

9. Other scatological references seem less gratuitous as a result of this nexus. Shumann's annoyance at Jiggs's drinking produces this insult: " 'One drink, huh?' Shumann said. 'There's a slop jar back there; why not get it and empty the jug into it and take a good bath?' " (115). Excrement and maternity coincide in the editor's grotesque comparison of the reporter's mother to "a canvas conceived in and executed out of that fine innocence of sleep and open bowels capable of crowning the rich foul unchaste earth with rosy cloud where lurk and sport oblivious and incongruous cherubim" (92–93).

10. Porter discusses Sutpen's design from the standpoint of slavery as an instrument of capitalism, and Sundquist emphasizes Faulkner's struggle in the thirties to acknowledge the economic and moral investment of the South in the ideology of racial separation.

11. Faulkner also uses a ménage à trois in "Honor," focusing on the attitudes of two pilots toward the woman who is wife to one and lover to the other.

12. Blotner (328–42) establishes the main resemblances between factual and fictional material in *Pylon*. More than many of his works, this novel drew on real

acquaintances of Faulkner, like Vernon Omlie and Jimmy Wedell, and on their experiences in barnstorming events. There were several mishaps at the Pan American games marking the inauguration of the Shushan International Airport during Mardi Gras of 1934; those Faulkner either witnessed or heard about after his arrival on February 15 are described partially in Millgate (138–49).

13. See Brinkley, especially 8–81.

14. See the account in the *Times-Picayune*, Feb. 20, 1934, 3.

15. Bleikasten brilliantly illuminates the problematics of signification, and Gresset the power of the silent gaze in the novel. Pitavy studies the gap of desire across which *écriture* seeks to move while admitting its own impossibility.

16. The narrator of *Absalom, Absalom!* describes Quentin and Shreve creating characters "out of the rag-tag and bob-ends of old tales and talking" (303).

17. On the allusions to T. S. Eliot, see Millgate (esp. 144).

WORKS CITED

Bakhtin, Mikhail. *Rabelais and His World.* Trans. Helene Iswolsky. Bloomington: Indiana University Press, 1984.

Bleikasten, André. "*Pylon*, ou l'enfer des signes." *Etudes Anglaises* 29 (1976): 437–47.

Blotner, Joseph L. *Faulkner: A Biography.* New York: Random House, 1984.

Brinkley, Alan. *Voices of Protest: Huey Long, Father Coughlin, and the Great Depression.* New York: Random House, 1982.

Deutsch, Hermann. "Huey Long of Louisiana." *New Republic,* Nov. 11, 1931.

Faulkner, William. *Absalom, Absalom!* New York: Random House, 1936.

———. *Collected Stories.* New York: Random House, 1950.

———. *Novels 1930–1935.* New York: Library of America, 1985.

Gresset, Michel. "Théorème." *Recherches anglaises et americaines* 9 (1976): 73–94.

Gwynn, Frederick L., and Joseph L. Blotner, eds. *Faulkner in the University.* Charlottesville: University of Virginia Press, 1959.

Millgate, Michael. *The Achievement of William Faulkner.* New York: Random House, 1966.

Pearce, Richard. "*Pylon, Awake and Sing!* and the Apocalyptic Imagination of the 30's." *Criticism* 13 (Spring 1971): 131–41.

Pitavy, François. "Le reporter: Tentation et dérision de l'écriture." *Recherches anglaises et americaines* 9 (1976): 95–108.

Porter, Carolyn. *Seeing and Being.* Middletown, Conn.: Wesleyan University Press, 1980.

Serres, Michel. *The Parasite.* Trans. Lawrence R. Schehr. Baltimore: Johns Hopkins University Press, 1982.

Sundquist, Eric J. *The House Divided*. Baltimore: Johns Hopkins University Press, 1983.
Torchiana, Donald T. "Faulkner's *Pylon* and the Structure of Modernity." *Modern Fiction Studies* 3 (Winter 1957–58): 291–308.

Willie's Wink and Other Doubtful

Paternal Texts in the Novels of

Robert Penn Warren

RANDOLPH PAUL RUNYON

The relationship between Willie Stark and Jack Burden began with an empty, indecipherable sign. Back in 1922 when the narrator of *All the King's Men* first met Stark in the back room of Slade's pool hall and Willie was a mere county treasurer, Burden could have sworn, at the moment of the handshake, that the future Boss gave him a wink. "Then looking into that dead pan, I wasn't sure."[1] It's an ambiguous sign that Stark gives young Burden, all the more difficult to interpret because its author refuses to acknowledge authorial intent. Twelve years later, Jack will ask him if it had been a wink or not.

> "Boy," he said, and smiled at me paternally over his glass, "that is a mystery."
> "Don't you remember?" I asked.
> "Sure," he said, "I remember."
> "Well," I demanded.
> "Suppose I just had something in my eye?" he said.
> "Well, damn it, you just had something in your eye then."
> "Suppose I didn't have anything in my eye?" (16)

Had Willie intended the wink it would have meant something: "maybe you winked because you figured you and me had some views in common about the tone of the gathering"—a gathering that included Tiny Duffy and Alex Michel, the kind of corrupt politicos Stark would later campaign to throw out of office. But since Stark refuses to say whether it was an expressive wink it means something else. It is a gift—a paternal one, to judge from the adverb that qualified his later smile—and for the giver to comment on it further would be to take it away: " 'Boy,' he said, 'if I was to tell you, then you wouldn't have anything to think about.' "

Jack Burden never did find out what he wanted to know about that wink. But the reader of Burden's narrative who has read Warren's other novels may know more than Jack ever could about it, and is given even more to think about. Such a reader could remember how Jason Sweetwater in *At Heaven's Gate,* thinking of the fetus in Sue Murdock's womb, began to think as well about mummies whose faces resembled what he imagined to be the fetus's face: they both had a kind of intent expression, a combination of wisdom and puzzlement. The reason for that seeming expressiveness, Sweetwater determined, was the nature of their squinting eyelids, whose squinting was due to neither wisdom nor puzzlement but to the fact that—in the case of the mummies—"there was nothing under them any more."[2] Like the mummy's squinting eyes, Willie's eye might, as Stark teasingly suggested, have only given the semblance of expressiveness, and have done so for a purely accidental, mechanical, and unintentional reason.

Later, in *Wilderness,* a son will gaze upon a dying man who seems a lot like his late father ("He felt as though, again, he sat beside a dying father")[3] and again the reader will encounter paradoxically expressive eyes: "Life showed only in the eyes [that] glittered with astonishing brilliance, as though some great excitement, some commanding thought, were taking hold. . . . But even when the eyes glittered, the cause, Adam came to feel, was not in anything that had passed between them, only some fluctuation of the fever or the transitory flicker of some old event in that fading brain" (119–20). Despite appearances, nothing had passed between the fatherly Hans Meyerhof and the filial Adam Rosenzweig; the semblance of some commanding thought in those eyes was not due to a desire to communicate but was simply either the result of the dying brain talking to itself or, worse than that, an involuntary fluctuation like the batting of Willie's eyelid (if indeed he had, as he said he might have, something in his eye). These paternal eyes can almost speak, not only in their unmerited expressiveness but in the sound they almost seem to make—a trick they share as well with the eye that winked at Burden: Adam "felt that he could almost hear . . . how the eyes, as they turned, would grind with tiny grittiness in the sockets" (121). And the eyes of a dying Willie Stark (in the hospital, mortally wounded by Adam Stanton) could give Jack Burden the same aural illusion: "the eyes turned toward me again, very slowly, and I almost thought that I could hear the tiny painful creak of the balls in their sockets" (400). Willie Stark clearly has a number of things in common with the man in *Wilderness* who reminds the protagonist of his father.

Still another thought crossing Adam Rosenzweig's mind as he stares at the dying Meyerhof may make it possible to piece together the meaning of the wink that puzzled Burden in the novel Warren published a decade and a half before: "Adam could not really talk with Hans Meyerhof. He was, clearly a dying man. Under the single sheet the body was nothing more than a heap of bones, lying almost as starkly obvious as they would lie in the earth, if a spade, some years from now, broke open the coffin" (119). This fantasy of breaking open the coffin had occurred to Cass Mastern, too, in the embedded tale in *All the King's Men*—in the text Jack Burden had tried to interpret before he entered Stark's employ. When Duncan Trice—whom Mastern had cuckolded—died a suicide and Cass served as one of the pallbearers, "The coffin which I carried [Mastern thought] seemed to have no weight. . . . [T]he fancy flitted into my mind . . . that it was empty. . . . I had the impulse to hurl the coffin to the ground and see its emptiness burst open" (172). Jonathan Baumbach, drawing upon the fact of Trice's greater age and that he had initiated Mastern into vice, sees the adultery of Cass and Annabelle Trice as "implicitly incestuous" and Duncan as "his 'substitute' father."[4] To Baumbach's analysis one could add the fact that Sadie Burke—Willie Stark's mistress—and Trice's wife were both, in a sense, "née Puckett": Annabelle literally (164), Sadie because before Stark came along she had belonged to "Sen-Sen" *Puckett* (73); to say still more about how the Mastern story suggests itself as a microcosm of the novel, one could point out that Stark's *other* mistress—the one whose jealous brother gunned him down—was *Anne* Stanton, who is quite clearly meant to be seen as another Annabel—Poe's—when Burden tells us that years ago he and Anne and Adam had once been "children by the sea" at Burden's Landing, where stormy weather "didn't chill us or kill us in the kingdom by the sea" (103). Cass would then be to Jack as Trice is to Stark, and the imagined emptiness of the coffin might have something to do with the physical emptiness of the mummies' eyes, with the figurative emptiness of the proto-father's eye in *Wilderness,* and with the potential emptiness of the sign Willie gave or didn't give Jack Burden through what looked like a wink.

It may take more than one novel for all the pieces to fall into place, but even within the one Burden inhabits there are instructive echoes of that original wink. One of them is what Jack imagines to be his last glimpse of Stark: "I must believe that Willie Stark was a great man. What happened to his greatness is not the question. . . . Perhaps he piled up his greatness and burnt it in one great blaze in the dark like a bonfire and then there wasn't anything but dark and the embers winking" (427)—wherein all that is left to see is a wink, the last trace of Willie Stark (like writing: *scripta manent*), like the smile of the Cheshire cat. Another is the twitch he saw on the face of the old man he picked up in New Mexico, a twitch that was the apparent prelude to a wink that never came: "The only thing remarkable about him was the fact that while you looked into the sun-brittled leather of the face, which seemed as stiff and devitalized as the hide on a mummy's jaw, you would suddenly see a twitch in the left cheek, up toward the pale-blue eye. You would think he was going to wink, but he wasn't going to wink. The twitch was simply an independent phenomenon, unrelated to the face or to what was behind the face or to anything in the whole tissue of phenomena which is the world we are lost in" (313–14). Jack Burden may think that the twitch is unrelated to anything else in the world because it is unrelated to the rest of that face, but this unrelatedness is precisely what relates it to a whole tissue of similar phenomena elsewhere in Warren's fiction: Willie's wink if he just had something in his eye, the feverish glitter of intelligence in Meyerhof's eyes in *Wilderness,* the paradoxically expressive eyes Sweetwater imagined in *At Heaven's Gate*—all the more so in the case of the latter for the fact that the twitch in this instance takes place on something like "the hide on a *mummy's* jaw."

So what we have is, on the one hand, instances of seeming expressiveness whose power to express is put into doubt because it is impossible to attribute intention to them; and on the other, a continuing accumulation of such instances (which not only accumulate but seem to allude to each other: mummy to mummy, eye to eye) in Warren's narratives that makes us wonder if some larger pattern might not emerge if we paid more attention to them (though we may fear that to look for meaning in such instances of meaninglessness would be to pursue a fool's errand). Something else Burden says, however, speaks precisely to such a situation: "It was only after the conclusion . . . when I had been able to gather the pieces of the puzzle up and put them together to see the pattern. This is not remarkable, for, as we know, reality is not a function of the event as event, but of the relationship of that event to past, and future, events. We seem here to have a paradox: that the reality of an event, which is not real in itself, arises from other events which, likewise, in themselves are not real" (383–84). And Warren, speaking in his own name, has said the same of poetry: "Does this not, then, lead us to the conclusion that poetry does not inhere in any particular element but depends upon the set of relationships, the structure, which we call the poem?"[5] The poem is that set of relationships; so is the "literariness" of Warren's fiction, whose reality thus emerges from the kind of relationships we have been paying attention to here.

The novel Warren published after the one about Willie Stark was *World Enough and Time,* in which a young man comes into possession of a text he thinks was written by the older man who seemed a father to him and acts upon his interpretation of that text and its presumed provenance to kill that father. That the victim of his misreading should bear a name— Fort—that is the equivalent in French (a language that has the privilege of bearing still other secrets in that novel)[6] of what Stark is in German strongly suggests that there is something going on here of the nature of what Warren says about relationships in poetry and Burden about gathering the pieces of a puzzle. If so, one might want to consider what parallels there may be between this text of doubtful paternity (though a paternity the young Beaumont never doubted) and the wink Willie gave Jack (a message for Jack to interpret, whose most puzzling aspect is its author's refusal to say whether or not it was a message). The text is a printed handbill that claims that the stillborn child to which Rachel Jordan—whom Jeremiah Beaumont married, but whom Cassius Fort had first seduced— gave birth was black, that its father wasn't the seducer Fort but a slave in the Jordan household. Fort in fact never wrote it, but Percival Skrogg and Wilkie Barron had, hoping that Beaumont would take the bait and murder Fort, which he did.

Jack Burden does not in fact murder Stark. But the man who does— Anne Stanton's brother Adam—does so because he too, like Beaumont, was manipulated by a pair of conspirators who carefully fed him a piece of news. Sadie Burke, acting through Tiny Duffy, wreaked her vengeance (for Stark's having left her for Anne) and Tiny's (for repeated humiliations) on Willie Stark by letting Adam know that Stark was sleeping with his sister, thereby goading him into a jealous rage. It is Adam, not Jack, who kills the father (if the father is Willie Stark; Jack, on the other hand, *is* responsible for the death of his actual [and secret] father, Judge Irwin— for it is the revelations Burden came up with about Irwin's past that made him, like Duncan Trice, shoot himself in the chest), but another Adam in

Warren—Adam Rosenzweig in *Wilderness*—provides yet another variation on these themes: like Jeremiah Beaumont, he tries to interpret a text
from the father.

Leopold Rosenzweig "had told his son that there was no nobler fate for
a man than to live and die for human liberty" (7). When he died, Adam
found himself meditating on a genuine paternal text, a poem his father
had written:

> If I could only be worthy of that mountain I love,
> If I could only be worthy of sun-glitter on snow,
> If a man could only be worthy of what he loves.

(5)

Adam soon left not only his Bavarian village but, in the eyes of his Orthodox uncle, the Jewish faith as well in order to try to live out his father's
concept of worth by fighting for the North in the American Civil War.
By his father's brother's interpretation of Mosaic law, it was blasphemy
to engage in secular hope for a better world instead of trusting in God's
plans for a Messianic future. His father had been guilty of that too, when
he fought in the revolution of 1848, but age and infirmity and his brother's
persistence brought him back to the faith of his fathers before he died,
though in his son's eyes he thereby betrayed his ideals.

Yet already it seems that Adam is burdened with not one but two paternal texts: his father's poem, the vessel of his political idealism, reducible
there (subsequent events will show why) to the thrice-written *worth;* but
also the text of the Law of Moses, the Book to which his Orthodox uncle
made his father return (Adam carries in his satchel something like that
text, the *seddur,* or prayerbook, he never opens until the end of the novel).
If the poem about worth is his father's text, then the Torah would be his
father's father's—a fact not without resonance when we consider a scene
in *Wilderness* that comes close to repeating the struggle the young Jeremiah Beaumont had with his *grandfather* in *World Enough and Time.*
Morton Marcher wanted to adopt Jeremiah for his heir, but only on the
condition that he renounce his father's name. A struggle ensued, in the
course of which Jeremiah warded off his grandfather's silver candlestick
with the cane he had wrested from the older man's grasp, but only after
"the lighted candle fell from it to the table" (22), as if the flame ("the
flame of the sperm candle" into which Marcher had stared before he said
he wanted an heir worthy of the estate) embodied the paternal virility

that would not now, the candle having been extinguished in its fall, be passed on. A cigar's flame does similar service in *Wilderness* when Aaron Blaustein asks Adam Rosenzweig to replace the son he lost in the war.

> "I really am not that bitter," he said, looking at his cigar, now dead, but not making any motion to relight it. . . .
> He flung the twisted, crumpled cigar to the red carpet, and stared down at it.
> "My son was killed," he said dully. . . . "I did not think I could live."
> He looked down at the broken cigar on the red carpet. (73, 75–76)

If the cigar's fall parallels his son's death, then Aaron's decision to replace it with another prepares the way for the delicate request he is about to make.

> Very carefully, he took out his cigar case, and prepared and lighted another cigar.
> He drew in the smoke, exhaled it. He inspected the cigar. "These cigars are very expensive," he said. (76–77)

When he made ready to make his proposal, he "dropped to one knee before Adam, letting the cigar fall from his fingers." This time the fallen cigar is still burning, like this would-be father's hope offered in all its vulnerability, the hope that the paternal line would not die out, but in such a way that it must risk the son's rejection: "Adam . . . stared at the cigar on the floor. He saw the red carpet about the lighted end of the cigar scorch to brown, then to black. . . . He saw the red winking of the blackened strands of the fabric as they were consumed and parted. . . . Adam rose abruptly from the chair. He thrust his left foot forward from under the touch of the old man crouching there, and ground his boot on the cigar and the smoldering spot of the carpet." (78–79) Like Willie Stark's greatness, Aaron Blaustein's paternity was reduced in the end to a winking flame. What is remarkable is what Adam so abruptly and violently does to it. Though clothed perhaps in the guise of protecting the carpet from further damage his gesture nevertheless represents the definitive stamping out of the winking paternal—or grandfatherly—flame.

Even in *Wilderness* winking had already enjoyed a particular significance: the sign, as it is here, of acceptance, but in an earlier episode made conspicuous by its absence. Earlier, on the voyage over from Europe, a certain Duncan's refusal to accept Adam into the Union Army took the form of a series of twitches that should have been followed by a wink but were not—a variation, that is, on Jack Burden's encounter with the mummy-jawed old man in New Mexico. What "twitches" is the surface of the ocean, which causes Adam to lose his balance and thereby display the pedal deformity he had hoped to conceal. "At that moment the ocean twitched again" and it was Sergeant Duncan's turn to display to all the assembled hands and potential enlistees what was wrong with *his* left leg by falling down into a sitting position, "ass-flat on the deck" (21). It appears that Adam might have passed muster if Duncan's impairment had not also been so embarrassingly revealed (the problem was that Duncan limped because he was shot from behind while running from the First Battle of Manassas). "If all these things had not happened in their unique pattern," the narrator tells us, "then things might have been all right, after all." But it seems that that unique pattern has something to do with the one we have been looking into here, something to do with twitching and winking. In the version Jack Burden remembered, the twitches should have led to a wink but did not. Likewise here: "There was, in fact, no logical reason why Meinherr Duncan should have been so outraged by Adam Rosenzweig's physical defect. He knew that the examiners did not really examine. He knew that he himself had *winked* at, and passed farther along, some rather poor specimens" (22, emphasis added).

Ultimately, Adam, who keeps running into images of the father—Duncan and the wink that wasn't, Aaron and the winking flame Adam extinguished, Hans Meyerhof with the paradoxically expressive eyes—will encounter an image of the text his father wrote, the poem whose call to worthiness ("If I could only be worthy . . . worthy . . . worthy") embodies the idealism that made him leave for America and which he saw his father betray when he returned to his uncle's brand of quietistic Judaism. "I have prayed that you may die within the Law," the uncle told Leopold, and his prayer was granted. What Adam discovers is an enigmatic text written on the hide of another Moses—Mose Talbutt, his fellow sutler's assistant in the employ of Jedeen Hawksworth, upon whose skin a single letter has been inscribed, one that stands for the very word most able to contradict the word that best sums up the text his father had written, the thrice-expressed *worthy* of his poem:

> On the man's right thigh, puckering and crinkling crudely up from the dark slickness of skin, was the brand. It was a big W.
>   . . . "You know what that is?" Jed Hawksworth demanded, turn-

ing on Adam. "Reckin that's one letter your prize scholar can read. W—W for worthless! That's what the Yankees put on 'em. Put on a soldier that ain't worth a damn." (217)

Talbutt's true identity was discovered by Hawksworth, who suspected it already, when he tore off the underclothes Mose would never remove and revealed the letter of guilt. His name wasn't Talbutt but Crawfurd, and he had been a deserter from the Union Army. But this revelation of hidden identity could well point out to us not only the constancy of his first name but its identity as well with that of the author of the received paternal (grandfatherly) text that Leopold Rosenzweig in his last days adopted as the palinode to the poem he had written, the Law of Moses. If one Moses can stand for the other—if there is a reason for the choice of names and this is it—then the text that contradicted the father's poem (the Law of Moses, transformed by its black incarnation into a palimpsest) can now be canceled out by something like the very text it once annuled.

The letter could mean any of a number of things (Wilderness, Warren, *w*ink); specifically one might have thought it could have meant *worthy* as much as *worthless* (though it wouldn't have existed in the first place in the form of a painful brand if it were not meant as a punishment). We have Jed Hawksworth's word for it, however—but what might it mean that the word for which he says it stands (or contradicts) should appear in the very name of this privileged interpreter? And what, one might also want to ask, is the *worth* of a *hawk*?

The publication a decade and a half after *Wilderness* of the poem Harold Bloom has termed "a deliberate and overwhelming self-interpretation of [Warren's] obsessive hawk-imagery" has made that question a little less difficult to answer.[7] "Red-Tail Hawk and Pyre of Youth" is the story of the murder and subsequent preservation of the corpse of a hawk who bears an astonishing resemblance to a complex of fetus, mummy, and paternal text that keeps recurring in Warren. Like the newspaper-wrapped infant in Percy Munn's dream in *Night Rider* ("she held out the bundle. . . . He saw that it was wrapped in old newspaper, stained and torn. . . . [It] began to flake away . . . as though disintegrating from its own sodden weight. . . . There . . . was a body, a foetus like those which he had seen suspended in liquid in great glass jars at the medical school"), the hawk in the poem is "cuddled / Like babe to heart. . . . Like a secret, I wrapped it in news-paper."[8] As a "chunk of poor wingless red meat," the hawk's body shares qualities with the stillborn fetuses of *World Enough and Time* ("Nuthin but a pore little piece of meat") and *The Cave* ("a piece of something like a dime's worth of cat meat from the butcher shop").[9] As a preserved corpse —the object of the poet's taxidermy—the stuffed hawk has something in common with the mummies that the fetus Sweetwater imagined in *At Heaven's Gate* reminded him of; the fact that it was the eyes, with their semblance of intelligent intent, that made him think of their resemblance is not without resonance here, for the yellow eyes of the preserved bird are what most haunt the poet: "the yellow eyes, / Unsleeping, stared as I slept" in the room where he had placed the hawk, like a text among texts, "on the tallest of bookshelves," in the company of "Blake and *Lycidas,* Augustine, Hardy and *Hamlet.*" And later, after he had left home, books and hawk behind, "with / Eyes closed I knew / That yellow eyes somewhere, unblinking, in vengeance stared." It is in those eyes that the hawk is most alive, his vengeful intent made apparent. Yet, paradoxically, those eyes are the poet's own creation, "glass eyes / Gleaming yellow" he had substituted for the unpreservable original "Gold eyes, unforgiving, for they, like God, see all." Not gold but yellow and not flesh but glass, they are perhaps the most visible sign of the taxidermist's artifice, of the absence of the real.

In this regard they resemble the eyes in the mummies Sweetwater remembered that squinted and thereby seemed intent "because there was nothing under them anymore." There was nothing beneath the glass eyes of the hawk either, only the skull "now well scraped / And with arsenic dried"; all that poor red meat gone too, replaced by "the clay-burlap body built there within." As *Wilderness* makes apparent, where Hans Meyerhof's eyes glitter with an astonishing brilliance that is merely the visible sign of a fading brain, this quality of seeming intent belongs to the eyes of not only Sweetwater's mummies but of Warren's fathers as well. In *Wilderness* too a certain winking can be expected from a father's eyes (withheld by Duncan, offered in the fading glow of Aaron Blaustein's cigar; both of them more recent versions of the wink Willie Stark refused to say if he intended), and in "Red-Tail Hawk" the hawk eventually becomes one-eyed too: the poet returns years later and finds it, no longer on the bookshelf but still among books—though with a difference, for it now lies not only with the Milton and *Hamlet* he had spoken of the first time but with a text that he has since then written: "a book / Of poems friends and I had printed in college." If the bookish company the stuffed hawk had always kept since it was first enshrined on that bookcase suggested that it was a text among texts, might the fact that it is now gathering dust in the company of a poem or poems like the one in which it appears mean that in that passage of time it had become something like the poet's poem? As it already clearly is an object of his own making, a reconstructed version of a now dead original, it had become a model perhaps for the kind of rewritten text that may be at the origin of what this poet writes.

> . . . the chunk of poor wingless red meat,
> That model from which all was molded.

It is true that in its present time-worn state, in its one-eyedness, the poet does recognize something of himself:

> That night in the lumber room, late,
> I found him—the hawk, feathers shabby, one
> Wing bandy-banged, one foot gone sadly
> Askew, one eye long gone—and I reckoned
> I knew how it felt with one gone.

Like the secret articulation that Warren wrote of in "The Circus in the Attic" and that only Time can reveal—"no one knows the meaning of the cry of passion he utters until the flesh of the passion is long since withered away to show the austere, logical articulation of fact with fact in the skeleton of Time"—the fact that Warren is blind in one eye has had to wait a long time to become part of what is publicly known about him, part of that text of which he says in *Being Here* "it may be said that our lives are our own supreme fiction" (108).[10]

What is the significance of the fact that the poet shares this one-eyedness with the stuffed hawk that is his own creation, or re-creation? It is more than a family resemblance. Warren would never have become a writer, at least according to the family romance his sister Mary tells, had it not been for the accident that led to his semiblindness, had not his brother Thomas thrown the rock in the air that sailed over the hedge to where Robert Penn was lying on his back, eyes open.[11] For it kept him from going to the Naval Academy, where he had already been appointed, and ultimately sent him to Vanderbilt instead, where he came under the influence of such teachers as John Crowe Ransom and Donald Davidson and such friends as Allen Tate.[12] One would like to think the writer in him would have won out over the naval officer anyway, but the way it happened the accident intervened like a stroke of fate.

Of more interest than the biographical fact alone is the articulation it finds in Warren's published work, of which his belated admission in "Red-Tail Hawk" ("I knew how it felt with one gone") is a highly privileged example, for it is the first time the secreted truth has broken through into direct expression in the text and it takes place in a poem where all the elements of the recurring pattern—the father as preserved corpse with paradoxically expressive eyes, as text (and rewritten text) and newspaper-wrapped fetal bundle—are present. What the resemblance between the stuffed hawk and the poet establishes is indeed a family resemblance, though—as we now know—an artificial one, for this half-blindness was not inherited from father to son.

But that the accident should have happened to the son alone and yet Warren's fiction be about fathers (Stark and Duncan) giving (or refusing to give) one-eyed looks to their sons and fathers whose eyes give the semblance of intent when they don't necessarily mean to (Hans Meyerhof, whose eyes were not only such signifiers without a referent, but who had the habit of lying on his back with his eyes open, in the same posture that was so unlucky for the young Warren: "I don't worry about him so much when he's asleep," Meyerhof's wife said. "It's when he just lies with his eyes open, looking out the way they do" [123]), suggests something almost like a hidden motive in that fiction, one in which the son projects his own one-eyedness onto the father, giving him the enforced wink that had really been his own, thereby inventing the text he pretends to decipher.

In a poem in which the poet climbs up to the nesting place of the hawk and finds that

> I am the father
> Of my father's father's father. I,
> Of my father, have set the teeth on edge [13]

the same kind of projection of a backward inheritance takes place.[14] "But / By what grape?" The fruit of such an effort in *Wilderness* is the reappearance of the initial letter of the word that so insisted in Adam's father's text on the skin of a Moses, so that by such stigmatization the text of his father's father might be rewritten, reinscribed with the letter of worth (or unworth) that in his father's text it had until now effectively obliterated. That Adam was aiming at the grandfather is already apparent from the fact that he inflicts an eventually mortal blow on Aaron Blaustein (grinding the winking flame to extinction with his boot; refusing to be his adopted son, and later realizing that that refusal was responsible for Aaron's death —a few months later, of a heart attack: "he thought now, if he had stayed with Aaron Blaustein, Aaron Blaustein would not have died" [301]) in the shadow of a mythic hero who killed his own grandfather—for that scene

was played out before a "great bronze of Perseus meditatively holding the
head of Medusa" (67). (Perseus killed his grandfather Acrisius acciden-
tally with a discus. In an analogous scene in Warren's later novel *A Place
to Come To,* the young protagonist will find a life-size copy of a matching
statue—the Discus-Thrower—in the home of the grandfatherly Professor
Stahlman.)[15] That his ultimate grandfatherly target is the Moses whose
text overcame his father's poem is apparent from the fact that Blaustein's
name is Aaron, for what better scripturally sanctioned substitute could
there be for Moses than Aaron, his brother and indispensable spokesman
on that other wilderness journey?

NOTES

1. *All the King's Men* (New York: Harcourt, Brace, 1946; repr. New York:
Bantam, 1974), 15.

2. *At Heaven's Gate* (New York: Harcourt, Brace, 1943), 317.

3. *Wilderness: A Tale of the Civil War* (New York: Random House, 1961), 120.

4. "The Metaphysics of Demagoguery: *All the King's Men* by Robert Penn Warren," in *Twentieth Century Interpretations of All the King's Men,* ed. Robert H.
Chambers (Englewood Cliffs, N.J.: Prentice-Hall, 1977), 139.

5. "Pure and Impure Poetry," in *Selected Essays* (New York: Random House,
1958), 26.

6. See Randolph Paul Runyan, "The Beech, the Hearth, and the Hidden Name
in *World Enough and Time,*" in *Southern Literary Journal* 17, no. 1 (1984): 68–81.

7. In a review of *Now and Then: Poems 1976–1978,* by Robert Penn Warren,
New Republic 30 (Sept. 1978): 34–35; repr. in *Critical Essays on Robert Penn
Warren,* ed. William Bedford Clark (Boston: G. K. Hall, 1981), 74–76. Other
poems, too, hint at the equation of father and hawk. Calvin Bedient has recently
argued that in "Evening Hawk" the hawk is "the phallus, here winged" as well
as "both father and son, in a crackling synthesis" (*In the Heart's Last Kingdom:
Robert Penn Warren's Major Poetry* [Cambridge: Harvard University Press, 1984],
167).

8. *Night Rider* (New York: Random House, 1939), 395. "Red-Tail Hawk and
Pyre of Youth," in *Now and Then: Poems, 1976–1978* (New York: Random
House, 1978).

9. *World Enough and Time: A Romantic Novel* (New York: Random House,
1950; repr. New York: Vintage, 1979), 204, 380; *The Cave* (New York: Random
House, 1959).

10. *The Circus in the Attic and Other Stories* (New York: Harcourt, Brace,
1946), 28; for the relevance of this sentence in the context of the story collection,

see Randolph Paul Runyan, "The View from the Attic: Robert Penn Warren's Circus Stories," *Mississippi Quarterly* 38, no. 2 (1985): 119–35. "Until recently," Floyd Watkins writes in *Then and Now: The Personal Past in the Poetry of Robert Penn Warren* (Lexington: University Press of Kentucky, 1982), 54, "it has not been widely known that Warren is blind in one eye, yet the accident was perhaps the most momentous event in his younger years." *Being Here: Poetry 1977–1980* (New York: Random House, 1980), 108.

11. Mrs. Mary Warren Barber, in an address to "The Nomads," a literary society in Maysville, Kentucky, 13 Feb. 1985.

12. Warren lends support to his sister's version of how he became a writer in a 1977 interview: "Then I had an accident. I couldn't go [to Annapolis]—an accident to my eyes—and then I went to the university instead, and I started out in life there as a chemical engineer. That didn't last but three weeks or so, because I found the English courses so much more interesting" (*Robert Penn Warren Talking: Interviews, 1950–1978*, ed. Floyd Watkins and John T. Hiers (New York: Random House, 1980), 243.

13. "The Leaf," in *Incarnations: Poems, 1966–1968* (New York: Random House, 1968).

14. As Harold Bloom has recently demonstrated in a brilliant analysis of the topos in Warren ("Sunset Hawk: Warren's Poetry and Tradition," in *A Southern Renascence Man: Views of Robert Penn Warren,* ed. Walter B. Edgar [Baton Rouge: Louisiana State University Press, 1984], 59–79).

15. *A Place to Come To* (New York: Random House, 1977), 61.

Addie's Continued Presence

in Faulkner's *As I Lay Dying*

PATRICK SAMWAY, S.J.

Oh, incompetence! Never can my dreams engender the wild beast I long for.
—Jorge Luis Borges, *Dreamtigers*

"A horse! a horse! my kingdom for a horse!"
—Shakespeare, *Richard III*

As I Lay Dying emerges from the depths of the modernist tradition, and though it appears to have a deceptively uncomplicated plotline that centers on honoring the request of a dying woman to be buried in her hometown, the narrative, structural, and semiotic techniques are so innovative and bold in terms of theories of art, film, language, communication, and even advances in recording technology that were going through unprecedented stages of change and development, that the total imaginative effect reaches cosmic proportions. Like *The Sound and the Fury,* this novel obliquely portrays a woman who dominates the thoughts and actions of her kin; by her absence (their loss) she has created a palpable void, one that is filled to a certain degree, however, by a continuation of her presence in another person—in the first novel by Miss Quentin and in the second by the duck-shaped woman. The mode of presence differs significantly in each case. While it is true that Caddy Caddy is mentioned in the appendix, and thus not entirely lost, her daughter becomes her alter-ego in the Compson household. Addie Bundren's place, on the other hand, as wife and mother, is taken by someone whose identity is revealed only in the last few pages of the text, someone completely unknown to the Bundren children.

The specific difference between these two modes of identity depends primarily on the structure and referential nature of *As I Lay Dying* as it fragments the four sections of *The Sound and the Fury* into a montage of fifty-nine sections, each enclosed by white space so as to create small, distinct units that the eye and the ear can master without much difficulty. Yet when the story is read sequentially, the chapters appear as fifteen choral voices that the reader-listener tries to interiorize globally once the final voice has ceased to speak. In a similar way, the fifteen voices function as fifteen cameras, which provide depth, perspective, and interlocking density, something a single camera could not achieve, since, even with good editing, the simultaneity of various responses and actions that make up the inner and outer drama of any particular scene would be lacking. In addition, the cubistic design of the novel forces the reader to rearrange the chapters into some type of linear pattern; as a result, the reader cocreates the novel with the author. The act of constantly rearranging the text and realigning images and dialogue, and thus reevaluating the personalities of the various characters, means that the reader must cope with and adapt to an expanding network of relationships, with the result that the newly constituted linear story and ensuing processes of aesthetic enjoyment will vary from reader to reader. Thus, Addie's presence is always in the process of transforming itself as she unremittingly repositions herself in the reader's mind, trying to lodge comfortably between ongoing moments of reflections.[1] The novel, like its historical counterpart, *The Scarlet Letter*, has a vitality of its own, which no one reader can seize and possess fully, since the novel's imaginative configurations will not allow it to stabilize in some permanent way—the same for all who read it.

The basis for the novel's modernity, however, rests not on specific techniques or devices, since that would imply, quite incorrectly, that Faulkner wrote the story without full and total regard to its intrinsic, organic development. Throughout the novel Addie is portrayed in a variety of ways; she is a woman, mother, wife, lover, corpse, fish, and horse. As he did with Caddy Compson, and a host of other women, Faulkner does not allow Addie to disappear; she is keep present by a subtle congeries and dynamic interplay of words and images.[2] In the most telling example, Vardaman makes a rather bizarre identity: "My mother is a fish."[3] This sentence, at once precocious, innocuous, pretentious, Joycean, and surrealistic, provides a marvelous counterpoint to Cash's thirteen-step syllogistic argument/poem that describes the proper way to make a coffin, a rational variant of the image that Tull proffers when he infers that Addie's funeral is perhaps the wedding she never had (p. 82). In *de-sign*ating Addie as a fish (not like a fish), her metaphysical being now, at least to Vardaman, encompasses two creatures; the imagination must thus expand to cope adequately with such an identity.

The identification with the fish has profound implications in this novel. Jung, for example, in his desire to explore transcultural symbols in *The Archetypes and the Collective Unconscious* devotes four full chapters to the symbolism of the fish. Though he explores the significance of the Babylonian fish-god Oannes and other Near Eastern fish myths in detail, his primary focus is on the Old and New Testaments, an area of scholarship that was in relatively early stages of development when he wrote. The popular Christian referent is to the acrostic 'IXΘTE ['Iησῦς Χριστος Θεοῦ Τιὸς Εωτήρ].[4] Fancifully Jung sees this reference as deriving from the Old Testament: "In later Jewish tradition the Leviathan that Yahweh fought in Isaiah develops a tendency . . . to become 'pure' and be eaten as 'eucharistic' food, with the result that, if one wanted to derive the Ichthys symbol from this source, Christ as a fish would appear in place of Leviathan, the monstrous animals of tradition having meanwhile faded into mere attributer of death and the devil."[5] Faulkner himself emphasized the identification of Addie-fish-Christ in the passage describing a log in the swollen river that stands *"upright upon that surging and heaving desolation like Christ"* (141); the Christian nature of this passage is reinforced in the description of the wagon as it shears "crosswise" (141) in the act of capsizing. This depiction of Addie as a fish provides another implied sign, ⊂⟨ , that the early Christians, tradition has it, used to identify themselves, especially during times of persecution. While the Old Testament does refer to fish (for example, according to Lv 11:9–12 and Dt 14:9ff., only fish that had both scales and fins could be eaten according to Jewish law), it does not do so in any great detail. Since few Israelites lived along the Mediterranean Sea, and the Dead Sea contained no fish, the Lake of Galilee became the prime local source for fish. It was from this locale that Jesus *trans-sign*ified fish; He gave a new, spiritual significance to these creatures by relating them to the Bread of Life.

Not only were some of the apostles fishermen from the Lake of Galilee (Mt 4:18–22), but Jesus as the Christ, the risen Lord, showed the reality of His resurrectional body by eating fish (Lk 24:42ff. and Jn 21:1–13). Jesus explicitly told Simon and Andrew, two fishermen, to follow Him and He would make them fishers of men, an announcement foreshadowing the abundant catch waiting them and all future disciples. Yet, it is precisely the New Testament references that Jung did not relate, dealing with the mysterious manner in which the Christ will be eternally present to His followers after His death and resurrection that are essential for an understanding of Jesus' presence in and to the world. During the feeding of the 5,000, at the Last Supper, in the inn at Emmaus, and at the dawn lakeside scene in the final chapter of John's Gospel, Jesus took bread, said a prayer, broke the bread and gave it to His followers, who ate it, even though the fulness of this particular act might have escaped them in the process. It should be noted that in the account in Luke's Gospel of the feeding of the 5,000 (9:10–17), two fish were also distributed and that twelve baskets full of broken pieces were left over, a symbolic number that refers to divine bounty.

Likewise the context should be noted in which the feeding of the 5,000 occurs (the only miracle in the New Testament to be recorded by all four evangelists): in the previous section (Lk 9:9) Herod said, "John I beheaded; but who is this about whom I hear such things?" In the following section (Lk 9:20), Jesus asked a crucial question to those following Him, "But who do you say that I am?" to which Peter answered, "The Christ of God." The distinctly apologetic nature of this passage shows a profound relationship between the changed bread (and by association the fish, though the theological exegesis of this would be different) and Jesus as the risen Lord. The words used by Jesus in changing bread (and also wine) particularly at the Last Supper, an act which theologians have traditionally called, using an honored Thomistic category, *transsubstantiation,* indicate that Jesus is present to His followers today the same way as He was to His disciples almost 2,000 years ago. For Christians, Jesus as the Christ does not bilocate or trilocate or exist other than He is; were He to do so, He would be two or more distinct persons. Thus, He is the same person after the Resurrection as He was before; this means that all Christians, and the characters in *As I Lay Dying* for the most part are self-proclaimed Christians with Addie being no exception, must dramatically alter their notion of personhood and personal presence. Since a key dimension of *As I Lay Dying* deals precisely with the problem of Addie's continued presence, Vardaman's solemn, priestly incantation, like Jesus', is one way Faulkner uses to indicate that, after Addie is buried, she will still be spiritually present and that in her resurrected state she will be recognized as being the same person who existed before she passed through death's portals.

Yet, Vardaman's sentence is only part of a wider network of references by members of the Bundren family to nonhuman creatures. When Vardaman repeats "*Jewel's mother is a horse*" (187), one simply cannot use the same theological methodology in determining the significance of the reference, for the simple reason that horses in the culture of the Israelites, unlike desert Arabs, were not popular animals. Yet in linking Addie-fish-horse together, Faulkner has established a significant part of the *ars poetica* of this novel and expanded even further the notion of personhood to create someone/something who could not exist in the world as we know it; only artistic language can so join and hold together these concepts, because outside of language one category of being mutually excludes the other. In terms of both Vardaman's and Darl's inner logic, however, which becomes more and more identical toward the end of the novel as Darl regresses, the equation of the horse with Addie seems reasonable. Just as Vardaman, a little boy lacking the primal experiences of this life, attempts to deal with Addie as a person in terms of the process by which the fish ceases to be "alive," so too Jewel, as perceived and noted especially by Darl, both lovingly maltreats and brutishly caresses his horse, a mother-surrogate, only to lose it when it is traded eventually by his father in order to procure a new team so the family can continue the funeral journey.

In the same way that the fish forced us to expand our notion of Addie's presence to her family, so too the horse presents another way of dealing with her existence; unlike the (eucharistic) fish—caught, cut-up, fried, and eaten—the horse presents a savage tableau that is at once "rigid, motionless and terrific," effecting not a spiritual, eternal presence, but on the contrary, a muscular, bulky statuesque presence, reminiscent of Bellerophon and Pegasus or of the bronzes of Frederic Remington, and that as an unruly terrestrial creature resists taming or control:

> Then Jewel is enclosed by a glittering maze of hooves as by an illusion of wings; among them, beneath the upreared chest, he moves with the flashing limberness of a snake. For an instant before the jerk comes onto his arms he sees his whole body earth-free, horizontal, whipping snake-limber, until he finds the horse's nostrils and touches earth again. Then they are rigid, motionless, terrific, the horse backthrust on stiffened, quivering legs, with lowered head; Jewel with dug heels, shutting off the horse's wind with one hand, with the other patting the horse's neck in short strokes myriad and caressing, cursing the horse with obscene ferocity. (12)

Yet like a movie that suddenly changes images, the mode of Addie's presence is *trans-formed* again from a Christian one to a Roman/Greek one, which is at the same time radically undercut by Addie's belief that Jewel "is my cross and he will be my salvation" (160). André Bleikasten rightly sees the transference of fish to horse as a "defense mechanism indicative of the incestuous nature of Jewel's love for his mother."[6] Jewel rides the horse, purchased at the price of much hard work, and also the coffin (as does Cash)—clearly indicating repressed eroticism.

By frequently being described in various ways as "wooden," Jewel's relationship to both his horse and his mother, most poignantly described in terms of statuary "like two figures in a Greek frieze, isolated out of all reality by the red glare" (211), evokes, in contrast to the biblical pericopes of Vardaman, other associations, particularly sex, death, and the coffin, as well as another modality of storytelling, that of the totem pole used by many native American tribes of the Northwest to relate their family histories.[7] It is interesting too in this context that the Greek word for a ceremonial pole φάλαγξ is a homonym for a phallus φαλλός; more apropos, Jung notes that a phallic symbol does not denote one sexual organ, but the libido in general.[8] Even the Christian connotation of "wooden" as related to Jewel's repressed sexuality is not lost, especially if one remembers that Jewel is Addie's salvation—her cross, the Christian tree of life and of death: "The fact that primitive Christianity resolutely turned away from nature and the instincts in general, and, through its asceticism, from sex in particular," Jung notes, "clearly indicates the source from which its motive forces came. So it is not surprising that this transformation has left noticeable traces in Christian symbolism. Had it not done so, Christianity would never have been able to transform libido."[9] Likewise, several important primitive myths tell us that "human beings were descended from trees, so there were burial customs in which people were buried in hollow tree-trunks, whence the German *Totenbaum*, 'tree of death'; for coffin, which is still in use today. If we remember that the tree is predominantly a mother-symbol, then the meaning of this mode of burial becomes clear. *The dead are delivered back to the mother for rebirth*."[10] From this perspective, *As I Lay Dying* is a totem pole interpositioning the signs, stories, and symbols recounting the life and death of Addie Bundren, the preoccupations of her family, and those of the larger community to the Bundrens' predicament; in this context, the fish and the horse are the primary totem animals used to relate and fix Addie's presence.

Faulkner has fused in *As I Lay Dying* two kinds of totem myths—those which were known by everyone (the Tulls, the Armstids, Dr. Peabody) and those which were the private property of particular families and could only be told by their members (the Bundrens themselves). Both of these myths in their original totemic forms tell of a primeval world when finite divisions between humans, animals, and spirits had not yet been created and beings could change themselves from one form to another; humans could become animals mysteriously by putting on skins, and animals could become humans by mysteriously taking off their skins. In addition, humans could marry animals and spirit beings. All realms of existence (water, earth, sky, and the land of the dead—and this is borne out by Addie in *As I Lay Dying* in her identification with the fish, horse, and buzzards) were interconnected by beings who could pass from one to another. What is particularly worth noting is that all boundaries of existence were fluid, where opposing categories (natural/supernatural, life/death, human/animal) were interchangeable. "It was a time when cosmic power accelerated the natural processes of change into miracles of transformation. It was a time now lost but remembered. . . . So, even though mythological time belonged to long ago, before mankind became separated and distinguished from animals and nature, the memory of it could be kept alive." [11] In fact some of the totem poles, containing the ashes of the deceased, served as mortuary poles, a phenomenon that has its counterpart in Cash's carefully constructed coffin.

Ancient, primitive civilizations, according to Jung and Freud, devoted considerable attention to the relationship between totems and taboos. Jung believed, for example, that in certain ritual actions if

> the libido connects with the unconscious, it is as though it were connecting with the mother, and this raises the incest-taboo. But as the unconscious is infinitely greater than the mother and is only symbolized by her, the fear of incest must be conquered if one is to gain possession of those 'saving' contents—the treasure hard to attain. Since the son is not conscious of his incest tendency, it is projected upon the mother or her symbol. But the symbol of the mother [Jewel's horse] is not the mother herself, so . . . there is not the slightest possibility of incest, and the taboo can therefore be ruled out as a reason for resistance. [12]

Jewel is pictured in his unique chapter as trying to protect his mother on a hill and make her secure; though this is characteristic behavior of a lover, Jewel does not wish to possess his mother sexually, and thus his treatment of the horse in Jungian terms does not *necessarily* mean that he has incestuous feelings toward her.

Freud, in contrast to Jung, takes a different view of totem and taboo; whereas Jung stayed close to the Freudian interpretation of myth and religion as sublimated sexuality (each of them as time went on feared that the other might anticipate the ideas of the other), Freud (undoubtedly familiar with Sir James Frazer's *Totem and Exogamy* and *The Golden Bough*) based his beliefs on the concepts of evolutionary anthropology, that is, on the doctrine of survival and the widely contested supposition that primitive man represents a fairly accurate picture of an early stage of our own development.[13] Freud saw totemism as a type of rule by which an animal stands in a peculiar relation to the whole clan. The totem is the common ancestor to the clan and its guardian-spirit or helper. And as a result one should not kill or eat the totem animal, nor should one marry within the totem clan. Freud concentrated on the social aspects of the second of these prohibitions, that dealing with exogamy or the law prohibiting marriage between persons of the same blood or stock as incest: if "we analyse the instincts at work in the neuroses, we find that the determining influence in them is exercised by the instinctual forcers of sexual origin; the corresponding cultural formations, on the other hand, are based upon social instincts, originating from the combination of egoistical and erotic elements."[14] Unlike Vardaman, Jewel has no intention of killing or mutilating his horse; on the contrary, even though he has a deep attachment to the horse, he heroically relinquishes it for the good of his dead mother, thus proving that the welfare of the family unit is above his personal interests or satisfaction. Freud speculated that the incest taboo does not correspond with the specific value of incest *sensu strictiori* any more than the sacredness of the totem corresponds with its biological value. "From this standpoint we must say that incest is forbidden not because it is desired but because the free-floating anxiety regressively reactivates infantile material and turns it into a ceremony of atonement."[15] Jewel's cooperation in trading the horse would confirm this hypothesis.

As Freud developed his ideas on totem and taboo, he came under the influence of Robertson Smith, who demonstrated in his *Lectures on the Religion of the Semites* the mythic and religious roots of Judaism, Christianity, and Islam; Robertson took exception to the contention that all religions could be explained by totemism, since he believed that ritual or practice preceded creed or belief. Both Smith and later Freud stressed the importance of the sacrificial meal: "The leading idea in the animal sacrifices of the Semites . . . was not that of a gift made over to the god, but of an act of communion, in which the god and his worshippers unite by partaking together of the flesh and blood of a sacred victim." [16] The bond of food is the cohesive mechanism and a communal meal of the totem animal unites the group in a special way. Jung notes that "many exemplars of the totem animal are killed and consumed during the totem meals, and yet it is only the One who is being eaten." [17] Thus, the eucharistic nature of the fish is not at odds with its totemic nature. In addition, anthropologists have long held that many primitive tribes considered the totem as a primal father, and when the real father is killed by the sons, they share his flesh and partake of his strength, though not without feelings of remorse; they revoke their deed by forbidding the killing of the totem. This element of parricide pervades the religious sensibility, since the sons in their relationship to the totem, or surrogate father, could attempt to bring about a sense of reconciliation; the totemic beliefs are thus father-oriented, since the sons wish to be protected by the father in the future. Thus totem religions grew out of a "filial sense of guilt, in an attempt to allay that feeling and to appease the father by deferred obedience to him." [18] In *As I Lay Dying*, Jewel's father is the Reverend Whitfield, while Anse is the father of Addie's other children: "I gave Anse Dewey Dell to negative Jewel. Then I gave him Vardaman to replace the child I had robbed him of. And now he has three children that are his and not mine. And then I could get ready to die" (168). Darl, intuiting the truth of the situation, badgers Jewel about his father: " 'Jewel,' I said, 'whose son are you?' . . . 'Your mother was a horse, but who was your father, Jewel?' " (202). Jewel's biological father remains unidentified and unnamed in this role, as if he did not exist. Likewise, Addie in her heart of hearts kills Anse: "Then I found out that I had Darl. At first I would not believe it. Then I believed that I would kill Anse. . . . He did not know that he was dead, then" (164). In both cases, an act of symbolic parricide occurs and the Bundren children, except for Darl, who could not endure the folly of the funeral trip, remain with their father once he has *re-formed* the family unit. In a rather bizarre scene that out-Freuds Freud, the three Bundren children consume the father-phallic-food (itself in the shape of a totem!) in the only communal meal the children have together: "there is about it that unmistakable air of definite and imminent departure that trains have, perhaps due to the fact that Dewey Dell and Vardaman on the seat and Cash on a pallet in the wagon are eating bananas from a paper bag" (244). It is precisely at this point in time, that Anse is undergoing his own marital transformation.

In creating a story that alludes to biblical notions of transubstantiation and corporeal resurrection and mythic notions of totemic storytelling and tribal taboos, Faulkner in focusing on Addie's continued presence to her family and neighbors is dealing with the age-old problem of the transmigration of souls, or as some cultures have termed it, of reincarnation (or, as James Joyce would put it, "met-em-pike-hoses" [metempsychosis]). The Greeks, for example, dealt with the notion that the soul of a dead person passes into an animal because the soul is immortal and cannot cease to exist. Herodotus wrote: "The Egyptians were the first to enunciate the following doctrine: the human soul is immortal, and when the body perishes the soul enters one animal after another in succession, and when it has made the rounds of all the land, sea, and air creatures [as in totem religions], it returns to a human being." [19] While this doctrine is probably not Egyptian, as Herodotus claims, but Pythagorean, it was important to many Mediterranean peoples, including the followers of the Orphic sects, Pindar, Empedocles, and most of all Plato. In the *Phaedo*, souls can be incarnated in animals, birds, and insects, though there is some reason to believe that this should be taken in an allegorical way.[20] The Neoplatonic writers, however, believed that their doctrine was by no means a uniform one, though obviously Christians, except for the Manichaeans and the Cathari, rejected it completely.

Though Faulkner stresses the fish, the horse, and the buzzards as the main nonhuman creatures that carry on Addie's presence, he is careful in his use of animals so that the overall pattern is not excessively rigid. The novel's title, for example, taken from the eleventh book of the *Odyssey*, evokes a relationship between a woman and a dog: "As I lay dying the woman with the dogeyes did not wish to close my eyes for my descent into Hades." If one postulates that the Faulknerian application of this is from Darl's perspective, then Addie has doglike characteristics, which in turn changes the image of her as fish-horse. Dr. Peabody, referred to as a "dipped rooster" (43), reinforces this relationship between Addie's eyes and animals; he "seen them [eyes] drive from the room them coming with sympathy and pity, with actual help, and clinging to some trifling animal to whom they never were more than packhorses" (44). Anse, too, shares this characteristic with a dog, since, when returning from the Snopeses, he is portrayed as "more hang-dog than common and kind of proud too" (179), a description that is repeated in the final view we have of him (250); he is also pictured as a "steer" (59, 69) and a "horse" (117). And Vardaman resembles a drowned "puppy" (68) when he goes to the Tulls to talk about his mother and the fish. Anse likewise breaks down normal human-animal categories when he says that "a man aint so different from a horse or a mule, come long come short, except a mule or a horse has got a little more sense" (176). Also in describing "something to be always a-moving," Anse associates the wagon bearing Addie with a horse and a snake (35). Jewel on his horse "is enclosed by a glittering maze of hooves as by an illusion of wings" as he "snake-limber" tries to hold the horse in check (12). A similar image is used later to refer to Jewel: "Motionless, wooden-backed, wooden-faced, he shapes the horse in a rigid stoop like a hawk, hookwinged" (89). Dewey Dell seems, as might be expected, to have a natural affinity with a cow (59–61).

The most difficult juxtaposition of animals and human beings occurs as Darl is on the train being taken to Jackson:

> They pulled two seats together so Darl could sit by the window. One of them sat beside him, the other sat on the seat facing him, riding backward. One of them had to ride backward because state's money has a face to each backside and a backside to each face, and they are riding on the state's money which is incest. A nickel has a woman on one side and a buffalo on the other; two faces and no back. I don't know what that is. Darl had a little spy-glass he got in France at the war. In it it had a woman and a pig with two backs and no face. I know what that is. "Is that why you are laughing, Darl?"
> "Yes yes yes yes yes yes." (244)

While it is not difficult to spot the variables here, Darl couples them together violently and in a way that implies bestiality and incest, implied motifs warranted in the novel but never realized. One attendant on the train "rides" (a word associated primarily with Jewel) backward, and because he does so he faces his partner; in this position, they seem to have an "incestuous" relationship. People, like coins, have a front and backside, and thus the buffalo and the woman on a nickel both are facing out and appear to have two faces no backsides. Darl cannot deal with this. Yet when thinking about the image of a woman and a pig in a spy-glass, he sees two backs, and like the two attendants, he thinks of incest. He knows what that is, and this is cause for his cosmic laugh.

Some outside sources might be helpful here. In *Othello* (1.1), Iago and Roderigo call to Brabantio, the father of Desdemona, to inform him of Othello's relationship with Brabantio's daughter: "*Iago.* 'I am one, sir, that comes to tell you your daughter and the Moor are now making the beast with two backs.'" His allusion is to sexual intercourse, though a more subtle reference could well be to the problem of the Gerasene demoniac in Lk 8:26–39 (also Mt 8:28–34), in which a rite of exorcism takes place and the evil spirits are displaced (perhaps a sublimated wish on Darl's part). Another suggestion is that it refers to the myth of Demeter, the corn-goddess, whom Faulkner could have read about in *The Golden Bough*.[21] As corn-goddess, pigs were sacred to Demeter and regularly sacrificed at the Thesmophoria autumn festival because of the destruction caused by the pigs in the corn fields. The following year, whoever ate the gatherings pulled up from the chasm would be assured of a good crop. Some versions of the myth say that the pigs even ate Demeter, and thus those who feasted on their remains were in effect participating in her divinity. One specific version portrays the Black Demeter as having the head of a horse on the body of a woman—an indirect echo of Darl's preoccupation with Jewel. Whatever, these images do not neatly coalesce to form a logical, manageable one—and that could well be the point that Faulkner is making. As Giliane Morell has noted, "Du regard interdit au regard qui rend fou, c'est le langage de la raison elle-même qui est mis en question dans *Tandis que j'agonise*, car on ne peut éviter de se demander avec Cash: qui sont les vrais fous?"[22] Darl's language is beyond his control; he no longer can create sentences, because the axis upon which they turn, the governing principle by which images are yoked together, the informing and transforming power, is missing.

In contrast to Darl, who will live out his life disturbed and alone, the Bundren family regroups to move into the future. Nothing is really said about the direction the family will take, but Anse seems pleased, especially that he has taken a new wife, "—a kind of duck-shaped woman all dressed up, with them kind of hard-looking pop eyes like she was daring ere a man to say nothing" (249). The comic effect changes the mood of the story tremendously; what is most fortuitous is that the shape of the new Mrs. Bundren will allow her to be at home either on land or on water. In this newest member of the Bundren family, Addie will still remain present to her husband and children. Not only do we have an intimation in the fish image that she will be resurrected on the last day, but her spirit has undergone a series of transmigrations, and though we have no guarantee that there will be a continuation of her personality, her karma will certainly be felt by the remaining Bundrens. Though Faulkner does not go so far as to apotheosize Addie or indicate her assumption into the heavens, the introduction of the new Mrs. Bundren by Anse takes place on the very last page of the novel, thus giving her a prominent place in the structure of the story, one that to a great extent must offset the events and dialogue that were part and parcel of Addie's death.

As a modern novel, *As I Lay Dying* is both easy to read, because of its short chapters, and difficult to cope with, because of the heavy use of montage. Sergei Eisenstein, the Russian film director, mastered hundreds of "whimsical hieroglyphic characters," as he put it, in order to appreciate the sign nature of film language. "How grateful I was later on to fate for having subjected me to the ordeal of learning an oriental language, opening before me that strange way of thinking and teaching me word pictography. It was precisely this 'unusual' way of thinking that later helped me to master the nature of montage."[23] He noted, for example, that in the late ideographic systems of Near Eastern cuneiform or of Tangut, the element of representationality, preserved in the semipictographic signs of early Sumerian or ancient Chinese writing, had almost disappeared. In the language of semiotics, Eisenstein was dealing with the problem of the transformation of iconic signs into symbolic ones. As Vjačeslav Ivanov has noted, the "evolution of iconic signs into symbolic ones takes place not only in the transformation of drawn pictograms into stylized ideographic symbols . . . but also in the development of rituals and social institutions."[24] The evolutionary nature of hieroglyphs, from the level of the representational to cosmic discourse, is underlined in Eisenstein's essay "Beyond the Shot," in which he shows how montage in particular expresses a concept, the result of multiple images: "The combination of two hieroglyphs of the simplest series is to be regarded not as their sum, but as their product, i.e., as a value of another dimension, another degree; each separately, corresponds to an *object,* to a fact, but their combination corresponds to a *concept*. From simple hieroglyphs has been fused—the ideogram. The combination of the two 'depictables' makes it possible to represent something graphically unpredictable."[25] From both a semiotic and cinemagraphic point of view, Eisenstein showed concretely in his films that the whole is more than the sum of its parts and different from what one finds in nature as the movement goes from the representational to the abstract.

Because it depicts humans, animals, fish, and birds as sign words, *As I Lay Dying* can be considered a hieroglyphic cartouche, the story of a "royal" person who has died and whose personal history is etched in stone.[26] The novel has a number of framing devices that enclose Addie's story, including the "circle" (164) outside of which are time, Anse, and love; the "shape to fill a lack" (164) like the word "love"; the shape of her body when she "used to be a virgin . . . the shape of a   and I couldn't think *Anse,* couldn't remember *Anse*" (165); the ominous configuration the buzzards make when they move in "little tall black circles of not-moving" (185); both the real shape of the coffin and the implied shape of the fish; the path which "turns and circles the cottonhouse at four soft right angles" (3); the circular nature of the book as Anse appears a "foot taller" (249) when introducing the new Mrs. Bundren, just as Jewel is a "full head" taller than Darl (3) when we are first made aware that Addie is dying.

In his letter of September 27, 1822, to M. Dacier, Jean-François Champollion noted the thrill he had when he discovered that hieroglyphs are basic ideographics, depicting the ideas, not the sounds, of language. As he explained, the "look of a hieroglyphic inscription is a veritable chaos. Nothing is in its place. There is no relation to sense. The most contradictory objects are put right next to each other, producing monstrous alliances."[27] Could the exact same words be used to describe *As I Lay Dying?* Yet Champollion knew that in deciphering the Rosetta Stone he must be on the right track, since the regularity of the script and the combination of signs indicated that sense must be intended. *As I Lay Dying* invites the same type of methodological investigation, of being able to "read" and "see" what has been there for many years. Addie's continued presence in this novel gives the lie to her father's belief that "the reason for living is getting ready to stay dead" (167).

NOTES

1. I am grateful to Professor John Matthews of Boston University for sharing with me his ideas on *As I Lay Dying* at the Third International Faulkner Colloquium held in Salamanca, Spain, Apr. 26–29, 1984. See Panthea Reid Broughton, "Faulkner's Cubist Novels," in *"A Cosmos of My Own": Faulkner and Yoknapatawpha, 1980,* ed. Doreen Fowler and Ann J. Abadie (Jackson: University Press of Mississippi, 1981), 59–94; Watson Branch, "Darl Bundren's Cubistic Vision," in *William Faulkner's "As I Lay Dying": A Critical Casebook,* ed. Dianne L. Cox (New York: Garland, 1985), 111–29; Stephen M. Ross, " 'Voice' in Narrative Texts: The Example of *As I Lay Dying,*" *PMLA* 94 (1979): 300–10; Karl F. Zender, "Faulkner and the Power of Sound," *PMLA* 99 (1984): 89–108; and two works by André Bleikasten, *Parcours de Faulkner* (Paris: Editions Ophrys, 1982), 165–214, and *Faulkner's "As I Lay Dying"* (Bloomington: Indiana University Press, 1973).

2. See Monique Pruvot, "Faulkner and the Voices of Orphism," in *Faulkner and Idealism,* ed. Michel Gresset and Patrick Samway, S.J. (Jackson: University Press of Mississippi, 1983), 127–43.

3. William Faulkner, *As I Lay Dying,* rev. under the direction of James B. Meriwether (New York: Random House, 1964), 79. All future references to this novel will be to this edition.

4. Carl Jung, *The Collected Works of Carl Jung: The Archetypes and the Collective Unconscious,* trans. R. F. Hull (Princeton: Princeton University Press, 1959), vol. 9, part 1, chaps. 6–9. The letters in Greek for the word "fish" refer to Jesus Christ, Son of God, Savior.

5. Ibid., 119–20.

6. André Bleikasten, *Faulkner's "As I Lay Dying,"* 93.

7. See Åke Hultkrantz, *The Religions of the American Indians,* trans. Monica Setterwall (Berkeley: University of California Press, 1979), 66–83; Marjorie Halpin, *Totem Poles: An Illustrated Guide* (Seattle: University of Washington Press, 1983), 21–22.

8. Jung, *Symbols of Transformation,* trans. R. F. Hull, vol. 5 of *Collected Works* (Princeton: Princeton University Press, 1956), 222.

9. Ibid., 229.

10. Ibid., 233.

11. Halpin, *Totem Poles,* 21.

12. See Edwin Wallace, *Freud and Anthropology: A History and Reappraisal* (New York: International Universities Press, 1983), 59–128.

13. Ibid.

14. *Freud and Anthropology,* 81–82.

15. Ibid., 106.

16. Ibid., 95.

17. Carl Jung, *Four Archetypes: Mother, Rebirth, Spirit, Trickster,* trans. R. F. Hull (Princeton: Princeton University Press, 1970), 62.

18. Wallace, *Freud and Anthropology,* 99.

19. See the article "Transmigration of Souls," in *New Catholic Encyclopedia* (New York: McGraw-Hill, 1967), 257.

20. Plato, *Phaedo,* 70A–73B.

21. For an interesting analysis of this myth as applied to this novel, see Mary Jane Dickerson, "Some Sources of Faulkner's Myth in *As I Lay Dying,*" *Mississippi Quarterly* 19 (Summer 1966): 132–42.

22. See Giliane Morell, " 'Pourquoi ris-tu,' Darl?—ou le temps d'un regard," *Sud* (Marseille) 15/15: 146.

23. See Vjačeslav Ivanov, "Eisenstein's Montage of Hieroglyphic Signs," in *On Signs,* ed. Marshall Blonsky (Baltimore: Johns Hopkins University Press, 1985), 222.

24. Ibid., 223.

25. Ibid., 225.

26. See Maurice Pope, *The Story of Decipherment: From Egyptian Hiero-glyphic to Linear B* (London: Thames and Hudson, 1975), 60–84; also John T. Irwin, *American Hieroglyphics: The Symbol of the Egyptian Hieroglyphics in the American Renaissance* (New Haven: Yale University Press, 1980).

27. See Pope, *The Story of Decipherment,* 75.

A Dialogic Hereafter:

The Sound and the Fury

and *Absalom, Absalom!*

OLGA SCHERER

Nearly all the available writings of Mikhail Bakhtin (1895–1975) are by now either published, or about to be, in English translation. More than anything, however, it is perhaps the simultaneous publication in 1984 of the second, probably definitive, English version of his *Problems of Dostoevsky's Poetics* and Katerina Clark and Michael Holquist's comprehensive biographical study of Bakhtin that has helped to intensify the familiarity with this great theoretician's ideas which I observe among American narratologists, including those inspired by deconstructionism. These developments are very encouraging to one whose central preoccupation, since my first reading, in 1968, of Bakhtin's book about Dostoyevsky's poetics, has been the study of the "post-Dostoyevskian" polyphonic novel, notably with reference to Faulkner.[1]

Here I want to examine the ways in which certain characters of any one work by Faulkner recur in another, or others, to yield in the end what has come to be known as a saga. In keeping with Bakhtin's distinction between the "monologic" narrative principle, crowned in the nineteenth century by the works of Tolstoy, and the radically new "dialogic" or "polyphonic" conception introduced into the novel by Dostoyevsky as the dominant principle governing all fundamental narrative relationships, I shall try to show that the devices for the reuse of narrative elements—characters in particular—fall similarly into one or the other of these two fundamental worldviews, resulting in (1) the *monologic* type of recurrence, which I shall call referential because it takes place (in the second text) by way of denotation within a *zone of reference* already signified by the first text; and (2) the *dialogic* type of recurrence which, bypassing actual referential material recorded by a first text, takes place in a *zone of significance* (a referential no-man's-land).

In the second of the two types of recurrence the first text produces a graft on the second by connotation. The recurring hero is thus protected against both the certainty of his "former" representation and his possible identification with an abstract idea. The recurrence itself, which is at no time denoted, not only frees the idea of the hero from potential nonincarnation, but also gives him the choice, as it were, of deciding whether he is the *same* or not.

It is therefore impossible in this type of recurrence to conceive of the recurring hero either as an independently existing idea or quality (jealousy, valor, patriotism, racism, incest), or as a real object simultaneously existing in all its contingencies. The world from which the hero is extracted (or, more exactly, ambivalently extracts himself) is no more paraphrasable than the one into which he is being inserted (= he inserts himself), the two worlds existing only by way of a connoted textual confrontation where the "idea" directly *signifies*.

Monologic recurrence, on the other hand, is accomplished without the "consent" of the recurring character himself. His reappearance, together with the traits which make his identity plausible—the referential material —is a message conveyed by the author directly to the reader "behind the character's back." His identity, then, is guaranteed in both works by the author's supreme authority from which the character is excluded. Thus the author alone has the power to impose a notion of an already identified and partly defined character upon the process of that character's reincarnation. The author alone is responsible for the preconceived idea which he wishes to use again. It is he who makes not only the name of the character he brings back to life serve as signifier of that idea, but also the behavior chosen for him in keeping with the earlier reference. Whereas the character himself, though obviously conscious of his name, possibly also of his behavior, may be completely unaware of the idea he represents. This may even be true if, while retaining certain traits, losing others and (most often) obtaining new ones, he remains, like many Faulknerian characters, in the foreground of both the old and the new context.

The mechanisms active in the referential type of recurrence seem to be inherent to the monologic conception of the individual narratives involved. In both the initial and the new text the character is structured, in Bakhtin's terms, as an object of authorial discourse.[2] The monologic character is inferior to the author both in knowledge (particularly concerning himself) and authority (with regard, among other things, to the axiological system the author is establishing). He may in extreme cases be caricatured as a mere meeting place of various externally given definitions (historical, social, psychological, etc.) which together assign him a place in a preconceived notion of a "world." But even in cases of behavior less deliberately determined by external factors, the given set of realities (even when represented as unstable) becomes the fixed point of the two texts, the invariable in relation to which the dependent elements of the variables are established and defined. And it is out of such conditions that the monologic author guarantees the *sameness* of the character in both novels.

The great majority of the mechanisms of recurrence in the different works of the Yoknapatawpha series are, like most of those works themselves, essentially monologic.[3] The series as a whole may therefore at first sight be said to resemble traditional sagas or romans-fleuve, such as those of Zola, Martin du Gard, Rolland. The rare dialogic recurrence I have found between *The Sound and the Fury* (1929) and *Absalom, Absalom!* (1936) thus acquires all the more importance.

The most flagrant illustration of monologic recurrence in Faulkner's later works is perhaps the restitution of Temple Drake (*Sanctuary,* 1931) in *Requiem for a Nun* (1951). The latter, a peculiar novel-play, not only exploits the development of an idea in the absence of its bearer, but also maximally reinforces the zone of reference in which the idea evolves. Endowed with a fearsome, all-powerful *Weltgeist,* this zone—essentially the author's zone and a mere guarantor at the outset (*Sanctuary*)—actually becomes the chief protagonist in *Requiem,* a kind of abstract character, not present in the cast but equipped with the most powerful and authoritative voice.

None of the three stories which are inserted as introductions at the beginning of the three acts of *Requiem* seems to be part of Faulkner's fiction, despite the recognizable proper names of characters (Grenier, Sutpen, Compson) of places (Nashville, north Mississippi), institutions (the Bureau of Indian Affairs), and the like. These signified realities fill the fictional space and the continuity of its ethos with such a historical or cosmic authority that the identity of a Temple Drake or a Nancy Mannigoe emerges as unmistakable authentic even before the protagonists are named or appear on the scene. They are thus made in advance to fit a situation, as if they were mere objects of the author's exclusive authoritarian interpretation, which to boot they are not allowed to take into account at the time of their own appearance. It is as if the author, singling out the epic aspect of his previous work, imposed upon it all the infallible signs of a preconceived mythical interpretation of his fiction—and this without his past and future characters' knowledge.

Like "The Custom House" (the introduction to Hawthorne's *The Scarlet Letter*,) the introduction to the first act of *Requiem* ("The Courthouse") purports to build a story, a fragment of history, as part of History itself, without consulting posterity about its impact or allowing the characters thus presented to be aware of its meaning. The author makes individual destiny penetrate the mythical destiny of Yoknapatawpha, and through it, that of America and the world. The heroine restored to life is confined to the "hinterland of America," which, without her knowledge, is to become her small place in the history of the world. The full meaning of the character's behavior and observations is, like that of Tolstoy's characters, externally presented.

Neither Temple nor Nancy, when their turn comes to begin their existence in the dialogue part of the first act, will try to question or confirm the function, which the author forces them to fulfill, of "merely adding one puny infinitesimal more to the long weary increment since Genesis" (44). Their utterances will never be contaminated by the initial passage which after all, in prefacing their performance, concerns them at least indirectly. They will never attempt, as dialogic heroes would, to exorcise or conjure the words of the preamble that threatens to lock them within a finished form and confine them to a specific role in the world. In other words, the "content" of the form, in separating the expository part from the dialogue part without allowing them to knit, negates the "form" of the content which, for its final effect, sets up an organic link between these two parts—again behind the heroines' backs. Never will the "character's zone" invade "the author's zone"—to use these Bakhtinian terms.[4] The character will never be allowed to assert his own, possibly recognizable signifiers in authorial discourse, let alone be given a chance to "have the last word."

Not only is Mrs. Gowan Stevens doomed never to know, never even to guess, what part she is made to play by being resuscitated, or in what project, prompted by what idealism (transcendental? dialectic?), she is to be enrolled, or what judgment might threaten her motives, but the author also whispers the answers to such questions directly into the reader's ear, blocking the character's access to this complicity. Moreover, the heroine must submit to being identified as Temple Drake *by another* and yield to "the idea" signified by this name. Falling back entirely on the *signified* of this identity, the heroine of *Requiem* cannot help accepting a state of affairs established outside herself, even in those scenes where she heaps abuse upon herself for all the wrongs done and designates herself in the third person by her own name (more exactly, by both her names). Thanks to a number of traits—signifiers of her previous identity—presented as indicators of a biographical sequence (a clearly metonymic technique), her awareness can absorb all the acts of debauchery, moral corruption, criminal complicity, false testimony, which she had committed with impunity in her youth.

There is Temple's famous declaration, which constitutes the only direct allusion to Dostoyevsky in Faulkner's work: "a good fair honest chance to suffer—you know: just anguish for the sake of anguish, like that Russian or somebody who wrote a whole book about suffering, not suffering for or about anything, just suffering" (*Requiem for a Nun,* 115). This declaration aims at an idea (a noble idea, of course) which exists *as* an idea and which it therefore suffices simply to signify in order to achieve at will its disincarnation and subsequent reincarnation. Faulkner is decidedly least "Dostoyevskian" when he refers to Dostoyevsky directly.

The strict linearity of biographical contiguity, justifying the reversal which takes place in the new Temple and which puts her on the path of expiation, precludes all possible metaphorization which might recreate the actual zone of this particular character through a strategic signifier borrowed directly from a crucial statement made in *Sanctuary.* Instead, the evolution of the incorrigible Mrs. Stevens, whom Nancy's salutary crime sets at last on the path of expiation, is carried out primarily within the zone of reference, the author's zone, where all the heroine's character traits, disembodied, had only been waiting to be placed again at any moment, unchanged (or advanced by one notch in an unchanged direction), within the new project of a biographically verifiable story. By accepting stages of nonincarnation the character accepts an external definition. She allows the author to have the last word.

Not only do both (implied) authors—that of *Sanctuary* and that of *Requiem*—directly communicate with both corresponding (implied) readers, but the single author, implied in what it is legitimate to consider as a single system composed of the two works, similarly bypasses the implied authors of the two component parts. He establishes an almost entirely denoted referential metacommunication, the urgency of which might have been dictated to him by a new stage in the real author's moral evolution. Having perhaps reread *The Brothers Karamazov* in a "monologic" state of mind, Faulkner borrowed a *signifying value* from that novel, only to apply it to *Requiem* as a *signified value*. The dialogue between Temple Drake and Mrs. Gowan Stevens becomes a monologue with every vestige of a possible open-endedness destroyed in advance.

I now turn to Faulkner's dialogic techniques applied to recurrence, as exemplified by *The Sound and the Fury* and *Absalom, Absalom!*, Faulkner's only fully-fledged polyphonic novel. I have so far assumed two theoretical categories: dialogic and monologic. But clearly these two categories cannot exist in a pure state in novelistic practice. The referential function cannot wholly exclude the function of significance from narrative discourse, just as connotation cannot completely replace denotation, a minimum of denoted information being obviously indispensible to generate subsequently connoted information. The opposite is equally true: some paradigmatic graft is inevitable, even in the most naive, "realistically" handled narratives. It is therefore best to speak of a relative dominance of one or the other type of recurrence, as indeed Bakhtin (1929–63) does when he discusses narrative monologism and dialogism in general.

This relativity becomes clearly visible in the characters in *The Sound and the Fury* who reappear in *Absalom, Absalom!* Some of them are manifestly referential adaptations; as such, while losing those traits which are inessential in the new context and gaining others, they remain compatible with their status in *The Sound and the Fury*. Yet almost all are drawn to a greater or lesser degree into the general project of *Absalom, Absalom!* through direct or indirect contact with Quentin Compson, the dialogic hero par excellence. It is their contact with Quentin that even sometimes makes their discourse acquire the paradigmatic mobility characteristic of dialogic communication.

A lengthy analysis is impossible here, and I can only give an outline of that most striking originality in *Absalom, Absalom!* which consists in establishing a subsidiary dialogue between the following two distinct projects:

1. a most intricate polyphonic system built up by the general narrator (a kind of "unreliable" author) and Quentin Compson (Faulkner's most consistently dialogic hero) through:
   a. Miss Rosa Coldfield—probably Faulkner's most Dostoyevskian

female character—whose long discourse, endowed with characteristic elements of a confession, such as those produced by Dmitri Karamazov or Stavrogin, is, furthermore, not unlike that of the narrator in *Notes from the Underground,* a vast polemic with authorial attempts to lock her within a zone of external definition;

b. the flippant dialogic instigator Shreve;

c. the "auxiliary narrator" Mr. Compson, a traditional, author-oriented figure who is gradually "forced" by his son to give in to polyphony;

d. the polyphonically reconstructed, highly dialogic trio composed of Charles, Henry, and Judith, who speak through the points of intersection created by their reconstructors' ambivalent, unsymmetrically overlapping zones;

2. the monologic, myth-generating system of Thomas Sutpen, whom no verbal instigation succeeds in pulling out of authorial discourse. [5]

Nor is it possible to demonstrate the essential complementarity—a monologic characteristic—of the relationship between the four sections of *The Sound and the Fury* in which, as in *As I Lay Dying* (1930), the "whole truth" withheld by the author is constituted by the sum of all the fragments of that whole furnished by individual character zones. Only Quentin (narrator and fully fledged coauthor of the second section, the only truly dialogic section in *The Sound and the Fury*) possesses knowledge of and authority with regard to essentials—especially those concerning himself —comparable to the author's. That is why in a study of dialogic relationships between *The Sound and the Fury* and *Absalom, Absalom!* it is the wholly connoted recurrence of Quentin Compson that must primarily be considered.

Obsession with incest obviously did not wait for a Bakhtin-oriented study to be observed as the principal common motif between the two novels. Anxious to extract the most complete meaning of Sutpen's story in Quentin's mind, Faulkner scholars make a case of utmost importance for this recurring theme. [6]

It is, however, necessary to insist that it is Quentin himself who imperceptibly suggests, as he now tries to reproduce one of the three possible reasons which motivated Henry Sutpen to kill his best friend, Charles Bon, in order to prevent Charles's possibly incestuous marriage to Henry's sister Judith, that he is particularly sensitive to the situation because of "his own" and perhaps Benjy's similar incestuous commitment to his sister Caddy, a predicament which will eventually lead him to suicide.

Quentin's suggestion of this crucial link between *The Sound and the Fury* and *Absalom, Absalom!* rests upon a single word: *door,* a word frequently denoted in his discourse in section 2, but always within the same, identically phrased, and often incomplete image: that of Caddy "at the threshold of an ultimate action."[7] Caddy's departure will break the "incestuous" Benjy-Caddy-Quentin trio, which the hero of the second section would have wished to preserve, just as Charles Bon would have wished to preserve the possibly similar one he formed with Henry and Judith Sutpen. Let us look at a few examples of Quentin's chief signifier repeatedly transferred from context to context in his internal dialogue which entirely fills the second section of *The Sound and the Fury:*

> *One minute she was standing in the door.* (76)

> *Moving sitting still. One minute she was standing in the door. Benjy. Bellowing. Benjamin the child of mine old age bellowing. Caddy! Caddy!* (83).

> *Did you ever have a sister? No but they're all bitches. Did you ever have a sister? One minute she was. Bitches. Not bitch one minute she stood in the door* Dalton Ames (86).

> *Sold the pasture. . . .*
> *Father will be dead in a year they say if he doesn't stop drinking and he won't stop since I since last summer and then they'll send Benjy to Jackson I can't cry I can't even cry one minute she was standing in the door the next minute he was pulling at her dress and bellowing his voice hammered back and forth between the walls in waves and she shrinking against the wall* (114).

> like when I was a little boy *hands can see touching in the mind shaping unseen door Door now nothing hands can see* My nose could see gasoline, the vest on the table, the door (157).

The last example, in light of the preceding ones, illustrates a fundamental phenomenon in dialogic communication: an idea which, instead of being signified, itself *signifies.* The hero multiplies the instances of his discourse, thus negating by anticipation a possible single view of himself —such as the authorial view, for example—whose partial truthfulness he nevertheless painfully recognizes.

A monologic author would have directly signified Quentin's ambivalence in his own threshold situation actually stating his hero's awareness of the fact that the past is more real to him than the present; that the concrete door which he now physically perceives among other objects of his present life (gasoline, the vest), all illusory, make him think of another door (by which his beloved sister, whom he is sure to have wronged, stood before disappearing forever), then of another door (Door), the ultimate door at the threshold of his destiny (suicide). Instead, the author multiplies the instances of Quentin's discourse through several signifiers among which the principal ones are:

1. *a lexical signifier: door,* which remains the same, appearing either with or without the definite article—a device designed to bestow upon the object at least two situational associations between which the "I" is split;

2. *a graphic signifier: Door,* where the capital letter introduces a third object which it turns into a symbol (of death);

3. *a grammatical signifier:* the present tense supplied to a situation in the past, connoting a feeling of reality, coupled with the past tense applied to a present situation, connoting a feeling of unreality, with death (*Door*) tied to the former, of course.

All these devices used to produce a *vertical* fragmentation of discourse (along the axis of significance) turn the discourse itself into an *idea,* rather than, as traditional narrative tends to do, turning an idea (*horizontally,* along a linear chain) into discourse. At the reception end—whatever the particular interpretation of this ambivalent idea (Freudian, Marxist)—the reading will always respect the vertical organization of syntactic relationships.

It will now be easy to demonstrate that the single word *door* constitutes a more solid bridge between Faulkner's two novels, as it recurs in *Absalom, Absalom!* through Quentin Compson's habitual self-conscious strategy, than does the *sameness* of his name, the similarity of his circumstances (for instance, his departure from the South and his life at Harvard), the compatibility of members of his family (Mr. Compson as skeptical and sensitive as ever) or his more general environment (Shreve as arrogant in his appreciation of the quaint South and as loyal a friend to Quentin as ever).

It is worth noting in this connection that strict referential compatibility is not always respected by Faulkner, who in his polyphonic narratives might have, and rightly so, paid less attention to the zone of reference than to that of significance. And so for instance, in *Absalom, Absalom!* Quentin and Shreve seem to share the same room, whereas *The Sound and the Fury* clearly indicates that each has his own ("through the wall I heard Shreve's bedsprings and then his slippers on the floor hishing" [73]). A simple slip of the pen or a deliberate error supposed to suggest how little importance details of this sort possess? Of course, between the time represented in *Absalom, Absalom!* and that, somewhat later, represented in *The Sound and the Fury,* the two friends could have ceased to be roommates and become neighbors. Such a detail could in fact have a certain informing value in a reading which accepts a situation of latent homosexuality between the two young men, suggested by a third one named Spoade. Such a state of affairs could moreover be projected upon an implicitly similar one possibly existing between Henry Sutpen and Charles Bon.

Another possible slip on the part of Faulkner—concerning a young black boy called Luster—considerably worries a number of scholars. One of Roskus's and Dilsey's four children in *The Sound and the Fury,* Luster helps his mother mind the retarded Compson boy, Benjy. We learn moreover that on April 8, 1928 (section 4) Luster was just beginning to learn to drive the surrey drawn by the docile mare Queenie. *Absalom, Absalom!* on the other hand, assures us that during a period which must be situated prior to 1909 Luster, again a very young man and Quentin's former playmate, handles horses with great mastery on a rainy day and in muddy soil at the cemetary where he drove Mr. Compson and his son just before the latter's departure for Harvard. While it is perfectly legitimate to speculate on the incompatibility of Luster's traits as he "passes" from *The Sound and the Fury* to *Absalom, Absalom!,* it is perhaps just as legitimate to suggest that a possibly deliberate act of sabotage committed by Faulkner through Luster on the body of his realia system might represent a metafictional authorial comment on the relative unimportance in polyphonic fiction of objectively verifiable data.[8]

Without denying the semantic weight, in the Yoknapatawpha series, of "realistically" recurrent items of specific information—a massive *signified invariant*—I venture to propose *signified variants,* such as the *door,* as a more reliable type of recurrence, at least for the polyphonic texts of the series. Thanks to this single word's high degree of contextual mobility it becomes the truly trustworthy though ambiguous *signifier of the invariant,* whatever the latter contains beside Quentin himself.

As Miss Rosa Coldfield's powerfully dialogic confession draws to its end in chapter 5 of *Absalom, Absalom!* the general narrator may be temporarily identified with Quentin, at least according to the formal appear-

ances of his discourse, a "substituted direct discourse," as Bakhtin/Vološi-
nov calls it.[9] In a key sentence the general narrator takes up the word
door, applying it presumably to the shut door—a typical threshold again
—against which the old maid stumbles at Sutpen's Hundred. Miss Coldfield's access is forbidden, first to the stairs, then to the landing, finally to
the room where lies the body of the illicit lover, Charles Bon, as is her own
access to love definitively forbidden because of Thomas Sutpen's violent
death. "But Quentin was not listening, because there was also something
which he too could not pass—that door, the running feet on the stairs
beyond it almost a continuation of the faint shot, the two women, the
negress and the white girl" (*AA,* 172).

That door! We are clearly in the presence of an object already known
to the reader: the shut door behind Charles Bon's corpse, of course. As he
revives in his mind "brother and sister [Henry, after killing Charles, and
Judith], curiously alike as if the difference in sex had merely sharpened the
common blood," Quentin apparently also lends his ear to Miss Coldfield's
last words, which reproduce the dramatic dialogue between brother and
sister:

> *Now you cant marry him.*
> *Why cant I marry him?*
> *Because he's dead.*
> *Dead?*
> *Yes. I killed him.*
> He (Quentin) couldn't pass that. He was not even listening to her
> (*AA,* 172).

What couldn't Quentin pass? That door again? And another door perhaps? We have here, as in large segments of the second section of *The
Sound and the Fury,* a classical example of autocommunication. It is in fact
the *intra*textual autocommunication of Quentin Compson's internal dialogue in *The Sound and the Fury* that makes the emergence of *inter*textual
autocommunication possible here.

The notion of autocommunication, borrowed from Iuri Lotman, adds
to Jakobson's famous diagram of communication another diagram which
points out the more seldom encountered existence of another itinerary the
message may take when a shift of context changes the initial code into
a different one (sometimes a "secret" code) and produces a second message which, as it reaches the addressee, identifies him with the speaker

("I" → "I"): the speaker and the addressee both undergo a contextual shift (*sdvig*, in the Russian original), creator of the new code by which the initial message is modified without itself disappearing. At the syntagmatic level asemantic segments are formed. A highly organized though asemantic discourse can be conducted. In such a discourse stress is put on its syntagmatic organization; the stricter the latter, the freer and more associative the semantic relationships become.

That door in *Absalom, Absalom!* illustrates intertextual autocommunication in which a hardly noticeable contextual shift to *The Sound and the Fury* produces an interference within a two-word syntagma. *That door* now belongs to two contexts, but the recognition of this fact is limited to those readers who ("I"), like Quentin Compson ("I"), possess not only the knowledge of the first code, but also an inkling of the second. The first contains an earlier part of Miss Rosa's confession, where the significance of the door at the top of a staircase is established for herself and, potentially also, for a half-listening Quentin, as an object which in the minds of both characters as well as in the minds of the characters conjectured by the reconstructed story (Charles-Judith-Henry) carries a symbolic meaning of a very complex, doubly overlapping, erotic situation. The second code relates to *The Sound and the Fury*.

Naturally, all the characters in *Absalom, Absalom!* other than Quentin are excluded from the second code. This exclusion even applies to the general narrator (whose total substitution for Quentin now seems doubtful) and may go as far as to give the illusion of affecting the author himself. Quentin Compson becomes for a moment the true author of both novels, sharing an intimate knowledge about himself with the readers (*AA* and *SF*) behind the author's (*AA*) back.

Readers excluded from the "contract" of intertextual autocommunication (that is, excluded from the game) may feel the sudden suspension of the referential function as an asemantic operation (= an arbitrary paradigmatic substitution). They will go back with relief to "the two women, the negress and the white girl [Clytie and Judith]" who, returning the discourse without ambiguity to the initial code, send the message back to the initial context of *Absalom, Absalom!*

For various reasons, which range from mystification to a simple joke, novelists frequently refer to their earlier works by availing themselves of hardly perceptible devices of intertextual autocommunication. Faulkner's ambiguous *door* may be one way of establishing a special kind of complicity with the readers of his "difficult" novels or, on the contrary, a way of chastizing the reader of *Absalom, Absalom!* for not having read *The Sound and the Fury* or for having read it inattentively.

Whatever the case, the initial relationship between signifier and signified is recovered at the end of chapter 5 in *Absalom, Absalom!* Had Faulkner let it go at that, we could easily slide over the operation without taking into account any shifts in meanings (other than those which exist for *AA* alone). But the author goes further. Two pages later, taking up the same narrative instance (the account of the general narrator, seemingly identified with Quentin), he transfers the same statement to another spatiotemporal situation (Harvard), where Quentin is faced with a world he anticipates as hostile, or at least insensitive, to the southern ethos. Quentin will now have to deal not only with Shreve's flippant interpretations, but also with the general narrator's recontextualized, North-oriented challenge.

The passage in question appears after the reading of the first half of Mr. Compson's letter announcing Miss Rosa Coldfield's death. It is immediately preceded by five short sentences torn out of Quentin's crypto-discourse—"*Tell about the South. What's it like there. What do they do there. Why do they live there. Why do they live at all*"—a sample of a highly concentrated polylogue maintained by Quentin with the mutually intersecting voices to which is added the voice of his own self-conscious anticipation of Shreve's (hostile?) instigation with regard to Quentin and his curious, "exotic" southern culture, possibly also the narrator's newly acquired tongue-in-cheek attitude toward southern problems.

As the narrator now begins to probe into the hero's past—in an almost satirical manner which Quentin had foreseen with some apprehension —he quickly proves unequal to the dialogic task. The hero has probably never viewed his personal drama (*SF*) in the narrator's terms of a ceremonious aestheticism which clashes with his own image of Caddy placed upon the ultimate threshold of her destiny. The narrator's excessively deliberate decorum, penetrating the demonstrative pronoun, "*that* door," defies Quentin's own feelings which are now hurt by an indiscreet and unjustified connivance with the reader, and which the narrator sets forth as a purely "external" observer ("that gaunt [. . .] face"), one whose knowledge of Quentin's tragedy is limited to its inessential aspects. The passage clearly begins within the context of *Absalom, Absalom!*, evoking Quentin's imminent departure with Miss Coldfield for Sutpen's Hundred, only to slide imperceptibly into the context of *The Sound and the Fury:*

that very September evening when Mr Compson stopped talking at last, he (Quentin) walked out of his father's talking at last because it was now time to go, not because he had heard it all because he had not been listening, *since he had something which he still was unable to pass: that door,* that gaunt tragic dramatic self-hypnotized youthful face like the tragedian in a college play, an academic Hamlet waked from some trancement of the curtain's falling and blundering across the dusty stage from which the rest of the cast had departed last Commencement, the sister facing him across the wedding dress which she was not to use, not even to finish, the two of them slashing at one another with twelve or fourteen words and most of these the same words repeated two or three times so that when you boiled it down they did it with eight or ten. (*AA,* 174, italics mine)

Here the initial intertextual autocommunication (quoted above) is now enlarged by a narrator boastful of his knowledge of Quentin's intimate problem, so much so that he can lend it a highly elaborate theatrical metaphor. The narrator's bragging impunity is reinforced in the new intratextual context (Harvard) by the somewhat commiserating flippancy which according to the hero the northern world displays toward him and which the narrator seems—or pretends—to share. Armed with a superiority of the monologic type, the narrator "takes advantage" of the hero's thus weakened position to put him into finished form, canceling his polyphonic open-endedness. But as he enlarges his field of knowledge and authority, convinced of sharing them with the other participants in the system of intertextual autocommunication, he fails to suspect that in so doing he has set off a real dialogue in which Quentin becomes the interpreter, perhaps even the judge, of the narrator whose presentation appears to him offensive and inadequate.

The narrator's challenge is, then, unworthy of a dialogic hero who refuses to let a monologic *other* extract from him acquiescence to a brutal judgment ("an academic Hamlet" and other ungenerous epithets determined by a global and finished worldview). The hero boldly refuses the narrator's invitation to a referential collaboration which he regards as unjustified, insulting, presumptuous. He will not allow the narrator to define him from outside or reduce him metaphorically to provincial hamletism. He forces the narrator to "mind his own business" by returning to Miss Coldfield and her preparations to set out in Quentin's company on her own ultimate venture. A venture for which, incidentally, the narrator is also inadequately equipped.

As for Quentin, he will wait for another, one like himself capable of engaging in a search for self-awareness through dialogue, the kind of "invisible other" or "hypothetical interlocutor" that Dostoyevsky insisted upon, another self perhaps, creator of a "fantastic" instance emanating from an area outside all denoted discourse, and whose voice sounds as if it were that of his other self: he will wait for Charles Bon and Henry Sutpen to speak to him of *sister*.

It is, then, without the aid of any general or auxiliary narrator that Quentin Compson listens to Charles Bon's written statement to Judith which his own groping hands that "now nothing *can* see" and his nose that "*could* see gasoline, the vest on the table, the door," have by contamination perhaps contributed to making temporally self-contradictory: "*I do not add, expect me. Because I cannot say when to expect me. Because what* WAS *is one thing, and now it is not because it is dead, it died in 1861, and therefore what* IS [. . .] *I cannot say when to expect me. Because what* IS *is something else again because it was not even alive then*" (*AA*, 131).

By the time this statement comes to the reader's knowledge it is already modified by Judith's overlapping comment which reshuffles the relationship between the two contrasting grammatical signifiers sufficiently in order not only to attenuate the skepticism of Bon's last words about himself and about the place of the world in his consciousness at the threshold of his ultimate disaster—"something, something that might make a mark on something that *was* once for the reason that it can die someday while the block of stone can't be *is* because it never can become *was*" (*AA*, 127–28, italics mine)—but also to "mobilize" Quentin's last metaphorization of metonymy by implanting, upon her own version of the *was/is* issue, his last words internally pronounced at the threshold of his own, somewhat similar disaster: "The peacefullest words. Peacefullest words. *Non fui. Sum. Fui. Non sum.* Somewhere I heard bells once. Mississippi or Massachusetts. I was. I am not. Massachusetts or Mississippi" (*SF*, 157).

May one be allowed to regard Quentin's hypothetical interference within an entirely extrareferential grammatical code, which only those three characters share ("I"), as an intertextual extension of the intratextual autocommunication between Charles Bon ("I") and Judith Sutpen ("I") in a polyphonic hereafter?

NOTES

1. See my following papers: "Absalon et Absalon," *Langues Modernes* 1 (1974): 1–24; "La contestation du jugement sur pièces chez Dostoïevski et Faulkner," *Delta* 3 (1976): 47–62; "Faulkner et le fratricide. Pour une théorie des titres dans la littérature," *Etudes Anglaises* 3 (1977): 329–36; "Texte-contexte-prototexte-métatexte," *Tréma* 2 (1978): 35–44; "Satire et autorité narrative," *Revue Française d'Etudes Américaines* 4 (1978): 50–55; "William Gass: Instances de la stylisation," *Delta* 8 (1979): 65–85; "Rosie Coldfield et Vanka Karamazov. Le diminutif au service de l'ambivalence," *Revue de Littérature Comparée* 3 (1979): 311–22; "Le héros extensible," First International Faulkner Conference, University of Paris VII, 1980; "A Polyphonic Insert: Charles's Letter to Judith," Second International Faulkner Conference, University of Paris VII, 1982 (forthcoming).

2. Even as great a monologic hero as Don Quixote is defined in his folly on the strength of the author's word, authorial appreciation of the folly's possible wisdom or desirability notwithstanding.

3. It may be interesting to note that one of the secondary characters in *Absalom, Absalom!* (*AA*), Wash Jones, Sutpen's loyal "poor white" who will end up by killing his master and is treated monologically in the novel, appears endowed with dialogic features in an earlier work, the short story "Wash" (1931), of which he is the principal character.

4. Bakhtin (1936–38 and 1937–38) distinguishes between these two zones and speaks of a possible invasion of the authorial zone by the character zone.

5. It seems that only a monologic character possesses the necessary equipment directly to enter an extraliterary universe of myth.

6. See, for instance, Cleanth Brooks, 318.

7. Bakhtin (1929–63) insists on the "threshold" situation prevalent in the presentation of all the heroes, and even some minor characters, in Dostoyevsky's novels. Instead of evolving through biographical stages, as characters normally do in traditional nineteenth-century fiction, Dostoyevsky's characters appear as fully developed, ideologically committed yet wavering individuals, placed on the threshold of an event of ultimate significance, like murder (inflicting murder or being murdered), suicide, insanity. I might add that, if on some occasions they do take time to die calmly in bed, as Tolstoy's heroes often do, they are made to do so in order to satisfy the author's parodic needs (e.g., the old Verkhovensky in *The Possessed*). The frequency of "threshold" characters in Faulkner's work is considerable.

8. Luster naturally passes unnoticed in the necessarily schematic analyses of the semiotic study of Faulkner's universe by Sorin Alexandrescu. A secondary character in *The Sound and the Fury* (*SF*) and *AA*, the young black boy does not appear on Alexandrescu's "table of roles" (314–15). Among more traditional scholars Cleanth Brooks speculates on the possibility of two different characters

both named Luster (472), while, according to the French translator of *SF,* Maurice Edgar Coindreau, Luster, unlike Frony, Versh, and T. P., is not Roskus's and Dilsey's child, but grandchild through Frony, who would thus be his mother (8). None of such speculations yields total representational compatibility.

9. "Substituted direct discourse" occurs when the author's rhetoric and that of the hero merge "and we get protracted passages that belong simultaneously to the author's narrative and to the hero's internal (though sometimes also external) speech [. . .]. If the personal pronoun 'he' were changed everywhere to 'I', and if the verb forms were adjusted accordingly, no dissonance or incongruity, whether in style or otherwise, would result" (Bakhtin, 138–39).

BIBLIOGRAPHY

Alexandrescu, Sorin. *Logique du personnage. Réflexions sur l'univers faulknérien.* Tours: Mame, 1974.
Bakhtin, Mikhail (V. N. Vološinov). *Marxism and the Philosophy of Language* [1929]. Translated from the Russian by Ladislav Matejka and I. R. Titunik. New York and London: Seminar Press, 1973.
———. *Problems of Dostoevsky's Poetics (Problemy poètiki Dostoevskogo* [1963], modified version of *Problemy tvorčestva Dostoevskogo* [1929]). Translated by R. W. Rotsel. Ann Arbor: Ardis, 1973. Also translated by Caryl Emerson. Minneapolis: University of Minnesota Press, 1984.
———. "Slovo v romane," "Discourse in the Novel." In *The Dialogic Imagination,* edited by Michael Holquist, translated by Caryl Emerson and M. Holquist, 259–422. Austin: University of Texas Press, 1981.
———. "Formy vremeni i xrononotopa v romane" (1975). In *The Dialogic Imagination,* 84–258.
Brooks, Cleanth. *William Faulkner: The Yoknapatawpha Country.* New Haven: Yale University Press, 1963.
Clark, Katerina, and Michael Holquist. *Mikhail Bakhtin.* Cambridge: Harvard University Press, 1984.
Coindreau, Maurice Edgar. Preface to *Le bruit et la fureur,* his translation of *The Sound and the Fury.* Paris: Gallimard, 1931.
Faulkner, William. *The Sound and the Fury.* New York: Cape and Smith, 1929.
———. *As I Lay Dying.* New York: Cape and Smith, 1930.
———. *Sanctuary.* New York: Cape and Smith, 1931.
———. "Wash." In *These Thirteen.* New York: Cape and Smith, 1931.
———. *Absalom, Absalom!* New York: Random House, 1936.
———. *Requiem for a Nun.* New York: Random House, 1951.
Holquist, Michael. See Clark, Katerina.

Lotman, Iuri. "O dvux model'ax kommunikatsii v sisteme kul'tury." In *Sèméi-otixè. Sbornik po vtoričnym modeliruiuščim sistemam,* 227–43. Festschrift for Mikhail Bakhtin. Estonia, U.S.S.R.: Tartu University, 1973.

Vološinov, V. N. See Bakhtin, Mikhail.

Peter Taylor's "Porte Cochère":

The Geometry of Generation

SIMONE VAUTHIER

There is something slightly baffling about the reception of Peter Taylor. As one critic put it, his place "in modern fiction is secure." His craftsmanship, in particular, is widely acknowledged but has received little critical attention. It is praised for its "purity," "quietness," "austerity," qualities that too often partake of the ineffable; in the words of Gene Baro, Peter Taylor "writes so simply and powerfully he seems scarcely to be exercising his craft."[1] Surely the ways in which the writer exercises his craft in order to create the illusion that he is not doing so deserve to be investigated. Peter Taylor himself, when speaking of his stories, stresses the element of deliberate construction that goes into their making. In one interview, he declared that he had "worked some stories out just the way you'd work out a theorem," and offered "Venus, Cupid, Folly and Time" as an example of his method.[2] Criticism ought to take the hint and attempt —at its own level and with its various tools—to "work out the stories systematically."[3] This paper is intended as a modest start to a reexamination of Peter Taylor's fiction which will depart from the usual thematic approaches.

Rather than "Venus, Cupid, Folly and Time," "Porte Cochère" will serve as my exemplum of what the author calls his "more schematic stories."[4] Though not so well known, this early story has the advantage of being shorter and easier to encompass within the scope of an essay. Even so, I make no claim to any sort of completeness in the present study. Here I investigate the story from the angle of spatial scheme and will not deal, for instance, with narrational processes except where they are relevant to the spatial approach.

At the threshold of the story, the title is an "Open Sesame," which enables us to enter the fictional world through a semantic code. Since like any door a porte cochère both delimits and links two areas, the phrase evokes the opposition outside/inside. In fact, better than any other door, it ties together a nexus of spatial relationships: insofar as it usually implies another entrance, and has to be located in relation to this, it brings in the opposition left versus right (horizontality); insofar as it denotes a carriage entrance going through a building, it sets up a double polarity of up above and down under (verticality) and of front versus back (prospectivity).[5] As a door involves a passing through, the phrase "porte cochère" strongly implies the larger category of directionality, and it clues us not simply into the semantics but into the syntax of the story to come.

Furthermore, as a synecdoche, the porte cochère connotes a certain kind of house, large and substantial, and as a metonym, a certain kind of life. Thus to any reader already familiar with the work of Peter Taylor, the title immediately relates to the author's fictional world, in which the house is "the central, the prismatic symbol,"[6] so that we can guess that the "topic space" (Greimas), the space of transformations, will be the inside rather than the outside of the house that boasts a porte cochère. As a lexical item, porte cochère is also arresting. A French phrase, it has been adopted into English to the extent that it is listed in dictionaries; yet it is not wholly anglicized and still often flaunts its foreign grave accent. Thus the word, though unambiguous, is not so transparent (if indeed words ever are) as an English equivalent would be. The title therefore has a "defamiliarizing" impact: it does not simply convey information, it draws attention to itself and to its linguistic status. The effect is not counteracted but, rather, strengthened when we are told in the second paragraph of the story that "porte cochère" was Mrs. Brantley's expression, Ben Brantley, the protagonist, and his children preferring for their part the more vernacular "drive-under." Since two phrases are used to denote the same object, more must be in question in the text than their fictional referent. The translation emphasizes the link between the phrase and its speaker, its connotative value for a particular locutor; or, to look at the problem from another angle, the double nomination draws attention to the relativity implied in a subject's perception and/or construction of his or her environment.

The warning is all the more needed because the short story builds the fictional space largely through the focus of perception of Old Ben. To summarize it briefly, "Porte Cochère" explores an elderly man's state of mind as he waits out in his study the half-hour before his birthday dinner party, for which his children have gathered from various parts of the country.

In this restricted time, Old Ben shifts from a complacent projection of himself as an undemanding liberal father to a realization of his devious possessiveness and tyranny and eventually to an acting-out of his inner rage against his children. The story is told by an undramatized narrator in external focalization.[7] But the narrator deprives himself of the freedom and scope which such a position normally entails by focalizing his narrative fairly strictly on Ben Brantley, and by choosing to see him from within. Thus he can present the narrated world as the focalized character turned focalizer perceives it. The spatial indications which we are given create the fictional character at the same time as they create the fictional world.

THE CONSTRUCTION OF SPACE

In fact, as gradually appears, Old Ben is involved in the construction of his space in more ways and on more levels than his present immobility and passivity would lead us to expect. Certainly, at first, he seems merely the point of reference around which the description of the various fictional loci can be organized: "Old Ben kept listening for Cliff's voice above the others. They were all down on the octagonal side porch, which, under its red tile roof, looked like a pagoda there on the side lawn. Old Ben was in his study" (7). The invisible observer, building a system of localizations ("down," "there") in relation to the place occupied by the old man, gives it a sort of self-evident quality, although the room itself is only named, as an afterthought, with the last word of the last paragraph. Then increasingly, as the narrator makes Ben the focus of perception, the character functions as a "discursive subject" through whose selective focalization a space is projected and produced.[8] Ben Brantley, "seventy-six and nearly blind" (388), might be considered an inadequate post of observation. Yet, if he cannot see through the walls and focuses only vaguely on those objects he can perceive, he is able at least to hear and interpret the noises that reach him and, perhaps more important, he *wants to know* what is going on in the house. "Old Ben could recognize Cliff's leave-taking and the teasing voices of the others, and then he heard Cliff's footsteps on the cement driveway, below the study—a hurried step. He heard Cliff in the side hall and then his footsteps at the bottom of the stairs" (389). The layout of the house—and the important fact that the study is above the driveway—becomes clearer to the reader, as do Ben's relation to his surroundings and his propensity to eavesdrop. The spatial indications provided are narratively motivated and authenticated because they enter into the cognitive program of the character which produces them (and is produced by them).

Given the choice of focalization, the extent of the area where the action takes place is of necessity very limited. With one exception no glimpse is afforded of the whole house. (The only view that is offered—introduced by the narrator-focalizer, though it could also contain a mental image emanating from the character—interestingly juxtaposes inside and outside, grounds and house: "he seemed to peer between the open draperies and through the pane of the upper sash, out into the twilight of the wide, shady park that stretched from his great yellow brick house to the Pike" [393]. The expanse of the park, the building material and its color, the Nashville location, all confirm what the reader had surmised: this is indeed a substantial house.) The study receives a good deal of attention but never in the form of a set description; the windows, the quality of light in the room when the draperies are drawn, the umbrella stand and the old-fashioned radio, such things are called up in the narration when they come under the notice of the character. Otherwise, the house exists only as a collection of loci, the side porch, the hall, the living room, the stairs. Rather than described, these are simply located in relation to one another: "the octagonal side porch which was beyond the porte cochère," "His study was above the porte cochère," "the cement driveway below the study," and so on. It will be seen that a double system of reference is operating here, according roughly to whoever is the focus of perception, the narrator-focalizer or the character. Whether focalized by the narrator or Ben, these other parts of the house, after the first expository paragraphs, are mentioned only as the character is made aware of them.

But the protagonist, intent on his cognitive program, is also led to remember other places. The strange quality of light in his study affects him: "For one moment, he felt that his eyes or his glasses were playing him some new trick. Then he dropped his head on the chair back, for the strange quality now seemed strangely familiar, and now no longer strange —only familiar. It was like the light in that cellar where long ago, he used to go to fetch Mason jars for Aunt Nelson" (389). One space calls up another space and another time. But this is no nostalgic dwelling on the past. Ben remembers how his aunt used to send for him all across town and "made him whistle the whole time he was down in the cellar, to make certain he didn't drink her wine," though he was but ten or twelve. The memory of the cellar leads him back to the present through the evocation of yet another space: "Where Aunt Nelson's house had been, the Trust Company now stood—a near-skyscraper. Her cellar, he supposed, had been in the space now occupied by the basement barbershop—not quite so deep or so large as the shop, its area without boundaries now, suspended in the center of the barbershop, where the ceiling fan revolved" (389). In Ben's mind, the two spaces coexist but, let it be noted, not the two times, and Aunt Nelson's cellar is now a ghostly area. Later he will recollect not the lost cellar but the present shop: "Old Ben's eyes, behind the smoked lenses, were closed, and he was visualizing the ceiling fan in the barbershop" (393). That he does not grieve over the destroyed place is already suggested in the word "visualizing," which here implies *vouloir-voir,* some sort of voluntary action. The associative train of his ideas immediately confirms the suggestion. "Presently, opening his eyes" —incidentally, the closing and opening of his near-blind eyes is itself most suggestive—"he reflected, almost with a smile, that his aunt's cellar was not the only Nashville cellar that had disappeared. Many a cellar!" (393) One lost place calling up another, he now remembers his father's cellar, "round like a dungeon" because it "had been a cistern in the very earliest days" (393). The memories lodged within that remembered space are much more traumatic than those linked to Aunt Nelson:[9] a more expanded flashback shows that descending into the cistern on a ladder was frightening to the boy, as "his father's voice, directing him, would seem to go around and around the brick walls and then come back with a hollow sound, as though the cistern were still half full of water" (393). One day, "in his fright at the very thought of water," he drops the lantern, which goes "whirling and flaming to the brick floor, which Ben had never before seen" (393). Though the flames quickly die out, his incensed father beats him mercilessly. The incident is told with a wealth of details, many of them concerned with spatial objects—notably walls.

Thus Old Ben is made responsible for the projection of a double space, an actual, immediately observable space and a recollected, absent space, which is itself composed of various places, including the present barbershop. (This, of course, enlarges the potential volume of the fictional space.) Because of Ben's role as the discursive subject, the actual and the mental spaces share many common features even though they are intended to stand in contrast to one another. Neither the present nor the past houses are evoked as living wholes. They are synecdochally or metonymically represented. The aunt's house is reduced to its cellar, the father's to the cistern, the porch, the carriage house, the kitchen window, and the yard with its big shade trees. Ben's house is actualized in slightly more detail but remains a collection of discrete, albeit related, loci. The places which Ben is mostly aware of are not, with the exception of the study, living rooms in the etymological sense. The Brantley children talk animatedly on the porch, the final confrontation with their father takes place on the staircase just as Ben had to confront his father's angry face over the rim of the cistern. Such areas are in-between areas, partaking of both inside and outside qualities, setting up a problematics of inside versus outside. They are transit places in which one never stays for long, however deeply Ben's expeditions into the two cellars have stamped his personality. Since the remembered places are located underground, and the actual places are above it but at different levels, verticality also becomes a prominent feature which, however, qualifies as much the position of the actors in the family scenes as the places themselves.

It is precisely the position of the actors which makes for the main contrast between the two spatial systems and can be said to account for the thymic quality of each, as we shall see in a moment.[10] But the characters' placing is first indicated in the neutral terms of the spots they happen to occupy. Thus while the Brantley children are *down* on the side porch, their father sits in his study *above* the porte cochère: their position is inferior and lateral. Moreover, Ben's study "open(s) off the landing halfway up the stairs," and is "not part of the second floor" (388). So, clearly, it is not only in a superior location but it is *aside* from the main or communal part of the house. From the very beginning, the distribution of the different parts of the house and of the characters in the fictional space shows that father and children, on this family occasion, are not really reunited and that even if the study is the focal point where the protagonist sits and registers the sounds that tell him what his children are doing, it cannot be thought of as the center of the house. In fact, although the house exists as the virtual surrounding of the study, it is never presented as a concentric area; on the contrary, the off-center placement of the few other parts that are mentioned is constantly underlined. As a consequence, the focalized focalizer's centrality appears as a narrative strategy which emphasizes his egocentricity but raises questions as to his role in his family. Now this off-sidedness contrasts with a recurring feature associated with the remembered places. Not that they are presented as central but, being repositories of food and drink, they are, perhaps, more directly related to the ongoing life in the respective houses, and strikingly they both carry circular associations. The father's cellar is "round like a dungeon"—a comparison which, of course, introduces suggestions of medieval tyranny and a two-fold male-female symbolism—and it has "circular shelves" (393). The aunt's is more conventionally rectangular but, in its ghostly state, it is associated both with centrality and circularity, being now "suspended in the center of the barbershop, where the ceiling fan revolve(s)," drawing another invisible circle (389). As a child, Ben willy-nilly had to go down into these underground places, while adults, listening like the aunt or looking at him like the father, kept close watch over him from above. Now, in the present of reference of the story, the situation has been reversed, Old Ben, from a topographical position of superiority, keeps his children under surveillance.

With such remarks, we have already touched upon another function of Ben in the narrative, one indeed that imposes itself more readily perhaps on the reader's attention. Being the protagonist, he is naturally an "actant," to whose actions we tend to pay attention. As it happens, the narrative program in which he is engaged has much to do with space. Before we examine this aspect of the narrative, we may note how the fictional space envisaged as a set of attributes already appears as an elaborate development of the polarities encapsulated in the compound noun of the title. In addition, the deployment of spatial indications around and/or through the character, the juxtaposition of loci with a different ontological status, the oppositions and parallels created—all contribute to the construction, together with the fictional space, of a number of connected themes—the interdependence of space and consciousness, the reciprocal definition of related places, the possibility of spatial change and variable topology, the temporal dimension of space. And, of course, the emblematic virtualities of spatial placement.

THE ACTOR'S USE OF SPACE

In the present of the story, apart from taking possession of his surroundings through hearing, Old Ben is the subject of two narrative programs. In the past, he was similarly involved in two programs, which, though they are not granted the same narrative volume, nicely balance the present ones, all the more nicely, indeed, since the narration embeds the former into the latter. The first program starts fairly early when Ben hears Clifford, his favorite son, leave his brothers and sisters. Sitting apart from the family circle by his own choice (he needs a nap and also finds

Laura Nell's "chatter" "particularly taxing and obnoxious" [388]), Ben is not content with his present isolation. He "longed to have Cliff come and talk to him about whatever he would" (390). The operative word here is "come," not talk. For "whatever Cliff was thinking about—his law, his golf, or *his wife and children*—would be of no real interest to Old Ben" (389–90, emphasis added). If he longs for his son's presence, he does so precisely at the moment when Clifford hurries up the stairs to go and write a letter to his wife. Ben's objective is to get his son into his study, thereby capturing his attention. Thus his first action, his calling out to Clifford, "almost despite himself," that the news will be on in a few minutes, is a matter of *proxemics*. It is not enough for Old Ben to know that his son is in the house: Clifford must be induced to come inside his own personal space. The development of the scene shows indeed that conversational exchange is not the desired end but rather the means to ensure that Clifford will first enter the study, then remain there. When Cliff claims he must go and write Sue Alice, "Old Ben felt that he didn't need good sight to detect his son's ill-concealed haste to be off and away" (390). So, enticement having failed, he tries aggressive baiting:

> Cliff had, in fact, turned back to the stairs when Old Ben stopped him with a question, spoken without expression and almost under his breath.
> "Why did you come at all? Why did you even bother to come if you weren't going to bring Sue Alice and the children? Did you think I wanted to see you without them?" (390)

Then he resorts to taunts and even to a form of blackmail, declaring that he is "not going to the club or anywhere else for supper," as is the family tradition on his birthday (391). In the battle of wills between father and son, Ben's victories are marked by Clifford's replies; even when the latter loses some of his self-control and tells his father, "Don't be so damned childish" (391), Ben avails himself of the opportunity to pursue the conversation: "I'm getting childish, am I, Clifford?" Upon which Clifford indulges in a lengthy analysis of his father's character. But Ben's victories (and occasional defeats) are also marked by Cliff's physical moves: "He stopped at the doorway" (victory); "he turned back to the stairs" (defeat); "he stopped with one foot on the first step of the second flight," "Clifford took several steps towards his father," "Clifford came even closer" (victories); "Clifford was turning away again" (new threat of defeat); "During his long speech he had advanced all the way across the room until he was directly in front of his father" (etc., 390–93). Clifford's bothering to reply is always a plus for Ben, who controls the exchange, but the young man's movements indicate his intentions and show more clearly that the battle is not easily won. On the whole, however, as Clifford advances into the study, he concedes more and more ground to his father. Ben, for his part, does not care to establish a real communication with his son. His only concern is to keep Clifford away from his room and writing table and to inveigle him into staying in the study. No matter how candid his son's part of the exchange becomes, Ben pays it only surface attention, as it were, because the only important thing is that their talk should not stop. When, provoked into saying a few home truths, Clifford asks a telling question, "What the hell do you want of us, Papa? I have thought about it a lot. Why haven't you ever asked for what it is you want? Or are we all blind and it's really obvious?" The old man does not trouble to answer and only enjoins him to go "write your spouse" (392). (Yet he will answer the question later, but when he makes his wishes known, his utterances, deprived of context, will not make sense to his children.) As a matter of fact, the deeper Clifford's emotional involvement in what he says to his father, the deeper his penetration of the study, and therefore the more satisfying the situation from the father's point of view. While Old Ben manipulates Clifford through words, verbal language is in fact simply an instrument the better to speak "the silent language" of proxemics.[11] And the message of this latent communication is, "I still am the Father, the master."

In the course of Clifford's expostulations, it appears that the silent language of proxemics has long been spoken between them, even if neither perhaps quite knows what it is all about. For the situation, Clifford notes, is a familiar one. When his father snaps that he is free to go, "You have all been free as the air, to come and go in this house," the son smiles: "Free to come and go, with you perched here on the landing registering every footstep on the stairs and every car that passed underneath. I used to turn off the ignition and coast through the drive-under, and then think how foolish it was, since there was no back stairway. No back stairway in a house this size! [. . .] And how like the old times this was, Papa—your listening in here in the dark when I came up!" (392). Although no reproach has been uttered, Clifford interprets the use which his father has made of their spatial environment, and the connotations of the drive-under come into full play in this passage.

In addition, the power play of the apparently helpless old man has a marked temporal dimension as well. Tactics are ever a question of space and timing. In this case, the whole episode starts with Ben's awareness of time: "It was almost time to begin getting ready for that expedition [to the club] now, and simultaneously with the thought of it and with the movement of his hand toward his watch pocket, he became aware that Clifford was taking his leave of the group on the side porch" (388–89). Throughout the meeting, he is conscious of time. "Old Ben held his watch in his hand, and he glanced down at it quickly" (391). "His fingers were folded over the face of the watch," he "slipped his watch back into his vest pocket nervously, then slipped it out again, constantly running his fingers over the gold case, as though it were a piece of money" (392). This byplay, however, stops when time ceases to matter because the interval which had to be bridged is now over. Old Ben interrupts Clifford in the midst of a tirade by moving in his turn: "Old Ben pushed himself up from the chair. He put his watch in the vest pocket and buttoned his suit coat with an air of satisfaction. 'I'm going along to the club for supper,' he said, 'since there's to be no-un here to serve me.' As he spoke, he heard the clock chiming the half hour downstairs" (392–93). His timing has been perfect. Because this revealing gesture and remark occur just as Clifford was attempting to express to his father and to himself the puzzling nature of their relationship, any doubt which a trusting reader might have entertained is dispelled: the father has engineered the confrontation so that he could while away the half-hour before supper time in an ego-gratifying manner. In order to kill time satisfactorily, he had to consume his son's time, and time, as the comparison between the gold watch and a coin reminds us, is money.

So far Old Ben's strategy has been successful. He has proved his competence in performing the program he had set himself—thus playing both Sender and Subject (Greimas). He has entrapped Clifford in a place and in a role—that of the Child of transactional analysis.[12] One is all the better reminded of Eric Berne's theories, since Clifford accuses his father of playing "sly games" with his children (392). In his part as Parent involved in a Crossed Transaction, instead of a transaction between Adults, Ben does not act the overbearing father, but in fact assumes the tolerant role of the benign father. He never gets indignant over Clifford's increasingly bitter accusations, he simply does not take them into consideration and can be said to sidestep the issue—and the relationship.

Before the narration comes to the second narrative program, which involves Ben in the present of reference, it introduces, by means of the two flashbacks, programs he had to engage in as a child. In both cases, the Sender is an adult dispatching the child on missions which require a change of space and are either boring or frightening. His recollections are of being ordered about. Aunt Nelson "would send for him all the way across town to fetch her Mason jars"; here, the distance between the two houses, the crossing of Nashville, are made to convey the unreasonableness of the aunt's demands. In his father's cellar, a similar chore exposes him to even greater ordeals, since the old cistern is intrinsically terrifying, the expedition more fraught with dangers, real and imaginary, and his callous authoritarian father ever ready to administer corporal punishment. The trials which the subject has to undergo in such places assign to them —and metonymically to the houses of which they are a part—a negative, dysphoric value. On the most fateful of his descents into the dungeonlike cellar, the memory of which still makes Old Ben draw back from the window "with a grimace" (393), the father's house appears as the locus of grievous power. When the lantern crashes to the floor, and sends up "yellow flames that momentarily lit the old cistern to its very top," the boy, looking upward, sees "the furious face of his father with the flames casting jagged shadows on the long, black beard and high, white forehead" (393). What with the contrast between yellow flames and shadows, black beard and white forehead, and the child's wish that "the flames might engulf him before he came within reach of those arms," the scene is reminiscent of hell. After the severe beating which he gets, Ben "remained for a long while standing with his face to the wall" then goes to the summerhouse —a place removed from the house. "There he had lain down on a bench, looked back at the house through the latticework, and said to himself that when he got to be a grown man, he would go away to another country, where there were no maple trees and no oak trees, no elms, not even sycamore and poplars; where there were no squirrels and no niggers, no houses that resembled this one; and most of all, where there were no children and no fathers" (394). The father as an individual has vanished from his son's thoughts but has been metonymically replaced by the house seen through latticework, which though denoting a typical building material may also connote something of the jail. The child has never found in the house *la coquille initiale,* the originary shell which offers those euphoric values of intimacy which Gaston Bachelard has so well analyzed.[13] Neither of the houses evoked in the flashbacks could have represented for the boy "le non-moi qui protège le moi," the non-I protecting the I. His childish desire, which makes him the Sender and the Subject of a fantasized program, is summed up in a double wish: to leave the familiar space in order to find another that would be different scenically, socially ("no niggers") and architecturally, *and* to be rid of family ties. The link between the two wishes is foregrounded in the juxtaposition of his simultaneous rejection of "houses that resembled this one" and of filial succession. Thus his fantasized program involves the transformation of space as a preliminary, if not a prerequisite, to the transformation of the world of generation.

Apparently, the adult has not left his region or even his hometown and he has got over his fear of family entanglements to the extent of fathering no less than five children. But the reader is made aware, even before the final recognition scene, that Ben has succeeded in transforming his immediate environment. The house in which he has raised his children and in which the present action unfolds is, in a sense, a counterhouse. Time could only destroy materially, indeed has destroyed, the hated environments of his childhood; his house does more than Time could insofar as it is a standing negation of the other places. As an actant, Sender, Subject, and—as we shall see—Receiver of his program, Ben has shaped a space in which he could be a different kind of father from his own father—which shows him to be a different kind of father. How different, however, is a matter of evaluation. As Ben boasts to Clifford, his children "have been as free as the air to come and go in this house" (392). In *his* view he has created a space of freedom.

The last narrative program in which he is involved results in a reevaluation of his space and his role. Now ready to go out to the club, Old Ben "stepped to the door" for the first time and "looked down the dark flight of steps at his four younger children" (394). Out of the shelter of his study, or almost out, he is in a new space which will prove the topic space of his new experience. For there he must confront his children: The four younger children "stood in a circle directly beneath the overhead light, which one of them had just switched on. Their faces were all turned upward in the direction of the open doorway where he was standing, yet he knew in reason that they could not see him there" (394–95). Though, looking down at them, he seems to be in his customary position of domination, his apartness and emotional isolation are indirectly shown in the contrast with his children's position. They stand "in a circle" "directly beneath the overhead light" so that the idea of the circle, a common metaphor for family life, is reinforced by the idea of the center that holds things together. While they stand in light, he is in darkness, looking at them through dark glasses. We are prepared for a change, moreover, because a link is established between Aunt Nelson's cellar and Ben's house through the iconic image of the circle defined by the overhead light. And though Ben is still in a position of domination, though he can dimly see them, he has to push away the idea that they can see him in their turn, which deprives him of his superiority as voyeur and eavesdropper and returns him to his childhood condition of being under surveillance. Though he can hardly distinguish their lowered voices, he is certain they are talking about him, certain that Clifford whom he can hear upstairs is thinking about him. This provokes an offended outburst: "Never once in his life had he punished or restrained them in any way. He had given them a freedom unknown to children in the land of his childhood, yet from the time they could utter a word they had despised him and denied his right to any affection or gratitude. Suddenly, stepping out onto the landing, he screamed down the stairs to them: 'I've a right to some gratitude!'" (395). Frustrated and feeling perhaps the need to make some connection, though it be only to claim his right rather than utter his desire, he shouts at the group what is in fact a belated answer to Clifford's earlier question, "What is it you want?" He wants, as he phrases it to himself, the affection and gratitude they have denied him, but characteristically he only demands gratitude, which must render his statement even more puzzling to his four younger children. Upon this, the children, at first stunned, start moving slowly toward the stairs while Clifford comes out into the upstairs hall. "The four children were advancing up the first flight, and Clifford was coming down from upstairs. Old Ben opened his mouth to call to them, 'I'm not afraid of you!' But his voice had left him" (395). Projecting his inner hostility against them he can only stand momentarily in fear of them. No longer the producer of spatial conditions, no longer the Subject of a program of which he is also the Sender and the Receiver, Old Ben perceives himself as the victim, the Object, of his children's aggression, expressed in their movement through the topic space.

The momentary fright triggers a flash of recognition: "in his fear that in their wrath his children would do him harm, he suddenly pitied them. He pitied them for all they had suffered at his hands. And while he stood there, afraid, he realized, or perhaps recalled, how he had tortured and plagued them in all the ways that his resentment of their good fortune had taught him to do" (395). In his self-awareness, he "even remember(s) the day when it had occurred to him to build his study above the drive-under and off the stairs, so that he could keep tabs on them. He had declared that he wanted his house to be as different from his father's house as a house could be, and so it was. And now he stood in the half darkness, afraid that he was a man about to be taken by his children and at the same time pitying them" (395). Ben realizes how he has used space and positions in space to torture his children mentally, though he has never abused them physically. He has manipulated space in order to gain some sort of power. The man Ben has enjoyed what the downtrodden child lacked, a location of superiority from which to control the members of his family. Thus he reproduces, by different means and without the physical harshness, the parental position as he symbolically remembers it, up above looking at, overseeing, the child down there. Until this moment of recognition, he has blinded himself to the role which he has ensured with his spatial arrangements. (Numerous references to his impaired vision and his dark glasses recur through the text.) Ben's preference for "drive-under" is not simply a liking for the more vernacular phrase; the expression really conveys what is the more or less hidden purpose of the drive-under, which is a means of domination and subordination.

Space, however, has betrayed him. The very layout that enabled him to spy upon his children now enables them to invest him from above and below. Just as his father's house was not safe for Ben the son, so now the house built to his own specifications is not safe for Ben the father.

Nor does the protagonist's flash of insight really lead to cathartic forgiveness, of self or of others. Significantly, the old man withdrew into his study, "closed the door and locked it," and then performed a belated acting out: "As the lock clicked, he heard Clifford say, 'Papa!' Then he heard them all talking at once, and while they talked he stumbled through the dark study to the umbrella stand. He pulled out the stick with his father's face carved on the head, and in the darkness, while he heard his children's voices, he stumbled about the room beating the upholstered chairs with the stick and calling the names of his children under his breath" (395). The foray into the area outside the study has failed to reunite him with his children for the family celebration of his birthday. But his retreat is not simply retrogression. Having regained the safe place where he has played voyeur for so many years, he resorts, on this occasion, to action. Having recognized in himself the unjust, oppressive father who exercises his authority over his children because they are his children, he now makes, vicariously, the paternal gesture of aggression, in a private ritual of repetition.

To sum up this part of my analysis, "Porte Cochère," for all that it deals with an almost motionless protagonist, is about changing space, and changing places, and also about the desire to change the world and the failure of this desire. Assuredly, no narrative can exist without reference to the spatial dimension, and fiction, as Ricardo Gullon has shown, is fundamentally a medium in which "absolute space is replaced by a context of changing space with precise functions." [14] Only in "Porte Cochère" this "context of changing space with precise functions" becomes the subject's narrative program. The hero's project has been to transform space, to shape it in order to position himself in it in such a way as to fulfill his inner needs. To this extent, spatialization can be said here to be an "intervention of the will" (Gullon), though this intervention is bound to the character's unconscious drives. Thus space appears to be the theme of the story as well as its shape. Or, rather, one of the story's themes. According to Greimas in *Sémiotique et sciences sociales,* we must regard "l'espace comme une forme susceptible de s'ériger en un langage spatial permettant de parler d'autre chose que de l'espace." [15] Even a thematics of space may, indeed, probably must, be the support of another thematics. One might, for instance, show that the many references to up versus down and to light versus darkness (features of the narrated loci that define the fictional space) support an axiology which indexes /up/ and /light/ positively, but since this does not depart from widely accepted valuations, it is not necessary to dwell on such an aspect of the narrative. One might more profitably demonstrate how the spatial language of the story enables the reader to construct an image of Ben which diverges from his early self-appraisal as a tolerant father who has treated his children as "equals" and approximates more closely his later self-image, without, however, coinciding with it entirely. On the one hand, the two topographical systems which establish the spatial lexicon of the narrative do not stand, as we have seen, in simple opposition. The present setting and the remembered places share some common features, in spite of their difference, so that Ben's world cannot be as unlike that of his father as he thinks. On the other hand, the spatial syntax of the story is deeply revealing of Ben's habitual strategy. In the course of the preceding developments, however, I have given enough examples of such functioning. It seems therefore more urgent to insist on what I shall call the geometry of the generational pattern.

THE GEOMETRY OF HUMAN RELATIONS

The theme of paternity is, needless to say, implemented through semantic clusters, figures, and narrative devices which are not always linked to space, but these, for one thing, do not function independently from the general context with its emphasis on space and placement. Furthermore, the temporal line of succession is itself spatialized. On the whole, therefore, the theme may be considered to be largely carried through the use of spatial elements.

Take, for example, the religious isotopy. Throughout the text a number of isolated items build a configuration that discreetly confers upon the father certain godlike attributes. First the comparison established between the octagonal side porch and a pagoda amplifies the symbolism of the octagon which Christianity inherited from the Greek tradition and which associates this geometric form with resurrection. Here, the children, gathered to celebrate their father's birthday, sit in the pagoda, while Ben from his study listens, a *deus absconditus,* to their talking, "his watery eyes focussed vaguely on the peak" of the red tile roof (a color the obvious realism of which does not mask its imperial and liturgical associations). Here, of course, the religious suggestions emanate from the spatial environment and the use the characters make of it. Since the house was conceived, if not designed, by Old Ben, the templelike structure reflects back on him in a new way. Another instance of religious imagery is to be found when Ben Junior teases his brother, "No letter written?" and Clifford answers him with a "Nope, no letter this day of Our Lord" (393). The old-fashioned turn of phrase, which clashes with the informal "Nope," transforms an obsolete way of dating into a joke against their almighty father. In this case, the religious allusion is playful, which is no reason for discounting it. Such scattered notes further enter into resonance with the gold watch insofar as gold is the metal of the gods. The byplay with the gold watch in the confrontation between Old Ben and Clifford, while serving as a narrative time-marker and as an index to Ben's motivation, gives to an object that is in itself highly symbolic a prominence that is arresting. Old Ben, fingering his watch, and devouring his son's time, becomes a trivialized, watered-down version of Kronos/Saturn, the god who devoured his children and became conflated with Chronos. I do not mean to intrude a mythological interpretation upon a text of such restrained elegance as "Porte Cochère," simply to say that, for this reader at least, the old gods that have symbolized the father-son relationship in Western culture hover in the intertext of Peter Taylor's story. On a different cultural plane, the devilish connotations that surround Old Ben's father develop further the religious isotopy and endow the paternal figure with similar power. Rounding off the religious paradigm, however, a latent metaphor deeply modifies the father image. This is even less obtrusive than the allusions to Father Time. Look at the narrator's description of Ben: "he stood motionless, at the window, his huge, soft hands held tensely at his side, his long body erect, his almost freakishly large head at a slight angle" (393). The hugeness, the posture, the freakishness, as well as the choice of words (singularly, "erect") make one think of a bear. (We may have been prepared for such a reading by his name, Old Ben, which is that of the bear in a famous story of Faulkner's.) A sacred animal in many parts of the world, regarded in several mythologies as the ancestor of mankind, the bear used to be feared and worshiped.[16] Thus, implicit as it is, the metaphor enhances the religious paradigm deployed through the story. The particular note it sounds (especially clear if one remembers "The Bear") is a hint, insofar as the bear often plays *sacrificial* god, at the ambiguous nature and fate of the father-god. Old Ben at the end is afraid of being "taken"—like a city or a hunted beast. The religious imagery, therefore, suggests the dual aspect of fatherhood, destroying and destroyed.

In the story, a sort of doubling affects the image of the liberal, good father, which turns into the mask of the oppressive, bad father. However different their means, Ben and his father seek to control their children. Whereas, about to punish him, Ben's father shouts "the deafening command: 'Attention!'" Ben demands attention from his children, which is, in truth, no small demand. Similarly the filial and parental roles of Ben combine in a dual performance. On the linear, irreversible development that transforms the son into a father—a permutation of roles in the diegesis —the narration, through the two flashbacks, the process of spatialization and the use of imagery, emphasizes commutations. Old Ben, while acting as father, remembers his suffering as son, indeed remains a son. A minor instance of this occurs when, in the dimmed-out study, Ben reaches for one of the walking canes in the umbrella stand. "His hand lighting on the carved head of a certain oak stick, he felt the head with trembling fingers and quickly released it" (393). Although the narration reveals only later that this was the father's stick with his head carved on the knob, the stick which he used to beat young Ben with, the overreaction of the character strongly intimates to the reader aware of the disciplinary use of canes and of their phallic symbolism that something of the sort might indeed be the case, so that the vagueness of the reference, "a certain oak stick," reveals more of the character's continuing fear of his father than it hides of the facts. More important, Ben as father attempts to wipe out what John Irwin aptly calls "the affront of sonship, the affront of dependency," compounded here by the affront of violence.[17] Through his very attempt to reject his father's model of fatherhood, and his failure to do away with some form of domination, Ben still behaves like a son. For he is seeking for revenge against his father. He is unable to treat his children as equals, notwithstanding his claims to the contrary, but in his "resentment of their very good fortune" he unconsciously aligns himself with them, as though they were his siblings. And through his lifelong behavior to them, of which his treatment of Clifford in the present is but an epitome, he has been seeking revenge against his father, making them substitutes for his father.

That the children serve as substitutes for the father is particularly evident in the case of Clifford: this son, "the real man among the others," Ben identifies with himself at least once when he notes that his footsteps are "heavy footsteps like his own" (388, 389). But the narration also links Cliff in unobtrusive ways with his grandfather. Old Ben admires his son's athletic physique, is very much aware of his body, the way he moves, turns around on the ball of one foot, and so on.[18] So was he aware, in the past, of his father's body; even as he was about to be caned, he noticed that the old man's coattails were "somehow clinging close to his buttocks and thighs, so that his whole powerful form was outlined—his black figure against the white brick and the door" (394). Furthermore, the only detail given about Clifford's apparel is that he wears white shoes, which implies that he is in white: now white is, together with black, strongly associated with Ben's father, his face and his house. Finally footsteps signal in both cases the coming of the two men. Such conflations between grandfather and grandchildren have long been observed by psychoanalysts, from Sigmund Freud and Ernest Jones on.[19] The fantasmatic doubling of grandfather and son offers a clue to the impact on Old Ben of the final confrontation with his children to which I would like now to come back.

The old man's fantasy of being "taken" by his children is indeed striking. With it, there hangs dimly over the decorous, bourgeois Nashville home the shadow of collective parricide, of the Freudian myth of the murder of the primal father. But one may be a little more precise. If Ben is unable to bear that position in between Clifford and his other children, it is partly because he is caught between (a fantasmatic image of) the powerful Father and his own offspring. The scene on the staircase, or rather the positioning of the actors, is emblematic of his situation in life. Although we only see him engaged in dual relations, with his aunt or with his father on the one hand, and with Clifford or with his children as a group on the other, Ben's experience depends on his place in the chain of generations and is triangulated by three terms, Father-Ego-Son. As Ego he is normally led to fear both Father and Sons because of the aggressive desires he has felt toward them and now projects upon them. His childish wish was to live in a country where there would be no children and no fathers, where he could be an isolated Ego, self-engendered and without descent—an old fantasy of mankind, at least as old as Melchisedec and Sophocles' own Oedipus.[20] And though he built his house in order to position himself differently from his father, up above and aside from the family he has reared after all, he eventually finds out that there is no place where one can transcend the positioning, the conflict of generations. Like all human beings, he is caught in the chain of generations, caught in the guilt of violence. Choosing his father's cane to beat his children by proxy, he still affirms himself a son in the very assertion of his fatherhood, of his right to victimize his children, and in the symbolic killing of the father whose phallic weapon he now has assumed. Just as he fears and pities his children, so now the reader must fear and pity the fictional character—must fear and pity in him the representative of the human plight.

For, of course, to fear generation is not simply to fear involvement and sexuality, whatever part this particular fear may play. (Significantly, women are almost absent in the story.[21] Ben's mother is not even alluded to; his dead wife mentioned only in connection with the naming of the "porte cochère." Needless to say, it is important that *her* word for it should stand at the threshold of the narrative, thus making the father's word the contextually marked one. The title, therefore, subtly undermines the language and the law of the father.) The ultimate fear proceeds from the fact that the succession of generations is succession in death. The fantasy of being *causa sui* is linked to a dream of immortality. "Without descent, without genealogy; no more generations; the world of generation and death transcended"—thus Norman O. Brown.[22] It is no coincidence that the family reunion should take place on the birthday which, celebrating Ben's entrance (or fall) into the world of generation, brings him closer to death. When he seizes his dead father's cane, the protagonist uses this symbolic weapon to punish his children for being his and being his successors. But the carved face on the head of the cane functions, for the reader, almost like a skull, as a *memento mori* which in his fury Old Ben does not heed.

"Porte cochère" and "drive-under" become symbols of the ineluctable conditions under which all human beings enter and experience life. Space as the setting for a microdrama turns, in Peter Taylor's brilliantly understated treatment, into the emblematic arena where the geometry of family relations regulates our positions, into a symbol of our existence in the world.

NOTES

1. Gene Baro, "A True Short-Story Artist," *New York Herald Tribune Book Review,* Dec. 6, 1959, 9, quoted by Barbara Schuler in "The House of Peter Taylor," *Critique* 9, no. 3 (1967): 17.

2. Stephen Goodwin, "An Interview with Peter Taylor," *Shenandoah* 24 (Winter 1973): 9.

3. Ibid., 14.

4. "Porte Cochère" was first published in the *New Yorker,* July 16 and 21–24, 1949, then reprinted in *Fifty-Five Stories from "The New Yorker"* (New York: Simon and Schuster, 1949). It has been included in the last collection of Peter Taylor's stories to date, *The Old Forest and Other Stories* (Garden City, N.Y.: Doubleday, 1985). It is a more expanded version, slightly different from that of the *New Yorker,* and some of the changes (the aunt's name is different, the presence of the narrator is more clearly felt, etc.) would have been relevant to my interpretation. Unfortunately, this edition is marred by a few typographical errors and what is clearly the omission of one line (263) so that the text is not reliable enough for my purposes. Nor do I know whether this represents the author's latest version. Under the circumstances, I have preferred to use the Simon and Schuster version; all the page citations, indicated within parentheses in the text, will refer to this edition.

5. I have borrowed these and other terms from A. J. Greimas, *Sémiotique, dictionnaire raisonné de la théorie du langage* (Paris: Hachette, 1979), but as my reader will soon discover, this reading of "Porte Cochère" does not pretend to be a semiotic reading of Peter Taylor's story.

6. Schuler, "House of Peter Taylor," 7.

7. The distinction between focalization (who perceives) and narration (who tells) has been introduced by Gérard Genette, *Figures III* (Paris: Seuil, 1972), and adopted with some modifications by Shlomith Rimmon-Kennan, whom I follow here (*Narrative Fiction: Contemporary Poetics* [London: Methuen, 1983]).

8. Again I borrow concepts, which I have found useful in my eclectic kind of analysis, from a confirmed semiotician, Denis Bertrand, *L'espace et le sens, Germinal d'Emile Zola* (Paris: Hadès-Benjamin, 1985).

9. I might have added that these places share a feature which is not intrinsically spatial but which characterizes space, namely, /light/: the aunt's cellar has

the same dim light as Ben's study, the father's cellar is dark. /Light/ is related to the major isotopy of /sight/ or, rather, /impaired vision/, which I shall only glance at but which would deserve further investigation.

10. The thymic category is articulated into euphoria/dysphoria; see Greimas.

11. "Proxemics" is the term Edward Hall coined for the "interrelated observations and theories of man's use of space as a specialized elaboration of culture" (*The Hidden Dimension* [Garden City, N.Y.: Anchor Books, 1969]). According to Greimas, "la proxémique est une discipline—ou plutot un projet de discipline —sémiotique, qui vise à analyser les dispositions des sujets et des objets dans l'espace, et plus particulièrement, l'usage que les sujets font de l'espace aux fins de signification."

12. Eric Berne, *Games People Play: The Psychology of Human Relationships* (New York: Grove Press, 1964).

13. Gaston Bachelard, *La poétique de l'espace* (Paris: Presses Universitaires de France, 1957), 24.

14. Ricardo Gullon, "On Space in the Narrative," *Critical Inquiry* (Autumn 1975): 112.

15. A. J. Greimas, *Sémiotique et sciences sociales* (Paris: Seuil, 1976), 130.

16. Jean Chevalier et al., *Dictionnaire des symboles* (Paris: Robert Laffont, 1969); Sir James Frazer, *The New Golden Bough*, abr. ed. (New York: New American Library, 1959), esp. 545–49, 551.

17. John Irwin, "The Dead Father in Faulkner," in Robert Con Davis, *The Fictional Father: Lacanian Readings of the Text* (Amherst: University of Massachusetts Press, 1981).

18. The motif of whirling or turning about is associated both with Clifford and Old Ben (390–91, 394).

19. The idea of the "identification" of grandfather and grandchild has received a more recent formulation in Alain de Mijolla, *Les visiteurs du moi* (Paris: Les Belles Lettres, 1981).

20. Cf. Heb. 7:3; Norman O. Brown, *Love's Body* (New York: Vintage Books, 1956), 54–55; and Claude Simon, *Le sacre du printemps* (Paris: Calmann-Levy, 1954).

21. In the Doubleday edition, Aunt Nelson is named Aunt Nell Partee and one of Ben's daughters is Nell instead of Laura Nell; the naming thereby strengthens a female line in the family.

22. Brown, *Love's Body*, 54.

The Framing of Charles W. Chesnutt:

Practical Deconstruction in the

Afro-American Tradition

CRAIG WERNER

First, three quotations.

Under exegetical pressure, self-reference demonstrates the impossibility of self-possession. When poems denounce poetry as lies, self-referentiality is the source of undecidability, which is not ambiguity but a structure of logical irresolvability: if a poem speaks true in describing poetry as lies, then it lies; but if its claim that poems lie is a lie, then it must speak true. (Culler, *On Deconstruction*, 202)

They ain't no different from nobody else. . . . They mouth cut cross ways, ain't it? Well, long as you don't see no man wid they mouth cut up and down, you know they'll all lie jus' like de rest of us. (Hurston, *Mules and Men*, 22)

The text is a beautiful, slender stream, meandering gracefully through a wide meadow of margin. (Chesnutt, "Baxter's *Procrustes*," 419).

As the Signifying Monkey and Brer Rabbit have always known, as Charles Chesnutt knew in 1890, as Euro-American literary theorists working in the wake of Jacques Derrida have discovered, truth lies in a lie. By focusing on the writing of Chesnutt, one of the most enigmatic figures of the post-Reconstruction era, I hope to prefigure a politically significant discourse between Euro-American literary theory and the Afro-American expressive tradition it has excluded from its premises.

But before I begin, two remarks on the premises. First, an anecdote explaining the hostility toward the theoretical enterprise, until recently my central position, which may emerge throughout this essay. As a graduate student, I participated briefly in a critical-theory reading group. At one meeting, a prominent theoretician responded to Missy Dehn Kubitschek's question concerning the relevance of theory to a nonspecialist audience with the contemptuous statement, "I don't much care what the guys at the corner garage think about my work." Juxtaposed with the frequently recondite and exclusive vocabulary of theoretical writing, this highlighted what I perceived, and to some extent continue to perceive, as an elitist stance which contributes to the effective power of the institutions that deconstruction ostensibly calls into question. As an aesthetic populist who takes James Joyce, James Brown, and George Clinton with equal comico-seriousness, I consigned the whole enterprise to the nether regions and went about my business. Only recently, inspired by the gentle chiding of autodidacts Geoff King and Charles Weir and academics Kathy Cummings of the University of Washington and Robert Stepto of the Afro-American Studies Department of Yale—a ritual ground given over to unspeakable forces in my neopopulist demonology—have I begun to realize that, professional argot and elitist individuals aside, the guys at the corner garage may have been telling lies about their true knowledge of deconstruction all along.

Second, and perhaps the paranoia inheres in the populism, I've felt for some time that I was standing alone in my reading of Chesnutt as an exceptionally complex modernist/postmodernist ironist situated on the margins of a literary marketplace conditioned first by the plantation-tradition stereotypes of Thomas Nelson Page and later by the virulent racist diatribes of Thomas Dixon. Standard literary histories evince almost no awareness of Chesnutt's complexity; *The Cambridge History of American Literature* (edited by Carl Van Doren et al., 1917) omits all mention of Chesnutt, while the fourth edition of *The Literary History of the United States* (edited by Robert Spiller et al., 1974) dismisses him as a minor plantation-tradition figure overshadowed by Joel Chandler Harris. Even William Andrews's sensitive study *The Literary Career of Charles W. Chesnutt* credits Chesnutt with relatively little awareness of structural irony or metafictional subtlety. Aesthetic isolation mocks my populist soul; on the other hand, originality intrigues my academic mind. Whatever the case, Afro-American novelist John Wideman's piece "Surfiction" in the Summer 1985 issue of the *Southern Review*—my copy of which was lost in the mail and arrived only this week, on All Souls' Day—seems to be a response to my unsounded call or a call for my unsounded response. I say "seems" because, upon recognizing the Chesnutt figure created by Wideman, who recently identified Brer Rabbit as his favorite literary character when questioned by the *New York Times Book Review*, I decided not to read the rest of his piece until I had figured out my own position. Incidentally, were I permitted (to quote one of Chesnutt's more famous black contemporaries), I might suggest some duplicity in the identification of Wideman's words as "fiction" in the table of contents of the *Southern Review*. (Space for future retrospective commentary: after reading both Wideman's essay and a version of this paper at a conference, I'm surer than ever that it's nothing but a lie.) With these positions in mind, we can begin.

Henry Louis Gates suggests the implicit connection between the Afro-American folk tradition from which Chesnutt drew many of his figures and the deconstructionist sensibility when he presents "the Signifying Monkey, he who dwells at the margins of discourse" as a figure embodying the "Afro-American rhetorical strategy of signifying [as] a rhetorical act which is not engaged in the game of information-giving. Signifying turns on the play and chain of signifiers, and not on some supposedly transcendent signified" (129–31). Locating his own position in the space between Euro-American theory and Afro-American signifying, Gates applies his insights concerning "folk deconstruction" to Afro-American literary history in a diagram centering on Hurston and including Jean Toomer, Sterling Brown, Ralph Ellison, Richard Wright, and Ishmael Reed. In response to this diagram—clearly intended by Gates as provisional rather than definitive—I would suggest that, especially in *The Conjure Woman* (1899) and the self-referential story "Baxter's *Procrustes*" (1905), Chesnutt prefigures both the Afro- and Euro-American understandings of literary signification in a way that we have only recently begun to comprehend. In advancing this argument, I am suggesting not simply that deconstructionist methodologies can be profitably applied to Chesnutt's work or that a general parallel exists between the Afro-American tradition and Euro-American theory. Rather, I am suggesting that Chesnutt consciously orients his discourse toward crucial elements of the deconstructionist project and that he anticipates constructive approaches to several issues which remain extremely problematic in contemporary theoretical discourse. From a deconstructionist perspective, it should come as no surprise that focusing on the excluded margin, the Afro-American literary tradition which has never enjoyed the social privilege allowing it to dismiss the masters from its awareness, should help cast light on the blind spots of Euro-American theory.

By focusing on the general (and to the extent possible, shared) understanding of deconstruction in contemporary academic discourse, I hope to lay some groundwork for future cross-cultural discussions oriented toward the articulation and refinement of specific implications of Derrida's positions. Terry Eagleton's chapter "Post-Structuralism" in *Literary Theory: An Introduction* and Culler's chapter "Critical Consequences" in *On Deconstruction*, two works which diverge sharply in their views of the larger significance of the movement, share a number of premises I shall treat as consensual positions. Both understand deconstruction as a philosophically grounded approach to thought which: (1) emphasizes the problematic relationship between the linguistic signifier and the "transcendent signified" (Eagleton, 131; Culler, 188); (2) challenges, and ultimately decenters, hierarchies of thought or expression based on binary oppositions which privilege one term over its ostensible opposite (Culler, 213; Eagleton, 132); (3) focuses on the "marginal" terms excluded from the discourse in order to recognize the way in which the text subverts its own meaning (Culler, 215; Eagleton, 132–33); (4) recognizes that all signifiers derive their meaning from "traces" of other signifiers and concentrates on the "play of signifiers," creating a theoretically endless chain which frustrates attempts at closure (Eagleton, 134; Culler, 188). Eagleton summarizes the deconstructive project as follows: "Deconstruction tries to show how such oppositions, in order to hold themselves in place, are sometimes betrayed into inverting or collapsing themselves, or need to banish to the text's margins certain niggling details which can be made to return and plague them. . . . The tactic of deconstructive criticism, that is to say, is to show how texts come to embarrass their own ruling systems of logic" (133). Culler echoes and extends this understanding when he writes of the deconstructionist interest in "previous readings which, in separating a text into the essential and marginal elements, have created for the text an identity that the text itself, through the power of its marginal elements, can subvert." Generalizing this approach in a manner consistent with Eagleton's insistence on the contextual determinants of textual meaning, Culler asserts, "One could, therefore, identify deconstruction with the twin principles of the contextual determination of meaning and the infinite extendability of context."

Chesnutt, whose active publishing career had ended by the time Ferdinand de Saussure delivered the lectures which would become the Course in General Linguistics between 1907 and 1911, derived his awareness of the problematical nature of binary oppositions, hierarchies in discourse, and the signifier-signified relationship from two basic sources: the folk tradition on which he drew, and the literary context in which he wrote. As Hurston, Ellison, and Gates have noted in quite different contexts, the Afro-American folk tradition encodes a profound suspicion of and resistance to Euro-American expression. Placed in a marginal position enforced by institutional structures and physical violence, Afro-Americans, especially those *without* access to the mainstream educational system, have always been acutely aware of the radical inadequacy of white figures of black experience. Experiencing what W. E. B. Du Bois called *double consciousness*—"this sense of always looking at one's self through the eyes of others, of measuring one's soul by the tape of a world that looks on in amused contempt and pity" (17)—Afro-Americans, individually and communally, learned quickly to manipulate the gap between signifier and signified. Constructing elaborate verbal "masks" in everyday discourse as well as in the spirituals and animal tales, "slaves" (to use the Euro-American signifier) continually (and because of their political oppression, implicitly) subverted the oppositional racist association of *white* with such privileged terms as "good," "God," "mature," and "civilized," and *black* with such excluded terms as "evil," "devil," "childlike" and "savage." Focusing on the "marginal" elements of the dominant discourse (i.e., themselves), they learned effectively to decenter social and political hierarchies in order to survive, psychologically and physically. Ultimately, as Ellison notes in his wonderfully titled essay "Change the Joke and Slip the Yoke" in his proto-deconstructionist book *Shadow and Act,* this shaped an expressive tradition based precisely on the closure-resisting play of signifiers articulating "a land of masking jokers" in which "the motives hidden behind the mask are as numerous as the ambiguities the mask conceals" (70). Chesnutt, probably the first Afro-American writer to assume the truth lying behind Ellison's signifying, incorporates this deconstructive folk sensibility into his literary productions in a highly self-conscious manner.

The specific manifestations of this self-consciousness, however, derive directly from the tradition of racial signification in the Euro-American writing of the 1880s and 1890s. When Chesnutt began to publish in mainstream magazines such as *Family Fiction* and the *Atlantic Monthly* in 1886 and 1887, he encountered editors and readers deeply influenced by Joel Chandler Harris's tales of Uncle Remus and Brer Rabbit. Harris remains one of the least understood, and perhaps least understandable, figures in one of the least understood and least understandable currents of the southern literary tradition: that of minstrelsy. On the surface, Harris appears to articulate a straightforward version of the plantation tradition in his tales of an essentially childlike black man gently harassed into telling charming animal stories by a young white boy who brings him sweets and affection from the big house. Occupying the center of the American consciousness of Harris—the Disney minstrel show *Song of the South* is only the most obvious of many examples—this image would seem to dictate dismissal of the Uncle Remus tales as the type of "blackface minstrelsy" Berndt Ostendorf describes as "a symbolic slave code, a set of self-humiliating rules designed by white racists for the disenfranchisement of the black self" (66).

Beneath both the benevolent and maleficent surface(s) of the minstrel tradition, however, lie unsuspected depths where Harris joins William Faulkner and Derrida to comprise a significant genealogy in which Chesnutt is the crucial and crucially unrecognized missing relation. The most powerful recent Faulkner criticism, that written by John Irwin and Eric Sundquist, recognizes a troubling link between the irresolvability of the Faulknerian text—Irwin calls Quentin's narration of *Absalom, Absalom!* "an answer that doesn't answer—an answer that puts the answerer in question" (8)—and the presence of unresolved psychological tensions originating in miscegenation, the denied actuality which unrelentingly subjects racial oppositions to the type of subversive interrogation Luce Irigaray directs against Freud's gender oppositions in "The Blind Spot of an Old Dream of Symmetry." Orienting his discussion specifically toward Faulkner's rejection of the binary oppositions inherent in "Manichaeanism," Sundquist writes: "The gothicism of *Absalom, Absalom!* is not by any means the sentimentality of a minstrel show—not the benign dream in which 'all coons look alike'—but the nightmare in which black *and* white begin all too hauntingly to look alike" (99). Harris and Chesnutt in fact prefigure this Faulknerian dilemma, a dilemma inherent in the minstrel show from the beginning. As Ostendorf writes:

> Minstrelsy anticipated on stage what many Americans deeply feared: the blackening of America. Minstrelsy did in fact create a symbolic language and a comic iconography for "intermingling" culturally with the African Caliban while at the same time "isolating" him socially. In blackening his face the white minstrel acculturated vol-

untarily to his "comic" vision of blackness, thus anticipating in jest
what he feared in earnest. . . . Minstrelsy is proof that negrophilia
and negrophobia are not at all contradictory. Minstrelsy is negrophobia staged as negrophilia, or vice versa, depending on the respective
weight of the fear or attraction. (67, 81)

To state this in specifically deconstructive terms, the minstrel show—
whether manifested in the Uncle Remus tales, Faulkner's novels, or, as
Charles Sanders brilliantly suggests, T. S. Eliot's *Waste Land*—subverts its
own meaning by deconstructing the binary opposition on which its hierarchical structures depend, creating a form of expression which demands
confrontation with an infinitely extensive/regressive chain of signifiers.
Which is to say: white minstrelsy deconstructs itself.

Nowhere is this clearer than in *Uncle Remus, His Songs and Sayings,*
the text through which Harris engendered a long line of Euro-American
negrophiles. As Harris seems to have sensed—he attributed the writing
of the Brer Rabbit tales to an internal "other fellow" who "is simply a
spectator of my folly until I seize a pen, and then he comes forward and
takes charge" (Martin, 92)—and as Bernard Wolfe first articulated in his
1949 essay "Uncle Remus and the Malevolent Rabbit," the volume in fact
presents a sequence of "answers that don't answer, that put the answerer
in question." Just beneath the negrophiliac surface of the "charming" tales
(most of them faithfully reproduced from the Afro-American oral tradition) that Harris expropriates from/to the benevolently asexual Uncle
Remus lies a world of violence, sexual energy, and barely subdued racial
drama in which the physically weak Brer Rabbit attains at least momentary mastery over the stronger but less aware Brers Bear, Wolf, and Fox
through his manipulation of the gap between verbal signifier and concrete
action. Encoded within the ordered hierarchy of the plantation tradition,
the trickster figure delights in the disruption of hierarchies, textual or contextual, almost without reference to their apparent significance. At times,
as in "The Wonderful Tar-Baby Story," this radically subversive delight
works to Brer Rabbit's detriment. When Brer Rabbit takes on the role of
the "master" demanding respect from the tar baby—a profoundly charged
figure for the "black" pole of oppositional racist thought (stupid, lazy,
very black, a thing)—his discourse subverts his own claims of privilege
as surely as his ability to turn Brer Fox into a riding horse elsewhere decenters the plantation-tradition hierarchy. This aspect of the Brer Rabbit
tales is particularly important in relation to the development of Afro-

American deconstruction because it protects against substituting one set of privileged terms for another. Although Wolfe's reading of the animal fables as slightly veiled allegories of racial hatred and sexual competition seems accurate, the random and frequently self-destructive manifestations of Brer Rabbit's deconstructive energies make it clear that the tales privilege *neither* the black nor the white position.

An understanding of Chesnutt, however, requires some attention to the unconsciously self-deconstructing aspects of Harris's adaptation of this already deconstructive material in *Uncle Remus, His Songs and Sayings,* which subverts its own intended meanings by encoding several thoroughly contradictory versions of its Afro-American subjects. The tension emerges clearly in a comparison of the three major sections of the book. The irascible minstrel-show darky signified by the name "Uncle Remus" in "His Sayings" and the loyal slave presented in the plantation-tradition short story "A Story of the War" evince nothing of the creative energy of the storyteller of "Legends of the Old Plantation." Within the "Legends," on which Harris's reputation depends almost entirely, a similar tension exists between the frame tales, written in standard English, and the animal tales, written in a linguistically accurate dialect which Harris contrasts in his introduction specifically with "the intolerable misrepresentations of the minstrel stage" (39). As Harris's comment concerning the "other fellow" intimates, an anxious but not quite articulated awareness that the linguistic and thematic tensions of the book cast his own identity as a unified subject into doubt, permeates *Uncle Remus.* The opening "Legend," "Uncle Remus Initiates the Little Boy," establishes not one but two narrative frames, suggesting the unbridgeable distance between Euro-American signification and Afro-American experience. The most obvious frame tale concerning Uncle Remus and the seven-year-old boy establishes a symbolic equality between the ostensibly childlike black man and the actual white child, Harris's pastoral version of an earlier self similar to that constructed by Mark Twain in *Tom Sawyer,* a construction which reveals a deep longing for the Old South (Martin, 92–96). Alongside this frame, however, another frame, almost entirely unrecognized, presents a "mature" perspective which "explains" how the collaboration between the two "childlike" figures happens to have been written down on paper. Presented only at the beginning of the first legend, this frame is in some ways as subversive of oppositional hierarchies as the Brer Rabbit tales themselves. The little boy is introduced as a figure of absence; his mother, "Miss Sally," a curiously asexual figure who will be refigured in the "Miz Meadows" of the Brer

Rabbit tales, "misses" her child. Arriving at Uncle Remus's cabin, she sees her "boys" together and steps back. Harris concludes the initial frame with the sentence: "This is what 'Miss Sally' heard." Although there is no evidence that he was doing so as part of a conscious rhetorical strategy, Harris has in effect decentered his presence into at least four components: Uncle Remus who as storyteller plays the role of "the other fellow" in charge of Harris's pen; the little boy who bears the most obvious biographical relationship to Harris; the passive "feminine" figure who resembles the Harris who collected the tales attributed to Uncle Remus from a number of Afro-American "informants"; and the silent scribe, Harris the *Atlanta Constitution* columnist, who attributes his tales not directly to the black tellers but to a white female intermediary. In this complex configuration, neither whiteness nor masculinity possesses the significance—as signifiers invoking a range of transcendent creative attributes—attributed them by the explicitly patriarchal and paternalistic plantation-tradition writers.

Given the multitude of "presences" mediating between "Harris" and his "subjects," it should come as no surprise to discover traces of mutually deconstructing forms of awareness throughout the "Legends." "The End of Mr. Bear," for example, betrays its own ruling system of logic in several ways. Most obviously, the text subverts the plantation-tradition opposition between benevolent white master and happy black slave through the contrast between the superficially stereotypical frame and the vicious tale. Culminating in the death of Brer Bear (on the level of racial allegory, the symbolic white man), whom Brer Rabbit tricks into sticking his head into a tree where it is stung by a swarm of bees, the text closes with an expression of barely veiled joy (attributed to Uncle Remus but consistent with the folk materials) derived from contemplation of this inverted lynching: "dar ole Brer B'ar hung, en ef his head ain't swunk, I speck he hangin' dar yit" (136). It seems almost unbelievable that no critic prior to Wolfe seems to have understood this even in part as a warning against the racial pride —ironically projected as a savage black desire for a "shrunken head"— which enforced the social privilege encoded in the black-white opposition.

Even without reference to the animal tale, "The End of Mr. Bear" provides clear evidence of the self-deconstructing tendency of Harris's text to "embarrass its own ruling systems of logic." When the little boy comes to the cabin, he finds Uncle Remus "unusually cheerful and good-humored" (133). Signifying this good humor in the way most dear to slaveholders and plantation-tradition writers who cited the slaves' oral performances as proof of their contentment, Uncle Remus sings a song, "a senseless affair so far as the words were concerned." Immediately after quoting a verse of this "non-signifying" song, however, Harris contradicts himself in a peculiar manner. Unconsciously underlining Harris's ever-shifting Brer Rabbit–like relation to his text, the following passage reads:

> The quick ear of Uncle Remus, however, had detected the presence of the little boy, and he allowed his song to run into a recitation of nonsense, of which the following, if it be rapidly spoken, will give a faint idea: "Ole M'er Jackson, fines' confraction, fell down sta'rs fer to git satisfaction; big Bill Fray, he rule de day, eve'ything he call fer come one, two by three. Gwine 'long one day, met Johnny Huby, ax him grine nine yards er steel fer me, tole me w'ich he couldn't; den I hist 'im over Hickerson Dickerson's barn-doors; knock 'im ninety-nine miles under water, w'en he rise, he rise in Pike straddle un a hanspike, en I lef' 'im dar smokin' er de hornpipe, Juba reda seda breda. Aunt Kate at de gate; I want to eat, she fry de meat en gimme skin, w'ich I fling it back agin. Juba!"

This curious passage begins with an intimation of a level of awareness in Uncle Remus, associated with his leporine "quick ear," which allows him to shift from the "senseless affair" into "a recitation of nonsense." The reasons for the shift or the difference between the two levels of non-signifying discourse are never stated. Emphasizing the insufficiency of his written text which can provide only a "faint idea" of the oral expression of "Uncle Remus," who exists only within the written text, Harris plunges into what, if recognized, would certainly have seemed a nightmarish minstrel show skit on the relationship between signifier and signified. Trapped within the hierarchical system which denies transcendence to the Afro-American subject, Harris can only dismiss Uncle Remus's words, albeit with a great uneasiness grounded on his sense that the black voice signifies something unavailable to any white "presence" in the text.

Clearly a version of the signifying rhetoric described by Gates, Uncle Remus's speech is best understood as a quintessentially Afro-American manipulation of the "play of signifiers," which includes numerous politically resonant images of conflict and/or Africanisms which subvert plantation-tradition images without concern for specific referential meaning. Accepting the divergence between signifier and signified, the black voice encoded in the text subverts the previous interpretation of the words as nonsense. Immediately after the performance, which creates "bewilderment" in the young boy and, presumably, in the white readership guided by Harris's remarks, Uncle Remus proceeds "with the air of one who had just given an important piece of information" (134). The black voice, aware that the destruction of an oppositional hierarchy resting on a simplistic sense of linguistic significance does not entail the destruction of all meaning, very nearly effects a successful revolution when Uncle Remus says: "Hit's all des dat away, honey. . . . En w'en you bin cas'n shadders long ez de ole nigger, den you'll fine out who's w'ich, en w'ich's who." Acutely uncomfortable with the confusion of identity established through the verbal play of the "black" voice in the "white" text, Harris seems unable to distinguish between his own voice and the voice of an "other" subverting the hierarchical system which privileges the written expression as a mark of civilization and humanity. Returning to the standard English of the frame tale, Harris attempts to reassert the plantation-tradition stereotype which ascribes superior "capacity" to whites and only child-like significance to black expression: "The little boy made no response. He was in thorough sympathy with all the whims and humors of the old man, and his capacity for enjoying them was large enough to include even those he could not understand." Even the reassertion reveals subversive traces, however; the boy is silenced, uncomprehending. Shortly, the angry black voice of the Brer Rabbit tales will assume the central position in the world of the text. The deconstructive black voice renders the white personae silent, thereby creating a space for articulation of the subversive animal tale ending with the lynching of Brer Bear, condemned by his inability to see through Brer Rabbit's masks. As ironic prelude, however, and apparently without any awareness on the part of Harris, Uncle Remus effects a role reversal which places the white child in the symbolic position of the subordinate attending to the marginal details of the master's work: "Uncle Remus was finishing an axe-handle, and upon these occasions it was his custom *to allow* the child to hold one end while he applied sand-paper to the other" (emphasis added). The final sentence of the frame story echoes, almost word for word, the standard plantation-tradition description of slavery as a system benefiting both black and white: "These relations were pretty soon established, to the mutual satisfaction of the parties most interested." Operating in the newly created textual space, the final clause of the final framing sentence specifically contrasts the nonsense of the previous sections with the significance of the animal tale to come: "the old man continued his remarks, but this time not at random." Even the frame tale, the section of *Uncle Remus* in which Harris attempts to impose the oppositional order of the plantation tradition on the Afro-American folk materials, is subject to the deconstructive energies of the black voice. As the frame story metamorphoses into Brer Rabbit tale, the white writer's voice surrenders itself to the black speaker's as written by the white writer. In effect, the text acknowledges a significance in the non-signifying nonsense. This infiltration of what Gates would call a signifying black voice into not only the tale but the frame itself recalls Ostendorf's comments on the minstrel show and prefigures the racial and aesthetic tensions of Faulkner's greatest work.

Appropriating the voice of the Euro-American figure who established the ground on which he worked, Chesnutt recognized and consciously manipulated the self-deconstructive form of *Uncle Remus*. Particularly in *The Conjure Woman,* Chesnutt employs a complex rhetorical strategy, based on a deep understanding of the deconstructionist principles of the contextual determination of meaning and the infinite extendability of context, anticipated in the southern literary tradition only (if indeed at all) by the best work of Poe and Twain. Superficially, Chesnutt's conjure stories mimic Harris's structure; a white narrator, writing in standard English, reports the charming but absurd tales of an old black man, presented in black dialect. Like Uncle Remus, Chesnutt's Uncle Julius seems motivated by childlike selfish concerns. Uncle Remus cajoles the little boy into bringing him sweets; Uncle Julius manipulates his white listeners, the relocated northern businessman John and his wife, Annie, into a variety of personal indulgences. Most critics who have discussed the relationship between frame tale and conjure story in *The Conjure Woman* concentrate on the economic dimension of the relationship between Julius and John, or on Julius's attempt to educate Annie concerning the realities of slavery (Ferguson, Andrews). While these observations shed light on the mimetic dimension of the text, they typically exclude those aspects which relate primarily to the communications process itself, the aspects which intimate Chesnutt's awareness of numerous deconstructive concerns.

The model of the rhetorical relationship between John and Julius in *The Conjure Woman* comments directly on Chesnutt's own position as an Afro-American writer working in a context dominated by Euro-American oppositional hierarchies, particularly the plantation-tradition stereotypes shaped by Harris, Thomas Nelson Page, and countless others publishing in the same magazines where "The Goophered Grapevine" and "The Conjurer's Revenge" first appeared. Recognition of this parallel hinges on an understanding of the significance of the "mask" in the signifying tradition. In *Mules and Men,* Hurston described masking as follows:

> The Negro, in spite of his open-faced laughter, his seeming acquiescence, is particularly evasive. You see we are a polite people and we do not say to our questioner, 'Get out of here!' We smile and tell him or her something that satisfies the white person because, knowing so little about us, he doesn't know what he is missing. . . . The theory behind our tactics: 'The white man is always trying to know somebody else's business. All right, I'll set something outside the door of my mind for him to play with and handle. He can read my writing but he sho' can't read my mind. I'll put this play toy in his hand, and he will seize it and go away. Then I'll say my say and sing my song. (4–5)

Most immediately, this rhetorical strategy creates a space, simultaneously physical, verbal, and psychological within which the Afro-American individual and community can survive within a hostile racist culture. At times, it can serve as a more active political tool allowing Afro-Americans access to information or situations from which they would be excluded if their true motives were recognized. Set against this background, the figure Chesnutt creates in *The Conjure Woman* comes into focus as an elaborate mask, or set of masks, designed to infiltrate Euro-American discourse and, in the long run, subvert the binary oppositions on which racial privilege depends. It should be noted in approaching this strategy that, as soon as an audience recognizes the mask as a mask, the mask loses all possible effectiveness. The nature of the masking strategy, therefore, depends on the trickster's ability to convince the audience that it sees his or her actual face. One of the conceptually simple but practically inexhaustible methods for attaining this goal is to construct "false" masks, masks over masks, which the audience is allowed to see through in order to convince it that it has seen the trickster's face when in fact it is encountering only another mask. In effect, Chesnutt uses such a strategy to construct a complex model of practical deconstruction in which the masking Julius, prefiguring the doubly conscious Afro-American modernist writer, manipulates his audience through his awareness of the structure and limitations of Euro-American oppositional thought and his understanding of the potential uses of a marginal position.

Reflecting his situation as a light-skinned "black" writer born in North Carolina but living in Ohio, Chesnutt creates two personae, textual masks:

John, with whom he shares geographical residence and a Euro-American literacy based on writing and knowledge of white institutional structures (Stepto, 167); and Julius, with whom he shares racial and geographical origins and "tribal literacy," based on oral expression and specifically black cultural patterns (Stepto, 167). Dividing "himself" into two figures who, in the binary oppositions of the plantation tradition, are mutually exclusive and irresolvable, Chesnutt anticipates Saussure in deconstructing the linguistic convention, crucial to mimetic fiction, which asserts the identity of signifier and signified. Nonetheless, Chesnutt's audience, excluding from its discourse any cultural traditions positing alternatives to oppositional thinking and assuming the identity of signifier and signified, was almost totally unprepared to understand his critique. Chesnutt's "solution" to the problem brought the implicitly deconstructive elements of the masking/signifying tradition of Afro-American culture very near the surface of *The Conjure Woman*.

What I am suggesting is that Julius in *The Conjure Woman*, like Chesnutt in the literary culture of his era, constructs a sequence of increasingly opaque masks, predicated on his knowledge of the structure of his audience's belief systems and implying a recognition of the underlying perceptions asserted in Culler's identification of deconstruction with "the twin principles of the contextual determination of meaning and the infinite extendability of context." On the surface the Julius of "The Goophered Grapevine" appears to be motivated by economic self-interest, telling the story of the haunted vineyard in an attempt to scare John off and keep the grapes for himself. But this mask is absurdly transparent. Julius, of course, has no hope of frightening John, the "hard-headed" businessman, with romantic fancy. If John grants Julius any economic concessions it is because he is an essentially well meaning "master." In fact, Julius seems aware of the actual economic dynamic when he stresses the past bounty of the vineyard and the crucial role played by blacks in maintaining its productivity. In addition to suggesting a less direct economic motive, this double voicing intimates Julius's awareness that his white audience is in fact less unified than it appears. Employing many of the standard images associated with the nineteenth-century sentimental fiction addressed primarily to a female audience—particularly those focusing on the division of families (Fiedler)—Julius addresses not only John but also Annie, whom he gradually educates concerning the inhumanity of the slave system of the Old South. Given the composition of Chesnutt's magazine audience, it seems likely that he perceived the parallel between Julius's rhetorical strategy and his own. Allowing male readers seeking escapist fantasy to perceive him, like Julius, as a simple storyteller who "seemed to lose sight of his auditors, and to be living over again in monologue his life on the old plantation" (12–13), Chesnutt simultaneously educated his "female" audience, which itself occupied a marginal position in patriarchal/paternalistic culture, concerning the actual brutalities of racial relations.

Adopting an essentially deconstructive narrative technique, Julius places his subversive criticism of the romantic image of the "Old South" in the margins of his tale. Frequently, his most pointed criticism occurs in the background descriptions of what life was like "befo' de wah," a common formula in the nostalgic stories of Page and others. In "The Goophered Grapevine," for example, Julius says: "I reckon it ain' so much so nowadays, but befo' de wah, in slab'ry times, a nigger did n' mine goin fi' er ten mile in a night, w'en dey wuz sump'n good ter eat at de yuther een'" (14). Contrasted with the illicit treats the boy gives Uncle Remus or with the slave banquet in Paul Laurence Dunbar's poem "The Party," the political point of Julius's marginal "literary criticism" seems unmistakable. Especially in the early tales, Julius makes political points obliquely since more direct approaches might alienate John and result in his exclusion from the situation in which he can address Annie. As Julius establishes himself within the structure of John and Annie's lives, however, he alters his strategy. "Mars Jeems's Nightmare," the third story in the collection, focuses on a harsh master whose attitudes change substantially after he is transformed into a slave for a period of time; clearly, Julius feels free to include much more explicit social commentary than he had previously. Although John retains his condescending belief in the childlike simplicity of blacks in his ironic comment "I am glad, too, that you told us the moral of the story; it might have escaped us otherwise," there is no danger that he will use his social privilege to exclude Julius from the discourse into which they have entered. The strategy of "Mars Jeems's Nightmare" depends, therefore, on that of "The Goophered Grapevine," which disarmed John by playing on his belief that he "understands" Julius when he has actually only seen through a transparent economic mask. The long-term success of the strategy, however, requires periodic reenforcement of John's assumption, evidence Julius provides in "The Conjurer's Revenge" when he tricks John into buying a blind horse. The real significance of Julius's interaction with John, then, lies not in the success or failure of a particular trick but in the control he attains over the context in which he can direct his "marginal" address to Annie to communal rather than individual benefits.

When he allows this mask to become transparent in the didactic "Mars Jeems's Nightmare," Julius extends the basic principle to another level of contextual complexity. By convincing relatively liberal whites such as Annie, who are willing to face the somewhat distanced reality of the brutality of the Old South (itself part of a binary opposition of North-civilized / South-primitive), that they have seen the true face of the black "petitioner," Chesnutt creates a context in which his more radically subversive deconstructive message can infiltrate the literary forum. Having entered this discourse, Chesnutt may in fact discredit both conservative Old South *and* liberal New South through the structural analogy between the whites in the fables Julius tells and those in the frame story Chesnutt writes. From this perspective, John and Annie can be seen as new incarnations of the old masters subjecting Afro-Americans to a system of discourse and institutional organization that denies their humanity. Allowing his readers to penetrate a sequence of transparent masks, Chesnutt articulated an extremely intricate parody which expands to deconstruct the ostensible opposition of "liberal North" and "reactionary South," both of which manifest a similar set of racist attitudes. Condescension, active oppression, and pity are equally compatible with the binary oppositions of the plantation tradition. Perhaps Chesnutt's final target, in his immediate context, is the predominantly northern readership who, like John and Annie, are willing to indulge the transparent "entertainments" of a charming black storyteller, perhaps even accepting a limited political critique, as long as it leaves the social framework undisturbed.

Each level of this process moves toward the actual context in which Chesnutt wrote, raising questions regarding the interaction of text and world and implicitly repudiating the traditional view of fiction as a privileged form of discourse. Extending this approach temporally, it would be possible to see Chesnutt as attempting to educate a future audience, or perhaps future Afro-American writers, in the methods of deconstructionist/masking reading and writing. Of course such reading writers, whites or "literate" blacks, themselves would be subject to interpretation as new incarnations of John and Annie determined to master Afro-American experience through ever more subtle techniques. At some point in this infinitely extendable context, Chesnutt's deconstructions flip over into a kind of structuralist (though not ahistorical) awareness of the persistence of the deeply ingrained oppositional structures characterizing Euro-American discourse and supporting oppressive institutions. In speculating on the long-term implications of the rhetorical structure of *The Conjure Woman,* I realize I have ventured forth onto shifting ground. The final stages of the process outlined above are unsupported and, by nature, unsupportable. The last mask must always remain opaque, at least to its immediate audience. Any evidence of its construction renders it partially transparent and subjects it to possible exclusion from the public forum, destroying any hope of political effectiveness. The play of signifiers must resist closure in order to resist the power of the dominant discourse. Nevertheless, Chesnutt provides enough textual evidence to suggest this approach is not simply a postmodernist imposition, an academic revoicing of the plantation-tradition distortion of the Afro-American voice. Both the contrast between John's and Julius's linguistic practices and the specific choices of material for the tales Julius tells intimate Chesnutt's conscious awareness of basic deconstructive approaches to discourse.

Possessing only a minimal sense of irony, John assumes the identity of signifier and signified. Because his attitude toward southern life has been shaped by literature, John perceives Julius in terms of the signifiers of the plantation tradition. Rather than leading to a relaxation of his belief in the adequacy of the signifiers, perceived discrepancies between signifier and signified are resolved by adjusting his conception of the signified. John's belief in the plantation-tradition stereotype attributing mental capacity solely to the white term of the white/black binary opposition leads him to create a mixed ancestry for Julius: "There was a shrewdness in his eyes, too, which was not altogether African, and which, as we afterwards learned from experience, was indicative of a corresponding shrewdness in his character" (9–10). Similarly, the frame story of "Mars Jeems's Nightmare" emphasizes the underlying structure of the binary opposition which defines blacks as subhuman. Extending the black-physical / white-mental dichotomy, John describes Julius's relationship with the "natural" world:

Toward my tract of land and the things that were on it—the creeks, the swamps, the hills, the meadows, the stones, the trees—he maintained a peculiar personal attitude, that might be called predial rather than proprietary. He had been accustomed, until long after middle life, to look upon himself as the property of another. When this relation was no longer possible, owing to the war, and to his master's death and the dispersion of the family, he had been unable to break

off entirely the mental habits of a lifetime, but had attached himself to the old plantation, of which he seemed to consider himself an
appurtenance. (64–65)

In addition to supporting politically destructive institutions, such reduction of the black subject reveals John's simplistic linguistic and philosophical premises. Foregrounding the deconstructionist tendencies implicit in
Uncle Remus, The Conjure Woman suggests ways of subverting the power
of the discourse resulting from such simplistic premises.

Recognizing John's tendency to confuse white metaphorical signification with the actuality of the "black thing" signified, Julius bases his
strategy on the manipulation of the unrecognized distance between signifier and signified. Where John assumes presence, Julius implies absence.
Frequently, Julius's speech implies the inadequacy of the signifier-signified
paradigm, drawing attention to the ways in which the linguistic position
serves institutional structures whose actual operations the language veils.
For example, Julius describes Mars Jeems's relations with his slaves as
follows: "His niggers wuz bleedzd ter slabe fum daylight ter da'k, w'iles
yuther folks's did n' hafter wuk 'cep'n' fum sun ter sun" (71). Rhetorically
accepting the distinction between "daylight ter da'k" and "sun ter sun,"
this sentence parodies the way in which white folks, especially when they
want to evade their own position in an unjust system, employ different
signifiers to obscure what from the Afro-American perspective appear to
be identical signifieds. Although the sun rises after light and sets before
dark, the distinction, which might be emphasized by a good master as evidence of his kindness, does nothing to alter the fact that in either case, the
enforced labor is of murderous duration. Frequently Julius bases his rhetoric on the apparent acceptance of a white signifier, as in "The Goophered
Grapevine," which identifies the slave Henry with the vineyard in much
the same way John identifies Julius with the "things" of the plantation. By
adapting John's preconceptions, Julius finds it much easier to construct an
effective mask. As Gates notes in his discussion of the "Signifying Monkey," who along with Brer Rabbit provides the closest analog for Uncle
Julius in the folk tradition, "the Signifying Monkey [Julius, Chesnutt] is
able to signify upon the Lion [John, the white readership] only because
the Lion does not understand the nature of the Monkey's discourse. . . .
The Monkey speaks figuratively, in a symbolic code, whereas the Lion
interprets or 'reads' literally" (133–34).

A similar dynamic is at work in relation to the "folk" tales which charmed and fascinated both Julius's auditors in the text and Chesnutt's readership. Because the tales are presented in dialect within a frame readily familiar to readers of Harris, most contemporary reviewers assumed that Chesnutt was presenting "authentic" Afro-American folktales; several hostile reviews criticized The Conjure Woman for simply repeating folk materials without adequate imaginative transformation. As Melvin Dixon demonstrates, however, only one of the tales ("The Goophered Grapevine") is an authentic folktale. While the remainder incorporate folk elements, Chesnutt transforms them in a way which deconstructs the hierarchy on which the negative judgments rest. The recurring images of transformation in the tales—Sandy turns into a tree, Mars Jeems into a slave, Henry into a kind of human grapevine, and so on—implicitly repudiate the identification of signifier with transcendent signified. Identity is multiple, shifting, a play of forces rather than a transcendent essence. Chesnutt charmingly plunges his readers into the Faulknerian minstrel show/ nightmare in which the answers place the answerers in questions, names surrender their significance, becoming a source of ironic play in which the devil turns from black to white: "Mars Jeems's oberseah wuz a po' w'ite man name' Nick Johnson,—de niggers called 'im Mars Johnson ter his face, but behin' his back dey useter call 'im Ole Nick, en de name suited 'im ter a T" (75). Deprived of their linguistic base, dichotomies collapse, including that of white-classical-written-civilized / black-vernacular-oral-savage. For, although Chesnutt used Afro-American folk materials, the clearest source of the charming stories in The Conjure Woman is Ovid's Metamorphosis. The illiterate former slave and the classical poet play one another's roles in the minstrel show in which black and white begin to look very much alike. In a rhetorical gambit worthy of "The Purloined Letter" or the Signifying Monkey, Chesnutt draws attention to the similarity between Julius's concerns and those of the Euro-American philosophical tradition at the beginning of "The Gray Wolf's Ha'nt" when John sits down with Annie and reads:

The difficulty of dealing with transformations so many-sided as those which all existences have undergone, or are undergoing, is such as to make a complete and deductive interpretation almost hopeless. So to grasp the total process of redistribution of matter and motion as to see simultaneously its several necessary results in their actual interdependence is scarcely possible. There is, however, a mode of rendering the process as a whole tolerably comprehensible. Though the genesis of the rearrangement of every evolving aggregate is in itself one, it presents to our intelligence. (163–64)

When Annie repudiates the passage as "nonsense," John claims that this is philosophy "in the simplest and most lucid form." His failure to understand either the deconstructive implications of the emphasis on transformation and interdependence or the similarity between the philosophical passage and Julius's tales would seem clumsily ironic were it not for the fact that Chesnutt's ostensibly "literate" Euro-American readership shared the blindness. In addition, Annie's impatience with the philosophical discourse, contrasted with her eager but simplistic acceptance of Julius's oral versions, suggests intriguing approaches to the problem of audience which effects both Afro-American writers and Euro-American theorists.

"Baxter's *Procrustes*," the last story Chesnutt published prior to the literary silence of his last twenty-seven years, reflects his growing despair over the absence of an audience sensitive to his concerns. Not coincidentally, the story provides clear evidence that, even as he wrote the "conventional" novels (*The House behind the Cedars, The Marrow of Tradition, The Colonel's Dream*) which have veiled the complexity of the works which frame them, Chesnutt continued to develop his awareness of concerns which have entered the mainstream of Euro-American literary discourse only with the emergence of the deconstructionist movement. To a large extent, the issues raised in "Baxter's *Procrustes*" are those described in Culler's chapter on the "Critical Consequences" of deconstruction. Culler catalogs four levels on which deconstruction has effected literary criticism, the "first and most important [of which] is deconstruction's impact upon a series of critical concepts, including the concept of literature itself" (180). Among the specific results of deconstruction he lists the following propositions. Deconstruction focuses attention on (1) the importance and problematic nature of figures, encouraging readings of "literary works as implicit rhetorical treatises, which conduct in figurative terms an argument about the literal and the figural" (185); (2) "intertextuality," the "relations between one representation and another rather than between a textual imitation and a nontextual original" (187); (3) the gap between signifier and signified, leading to the conclusion that there "are no final meanings that arrest the movement of signification" (188); (4) the *parergon*, the "problem of the frame—of the distinction between inside and outside and of the structure of the border" (193); and (5) the problematic nature of self-reflexivity, which implies "the inability of any discourse to account for itself and the failure of performative and constative or doing and being to coincide" (201).

"Baxter's *Procrustes*," a parody of a literary club tricked into publishing and giving glowing reviews to a book which contains no words whatsoever, reads from a contemporary perspective as a treatise on the deconstructive issues Culler identifies. The "figural" descriptions of the reviewers, including the narrator, entirely supersede the book's "literal" contents, underlining the problematic relationship between signifiers and signified. The text's emphasis on the value of "uncut copies" of the book, ostensibly a printing of a poem parts of which Baxter has presented orally, draws attention to the problem of intertextuality. In Chesnutt's configuration, written copy and verbal "original" assume significance only intertextually, as they relate to one another; the probability that no "original" of Baxter's *Procrustes* exists renders the concept of "final meanings that arrest the movement of signification" absurd. Even the critical attempts to construct a final meaning are presented in terms of intertextuality. Responding to the comments of a fellow critic, the narrator observes: "I had a vague recollection of having read something like this somewhere, but so much has been written that one can scarcely discuss any subject of importance without unconsciously borrowing, now and then, the thoughts or the language of others" (419). Especially in regard to a "text" that consists entirely of absence, the most promising field of play for original critical thought, no definitive interpretation is possible. At his most insightful, the narrator half-recognizes the distance between his figuration and the actual text, writing that he "could see the cover through the wrapper of my sealed copy" (420). Chesnutt seems explicitly aware that this deconstruction of critical/philosophical certainties implies a parallel deconstruction of the idea of the unified transcendent subject. The interrelationship between psychological and linguistic realities assumes a foreground position when the narrator claims that Baxter "has written himself into the poem. By knowing Baxter we are able to appreciate the book, and after having read the book we feel that we are so much the more intimately acquainted with Baxter—the real Baxter" (418). Like all "subjects" of deconstructive thought, Baxter's significance can be perceived only through recognition of his absence.

The most interesting aspects of "Baxter's *Procrustes*," however, involve framing and self-reflexivity. Tracing the concept of the *parergon*—the "supplement" or "frame" of the aesthetic work—to its il/logical extreme, Chesnutt again anticipates the deconstructive perception summarized by

Culler as follows: "The supplement is essential. Anything that is properly framed . . . becomes an art object; but if framing is what creates the aesthetic object, this does not make the frame a determinable entity whose qualities could be isolated" (197). "Baxter's *Procrustes*" foregrounds this issue; frame and object simultaneously give one another significance—a significance derived purely from the traces each leaves in the other's field of absence—and deconstruct the hierarchical relationship between "ground" and "figure." The binding, which is the sole concern of the narrator's "review" is decorated with the fool's cap and bells, in effect becoming the "work" which derives its meaning from the *parergonal* absence of the empty pages. The narrator's description of the form of the words on the page in Baxter's *Procrustes,* based entirely on intertextual hearsay, articulates both his blindness and his insight: "The text is a beautiful, slender stream, meandering gracefully through a wide meadow of margin" (419). This recognition in turn suggests an awareness of context as frame. Extending the concern with the audience introduced in *The Conjure Woman*, "Baxter's *Procrustes*" presents a model of a literary discourse in which cultural frame and literary text cannot be clearly distinguished.

Published in the *Atlantic Monthly,* this openly self-reflexive text comments on itself and its audience, anticipating the deconstructive concern with the way "texts thematize, with varying degrees of explicitness, interpretive operations and their consequences and thus represent in advance the dramas that will give life to the tradition of their interpretation" (Culler, 214–15). Sharing a title with an empty book reviewed by fools who drive the author out of their community while they continue to profit from his production—a "sealed copy" of Baxter's *Procrustes* is sold for a record price at a club auction after Baxter's expulsion—Chesnutt's "Baxter's *Procrustes*" anticipates its own "misreadings." Interestingly, it also anticipates future "positive" readings in the club president's suggestion that Baxter "was wiser than we knew, or than he perhaps appreciated" (421). The retrospective appreciation of Baxter's "masterpiece" (420), however, relates solely to its economic value. Suspended in a context in which Uncle Julius's original auditors, Chesnutt's contemporary readers, and, perhaps, even his future (deconstructionist) critics share an inability to perceive the true values of an Afro-American text, (")Baxter's *Procrustes*(") seems acutely aware that its self-reflexivity does not transcend the gap between signifier and signified, attain closure, or imply self-possession. In this recognition, as in so much else, Chesnutt seems much more proto-deconstructionist than the marginal plantation-tradition figure he has traditionally been seen to be.

To remark Chesnutt's engagement with deconstructive concerns does not imply his ability to resolve their more disturbing implications. Confronting his marginalization and the failure of his audience to respond to anything other than the surface of his texts, Chesnutt fell into a literary silence like that of another premodernist American deconstructionist, Herman Melville, or those of the women writers whom Tillie Olsen discusses in her profoundly moving essay "Silences." Olsen catalogs a number of professional circumstances which drive marginal writers into giving up their public voices. Among the most powerful forces are "devaluation" ("books of great worth suffer the dearth of being unknown, or at best a peculiar eclipsing" [40]); "critical attitudes" ("the injurious reacting to a book, not for its quality or content, but on the basis of its having been written by a woman [or black]" [40]); and, perhaps most important, the "climate in literary circles for those who move in them" ("Writers know the importance of being taken seriously, with respect for one's vision and integrity; of comradeship with other writers; of being dealt with as a writer on the basis of one's work and not for other reasons" [41]). Chesnutt clearly confronted each of these problems without finding an adequate solution.

This breakdown (or absence) of contact between artist and audience parallels a similar situation, also leading to withdrawal from engagement with the context, which some observer/participants, myself among them, see as a major problem of contemporary theoretical discourse. Critics whose insights would seem to possess profound social significance find themselves in the situation of John reading to Annie; the form of their discourse and lack of contextual awareness alienate their audience, and, all too frequently, the critics respond by retreating into a contemptuous solipsism which guarantees that the subversive implications of their work will not have substantial effect on the context. One particularly unfortunate manifestation of this pattern has been the almost unchallenged alienation of Euro- and Afro-American discourse, an alienation addressed but not yet contextualized, by a small group of Afro-American (Stepto, Gates) and feminist (Johnson, Rich) theorists. Still, further work toward a context which allows, to use Culler's phrase, "these discourses to communicate with one another," offers intriguing possibilities for avoiding the nihilistic impasse and tapping the political potential of deconstructive thought. To begin, deconstruction possesses the potential for substantially alleviating the conditions which forced Chesnutt—and a long line of successors, including Hurston, Wright, Baldwin, and William Melvin Kelley—into exile. By focusing attention on the margin and articulating the recurring concerns of the folk-based Afro-American tradition in a vocabulary which can be recognized by the educated Euro-American readership which continues to comprise the majority of the literary audience, deconstruction at least theoretically could help create an audience sensitive to the actual complexities of Afro-American expression. At present, this potential remains unrealized, in large part because the literary community in which deconstruction has developed continues to exercise its social privilege in a manner which suggests a continued belief, clearly inconsistent with its articulated perceptions, that its own cultural tradition serves as the center of serious literary discourse.

Precisely because Afro-American culture continues to be excluded from, or marginalized in, Euro-American discourse, writers working in the wake of Chesnutt offer a great deal of potential insight into the blindness of the Euro-American theoretical discourse (which most certainly offers an analogous set of insights in return). A passage from Derrida's *De la grammatologie* quoted in Culler's chapter "Writing and Logocentrism" provides suggestive evidence of both the actuality and the implications of the Euro-American exclusion of Afro-American expression. Referring to the privileging of speech found in numerous European discussions of the nature of writing, Derrida writes: "The system of 'hearing/understanding-oneself-speak' through the phonic substance—which *presents itself* as a non-exterior, non-worldly and therefore non-empirical or non-contingent signifier—has necessarily dominated the history of the world during an entire epoch, and has even produced the idea of the world, the idea of world-origin, arising from the difference between the worldly and the non-worldly, the outside and the inside, ideality and non-ideality, universal and non-universal, transcendental and empirical" (107). Asserting that a particular European philosophical discourse "necessarily" dominates the "history of the world," Derrida excludes a wide range of cultural traditions based on relational conceptions of identity which treat significance as derived from process. Contrasting with the beliefs in individual subjectivity and transcendental signification characteristic of the system Derrida deconstructs, many African-based discourses (while no doubt subject to analogous deconstructions) suggest approaches to impasses in thought and action which, at the very least, should be of interest to those members of the deconstructionist movement concerned with the practical impact of their perceptions. Specifically, the conception of performance embedded in Afro-American aesthetics (Jones, Sidran, Scheub), particularly as articulated in music and verbal signifying, suggests that the feeling of alienation characteristic of many deconstructionist texts is not a necessary product of the recognition that speech does not create a "non-exterior, non-worldly and therefore non-empirical or non-contingent signifier." From the perspective of the excluded tradition which uses "call-and-response," the performative dynamic in which the meaning of any signification derives from the interaction of individual and community in relation to a specific set of social circumstances, the inadequacy of the Euro-American system which Derrida deconstructs seems obvious. More important than the parallel perception as such is the fact that Afro-American writers, experiencing the "double consciousness" which makes it impossible for them to exclude the Euro-American tradition from their expression even if they so desire, have been exploring the practical implications of the intersection of modes of thought for nearly a century. Opening theoretical discourse to consideration of complex Afro-modernist texts such as Melvin Tolson's *Harlem Gallery,* Langston Hughes's "Montage of a Dream Deferred," and Hurston's *Moses Man of the Mountain* might substantially alter the "feel" if not the conceptual underpinnings of contemporary theoretical discourse.

Perhaps the most important result of such consideration, derived from the origins of the Afro-American concern with deconstruction in both the relational conception of signification characteristic of the African continuum and the political circumstances of slavery and continuing oppression (based on the continuing dominance of the binary oppositions of American racial thought), would be to caution against (1) a relapse into the solipsistic withdrawal available primarily to those capable of exercising social privilege and (2) the separation of deconstructionist discourse from engagement with the institutional contexts in which it exists. Despite the prevalence of such separation in American academic discourse, it is not in fact inherent in deconstruction, a point made by both Eagleton and Culler. Attributing such separation to Anglo-American academicians (aka the demons of Yale), Eagleton stresses that "Derrida is clearly out to do more than develop new techniques of reading: deconstruction is for him an ultimately *political* practice, an attempt to dismantle the logic by which a particular system of thought, and behind that a whole system of political structures and social institutions, maintains its force" (148).

Similarly, Culler emphasizes that "inversions of hierarchical oppositions expose to debate the institutional arrangements that rely on the hierarchies and thus open possibilities of change" (179). Acutely aware of the ways in which even his sympathetic readers, and I suspect that would include many of the critics (I would not except myself) working toward an opening of discourses, continued to reenact the hierarchical minstrel show of the plantation tradition, Charles Chesnutt sensed this significance nearly a century ago. Like the guys at the garage—and, I suspect, the "girls" at the grocery—he knew that the man's mouth is cut crossways and that the cross cuts a figure flattering to the man. Now we can begin to figure out where the meanings lie.

WORKS CITED

Andrews, William. *The Literary Career of Charles W. Chesnutt.* Baton Rouge: Louisiana State University Press, 1980.

Chesnutt, Charles W. "Baxter's *Procrustes.*" In *The Short Fiction of Charles W. Chesnutt,* ed. Sylvia Lyons Render, 413–22. Washington, D.C.: Howard University Press, 1974.

———. *The Conjure Woman.* 1899. Ann Arbor: University of Michigan Press, 1969.

Culler, Jonathan. *On Deconstruction: Theory and Criticism after Structuralism.* Ithaca: Cornell University Press, 1982.

Dixon, Melvin. "The Teller as Folk Trickster in Chesnutt's *The Conjure Woman.*" *CLA Journal* 18 (1974): 186–97.

DuBois, W. E. B. *The Souls of Black Folk.* 1903. Greenwich, Conn.: Fawcett Publications, 1961.

Eagleton, Terry. *Literary Theory: An Introduction.* Minneapolis: University of Minnesota Press, 1983.

Ellison, Ralph. *Shadow and Act.* 1964. New York: New American Library, 1966.

Ferguson, SallyAnn. "Chesnutt's 'The Conjurer's Revenge': The Economics of Direct Confrontation." *Obsidian* 7, no. 2–3 (1981): 37–42.

Fiedler, Leslie. *The Inadvertent Epic: From "Uncle Tom's Cabin" to "Roots."* New York: Simon and Schuster, 1979.

Gates, Henry Louis, Jr. " 'The Blackness of Blackness': A Critique of the Sign and the Signifying Monkey." *Studies in Black American Literature* 1 (1984): 129–82.

Harris, Joel Chandler. *Uncle Remus: His Songs and Sayings.* 1880. New York: Penguin Books, 1982.

Hurston, Zora Neale. *Mules and Men*. 1935. Bloomington: Indiana University Press, 1978.

Irigaray, Luce. *Speculum of the Other Woman*. 1974. Trans. Gillian C. Gill. Ithaca: Cornell University Press, 1985.

Irwin, John T. *Doublin and Incest / Repetition and Revenge: A Speculative Reading of Faulkner*. Baltimore: Johns Hopkins University Press, 1975.

Jones, LeRoi. *Blues People*. New York: William Morrow, 1963.

Martin, Jay. "Joel Chandler Harris and the Cornfield Journalist." *Critical Essays on Joel Chandler Harris*. Ed. R. Bruce Bickley, Jr. Boston: G. K. Hall, 1981.

Olsen, Tillie. *Silences*. New York: Delta/Seymour Lawrence, 1978.

Ostendorf, Berndt. *Black Literature in White America*. Totowa, N.J.: Barnes and Noble, 1982.

Rich, Adrienne. "Disloyal to Civilization: Feminism, Racism, Gynephobia." *On Lies, Secrets, and Silence*. New York: Norton, 1979.

Sanders, Charles. "*The Waste Land:* The Last Minstrel Show?" *Journal of Modern Literature* 8 (1980): 23–38.

Scheub, Harold. "Oral Narrative Process and the Use of Models." *Varia Folklorica*. Ed. Alan Dundes. Paris: Mouton, 1978.

Sidran, Ben. *Black Talk*. 1971. New York: Da Capo, 1981.

Spiller, Robert, et al., eds. *The Literary History of the United States*. 4th ed. 1974.

Stepto, Robert B. *From Behind the Veil: A Study of Afro-American Narrative*. Urbana: University of Illinois Press, 1979.

Sundquist, Eric J. *Faulkner: The House Divided*. Baltimore: Johns Hopkins University Press, 1983.

Van Doren, Carl, et al., eds. *The Cambridge History of American Literature*. 1917.

Wideman, John E. "Surfiction." *Southern Review* 21 (1985): 633–40.

Wolfe, Bernard. "Uncle Remus and the Malevolent Rabbit: 'Takes a Limber-Toe Gemmun fer ter Jump Jim Crow.'" In *Critical Essays on Joel Chandler Harris*. Ed. R. Bruce Bickley, Jr. Boston: G. K. Hall, 1981.

The Contributors

WILLIAM L. ANDREWS is Joyce and Elizabeth Hall Professor of English at the University of Kansas. He is the author of *The Literary Career of Charles W. Chesnutt* and *To Tell a Free Story: The First Century of Afro-American Autobiography, 1760–1865* and the editor of *Literary Romanticism in America* and *Sisters of the Spirit: Three Black Women's Autobiographies of the Nineteenth Century.*

JAMES APPLEWHITE is a professor of English and former director of the Institute of the Arts at Duke University. He is the author of four highly acclaimed volumes of poetry and has received several poetry awards, as well as writing fellowships from the National Endowment for the Arts and the Guggenheim Foundation.

HAROLD BLOOM is Sterling Professor of the Humanities at Yale University. He is the author of many books, among them *Shelley's Mythmaking, The Visionary Company, Blake's Apocalypse, The Ringers in the Tower, Yeats,* and *The Anxiety of Influence.* He is also the editor, with Lionel Trilling, of *Romantic Poetry and Prose* and *Victorian Poetry and Prose.*

GALE H. CARRITHERS, JR., is a professor of English at Louisiana State University. He is the author of *Donne at Sermons* and articles published in *ELH, Milton Studies, College English, Genre,* and *ADE Bulletin.*

FRED CHAPPELL is a professor of English at the University of North Carolina, Greensboro, and author of five novels, a collection of stories, and numerous volumes of poetry. Among his many honors are the Bollingen Prize in Poetry and the Award in Literature from the National Institute of Arts and Letters.

GINA MICHELLE COLLINS is a visiting assistant professor of English at the University of Iowa. Her essays on translation and feminist discourse have appeared most recently in *Translation Perspective* and *Translation Review.*

KATE M. COOPER has published numerous essays and translations treating both the vernacular writings of medieval France and French post-structuralist theory. Her articles have appeared in such journals as *Mosaic, Romanic Review, Sub-stance,* and *Romance Notes.*

JOAN DeJEAN is a professor of French at the University of Pennsylvania. Her most recent book is *Libertine Strategies: Freedom and the Novel in Seventeenth Century France*.

CARL FREEDMAN is an associate professor of English at Louisiana State University. He has been an Andrew Mellon Fellow. His essays have appeared in *Modern Fiction Studies, College English, The Minnesota Review,* and other journals.

HENRY LOUIS GATES is at Harvard University. He has held fellowships from the Rockefeller, Mellon, Carnegie, and MacArthur Foundations, and received grants from the Menil Foundation and the National Endowment for the Humanities. He is the author or editor of a number of books, including *Black Literature and Literary Theory, The Signifying Monkey,* and *Figures in Black: Words, Signs, and the Racial Self.*

JEFFERSON HUMPHRIES is a professor of English, French, and Comparative Literature at Louisiana State University. He is the author of *The Otherness Within: Gnostic Readings in Marcel Proust, Flannery O'Connor and François Villon; Metamorphoses of the Raven: Literary Overdeterminedness in France and the South Since Poe; Losing the Text: Readings in Literary Desire;* and *The Puritan and the Cynic.* His essays, poems, and short stories have appeared in a number of literary quarterlies.

MICHAEL KREYLING is a professor of English at Vanderbilt University. He is the author of *Eudora Welty's Achievement of Order* and

the *Figure of the Hero in Southern Narrative.* His essays have appeared in the *Southern Review, Mississippi Quarterly,* and other periodicals.

JOSEPH G. KRONICK is an associate professor of English at Louisiana State University. He is the author of *American Poetics of History* and articles in *Boundary 2, American Literature,* and other journals.

ALEXANDRE LEUPIN received his doctorate in letters from the University of Geneva. He is the author of *Le Graal et la littérature* (L'Age d'Homme) and *Barbarolexis.* His articles have appeared in *L'Ane, Poétique, Diacritics, Yale French Studies,* and other journals.

JOHN T. MATTHEWS is an associate professor of English at Boston University. He is cofounder and coeditor of the journal *Faulkner,* and author of *The Play of Faulkner's Language.*

RANDOLPH PAUL RUNYON is a professor of French at Miami University in Oxford, Ohio. He is the author of *Fowles/Irving/Barthes: Canonical Variations on an Apocryphal Theme* and *The Braided Dream: Robert Penn Warren's Late Poetry* and has also published on Robert Penn Warren in the *Southern Literary Journal* and *Mississippi Quarterly.*

PATRICK SAMWAY, S.J., is literary editor of *America* and a professor of English at Lemoyne College in Syracuse, New York. He has edited, or coedited, a number of books, including *Stories of the Modern South,* and has contributed articles and reviews to literary journals as well as to popular magazines such as *Commonweal*.

OLGA SCHERER teaches American literature at the University of Paris. She has published articles in a number of European periodicals and in *Intertextuality in Faulkner*.

SIMONE VAUTHIER teaches at the University of Strasbourg. She is the editor of *Recherches anglaises et américaines* and has published numerous essays on southern writing in

French and American periodicals, including *Mississippi Quarterly* and *Delta*.

CRAIG WERNER is on the faculty of the Department of Afro-American Studies at the University of Wisconsin. He is the author of *Paradoxical Resolutions: American Fiction Since James Joyce* and essays that have appeared in periodicals such as the *Southern Review, Mississippi Quarterly, Studies in Black American Literature,* and *Obsidian*.

Index